Cinema and the
Invention of Modern Life

Cinema and the Invention of Modern Life

EDITED BY

Leo Charney
Vanessa R. Schwartz

UNIVERSITY OF CALIFORNIA PRESS
Berkeley   Los Angeles   London

University of California Press
Berkeley and Los Angeles, California

University of California Press
London, England

Copyright © 1995 by
The Regents of the University of California

Library of Congress Cataloging-in-Publication Data

Charney, Leo.
    Cinema and the invention of modern life / edited by Leo Charney,
Vanessa R. Schwartz.
        p.   cm.
    Includes bibliographical references and index.

    ISBN 978-0-520-20112-5 (pbk.: alk. paper)

    1. Motion pictures—Social aspects.   2. Popular culture—History—
20th century.   I. Charney, Leo.   II. Schwartz, Vanessa R.
PN1995.9.S6C47   1995
302.23'43—dc20   95-10821
                                                                                CIP

Printed in the United States of America

11 10 09 08 07

8   7   6   5   4   3

CONTENTS

ACKNOWLEDGMENTS

The editors thank Edward Dimendberg for his encouragement and enthusiasm from the start of this project. We would also like to express our gratitude to Rebecca Frazier, Stephanie Emerson, Diana Feinberg, Barbara Jellow and the rest of the University of California Press staff. Jim Loter deftly compiled the index, Angela Blake provided research assistance, and the American University College of Arts and Science, especially Dean Betty T. Bennett, supplied generous support.

Chapter 11, "Cinematic Spectatorship before the Apparatus" by Vanessa Schwartz, was first published in *Viewing Positions*, Linda Williams, editor, copyright © 1994 by Rutgers, The State University

Introduction

Leo Charney and Vanessa R. Schwartz

"Triumphant, exultant, brushed down, pasted, torn in a few hours and continually sapping the heart and soul with its vibrant futility, the poster is indeed the art . . . of this age of fever and laughter, of violence, ruin, electricity, and oblivion."[1] The rush of adjectives used by this French social commentator in 1896 to describe the poster as product of the "modern age" typifies the way in which modernity has elicited vigorous discourses that have attempted to construct, define, characterize, analyze, and understand it.[2] "Modernity," as an expression of changes in so-called subjective experience or as a shorthand for broad social, economic, and cultural transformations, has been familiarly grasped through the story of a few talismanic innovations: the telegraph and telephone, railroad and automobile, photograph and cinema. Of these emblems of modernity, none has both epitomized and transcended the period of its initial emergence more successfully than the cinema.

The thirteen essays in this volume present cinema and modernity as points of reflection and convergence. All of the essays generate from the premise that cinema, as it developed in the late nineteenth century, became the fullest expression and combination of modernity's attributes. While some essays more than others directly address the links between the cinema and other modes of modernity, all presume that modern culture was "cinematic" before the fact. Cinema constituted only one element in an array of new modes of technology, representation, spectacle, distraction, consumerism, ephemerality, mobility, and entertainment—and at many points neither the most compelling nor the most promising one.

These essays collectively argue that the emergence of cinema might be characterized as both inevitable and redundant. The culture of modernity rendered inevitable something like cinema, since cinema's characteristics

1

evolved from the traits that defined modern life in general. At the same time, cinema formed a crucible for ideas, techniques, and representational strategies already present in other places. These essays identify a historically specific culture of the cinematic which emerged from—yet also ran parallel to—other transformations associated with modernity in the late nineteenth and early twentieth centuries in such countries as France, Germany, England, Sweden, and the United States.

This collection juxtaposes the work of scholars in a variety of disciplines in the hope of bridging the frequent divide between the history of cinema and the history of modern life. By drawing on scholarship from a range of fields, we hope to enrich such areas as Cultural Studies, Film Studies, Literature, Art History, and Cultural History by insisting that studies of modern life can be enhanced when read through and against the emergence of film. Indeed, these essays will suggest that modernity can be best understood as inherently cinematic.

Despite the multiple connections and points of confluence linking these essays, we have grouped them into four broad conceptual areas: "Bodies and Sensation," "Circulation and Consumer Desire," "Ephemerality and the Moment," and "Spectacles and Spectators." These headings are meant not to provide an exclusive or restrictive framework but to highlight common threads among the topics considered by these authors.

In "Bodies and Sensation," essays by Tom Gunning, Jonathan Crary, and Ben Singer address new bodily responses to stimulation, overstimulation, and problems of attention and distraction. From the perspective of these analyses, perception in modern life became a mobile activity and the modern individual's body the subject of both experimentation and new discourses. The essays explore such techniques as photography, detective fiction, scientific psychology, Impressionist painting, the mass press, and "thrilling" entertainments, all of which endeavored to regulate and manage the newly mobilized subject.

Both mechanical reproduction and the mobility of products, consumers, and nationalities characterized forms of commercial culture at the turn of the century. The essays by Marcus Verhagen, Erika Rappaport, Alexandra Keller, and Richard Abel in "Circulation and Consumer Desire" elaborate a culture of market mechanisms that challenged boundaries between private and public spheres and reconstituted gender and national identities. These essays also make clear that cinema participated in but did not create an urban leisure culture that pivoted on women's active participation.

In "Ephemerality and the Moment," Margaret Cohen, Jeannene Przyblyski, and Leo Charney suggest that modernity resided in an immersion in the everyday; yet the everyday was, by definition, ephemeral. In response to this problem, such forms as panoramic literature, photography, and film endeavored to freeze fleeting distractions and evanescent sensations by identifying isolated moments of "present" experience. In these literary, artistic, and philosophical discourses, the negotiation between ephemerality and stasis emerged as a defining feature of modernity.

In "Spectacles and Spectators," essays by Vanessa R. Schwartz, Mark Sandberg, and Miriam Bratu Hansen investigate the allure of such diverse phenomena as wax museums, folk museums, amusement parks, and cinema in the development of a mass audience. While the first two essays focus on the fin de siècle, Hansen pushes forward into the twentieth century. Each essay elaborates from a different perspective what Hansen calls "the liberatory appeal of the 'modern' for a mass public—a public that was itself both product and casualty of the modernization process."

As a group, the essays in this volume map a common terrain of problems and phenomena that defines the "modern." In the remainder of this introduction, we identify six elements that emerge from the essays as central to both the cultural history of modernity and modernity's relation to cinema: the rise of a metropolitan urban culture leading to new forms of entertainment and leisure activity; the corresponding centrality of the body as the site of vision, attention, and stimulation; the recognition of a mass public, crowd, or audience that subordinated individual response to collectivity; the impulse to define, fix, and represent isolated moments in the face of modernity's distractions and sensations, an urge that led through Impressionism and photography to cinema; the increased blurring of the line between reality and its representations; and the surge in commercial culture and consumer desire that both fueled and followed new forms of diversion.

Modernity cannot be conceived outside the context of the city, which provided an arena for the circulation of bodies and goods, the exchange of glances, and the exercise of consumerism. Modern life seemed urban by definition, yet the social and economic transformations wrought by modernity recast the image of the city in the wake of the eruption of industrial capitalism in the second half of the nineteenth century. As the German sociologist Georg Simmel remarked in his landmark 1903 study "The Metropolis and Mental Life," the modern city occasioned "the rapid crowding of changing images, the sharp discontinuity in the grasp of a single glance, and the unexpectedness of onrushing impressions."[3]

It is not an accident that Simmel's words could double as a description of the cinema, since the experience of the city set the terms for the experience of the other elements of modernity. In a tradition that began with the work of the French poet Charles Baudelaire, this modern city has most frequently been allied to post-1850 Paris, which Walter Benjamin called the "capital of the nineteenth century."[4] The city's mid-century redesign, now known as "Haussmannization," was contrived by Napoleon III and his prefect of the Seine, Baron Georges Haussmann, to "modernize" the city's infrastructure, creating sweeping boulevards, a new sewer system, and a reconstructed central market.[5] These controversial changes made a formerly labyrinthine geography more legible, orienting Paris toward greater visibility. As T. J. Clark has put it, Paris became, for its inhabitants, "simply an image, something occasionally and casually consumed."[6]

Paris was later reclaimed as the source of modern life by such critics as Benjamin and Siegfried Kracauer, who allied it to the phenomena that surrounded them in Twenties and Thirties Berlin.[7] Miriam Hansen's essay in this volume comprehensively assesses Kracauer's evolution from a "pessimistic discourse on modernity" before 1925 to a view of mass culture as allegory for and symptom of the changes transforming German society. Kracauer began to see that mass cultural forms, as the specimen of modernity, gave viewers the potential to understand the conditions in which they were living and thereby to acquire the capacity for self-reflection (at least) or enlightened emancipation (at best).

From the contrast between Kracauer's focus on contemporary phenomena of the twentieth century and Benjamin's projection of modernity back toward nineteenth-century Paris, Hansen draws a distinction between a nineteenth-century modernity, primarily associated with the culture of Paris, and a twentieth-century modernity of "mass production, mass consumption, mass annihilation, of rationalization, standardization and media publics" identified with America and epitomized by the interdependence of mass culture and factory production.

If Paris initiated the transformation of the modern city into a showplace of visuality and distraction, the teeming New York of the turn of the century set the pace for frenzy and overstimulation. As Ben Singer writes in this volume,

> Cities . . . had never been as busy as they rapidly became just before the turn of the century. The sudden increase in urban population density and commercial activity, the proliferation of signs, and the new density and complexity of street traffic . . . made the city a much more crowded, chaotic and stimulating environment than it had been in the past.

The photographs and cartoons from mass-circulation newspapers and magazines that accompany Singer's essay testify to this sense of the city as an overflowing cauldron of distraction, sensation, and stimulation. The city in this way became an expression and site of the modern emphasis on the crowd. Whether one's aim was to tame it, join it, or please it, the crowd, in the form of the masses, became a central player in modernity. The emergence of modern life went hand in hand with the rise of a "mass society" that resulted, in part, from the growth of industrial capitalism. Additionally, in Europe and America the second half of the nineteenth century witnessed the birth of fervent nationalism and imperialism, as liberal bourgeois democracies dominated by elites gave way to societies in which the vast majority of the population was slowly enfranchised. The masses became recognized as a key constituency, imagined and figured as an often-undifferentiated grouping with putatively common desires and aspirations.

The possibility of a mass audience, combined with the atmosphere of visual and sensory excitement, opened the door for new forms of entertainment, which arose both as a part of the culture of sensation and as an effort to relieve it. The turn-of-the-century emergence of Coney Island, for example, ironically re-created the city's exhausting sensations and frenzied tempo in a seemingly more leisurely atmosphere.[8] The aura of seaside strolling allowed producers of the Coney Island distractions to draw on the increased appetite for mobile, kinetic sensation while packaging that appeal in the guise of a break from those sensations. In the same way, in its early years as an urban phenomenon, cinema served multiple functions: as part of the city landscape, as brief respite for the laborer on his way home, as release from household drudgery for women, and as cultural touchstone for immigrants.[9]

As a result of all this stimulation, notes Singer, "observers around the turn of the century were fixated on the notion that modernity has brought about a disturbing increase in nervous stimulation and bodily peril." In this environment, the body became an increasingly important site of modernity, whether as viewer, vehicle of attention, icon of circulation, or location of consuming desire. This sensual experience of the city has been embodied in the figure of the flâneur, the emblematic persona of nineteenth-century Paris, who strolled the city streets, eyes and senses attuned to the distractions that surrounded him. The flâneur's activity, at once bodily, visual, and mobile, set the terms for film spectatorship and the other forms of spectatorship that dominated the period's new experiences and entertainments.[10] As a Parisian type, the flâneur exemplified the masculine privilege of modern public life. In Janet Wolff's formulation, "There is no question of inventing the flâneuse: . . . such a character was rendered impossible by the sexual divisions of the nineteenth century."[11] Others have argued that the prostitute, who shared the sidewalk with the flâneur, represented his female counterpart.[12]

Several of the essays in this volume address flânerie and the gendered nature of public life. In his treatment of the late nineteenth-century posters of Jules Chéret, Marcus Verhagen shows how the artist's whimsical character, the *chérette*, was figured as a prostitute, and how the representation of female sexuality was thereby mobilized in the service of consumption. By contrast, Erika Rappaport's essay on the department store indicates how, for commercial ends, new forms of consumer culture enticed women into urban space and cultivated female desire. And in Alexandra Keller's analysis of turn-of-the-century mail-order catalogs, women similarly become both object and subject of this new form of consumer activity.

As typified by flânerie, modern attention was conceived as not only visual and mobile but also fleeting and ephemeral. Modern attention was vision in motion. Modern forms of experience relied not simply on movement but on the juncture of movement and vision: moving pictures. One obvious precursor of moving pictures was the railroad, which eliminated traditional barriers of space and distance as it forged a bodily intimacy with time, space, and motion.[13] The railroad journey anticipated more explicitly than any other technology an important facet of the experience of cinema: a person in a seat watches moving visuals through a frame that does not change position.[14]

In this way, modernity's stimulations and distractions made focused attention more vital yet less feasible. In Jonathan Crary's account in this volume, modern attention was explicitly predicated on its potential for failure, resulting in inattention or distraction. "Attention," writes Crary in light of the period's scientific psychology on the subject, "was described as that which prevents our perception from being a chaotic flood of sensations, yet research showed it to be an undependable defense against such chaos. . . . Attention always contained within itself the conditions for its own disintegration." In this view, "attention and distraction were not two essentially different states but existed on a single continuum." Crary traces this ambiguity through both the discourse of scientific psychology and Claude Manet's 1879 painting *In the Conservatory,* in which Manet struggled to channel the viewer's potential for both attention and distraction.

The tension between focus and distraction set the terms for a wider interchange between mobility and stasis, between the ephemerality of modernity's sensations and the resulting desire to freeze those sensations in a fixed moment of representation. Leo Charney's essay investigates the attempt "to rescue the possibility of sensual experience in the face of modernity's ephemerality" which links philosophical and critical work on modernity from Walter Pater in the 1870s through Martin Heidegger in the 1920s and Walter Benjamin in the 1930s. This concern emerged in film both through Jean Epstein's concept of *photogénie*—evanescent instants of cinematic pleasure—and through the precinematic motion studies of Eadweard Muybridge and Etienne-Jules Marey which broke down continuous movements into their component moments. These writers and artists crystallized ephemerality as not just an abstract concept but an active problem of bodily sensation, cognition, and perception. The present moment could exist "only as the site where past and future collide," since ephemerality would always outrun the effort to stabilize it, and the body's cognitive awareness of its "present" sensations could never coincide with the initial moment of sensation.

In nineteenth-century Paris, the impulses to freeze the moment and represent the present took early form in the development of photography and the corresponding aesthetic of Impressionism.[15] The essays of Tom Gunning and Jeannene Przyblyski in this volume suggest some of the complex uses made of photography in this period. Gunning locates photography as a multiply determined crossroads of new modern concerns. The photograph aided police detection by identifying individuals in the midst of the circulation and anonymity that otherwise marked modern life. By re-presenting the appearance of the putatively unique individual, the photograph destabilized traditional conceptions of personal identity by making the body "a transportable image fully adaptable to systems of circulation and mobility that modernity demanded."

As Gunning's essay makes clear, these new techniques of representation did not simply reproduce a self-present "reality." In the case of police photography, the photograph broke down the individual body into component parts and then processed it through new regimes of information organization. More important, the blurring of representation and reality gave rise to one crucial aspect of modernity—the increasing tendency to understand the "real" only as its re-presentations.[16] Analyzing photographs of the 1871 Paris Commune uprising, Jeannene Przyblyski notes "the growing tendency throughout the 1860s and 1870s to turn the camera upon contemporary events." Przyblyski's discussion indicates that as photography began to capture the real, the "real" became inconceivable and unimaginable without the photograph's verifying presence. "What was apparently asked of photographic *actualités* in 1871," Przyblyski writes, "was . . . that they exhibit bits of the 'real,' that they operate fragmentary and relic-like, with a metonymical claim to authenticity. In their almost mummified condition midway between historical artifact and simulated re-creation, there is something . . . particularly modern."

Many of this volume's essays echo Przyblyski's claim that representation as the re-presentation of the "real" marked the defining form of modernity; or, more exactly, that with the advent of a chaotic and diffuse urban culture, the "real" could increasingly be grasped only through its re-presentations. In addition to Gunning's and Przyblyski's accounts of the uses of photography, essays by Margaret Cohen, Vanessa R. Schwartz, and Mark Sandberg outline instances of this new form of re-presentation. Cohen analyzes French panoramic literature of the July Monarchy (1830–1848), a genre that aimed to provide a visual and verbal overview of contemporary life. These books were "everyday genres for representing the everyday,

genres with minimal transcendent aesthetic claims. . . . the close attention
to external and particularly visible material details . . . gives the reader
vivid access to the sensuous materiality of contemporary Parisian reality."

Cohen calls this zone between representation and reality the "epistemological twilight," a striking phrase that captures the ambiguity of the interaction between a reality that can be grasped only in its representations
and the representations that feed off and form part of that ongoing reality. Schwartz's essay indicates several phenomena of late nineteenth-
century Parisian culture that were popular because they transfigured and
re-presented a vision of "reality": wax museums, panoramas, the mass press,
and the public display of corpses at the Paris Morgue. "To understand cinema spectatorship as a historical practice," argues Schwartz, "it is essential
to locate cinema in a field of cultural forms and practices associated with
the burgeoning mass culture of the late nineteenth century." Like cinema,
these other new diversions compelled the spectator to negotiate spectacle
and narrative to produce a "reality-effect."

In similar fashion, Mark Sandberg's essay locates turn-of-the-century
Scandinavian folk museums as part of a broader "roving patronage of visual culture." These museums presented nostalgic dioramas as a way to
compensate for the threatening losses of a modernity that came relatively
late to Scandinavia. The folk museum's display of frozen moments and the
resulting reliance on the spectator to fill voids in the spectacle anticipated
cinema in indicating how narrative could serve a stabilizing function in
the face of modern evanescence. "It may well be," Sandberg proposes
at the end of his essay, "that narrative was more important to spectating at
the turn of the century than has often been assumed, serving as the unobtrusive safety net that made the unmooring of the eye in modernity possible and pleasurable. . . . Narrative helped make modernity attractive,
turning a sense of 'displacement' into 'mobility' and 'rootlessness' into
'liberation.'"

Narrative and visuality endeavored to channel the subject's floating attention not just as a viewer but also as a consumer. The forms analyzed by
Gunning, Przyblyski, Cohen, Schwartz, and Sandberg were all commercial
enterprises, as were the railroad, the telegraph, and virtually every other
icon of modernity. Consumerism's role as engine of modernity comes forward in the essays by Marcus Verhagen, Richard Abel, Erika Rappaport,
and Alexandra Keller. For Verhagen, the explosion of the poster onto the
late nineteenth-century Parisian landscape "revolutionized the Parisian
entertainment business" as both a "manifestation of the emergence of
mass culture . . . and a catalyst in the development of other mass cultural
forms." In Verhagen's analysis, moralistic responses to the poster's popularity echoed both early objections to the cinema and the generally fear-

ful reactions to new forms of a consumer culture "whose market mechanisms threatened to wear away the foundations on which class society was built."

In Abel's essay, the development of American cinema in the early years of the twentieth century cannot be understood outside the marketplace pressures that impelled film studios to differentiate their product from the potentially more popular French films of the Pathé studio. In response to both the saturation of the American market by "the Gallic red rooster" and an audience of newly arriving immigrants in need of "Americanization," American studios positioned Pathé as a suspicious and demoralizing "other," a formation that intertwined national and commercial identities. Abel's discussion underscores the interdependence of capitalism and nationalism, as a capitalist industry (emblematized by a film studio) could both distribute its products internationally and intercede in its own national markets. In this way, writes Abel, "cinema as a specific instance of modernity . . . was inscribed within the discourses of imperialism and nationalism and their conflicted claims, respectively, of economic and cultural supremacy."

In similar fashion, Rappaport and Keller investigate how consumer desires were mediated by the written texts that surrounded and incited them. Rappaport demonstrates how, in early twentieth-century London, "the press produced Edwardian commercial culture in partnership with men such as Gordon Selfridge." Selfridge, the owner of the department store that bore his name, cannily employed advertising and newspaper articles to promote himself, his store, and the vision of women as consumers and London as a commercial metropolis that would support them. By shifting focus from the stores to the manipulations of discourse that surrounded them, Rappaport illustrates that modernity's social phenomena can be understood only through the representations that constructed them.

Keller's essay on early Sears Roebuck mail-order catalogs expands this interdependence of text and consumerism to suggest that the mail-order catalog offered only text as the basis for desire, as the catalog's illustrations evoked the absent products wanted by the consumer. These ghostly images, like the catalog's mass dissemination, made the mail-order catalog a phenomenon parallel to cinema. Keller goes on to indicate that mail-order catalogs "effected a kind of rural flânerie for those who browsed its pages." The catalog's rural reader could stroll through products as the flâneur roamed the city. Like the modern city, the "world as brought into the rural home by the mail-order catalog was an abundant and crowded place, jammed with goods, the representation of a marketplace whose fleshly embodiment would be equally jammed with vendors, consumers, and gawkers."

Cinema, then, marked the unprecedented crossroads of these phenomena of modernity. It was a commercial product that was also a technique of mobility and ephemerality. It was an outgrowth and a vital part of city culture that addressed its spectators as members of a collective and potentially undifferentiated mass public. It was a representational form that went beyond Impressionism and photography by staging actual movement; yet that movement could never be (and to this day still is not) more than the serial progression of still frames through the camera. It was a technology designed to arouse visual, sensual, and cognitive responses from viewers beginning to be accustomed to the onslaught of stimulation.

Most important, cinema did not simply provide a new medium in which elements of modernity could uncomfortably coexist. Rather, it arose from and existed in the intertwining of modernity's component parts: technology mediated by visual and cognitive stimulation; the re-presentation of reality enabled by technology; and an urban, commercial, mass-produced technique defined as the seizure of continuous movement. Cinema forced these elements of modern life into active synthesis with each other; to put it another way, these elements created sufficient epistemological pressure to produce cinema.

Cinema, therefore, must not be conceived simply as the outgrowth of such forms as melodramatic theater, serial narrative, and the nineteenth-century realist novel, although all of these modes influenced its form. Nor can technological histories sufficiently explain the emergence of cinema. Rather, cinema must be reunderstood as a vital component of a broader culture of modern life which encompassed political, social, economic, and cultural transformations. This culture did not "create" cinema in any simple sense, nor did cinema advance any new forms, concepts, or techniques that were not already available along other avenues. In providing a crucible for elements already evident in other aspects of modern culture, cinema accidentally outpaced these other forms, ending up as far more than just another novel gadget.

These essays, finally, help us reconsider the lineage from modernity to postmodernity and the technologies, distractions, and representations of our own turn of a century. By specifying a particular culture of modern life, this volume will ideally initiate a more rigorous interrogation of the contrasts and resemblances between the "modern" and the putatively "postmodern." While postmodernism has often been conceived as the sequel to Modernism as an artistic movement, these essays create a context through which to reimagine postmodernity as the outgrowth of modernity, a broader social, political, and cultural transformation of which Modernism formed only one aspect. While the implications of this distinction have yet to be fully explored, the framework of modernity articulated in these essays encourages future scholars to begin from and return to the cinema as a common denominator bridging the nineteenth, twentieth, and (potentially) twenty-first centuries, at each turn uncanny repository of times gone by and prescient oracle of things to come.

NOTES

1. Maurice Talmeyr, "L'Age de l'affiche," *La Revue des deux mondes*, 1 September 1896, p. 216; cited by Verhagen in the present volume.

2. Three works that provide an overview of modernity and modern life are Stephen Kern, *The Culture of Time and Space, 1880–1918* (Cambridge: Harvard University Press, 1983); Marshall Berman, *All That Is Solid Melts into Air: The Experience of Modernity* (New York: Penguin Books, 1988); and Christoph Asendorf, *Batteries of Life: On the History of Things and Their Perception in Modernity*, trans. Don Reneau (Berkeley, Los Angeles, London: University of California Press, 1993).

3. Georg Simmel, "The Metropolis and Mental Life," in *The Sociology of Georg Simmel*, ed. Kurt Wolff, trans. H. H. Gerth (1903; reprint, New York: Free Press, 1950), p. 410.

4. Charles Baudelaire, *The Painter of Modern Life and Other Essays*, ed. and trans. Jonathan Mayne (London: Phaidon, 1965); Walter Benjamin, *Charles Baudelaire: A Lyric Poet in the Era of High Capitalism*, trans. Harry Zohn (London: Verso, 1983); and *Paris, Capitale du XIXme siècle*, ed. Rolf Tiedmann, trans. Jean Lacoste (Paris: Editions du Cerf, 1989).

5. See especially David Pinkney's classic study, *Napoleon III and the Rebuilding of Paris* (Princeton: Princeton University Press, 1958). Haussmannization was also an important act of social control; the boulevards divided working-class enclaves, impeded the building of barricades, and facilitated the deployment of troops in case of insurrection.

6. T. J. Clark, *The Painting of Modern Life* (Princeton: Princeton University Press, 1984), p. 36.

7. Works by and about Kracauer and Benjamin are cited throughout the essays in this volume, especially those by Hansen and Charney. On Kracauer, Benjamin, and modernity, see David Frisby, *Fragments of Modernity: Theories of Modernity in the Work of Simmel, Kracauer, and Benjamin* (Cambridge: MIT Press, 1986); Martin Jay, *The Dialectical Imagination: A History of the Frankfurt School and the Institute for Social Research, 1923–1950* (Boston: Little, Brown, 1973).

8. The pivotal work on leisure and urban culture at the turn of the century is Kathy Peiss, *Cheap Amusements: Working Women and Leisure in Turn-of-the-Century New York* (Philadelphia: Temple University Press, 1986). Also see John Kasson, *Amusing the Million: Coney Island at the Turn of the Century* (New York: Hill & Wang, 1978), and David Nasaw, *Going Out: The Rise and Fall of Public Amusement* (New York: Basic Books, 1993).

9. On these points, among many potential sources, see Miriam Hansen, *Babel and Babylon: Spectatorship in American Silent Film* (Cambridge: Harvard University Press, 1991); Charles Musser, *The Emergence of Cinema: The American Screen to 1907* (New York: Scribner's, 1990); and Eileen Bowser, *The Transformation of Cinema, 1907–1915* (New York: Scribner's, 1990).

10. On film, flânerie, and the modern city, see Anne Friedberg, *Window Shopping: Cinema and the Postmodern* (Berkeley, Los Angeles, London: University of California Press, 1992); and Giuliana Bruno, *Streetwalking on a Ruined Map: Cultural Theory and the City Films of Elvira Notari* (Princeton: Princeton University Press, 1992).

11. Janet Wolff, "The Invisible *Flâneuse*: Women and the Literature of Modernity," in Wolff, *Feminine Sentences* (Berkeley, Los Angeles, London: University of California Press, 1990), p. 47. On the interactions among women, film, and public space in modernity, see Bruno, op. cit.; Hansen, op. cit.; and Patrice Petro, *Joyless Streets: Women and Melodramatic Representation in Weimar Germany* (Princeton: Princeton University Press, 1989).

12. See Benjamin, "Paris, Capital of the Nineteenth Century," in *Baudelaire*, pp. 155–176; Susan Buck-Morss, *The Dialectics of Seeing: Walter Benjamin and the Arcades Project* (Cambridge: MIT Press, 1989). See also Priscilla Parkhurst Ferguson, "The *Flâneur*: Urbanization and Its Discontents," in *Home and Its Dislocations in Nineteenth-Century France*, ed. Suzanne Nash (Albany: State University of New York Press, 1993), pp. 45–64.

13. The indispensable work on the transformation of perception associated with the railroad is Wolfgang Schivelbusch, *The Railway Journey: The Industrialization of Time and Space in the Nineteenth Century* (1977; reprint, Berkeley, Los Angeles, London: University of California Press, 1986).

14. On film and the railroad, see Lynne Kirby, *The Railroad and the Cinema* (Durham, N.C.: Duke University Press, forthcoming); idem, "Male Hysteria and Early Cinema," *Camera Obscura* 17 (May 1988); and Mary Ann Doane, "The Moving Image," *Wide Angle* 7, 1–2 (1985).

15. On Impressionism, see Asendorf, op. cit., chapter 6; Clark, op. cit.; and Robert Herbert, *Impressionism: Art, Leisure, and Parisian Society* (New Haven: Yale University Press, 1988).

16. See Miles Orvell, *The Real Thing: Imitation and Authenticity in American Culture, 1880–1940* (Chapel Hill: University of North Carolina Press, 1989).

PART ONE

Bodies and Sensation

ONE

Tracing the Individual Body:
Photography, Detectives,
and Early Cinema

Tom Gunning

for Giuliana Bruno

CIRCULATION, MOBILITY, MODERNITY, AND THE BODY

A generation that had gone to school on a horse-drawn streetcar now stood under the open sky in a countryside in which nothing remained unchanged but the clouds, and beneath these clouds, in a field of force of destructive torrents and explosions, was the tiny, fragile human body.
WALTER BENJAMIN, "THE STORYTELLER"

It could be argued that techniques of circulation define the intersecting transformations in technology and industry that we call modernity. By "modernity" I refer less to a demarcated historical period than to a change in experience. This new configuration of experience was shaped by a large number of factors, which were clearly dependent on the change in production marked by the Industrial Revolution. It was also, however, equally characterized by the transformation in daily life wrought by the growth of capitalism and advances in technology: the growth of urban traffic, the distribution of mass-produced goods, and successive new technologies of transportation and communication. While the nineteenth century witnessed the principal conjunction of these transformations in Europe and America, with a particular crisis coming towards the turn of the century, modernity has not yet exhausted its transformations and has a different pace in different areas of the globe.

The earliest fully developed image of this transformation of experience comes, I believe, with the railway, which embodies the complex realignment of practices which modern circulation entails. As Wolfgang Schivelbusch has demonstrated, the railway not only depended upon but also allowed expansion of industrial production, with broad networks for transportation of both raw materials and commodities, as well as the restructuring of both rural and urban space as the site of circulation. This new landscape, which was organized according to circulatory needs, exemplifies the perceptual and environmental changes which define the experience of modernity: a new mastery of the incremental instants of time; a collapsing of distances; and a new experience of the human body and perception shaped by traveling at new rates of speed and inviting new potentials of danger.[1]

Any number of the *topoi* of modernity that cluster around the second half of the nineteenth century can be approached as instances of circulation: the boulevard system in the Haussmannization of Paris, which allowed a previously unimaginable expansion of traffic; the new modes of production of goods in the work process of the "new factory system," which demanded that individual workers perform simple and repetitive tasks as material passed before them; or innovations in systems of rapid transportation, such as the moving sidewalks unveiled at the Chicago Columbian Exposition of 1893 and the Paris Exposition of 1900. In all of these new systems of circulation, the drama of modernity sketches itself: a collapsing of previous experiences of space and time through speed; an extension of the power and productivity of the human body; and a consequent transformation of the body through new thresholds of demand and danger, creating new regimes of bodily discipline and regulation based upon a new observation of (and knowledge about) the body.

Cinema nestles into this network of circulation as both technology and industry, but also as a new form of experience. As a mass-produced entertainment industry with a national system of distribution by 1909, film distribution and exhibition exploited railway networks pioneered by vaudeville circuits and circus trains. The early genres of cinema, especially such seemingly diverse forms as travel actualities and trick films, visualized a modern experience of rapid alteration, whether by presenting foreign views from far-flung international locations or by creating through trick photography a succession of transformations which unmoored the stable identity of both objects and performers. Early actuality films frequently presented a simulacrum of travel not only by presenting foreign views but also through "phantom rides" films, which were shot from the front of trains or prows of boats and which gave seated, stationary spectators a palpable sensation of motion. This contradictory experience was as much the attraction of these films as was the representation of foreign tourism.

While actuality films depended directly on the new technology of both cinema and transportation to image the collapse of the space and time formerly required for an experience of global tourism, the phantasmagoria of the trick film with its magical metamorphoses echoes the transformation of raw material into products achieved nearly instantaneously through the rapid succession of tasks in the new factory system. The amazement experienced by Upton Sinclair's Lithuanian worker Jurgis Rudkus in

The Jungle, as he watched hogs transformed into hams and other products by the concatenation of actions of a score of workers in a few minutes of time, recalls the astonishment of a gawker at a magic show spellbound by an unbelievable succession of transformative wonders.[2] Peter Finley Dunne's Irish dialect character "Mr. Dooley" echoed this wonder when he ironically described the process: "A cow goes lowin' softly into Armours and comes out glue, gelatine, fertylizer, celooloid, joolry, sofy cushions, hair restorer, washin' sody, soap, lithrachoor, and bed springs, so quick that while aft she's still cow for'ard she may be anything fr'm buttons to pannyma hats."[3]

The speed of such industrial transformation made it appear magical, occluding the unskilled labor regulated by the factory system to perform repetitive and limited tasks. Skill seemed to be absorbed by the circulatory logic of the factory itself, as each task took place within a chain of rationalized labor. This new arrangement of production seemed able to make anything out of anything, without the laborious effort of skilled handicraft. In such new systems of labor, objects were transformed rapidly before one's eyes, and the stable identity of things became as uncertain as a panoply of magician's props.

Although the technical innovation of *motion* pictures introduced the literal possibility of portraying speed and movement, cinema's place in a new logic of circulation had been anticipated by the commodification of still photographs, especially the postcard and the stereoscope. As Jonathan Crary has indicated, we must rethink the history of photography by not focusing solely on the mode of new technological representation that it introduced but by considering its role in "the reshaping of an entire territory on which signs and images, each effectively severed from a referent, circulate and proliferate."[4] While the debate on the ontology of the photographic image has centered on the indexical tie a photograph maintains with its referent, Crary directs our attention to the actual use of photographs, in which this connection to a referent interrelates with the image's detachable nature, with its ability to gain a mobility its referent never possessed and to circulate separately.

Images of the Sphinx or the Wall of China could thus be viewed through a stereoscope in middle-class parlors, sent through the international mail as postcards, and projected on walls and screens as lantern slides in schools and churches throughout the Western world. In his famous essay on the stereoscope, Oliver Wendell Holmes, Sr., speculated in 1859 on the dissolving power of this new traffic in images. With deliberate irony, he claimed:

> Form is henceforth divorced from matter. In fact, matter as a visible object is of no great use any longer, except as the mould on which form is shaped. Give us a few negatives of a thing worth seeing, taken from different

points of view, and that is all we want of it. Pull it down or burn it up, if you please. . . .

There is only one Colosseum or Pantheon; but how many millions of potential negatives have they shed—representatives of billions of pictures—since they were erected. Matter in large masses must always be fixed and dear; form is cheap and transportable. . . .

. . . There may grow up something like a universal currency of these bank-notes, or promises to pay in solid substance, which the sun has engraved for the great Bank of Nature.[5]

Holmes's description of photographs as a new universal currency is more than a clever metaphor. It recognizes in photography the dominant characteristics of the modern capitalist economy, the role of money in ever increasing the pace of circulation. As Georg Simmel has indicated, "The modern view of life rests upon money whose nature is fluctuating and which presents the identity of essence in the greatest and most changing variety of equivalents."[6] Like the modern circulation of currency, photography abolished spatial barriers and transformed objects into transportable simulacra, a new form of the universal equivalent.

As Holmes's discussion demonstrates, photography could be understood in the nineteenth century not simply as the latest stage in realistic representation but also as part of a new system of exchange which could radically transform traditional beliefs in solidity and unique identity. Such fixed ideas could disintegrate in the solvents circulating through the modern networks of exchange and transportation. The body itself appeared to be abolished, rendered immaterial, through the phantasmagoria of both still and motion photography. This transformation of the physical did not occur through the sublimation of an ethereal idealism. The body, rather, became a transportable image fully adaptable to the systems of circulation and mobility that modernity demanded.

DRAMAS OF IDENTITY:
RATIONALIZING PHOTOGRAPHY'S INDISCRETION

"Then I fail to follow your Majesty. If this young person should produce her letters for blackmailing or other purposes, how is she to prove their authenticity?"
"There is the writing."
"Pooh, pooh. Forgery."
"My private note-paper."
"Stolen."
"My own seal."
"Imitated."
"My photograph."
"Bought."
"We were both in the photograph."

"Oh dear. That is very bad. Your Majesty has indeed committed an indiscretion."

CONVERSATION BETWEEN SHERLOCK HOLMES AND THE
GRAND DUKE OF CASSEL-FELSTEIN IN A. CONAN DOYLE,
"A SCANDAL IN BOHEMIA"

In this delightful exchange, Sherlock Holmes makes it clear that the Grand Duke's indiscretion lies in having been photographed with his mistress, rather than in having had a love affair. Holmes claims more here than the old saw that a criminal's only crime lies in getting caught. As a mode of evidence that cannot be denied, photography is indeed indiscreet, capturing information that could otherwise be hushed up or explained away. The photograph mediates between the public and the private, attesting to an intimacy of bodies that has now become a matter of record. The only recourse Holmes and his royal client have is discovering and suppressing the photograph before it is made public.

Photography operates as one of the most ambiguous emblems of modern experience. Modernity (and particularly modern capitalism) contains a tension between forces which undo older forms of stability in order to increase the ease and rapidity of circulation and of those forces which seek to control and make such circulation predictable and, therefore, profitable.[7] Photography participates dramatically in both of these often-opposed impulses. While the mechanical reproduction and multiplication of photographic images undermined traditional understandings of identity, within the practice of criminology and detective fiction the photograph could also be used as a guarantor of identity and as a means of establishing guilt or innocence. Within systems of power and authority, the circulatory possibilities of photography could also play a regulatory role, maintaining a sense of the unique and recognizable, tying the separable image back to its bodily source. In both the legal process of detection and its fantasy elaborations in detective fiction, the body reemerges as something to grab hold of, and the photograph supplies one means of gaining a purchase on a fugitive physicality. But the grasp afforded by this new technology of the image relied on new systems of knowledge and a modern concern with classification which could convert the image into effective information.

Photography stands at the intersection of a number of aspects of modernity, and this convergence makes it a uniquely modern means of representation. As the product of modern technology, photography evokes both admiration and opprobrium as an objective mechanical means of making an image with only minimal human intervention. The practical application of the accurate and detailed quality of this machine-made image was immediately recognized. Photography could, in Baudelaire's phrase, serve as "the secretary and clerk of whoever needs an absolute factual exactitude in his profession."[8] And this record-keeping accuracy depended on the photograph's unique bond with its referent, on its indexicality.

Photography became the ideal tool of the process of detection, the ultimate modern clue, due to three interlocking aspects: its indexical aspect, which comes from the fact that since a photograph results from exposure to a preexisting entity, it directly bears the entity's imprint and can therefore supply evidence about the object it depicts; its iconic aspect, by which it produces a direct resemblance to its object which allows immediate recognition;[9] and its detachable nature, which allows it to refer to an absent object separated from it in space and time. As a clue, the photograph entered into a new discourse of power and control.

In criminology, the photograph worked in two directions. One staked out the photograph's ability to capture evidence of a crime, the deviant act itself. The other practice (less direct, but much more common) used the photograph to mark and keep track of the criminal, serving as an essential element in new systems of identification. We will find both directions pursued not only in criminology but also in the mythmaking processes of detective fiction.

The narrative form of the detective story, rather than serve simply as an exercise in puzzle-solving, depends explicitly upon the modern experience of circulation. While circulation relies on an evolving process of rationalization of time and space, the very intricacy and speed of these routes of transfer and exchange create a counterthrust in which stability and predictability can be threatened. The detective story maps out two positions in this dialectical drama of modernity: the criminal, who preys on the very complexity of the system of circulation; and the detective, whose intelligence, knowledge, and perspicacity allow him to discover the dark corners of the circulatory system, uncover crime, and restore order.

Walter Benjamin located the origin of the modern detective story in the mobile transformation of identity, in the "the obliteration of the individual's traces in the big city crowd"[10] allowed by the modern environment. Attempts to reestablish the traces of individual identity beneath the obscurity of a new mobility were central to both the actual processes of police detection and the genesis of detective fiction. Techniques for identifying criminals became a central preoccupation for nineteenth-century police. In new systems of mobility and circulation, the criminal who could hide beneath an assumed identity functioned like a forged banknote, exploiting the rapid exchange of modern currency while undermining the confidence on which it depended. In the modern drama of detection, photography, through its indexicality, iconic accuracy, and mobility of circulation, provides the ultimate means of tying identity to a specific and unique body. In this way the process of criminal identification represents a new aspect of the disciplining of the body which typifies modernity. Systems of power were thus able to channel the free-floating insubstantiality of the photograph at which Oliver Wendell Holmes had so marveled into the orderly grooves of maintaining identity through surveillance.

Previously, the identification of criminals had frequently depended upon a direct and visible mark applied by legal authorities to the criminal's body, the equivalent of the scriptural mark of Cain. Many early nineteenth-century adventure novels turn on the discovery of the scar of the branding iron which in France had been used to mark malefactors for life (for example, the brand of Milady's shoulder in Dumas's *Three Musketeers* which reveals her criminal past). Such branding and marking of the flesh was countered on the criminal side by extreme physical disfiguration, such as the brigand's carving of his own nose and treating his face with acid to render himself unidentifiable in Eugène Sue's *Mysteries of Paris*. Law and outlaw thus fought a battle over legibility and culpability upon the body itself.

But the nature of the marks of criminality change in the nineteenth century. Michel Foucault describes the transformation of punishment from a prolonged public spectacle that violently demonstrates power and sovereignty on the criminal body to the surreptitious practice of embodying power in the disciplined body and in the creation of information archives.[11] Although Foucault traces the beginnings of this transformation to an earlier era, the nineteenth century sees its final achievement, at least in the West, with the mark of the branding iron officially suppressed in France in 1832.[12] Likewise, in the later nineteenth century, actual detection and detective fiction both witnessed an increased complexity and rarefication in the play of identification and disguise. The body at issue was traced and measured rather than marked, as the criminal employed means of evasion more subtle than disfiguration.

As Benjamin indicates, photography played an important role in both reality and fiction in this new regime of identity and concealment:

> The invention of photography was a turning point in the history of this process. It is no less significant for criminology than the inventing of the printing press is for literature. Photography made it possible for the first time to preserve permanent and unmistakable traces of a human being. The detective story came into being when this most decisive of all conquests of a person's incognito had been accomplished. Since then the end of efforts to capture a man in his speech and actions has not been in sight.[13]

The early proponents of police photography recognized that the new procedure both mimicked the earlier application of the branding iron and improved upon it technologically. In 1854 the inspector general of French prisons, Louis-Mathurin Moreau-Christophe, promoted the adoption of photographing the prison population as the "infliction of a new *mark*."[14] The apparent lack of violence involved in photography led Yves Guyot, a later proponent of police photography, to contrast the new method with the brutal procedures associated with the legendary head of the Sûreté at the beginning of the century, François Vidocq. Writing in 1887, Guyot declared: "In place of a police that is irritable, brutal, theatrical and dramatic, seeking publicity, there would appear a calm and stable police force, working in silence, proceeding by gentle strokes, noiselessly, but with the precision of a well-designed machine precisely assembled and made of first-class material."[15] Photography helped a new regime of control to emerge, armed with modern techniques.

While photography supplied the most powerful form of modern identification, the attempt to read the signs of identity in a new manner did not derive entirely from the introduction of new technology, nor was new technology sufficient for a new system of identification. Rather, we can see a modern concept of evidence appearing in criminology and detective fiction which embraced both photography and the method of detection. The nineteenth century witnessed a rearrangement of the hierarchy of judicial proof, as the value previously accorded to witness testimony was replaced by the scientific reputation of the analysis of indices.[16] As Ernst Bloch has pointed out, the *sine qua non* of a hunt for clues, a trial based on evidence as opposed to testimony and confession, dates only from the middle of the eighteenth century.[17] This new concept of evidence transformed both the narrative logic of signs of guilt and the methods of recognition. Instead of reading conventional signs imprinted on the criminal body with the force of sovereign power, detection was approached as a science, employing careful measurement and observation, privileging regimes of knowledge over brute force.

For example, in the famous late-nineteenth-century melodrama *The Ticket of Leave Man,* the paroled convict, Bob Brierly, is no longer recognized by an actual mark burned or cut into his flesh but by the fact that his prison haircut has not yet grown out completely.[18] Detection follows a fading trail of cause and effect rather than exposing an indelible mark. While such signs are more circumstantial and less overtly visible, they may also betray a man without his knowing it. The modern detective thus finds his or her model in Conan Doyle's Sherlock Holmes, who, as the semiotician Thomas Sebeok has emphasized, founded his method upon "the observation of trifles."[19]

The reading of these all-important trifles does more than demonstrate the detective's eye for details. Holmes's method opens onto a peculiarly modern world in which the forces of everyday life can mark people as deeply as an officially applied branding iron. While the complex maze of urban circulation provides a thicket in which individual identity can be concealed, it also marshals a range of factors which imprint the bodies of individuals with their own history. As Sebeok and others have pointed out,

Conan Doyle patterned Holmes on his professor of medicine, Dr. Joseph Bell of the Royal Infirmary of Edinburgh, who astonished students and patients with his ability not only to diagnose diseases from symptoms but also to read a person's occupation and background from details of body, gait, and clothing. In 1893 Bell described his method in terms that parallel Holmes:

> Racial peculiarities, hereditary tricks of manner, accent, occupation or the want of it, education, environment of every kind, by their little trivial impressions gradually mold or carve the individual, and leave finger marks or chisel scores which the expert can detect.[20]

This method of reading persons opens onto the new world of mobility and rapid circulation which we have been tracing, in which signs of class and occupation have moved below the threshold of immediately recognized conventional signs to reach the level of unintentional—and often unrecognized—symptoms. Thomas Brynes, chief of detectives in New York City, emphasized in 1886 that "there is nothing to mark people of that stamp [criminals] as a class"[21] and added that it was useless to construct a general physiognomic criminal type since there were no consistent physical features specific to criminals. Only the unique body imprinted with its particular, inherited physiology and, especially, its unconscious habits and adaptations to the life it has led could betray an identity which has become the product and residue of a life history. The role of the modern detective did not correspond to the earlier "physiologies" which subsumed criminals under ideal physical types. Identification, rather, relied on the absolute and ineradicable individuality (and unique culpability) of a specific criminal. As Gallus Muller, an American proponent of Alphonse Bertillon's method for identifying criminals, stated, the goal of such identification was "to fix the human personality, to give each human being an identity, an individuality, certain, durable, invariable, always recognizable, and always capable of being proven."[22]

Christian Phéline, in his brilliant study L'Image accusatrice, relates the emergence of criminal photography to other uses of photography within the modern world of anonymous crowds which devised bureaucratic means to trace and identify, such as medical documentation and the growing use of photographs in identity cards and passports, all of which demarcate a person as a unique entity. Phéline declares that "the photographic image contributes to the very constitution of such identity as social identity and therefore participates in the emergence of the individual in the modern sense of the term."[23] Such techniques of identification became necessary in the new world of rapid circulation and facilitated the circulation of the newly constituted individual through its circuits with a traceable accountability.

The detective story structures itself around two essential moments: one plays on the possibility of exploiting the loss of the immediate signs of identity and place in society, while the second tries to restore and establish identity and social status beyond a shadow of a doubt. The criminal can use disguise and alias to elude recognition. However, the detective can identify the criminal precisely by focusing on marks that the criminal might not be aware of or would find difficult or impossible to conceal. The drama of this new form of evidence lies less in stripping the criminal of his disguise (like the chief of the Sûreté who knocks off Vautrin's wig and reveals his shock of red hair in Balzac's *Père Goriot*) than in capturing the criminal in an act of unconscious revelation.

While the clearest and ultimately most successful example of new systems of criminal identification was the gradual adoption of the fingerprint,[24] throughout the latter part of the nineteenth century (and into the twentieth) photography was used both as a means of identification and as a means of gathering evidence of crime. The collection of photographs of criminals under arrest began soon after the invention of photography. Phéline cites examples from Brussels in 1843 and 1844, Birmingham in 1850, and the use of a photograph as legal evidence in Lausanne in 1854.[25] The Paris prefecture created an official photographic service department in 1873.[26]

Rogues' galleries (as these collections of photographs were called) were quickly instituted by modern city police departments and immediately caught the public imagination (figs. 1.1, 1.2). The public display of portraits of professional criminals (who sought anonymity and concealment) became one of the most popular forms of photographic galleries, with tourists flocking to them as an urban sight and Barnum displaying them in his museum.[27] Apprehension of criminals, both in reality and in detective fiction, often hinged on recognizing them from these photographs; *Le Pickpocket mystifié*, a Pathé film from 1911, for instance, shows detective Nick Winter trailing a pickpocket he has identified from a book of criminal photos he carries with him.

However, the very nature of the photograph, its detailed accuracy and instantaneity, created both organizational and procedural problems. Rogues' galleries were assembled by police departments around the world before a theory was devised to underpin their organization and method. Such photographic collections demanded regulation by systems of knowledge and classification. This new medium, so rich in indexical and iconic information, had to be systematized in order actually to supply the identifications they seemed to promise. How could this new method for producing an accurate image that could be made quickly and circulated widely fulfill its promise of universal surveillance?

An initial problem came from criminal resistance to the process. Criminals posed by police for such portraits would distort their facial expres-

Fig. 1.1. Male mug shots from a rogues' gallery, reproduced in Brynes's *1886 Professional Criminals of America.*

Fig. 1.2. Female mug shots from a rogues' gallery, reproduced in Brynes's *1886 Professional Criminals of America.*

sions in the hope of rendering their photographs unidentifiable. The slow speeds of early photography made possible this painless equivalent of the self-disfiguration of Sue's brigand. The face needed only to be contorted briefly in order to create a grotesque photograph.[28] A famous caricature (which also appeared as a comic photograph) captured the scene of guards holding a grimacing and struggling prisoner as a photographer takes his picture (figs. 1.3, 1.4). Although some commentators claimed that this image was purely fictional, a number of photographs included in Gustave Macé's "criminal museum" (a collection of mug shots published in 1890) show criminals similarly restrained or making bizarre grimaces.[29] However, the practice, made more difficult by even greater camera speeds, seems to have been short-lived. In 1886 Inspector Brynes declared:

> The very cleverest hands at preparing a false physiognomy for the camera have made their grimaces in vain. The sun has been too quick for them, and has imprisoned the lines of the profile and the features and caught the expression before it could be disguised. There is not a portrait here but has some marked characteristic by which you can identify the man who sat for it. That is what has to be studied in the Rogues' Gallery—detail . . . the skilled detective knows all this and looks for distinguishing marks peculiar to his subject.[30]

The caricature of prisoner resistance to photographic methods of fixing identity received a cinematic treatment (with some fascinating transformations) in an early film produced by the American Biograph Company. The single shot of A Subject for the Rogue's Gallery (1904) shows a woman criminal held (as in the caricature prototype) by a pair of cops as her photo is taken. The woman contorts her face comically, attempting to render any likeness unrecognizable. However, as she attempts to subvert the fixing of her image, the Biograph camera closes in on her, tracking forward, its gradually closer framing seeming to underscore the ineffectiveness of her attempt. As the film ends, the frustrated woman weeps, framed in medium close-up.

This early masterpiece marshals the device of camera movement in what can only be seen as a self-reflective moment, dramatizing both the film viewer's growing curiosity about this female spectacle and the oppressive power of the diegetic camera as it relentlessly sees through the woman's performance. Instead of a single contortion, the film presents a gamut of grimaces, until the prisoner gives up in exhaustion before the unblinking cinema camera. Perhaps more eloquently than any still photograph, this brief film acts out the drama implicit in all police photography which Phéline describes as "the exercise of political power on the individual's body and image."[31]

If the criminal's attempt to evade the photographic lens supplied only

Fig. 1.3. Police photographing a recalcitrant criminal. Staged photograph from Brynes's *1886 Professional Criminals of America.*

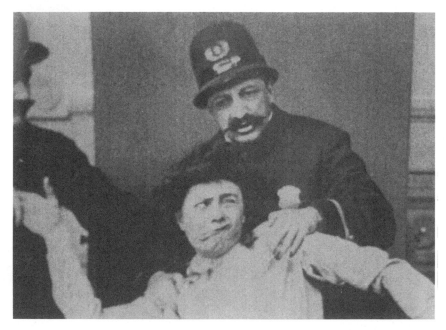

Fig. 1.4. Frame enlargement from Biograph's 1904 film *A Subject for the Rogue's Gallery,* shot by the cameraman A. E. Weed.

a temporary and largely ineffectual check on the use of photography in criminal identification, a more serious obstacle came from the nature of photography itself. Constructing a method which could use photography and other means of physical description and measurement in order to permanently fix an identity and individualize a subject depended on overcoming photography's tendency to capture the contingent and ephemeral, on substituting some core of identity for the mobile play of features. As Phéline phrases it, the photograph was simultaneously too poor and too rich a form of evidence to supply the easy means of identity a modern police department required.[32] The French police statistician Alphonse Bertillon introduced the most thorough and influential nineteenth-century systematization of photographic identification of criminals. As Alan Sekula puts it:

> Bertillon sought to break the professional criminal's mastery of disguises, false identities, multiple identities, and alibis. He did this by yoking anthropometrics [the precise measurement of body parts], the optical precision of the camera, a refined physiognomic vocabulary and statistics.[33]

Bertillon directly confronted the information chaos that an ever-expanding rogues' gallery of photographs presented for modern detective bureaus:

> During the last ten years the Parisian police have collected over 100,000 photographs. Do you suppose it possible to compare successively each of these 100,000 photographs with each of the 100 individuals who are arrested daily in Paris? . . .
> There was need of a method of elimination analogous to that employed in the sciences of botany and zoology; that is to say, taking as its basis the characteristic elements of the individuality, and not the name, which is liable to falsification.[34]

As Carlo Ginsburg, Alan Sekula, and John Tagg have shown,[35] the use of photography as a means of establishing identity depended on placing it within an archive of information on individuals which became the basic tool for the assertion of control in modern society. Such indexical signs as the fingerprint and the photograph played a key role in relating this archive of information to an actual individual body, but such indices could be effective only within a system that had already been rationalized in such a way that a match between indices and individuals could be made quickly and effectively. As Sekula deftly states, the "central artifact of this system is not the camera but the filing cabinet."[36]

The mere possession of a criminal's image could be useless, or at least unwieldy, Bertillon maintained. First, Bertillon systematized the process of police photography. He standardized the distance of subject from camera; created a special chair on which the subject would sit and which would

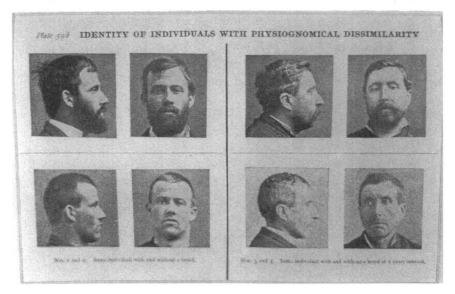

Fig. 1.5. Bertillon's use of photographic comparison to demonstrate the difficulties of an identification based on a general visual similarity, from his *Signaletic Instructions.*

control physical position and posture; determined the type of lens, thereby introducing a closer and unvarying framing; and established the directly frontal and profile angles of the now-familiar mug shot (fig. 1.5).[37] These procedures gave criminal photography a consistency that facilitated its use as information and evidence. Further, it established the process of photography as a disciplinary process, asserting the system's power over the criminal's body and image. The system determined the look and posture within the photograph; the criminal simply delivered up the facticity of his or her body.

But the photographic session was only one aspect of the rationalizing of the body which the Bertillon method entailed. The file of photographs had to be supplemented by the process of anthropometric measurement, a system of measurements of different body parts which allowed a statistical classification of the criminal which the mere resemblance of the photographic image could not deliver. By creating a system based on norms and deviations of separate parts of the body, Bertillon supplied the means of organizing and filing which the rogues' gallery could not supply in itself.

To fit into this schema, the body had to be broken down into comparable parts. Bertillon's measurement system tackles precisely the paradox of photography within modern systems of circulation. Photography serves the purposes of surveillance and identification necessary to a bureaucratic police system by establishing identity through its mesh of iconic resemblance and indexical reference. However, the photograph remains *too* individual, too specific, to be processed as thoroughly as rapid modes of information circulation demanded. Therefore, the analogic photograph needs, in effect, to become digitalized, supplemented by quantifiable data that assign each photograph a unique position within a rationalized system of information. Even the photograph itself had to be analyzed and rationalized:

> The photographic portrait would become a much more efficacious instrument of *search* and *recognition* if detectives were more familiar with the manner of using it; of *analyzing* it, *describing* it, *learning it by heart,* and, in a word, of drawing from it all that it is possible to draw from it; for it is necessary in order to see well, or rather to *perceive* what one *sees,* to know beforehand what are the points to be looked at.[38]

Bertillon rationalized the photograph's iconicity by supplementing it with a battery of bodily measurements and by dissecting the body into a series of features which would allow paradigmatic comparison. The photograph and the body it portrayed became, in Bertillon's system, a text that is articulated into morphological features and which can be "learned by heart." Central to this method was the "verbal portrait," in which the detective did not depend on visual recall but translated the bodily into linguistic signs. A series of preestablished physical traits would be described in a standardized vocabulary. The troubling mass and variety of the physical body so faithfully transcribed by a photograph was thus reduced and translated through a limited code—simple, unvarying, and precise.[39]

Bertillon called his system "signaletics" and called the process "signalizing," indicating that the body of the apprehended person underwent a process by which his or her body was transposed into a series of signs. The chaos of individual bodies was resolved in a truly structuralist manner as an interplay between an articulated system of oppositional elements (the parts of the body chosen for specific measurement) and their actualization in specific individual bodies. Not only could the measurement and morphological description of the different bodily elements be cross-referenced but they could also be arranged against a curve of statistical norms. Bertillon's American disciple Muller explained the method:

> Suppose, again, that a criminal is arrested under an assumed name, and we wish to ascertain whether he has been measured and photographed before. We take an exact measurement of the length of his head and will know at once in which of the main divisions we can find his name. The width of his head will lead us more specifically to the place his photograph can be found. The length of his middle finger, or his foot, forearm, height, little finger,

ear, etc., will enable us to arrive at the exact place where his photograph and description have been filed—if at all.[40]

Bertillon's comparative photographic charts of physical features (with rows upon rows of ear shapes, for instance) seem at first to further dissolve any sense of a unified identity rather than to confirm it (fig. 1.6). But this impression confuses the apparatus with its application. The range of possible ear formations shown on a Bertillon chart remains a fund of paradigmatic possibilities within the investigator's filing system, paradigms to be actualized in a syntagm of a particular body in order to catch within their intersection the guilty individual. Under the Bertillon system, the photograph finds its place within a logic of analysis into paradigmatic components, which are separated from a specific singular body in order to be circulated, compared, and then combined in order to point the finger of guilt. While a criminal possessing the sangfroid of Sue's brigand might alter ear shape, the complex interlocking specifications of a Bertillon chart would be beyond reach, short of total mutilation. The body has become a sort of unwilled speech, an utterance whose code is in the possession of a figure of authority rather than controlled by its enunciator. Although the criminal may assume an alias or seek to camouflage his or her identity through changing hair color or through other disguises, the specialist guided by the Bertillon code sees through this false body language and uncovers an indelible identity residing in a fixed arrangement of bodily elements.

The use of photography in detection in the nineteenth and twentieth centuries turned primarily upon this regulation of the body through close observation founded on systematic classification. In addition to its actual use for the identification of repeat offenders (political radicals as well as criminals—one of Bertillon's first successes was the use of signaletics to capture the anarchist Ravachol in 1892),[41] these new methods were elaborated in modern detective fiction. Bertillon himself recognized the congruence between his method and the plot mechanism of nineteenth-century melodrama. "Is it not a problem of this sort," he asked, "which forms the basis of the everlasting popular melodrama about lost, exchanged, and recovered children?"[42]

The photographic charts of the Bertillon method (with their rows of body parts arranged for observation, comparison, matching, and final identification) provide an emblematic image of the body of modernity, a body resolved into paradigmatic elements, parsed and arranged into an order that the teeming mass of individual bodies could never possess. The truth of the body, its confession of guilt, no longer lies simply in the "indiscretion" of allowing itself to be photographed but in its processing by experts and authorities. The individual body now appears simply as the realization

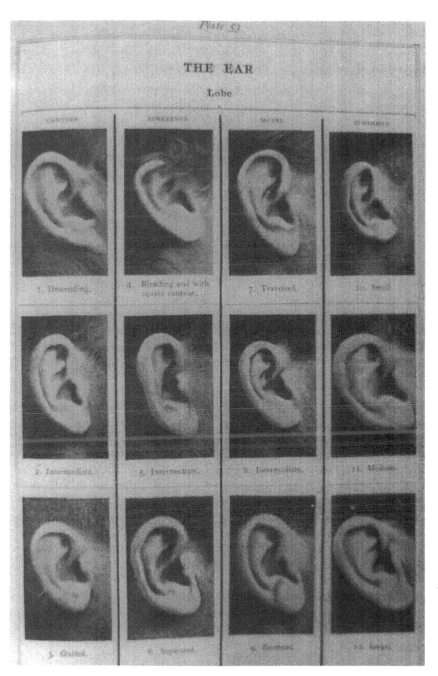

Fig. 1.6. Bertillon photographic chart of ear types, from his *Signaletic Instructions Including the Theory and Practice of Anthropometric Identification.*

of a limited number of measurable types. This systematization brings order and control to the chaos of circulating bodies, tamed through the circulation of information.

FIXING AN IMAGE OF GUILT:
THE BODY CAUGHT IN THE ACT

"He doesn't know the sentence that has been passed on him?"

"No," said the officer again, pausing a moment as if to let the explorer elaborate his question, and then said: "There would be no point in telling him. He'll learn it upon his body."

FRANZ KAFKA, "IN THE PENAL COLONY"

Phéline argues that photography became encoded in the nineteenth century as a ritual of power in which the body of the deviant (including, in addition to criminals, such troubling populations as the invalid, the mad, and the politically suspect) was subjected to a gaze and a recording apparatus possessed by authority.[43] As we have seen in Bertillon's method, this camera trained on the deviant body does not simply record it but also filters it through a new standardized vocabulary of description and classification. In this way the gaze of the law may know the criminal's body more thoroughly than the criminal does. The photograph acted as a "new mark," one which inscribed the deviant body with a socially defined individuality, an individuality which rested ultimately on its structural differentiation from all other recorded individual bodies. Through photography each body was stamped with this ineradicable individuality, but the marks of this difference also had to be rationalized, made systematic, to allow comparisons and identifications. Modern individuality was fashioned as the unique intersection of a limited (and therefore knowable) series of variables.

Systems of classification made the photograph responsive within this modern method of identification, marking each body through a regulated process of classification so thorough that Bertillon even downplayed the necessity of photography to the process.[44] However, the indexical nature of the photograph, its role in actually connecting an individual to his or her own image, still underpinned the whole system. The photograph remained the imprint of the individual body it imaged. Maintaining its identity as a clue, it pointed back to the body that caused it. Reversing the process of the branding iron imprinted directly on the flesh, the "new mark" of the photograph imprinted the sensitive emulsion with the image of the body.

In the modern process of ascertaining guilt and identity, the body thus unconsciously betrays itself by leaving its unalterable and already classified aspects of individuality (an ear of *this* shape, a nose of *that* sort of profile) in the hands of those with power and knowledge. The photograph reveals to the trained eye of the specialist the imprint of individuality upon the criminal body. In a sense, by falling under the regime of photography, the criminal became a *corpus delicti,* his own body supplying evidence of his guilt. The vulnerability of one's body to recording and classification developed into fantasies of universal observation not only through being photographed while under arrest but also through being caught in the act by photography.

Beyond photography's ability to present the likeness of a culprit when the actual culprit might still be at large, the camera could play an essential role as the mute yet unassailable witness of a crime. The camera recording the very act of malefaction appears in drama, literature, and early film before it was really an important process of criminal detection. While the perfection of video has now made the recording of a crime a pervasive and effective form of surveillance (as well as a form of media entertainment), a fascination with photographic evidence of misdeeds seems to predate considerably its widespread application in reality. The element of fantasy involved here leads less to the filing cabinet of governmental power than towards narratives of righteous vindication as well as paranoid plots of entrapment and blackmail.

The photograph as witness did not have to wait long to appear in melodramatic fiction. In 1859 Dion Boucicault, the master of melodramatic theater in England and the United States, used the device of a camera capturing a murderer in the act in *The Octoroon.* At the trial of the wrongly accused innocent, a photographic plate accidentally exposed at the instant of the crime overturns the case and is greeted with the exclamation, "'Tis true. The apparatus cannot lie."[45] While the use of photographs for recognition or for the preservation of evidence (the scene of the crime or elements difficult to transport or preserve, such as fingerprints or corpses)[46] became standard police procedure, capturing the instant of guilt on film remained more the stuff of fiction-making fantasy. But even as fantasy, the photographing of guilty acts reveals central aspects of the mythology of detection or the apparent powers of photography in a world of shifting identities and increased surveillance.

Many early films rework the climax of *The Octoroon.* Biograph's *Falsely Accused* (1908) deals with the murder of an inventor of a motion picture apparatus whose daughter is "falsely accused." At her trial, it is discovered that the murder was filmed by the inventor's camera, and the film is projected, absolving the daughter and condemning the true villain.[47] A more intentional device can be found in *Zigomar vs. Nick Carter,* produced by the French company Eclair in 1912. A banker concerned about theft rigs his safe with a photographic device which will snap the picture of anyone who tries to rob it. The photo thus obtained of Zigomar, the mysterious bandit and master of disguise, when he attempts to rifle the safe, allows detective

Nick Carter not only to establish Zigomar's guilt but also to become aware of his whereabouts and to obtain a clear image of his undisguised face.[48]

Perhaps the most frequent use of photography as evidence of criminal action in early cinema (as well as in real life) deals with sexual rather than violent behavior. Numerous early films, such as Edison's *Getting Evidence* (1906), detail a divorce detective's attempt to photograph a couple's illicit behavior. Although still photography undoubtedly served real-life divorce detectives as well as simple blackmailers, this scenario taps into a deep fascination with the recording of guilt, whose potential for fantasy outruns its actual use. In 1915 Freud analyzed a case of paranoia in which a woman was sure that her meetings with a lover were being photographed.[49] Although early motion picture cameras would hardly seem the optimal tool for capturing evidence of adultery (given their relative bulk, complexity, and noise), Stephen Bottomore has shown that the turn of the century produced dozens of works (short stories and plays as well as films) in which moments of private and surreptitious lovemaking were filmed and then shown publicly, resulting in embarrassment or worse.[50] Frequently, as with Biograph's *Story the Biograph Told* (1904), the filming results from a prank rather than from a detective's surveillance.

In all these cases, however, photographic evidence bears certain recurrent features that define its modernity. First, since the witnessing is technological rather than human, its evidence has a correspondingly greater claim to truth, since the "apparatus cannot lie." The sense of the camera as the nonhuman agent of truth is emphasized by the fact that the filming of certain scenes is often accidental (as in *Falsely Accused*) or unwittingly triggered by the guilty party (as with the camera/safe device in *Zigomar vs. Nick Carter*). The lack of human intention in the operation of the camera mirrors an equally important aspect of the photography of guilt which connects it to the detective's other techniques of evidence and identification. In most cases, the camera takes the culprit's photo when he is caught unawares. Therefore, like Holmes's keenly perceived trifles, the camera captures the guilty one in a moment of unconscious self-betrayal. As an index of guilt, the camera penetrates behind conscious concealment and uncovers a guilty image that the criminal cannot obfuscate, not only because of its indexicality and iconicity but also because the criminal remains unaware that a photo was being taken. As Foucault's discussion of the Panopticon establishes, the regime of the visible as the instrument of power is partly founded on concealing the apparatus of the gaze from view.[51] The photographed party, on the other hand, is inflicted with an ineradicable visibility, betrayed by a body he or she cannot conceal but which is available and readable to the detection specialist.

If the common denominator linking the use of photographic evidence in fantasies and fictional narratives with the regimen of the Bertillon method lies in the fixing of the body as sign of guilt, we also find a fantastic merging of the body with the apparatus, so that the *corpus delicti* becomes identified with the production of an image. In the case of female paranoia, analyzed by Freud, the young woman was convinced she was being photographed largely because she heard a knock or click that she believed came from the snapping of a camera shutter. In analyzing this aural hallucination, Freud identified its likely source as the woman's body, the click being an aural displacement of the throb of her excited clitoris.[52]

Freud does not dwell on this extraordinary bodily identification with the camera apparatus. Certainly, most claims of "I am a camera" rest primarily on the visual rather than the sexual organs. However, when photographs are approached as evidence, the issue rests less on a simulacrum of perception than on the act of recording, the retaining of the indexical trace. The body as the repository of evidence shifts from the body of the criminal to that of the victim which holds evidence of the violence done against it.

The conflation of the body with the processes of the camera are not limited to paranoid fantasies or Freudian interpretations. The most fantastic of such identifications appeared not in the annals of psychoanalysis but from within medical criminology, although the fascination it exerted soon spread to fiction, where it continued to appear after it was scientifically discredited. In 1870 a certain Dr. Vernois, a member of the Society for Legal Medicine of Paris, published his theory of the *optogramme*. Surgically removing the retinas of murder victims and scrutinizing them under a microscope, Doctors Vernois and Bourion claimed to have discovered the imprint of the victims' last sight—an image of their murderers.

As Philipe Dubois has pointed out, the *optogramme* produced a fantasy scenario of guilt involving a number of powerful condensations.[53] The body of the victim becomes a photographic apparatus at the moment of death. For the murderer, the act of being seen collapses into the act of being identified by producing ineradicable evidence, both indexical and iconic, of his guilt. The very act of murder produces its own record. And the instant of death fixes a final, latent image as a mute testimony, one which only modern science and medical technology can bring to light, analyze, and circulate.

We find here an extraordinarily modern transformation of the mark of guilt. The mark is imprinted indexically on the body of the victim rather than symbolically branded on the criminal body by state power. Without even being processed by the Bertillon method, the body itself becomes the source of information, transformed into an iconic index of its own murder. But the information the victim holds hides deeply within the body, which, as Dubois emphasizes, must be surgically opened to obtain it.[53] The murderer, unawares, has left his image behind through a physical reaction that modern science can trace. Once extracted from what Foucault calls "the dark coffer of the body,"[54] this physiological photograph can be placed by the technicians of detection within a broader system of classification in order to identify and convict. In actual fact, as Dubois points out, the images Vernois and Bourion claimed as optogrammes were incredibly obscure and never officially recognized by legal systems.[56] But the fantasy of the murderer leaving behind his image like a wound in the victim's body continued to grab the public imagination. Retina images appeared in the tales of the popular French detective Rocambole in the late nineteenth century, and played a key role in such early twentieth-century works of popular fiction as Thomas Dixon's 1905 novel *The Clansman* (the source for *The Birth of a Nation*), and such films as Pathé's *La Decouverte du docteur Mitchoff* (1911).[57]

In 1867 Villiers de l'Isle-Adam[58] used the concept of the optogramme for the climax of his fantastic tale "Claire Lenoir," inspired apparently by claims made a few years before Venois's publications that an English photographer had discovered an image of their final glance imprinted on the retina of slaughtered cattle.[59] In the tale's final scene, this pseudoscientific theory combines with occult and spiritualist theories to produce an image of Claire Lenoir's reincarnated husband on her retina at the moment of her death, the imprint of a supernatural vision. Her husband's phantom appears to Claire to terrorize her to her death and thus avenge her suspected marital infidelity.

The description given by the story's narrator, a rationalist doctor named Tribulat Bonhomet, as he makes his examination of her retina, evokes an uncomfortable physicality with overtones of necrophilia. It also reveals a highly gendered encounter, as the female body is probed for evidence by a masculine eye. The conflation of photographic evidence with the body merges here with the motif (discussed by Ludmilla Jordanova and Giuliana Bruno)[60] of the "sexual vision" of medical knowledge, the dissection of a woman's body by a male physician. Photography, autopsy, evidence of female guilt, and occult theories collapse into a delirium of condensations to form this morbid and uncanny tableau. As the female crook in *A Subject for the Rogue's Gallery* becomes subjected to the onslaught of the advancing camera, here a woman is probed to yield up photographic evidence of her own guilt.

Although Bonhomet uses an ophthalmoscope to examine directly the recently deceased woman's retina rather than extract it surgically, an atmosphere of physical violation overwhelms the description of this investigation of the woman's body. Bonhomet confesses to discomfort as he approaches the cadaver, even though he knows that the corpses of thousands of women (although belonging to the lower classes, he admits) are explored in European surgery amphitheaters, morgues, and hospitals each day. Overcoming his sense of indiscretion, he picks up the corpse of Claire Lenoir and wanders about her death chamber until he conceives of placing her across her bed with her head hanging down. This position facilitates his examination and reverses the upside-down retinal image. Declaring "I must see, I must see," he performs his examination, feeling as if he were "peering at the infinite through a keyhole." The supernatural vision he sees, the image of Claire's dead husband reincarnated as a vengeful savage, nearly drives him mad with fright.

In this imaginative and decadent tale Villiers weaves together elements of a modern obsession composed of visual curiosity and the desire for knowledge.[61] Bonhomet gazes into the darkness of the female body and discovers evidence of a supernatural he had previously scorned. More than the eccentric evidence of survival after death that this vision presents, this final scene brings together a peculiarly modern conjunction between the image of female dissection discussed by Jordanova and Bruno and the fantasy of the image as evidence, captured here within the ultimate camera obscura, a corpse.

This climax crystallizes gender relations of the female body and the masculine gaze through its invocation of the dissecting room and operating theater. But it also brings the unique evidence of the photographic imprint into alignment with the new importance accorded the autopsy (and the anatomic pathological knowledge that resulted from it) in nineteenth-century medicine. Like photography, when subjected to the Bertillon method of analysis, this process focused on the analysis of individuals. As Foucault has phrased it, this new medical perception lifted "the old Aristotelian law, which prohibited the application of scientific discourse to the individual," revealing its true locus precisely in "the differentiated form of the individual."[62] As the method of observing "trifles" described by Sherlock Holmes's prototype, Dr. Joseph Bell, had already shown, the modern concepts of guilt and disease rested on constructing a differentiated individual. Photography could provide a technology uniquely capable of constructing the image of this new unit of society (as the extension of Bertillon's photographs to identity cards demonstrates).[63] And the power of photography could range from the mapping of the surface physical characteristic to fantasies of invading the body's depth in order to fix an image of guilt.

Villiers's decadent symbolist tale may not fall precisely within the detective genre (although its frequent references to Poe signals its debt to one of the fathers of the detective story), but a similar conjunction of themes does appear in what I consider the most complex instance of an early film engaging the ambiguities of photographic evidence—Louis Feuillade's *Une erreur tragique* (1913). This two-reel film replays and complicates the scenario of the camera's accidental exposure of marital infidelity which Bottomore isolated. But here the masculine scrutiny of the image of female guilt becomes displaced onto the actual body of a film, on still images on a celluloid strip which repeatedly appear in close-up.

Watching a comic film[64] while on a business trip, a newlywed recognizes his wife, who, caught in the scene on the screen, is shown passing by in the street, arm in arm with a man the husband does not recognize. This possibility of an illicit affair caught unawares comes from an era in which a film shot in the street could still capture a random passerby rather than carefully arranged film extras, and in which a viewer's gaze might linger over such subsidiary action rather than simply attend to the narrative thread and main character.

Obsessed with this photographic evidence of an intrigue, the husband buys a print of the film from the exhibitor. Feuillade cuts to a close-up of the celluloid strip as the husband frantically examines with a magnifying glass the frames of film which bear his wife's image. Although it is his wife's body (and its possible waywardness) that is at issue here, the husband, unlike Tribulat Bonhomet, performs his examination only on the body of the film. Nonetheless, the frantic way he handles and scrutinizes the frames of film (referring to them several times) provides another tableau of a man examining and manhandling the visual evidence of female misconduct.

Feuillade's narrative of jealousy and apparent betrayal follows a different path of development from the earlier infidelity farces (or Villiers's tale of supernatural revenge) by revealing that the unidentified man photographed with the man's wife is, in fact, her brother, something the husband discovers only after he has set in motion his revenge and punishment of his wife. The arrival of the man who announces himself as his wife's brother forces the husband to scrutinize the film frame one more time, finally matching this image of an unknown man with an actual person, who only now is identified as a legitimate family member. Not only does this discovery raise the essential question of the need to interpret properly the evidence offered by a photograph, it also reveals the ease with which an image can be pushed inappropriately into a scenario of guilt. The image of the husband obsessively scrutinizing the frame of the film reveals him mistaking a process of recognition for actual evidence of wrongdoing. It is not surprising that Jean-Luc Godard has in recent years frequently referred to this film, which seems to anticipate his crucial maxim about the cinema: "This is not a just image—it is just an image."[65]

Still photography's ability to arrest an image served several purposes within both the process of criminal detection and its fictional representations. As *A Subject for the Rogue's Gallery* shows, police photography could stem the flow of transformation a criminal might use to elude legal recognition. To the mobility of the urban crowd and the phantasmagoria of false identities and aliases, the legal system opposed a regulated circulation of information and imagery. Such regulation rested upon a classification and disciplining of the body which photography aided but did not, by itself, determine. The photograph must be processed in order to become usable information.

Just as cinema itself developed from technology designed to analyze the flow of bodily motion into calculable segments and observable poses in the early motion studies of Muybridge and Marey, *Une erreur tragique* shows that the motion picture's succession of images can also be stilled, fixing an image of guilt. The image of the body in motion can become that of the body arrested and analyzed, available for comparison and identification. But if cinema is truth twenty-four (or sixteen) frames per second, it is also just a bunch of images. Still and motion photography's most frequent use as evidence lies less in establishing veracity than in regulating the flow of recognition and the assignment of blame, so that it moves in the predetermined circuits of power, as we—and Rodney King—discovered all too recently.

NOTES

A version of this essay was presented at the 1993 Society for Cinema Studies conference in New Orleans. I would like to thank Robert Ray, Miriam Hansen, Mark Sandberg, Roberta Pearson, and Phil Rosen for their comments to me.

1. Wolfgang Schivelbusch, *The Railway Journey: Trains and Travel in the Nineteenth Century* (New York: Urizen Books, 1979). The concept of circulation is discussed on pp. 180–188. On the transformation of space and time in modernity, see also Stephen Kern, *The Culture of Space and Time, 1880–1918* (Cambridge: Harvard University Press, 1983).

2. Upton Sinclair, *The Jungle* (New York: New American Library, 1963), pp. 39–45. The routing of material and work processes within the "new factory system" at the turn of the century is described by Daniel Nelson in *Managers and Workers: Origins of the New Factory System in the United States, 1880–1920* (Madison: University of Wisconsin Press, 1975), pp. 19–25.

3. Quoted in Harold M. Mayer and Richard C. Wade, *Chicago: Growth of a Metropolis* (Chicago: University of Chicago Press, 1969), p. 52.

4. Jonathan Crary, *Techniques of the Observer: On Vision and Modernity in the Nineteenth Century* (Cambridge: MIT Press, 1990), p. 13. Crary's exciting new conception of the role of photography and of the modern body has been highly influential on my essay.

5. Oliver Wendell Holmes, "The Stereoscope and the Stereograph," in *Classic Essays on Photography,* ed. Alan Trachtenberg (New Haven: Leete's Island Books, 1980), pp. 80–81.

6. Georg Simmel, *The Philosophy of Money,* ed. David Frisby, trans. Tom Bottomore and David Frisby, 2d ed., rev. and enl. (London: Routledge, 1990), p. 234.

7. This aspect of capitalism and modernity is treated in Marshall Berman, *All That Is Solid Melts into Air: The Experience of Modernity* (New York: Penguin Books, 1988), especially pp. 87–129.

8. Charles Baudelaire, "The Salon of 1859," in *Art in Paris, 1845–1862,* ed. and trans. Jonathan Mayne (London: Phaidon, 1965), p. 154.

9. The semiotic terms "index" and "icon" come from the work of the philosopher C. S. Peirce. They have been applied to photography by numerous scholars, including Peter Wollen in *Signs and Meaning in the Cinema* (Bloomington: Indiana University Press, 1969), pp. 120–126.

10. Walter Benjamin, *Charles Baudelaire: A Lyric Poet in the Era of High Capitalism,* trans. Harry Zohn (London: NLB, 1983), p. 43. In addition to the many tales of criminals as masters of disguise (from Eugène Sue to *Fantômas*), one could also point to the role disguise plays in a number of Sherlock Holmes tales, such as "The Man with the Twisted Lip," in which a change of identity allows a different relation to city life.

11. Michel Foucault, *Discipline and Punish: The Birth of the Prison* (New York: Vintage Books, 1979).

12. Christian Phéline, *L'Image accusatrice* (Paris: Cahiers de la Photographie, 1985), p. 10. All translations from Phéline are my own.

13. Benjamin, *Baudelaire,* p. 48.

14. Phéline, op. cit., p. 17.

15. Quoted in ibid., p. 37.

16. Ibid., pp. 57–58. Phéline refers to Edouard Bonnier's *Traité theorique et pratique des preuves,* which was commonly used as an authority in the second half of the eighteenth century.

17. Ernst Bloch, "A Philosophical View of the Detective Novel," in *The Utopian Function of Arts and Literature* (Cambridge: MIT Press, 1989), p. 246.

18. Tom Taylor, *The Ticket of Leave Man,* in *Nineteenth-Century Plays,* ed. George Rowell (London: Oxford University Press, 1972), p. 318.

19. Holmes's statement is quoted and discussed by Thomas A. Sebeok and Jean Umiker-Sebeok in "'You Know *My* Method': A Juxtaposition of Charles S. Peirce and Sherlock Holmes," in *The Sign of Three: Dupin, Holmes, Peirce,* ed. Thomas Sebeok (Bloomington: University of Indiana Press, 1983), p. 23. An extremely interesting treatment of the issues of photography and the detective story appears in Robert Ray, "Snapshots: The Beginnings of Photography," in *The Image,* ed. Dudley Andrew (Austin: University of Texas Press, forthcoming).

20. Bell is quoted in Sebeok and Umiker-Sebeok, op. cit., p. 35.

21. Thomas Byrnes, *1886 Professional Criminals of America* (1886; reprint, New York: Chelsea House, 1969), p. 55. I would like to thank James Swoch for making this work available to me.

22. Alphonse Bertillon, *Instructions for Taking Descriptions for the Identification of*

Criminals and Others by Means of Anthropometric Indications, trans. Gallus Muller (Chicago: American Bertillon Prison Bureau, 1889), p. 15. This quote comes from Muller's introduction. Alan Sekula also stresses the individualizing intention of the Bertillon method (in contrast to theorists of the "criminal type," such as Galton and Lombroso) in "The Body and the Archive," *October* 39 (winter 1986): 3–64. In "Snapshots," Ray explores the relations among photography, the detective story, and *physiologies,* although I find the modern practice of identifying a unique individual rather different from the earlier tradition of defining character *types* through physical characteristics.

23. Phéline, op. cit., p. 24.

24. On the adoption of the fingerprint as the sign of identity, see Carlo Ginsburg, "Clues: Morelli, Freud, and Sherlock Holmes," in Sebeok, op. cit., pp. 106–109. Resistance to fingerprints as a standard means of identification (he preferred using the shape of the ear as a distinguishing characteristic), combined with his dubious testimony as a handwriting analyst as a witness for the army at the Dreyfus trial, led to Bertillon's later loss of status as a leader in criminal identification. See Phéline, op. cit., pp. 38–42.

25. Phéline, op. cit., p. 15.

26. Ibid., p. 20.

27. Maren Stange quotes Jacob Riis on the popularity of the rogues' gallery as a tourist attraction, in *Symbols of Ideal Life: Social Documentary Photography in America, 1890–1950* (Cambridge and New York: Cambridge University Press, 1989), p. 19. For their display by Barnum, see the *Hartford Daily Courant,* 29 March 1858, P. T. Barnum file, Billy Rose Theater Collection, New York Public Library. I thank Iris Cahn for this reference.

28. One version of this caricature is reproduced in Phéline, op. cit., p. 106. It appears as an obviously staged photograph on p. 53 of *Professional Criminals.* Ben Singer has indicated to me in conversation that there is a long tradition of such caricatures, and I thank him for first alerting me to this.

29. Phéline quotes Ernest Lacan denying the veracity of this caricature in 1877, but reproduces the grimacing photographs from Macé. (Phéline, op. cit., pp. 106–107.)

30. Brynes, op. cit., p. 53.

31. Phéline, op. cit., p. 115.

32. Ibid., p. 84.

33. Sekula, op. cit., p. 27.

34. Alphonse Bertillon, *Signaletic Instructions, Including the Theory and Practice of Anthropometric Identification,* ed. R. W. McClaughry (Chicago: The Werner Company, 1896), pp. 12–13.

35. See Ginsburg, op. cit., p. 106; Sekula, op. cit.; and John Tagg, "Power and Photography: Part One, A Means of Surveillance: The Photograph as Evidence in Law," *Screen Education* 36 (winter 1980): 17–55.

36. Sekula, op. cit., p. 17.

37. Phéline, op. cit., pp. 12–13, 95.

38. Bertillon, op. cit., p. 4. Emphasis in original. It is interesting to note Sherlock Holmes's comment to Dr. Watson concerning his method: "You see, but

you do not observe" ("A Scandal in Bohemia," in *The Complete Sherlock Holmes* [Garden City: Doubleday and Co.], p. 162).

39. Phéline, op. cit., p. 118.

40. Bertillon, op. cit., pp. 8–9.

41. Phéline, op. cit., p. 38. Phéline also stresses the importance of photography in the suppression of the Commune (pp. 28–32).

42. Bertillon is quoted in Sekula, op. cit., p. 34. One can't help but see his sentiment fulfilled in the contemporary circulation of photographs and descriptions of missing children on milk cartons. In a period of late capitalism, only the containers of commodities circulate as widely and are as easily disposable as children.

43. Phéline, op. cit., p. 20.

44. Ibid., p. 130.

45. In *Plays by Dion Boucicault,* ed. Peter Thompson (Cambridge: Cambridge University Press, 1984), p. 163. It is worth noting that this play also turns on the difficulty of determining racial identity.

46. See Tagg, op. cit., pp. 23–24. The unclaimed dead in the morgue began to be photographed in France in 1874, to preserve evidence that decay might render unrecognizable (Phéline, op. cit, p. 103).

47. For a treatment of *Falsely Accused* in relation to early point-of-view films and several of the issues raised in this paper, see Tom Gunning, "What I Saw from the Rear Window of the Hôtel des Folies-Dramatiques, or, The Story Point of View Films Told," in *Ce que je vois de mon ciné,* ed. André Gaudreault (Paris: Méridiens Klincksieck, 1988), pp. 39–41. As Eileen Bowser points out in her discussion of the film, the police officer who hangs the screen for the courtroom showing of the film is played by D. W. Griffith in his screen debut ("Griffith's Film Career before *The Adventures of Dollie,"* in *Film Before Griffith,* ed. John Fell [Berkeley, Los Angeles, London: University of California Press, 1983], p. 367).

48. For a discussion of this scene in the context of the detective and criminal's use of disguise, see Tom Gunning, "Attractions, Detection, Disguise: Zigomar, Jasset and the History of Film Genres," *Griffithiana* 47 (May 1993): 137–156.

49. Sigmund Freud, "A Case of Paranoia Running Counter to the Psycho-Analytic Theory of the Disease," in *The Standard Edition of the Complete Psychological Works,* trans. and ed. James Strachey (London: The Hogarth Press and the Institute of Psychoanalysis, 1966), 14: 261–272.

50. Stephen Bottomore, "Les Thèmes du témoignage dans le cinéma primitif," *Les Premiers ans du cinéma francais,* ed. Pierre Guibbert (Perpignan: Institute Jean Vigo, 1985), pp. 155–161.

51. Foucault, *Discipline and Punish,* pp. 195–228.

52. "A Case of Paranoia," in Freud, op. cit., pp. 268–271.

53. Philippe Dubois, "Le Corps et ses fantômes: Notes sur quelques fictions photographiques dans l'iconographie scientifique de la second moitié du XIXème siécle," in *L'Acte photographique et autres essais* (Paris: Nathan, 1991), pp. 212–216.

54. Ibid., p. 215.

55. Michel Foucault, *The Birth of the Clinic: An Archaeology of Medical Perception* (New York: Vintage Books, 1975), p. 166.

56. Dubois op. cit., pp. 214–215.

57. See A. E. Murch, *The Development of the Detective Novel* (London: Peter Owen,

1958), p. 120. The poster for the Pathé film shows a bizarre apparatus for the obtaining of the retinal image, consisting of a camera and a magnifying glass focused on a dead man's eye. I would like to thank Yuri Tsivian for pointing this out to me.

58. Villiers's 1886 novel *L'Ève future* prophetically envisioned Thomas Edison's invention of motion pictures as preparation for the creation of a female android. For an extraordinary discussion of Villiers's novel as well as the female body as object of scientific curiosity and the cinematic apparatus, see Annette Michelson, "On the Eve of the Future: The Reasonable Facsimile and the Philosophical Toy," *October* 29 (summer 1984): 3–20.

59. "Claire Lenoir," in Villiers de l'Isle-Adam, *Oeuvres complètes*, ed. Alain Raitt et al. (Paris: Bibliothèque de la Pléiade, 1986), 2: 145–221. The sources for Villiers's use of the retinal image are discussed on p. 1,129 of this critical edition. Samuel Weber discusses "Claire Lenoir" in relation to Freud's notion of the uncanny in "The Sideshow, or Remarks on a Canny Moment," *MLA* 88 (1973): 1,124–1,131. I would like to thank Mikhail Yampolski for first directing me to Villiers's tale.

60. These tableaux are analyzed by Ludmilla Jordanova in *Sexual Visions: Images of Gender in Science and Medicine between the Eighteenth and Twentieth Centuries* (Madison: University of Wisconsin, 1989), pp. 98–110. This theme is further explored through a discussion of silent film and other narrative traditions in Giuliana Bruno's extraordinary *Streetwalking on a Ruined Map* (Princeton: Princeton University Press, 1992), pp. 58–78.

61. For a discussion of a similar obsession, in the nearly contemporaneous theater work of André de Lorde, with the knowledge a woman's body can yield, see my essay "The Horror of Opacity: The Melodrama of Sensation in the Plays of André de Lorde," in *Melodrama Stage, Picture, Screen*, ed. J. S. Bratton, Jim Cook, and Christine Gledhill (London: British Film Institute, 1994).

62. Foucault, *Birth of the Clinic*, p. 170.

63. For a discussion of the origin and growth of the photographic identity card, see Phéline, op. cit., pp. 22–23, 135–138. The most insightful treatment of the use of motion photography in medicine is offered in Lisa Cartwright, "'Experiments of Destruction': Cinematic Inscriptions of Physiology," *Representations* 40 (fall 1992): 51–70.

64. Richard Abel has identified this film as Gaumont's *Onésime vagabond*, in "An Economy of Framing: Photographs and Films in Early French Melodrama, 1909–1913" (Paper delivered at conference of the British Film Institute, "Melodrama: Stage, Picture, Screen," London, July 1992). Besides its analysis of *Une erreur tragique*, this paper includes extremely interesting discussions of the use of photographs in other early French films.

65. See *Jean-Luc Godard: Son + Image, 1974–1991*, ed. Colin McCabe and Mary Lea Bandy (New York: Museum of Modern Art/Harry Abrams, 1992), pp. 149, 162. Godard, in an interview with Serge Daney, speculates—with his usual synchronic sense of chronology—that Mallarmé wrote of the blank page after having just seen *Une erreur tragique*. Gilles Deleuze quotes Godard's maxim ("Pas une image juste, juste une image") on p. 35 of this volume.

TWO

Unbinding Vision: Manet and the Attentive Observer in the Late Nineteenth Century

Jonathan Crary

One of the most important developments in the history of visuality in the nineteenth century was the relatively sudden emergence of models of subjective vision in a wide range of disciplines during the period from 1810 to 1840. Dominant discourses and practices of vision, within the space of a few decades, effectively broke with a classical regime of visuality and grounded the truth of vision in the density and materiality of the body.[1] One of the consequences of this shift was that the functioning of vision became dependent on the contingent physiological makeup of the observer, thus rendering vision faulty, unreliable, and even, it was argued, arbitrary. From the midcentury on, an extensive amount of work in science, philosophy, psychology, and art was coming to terms in various ways with the understanding that vision, or any of the senses, could no longer claim an essential objectivity or certainty. By the 1860s the work of Hermann Helmholtz, Gustav Fechner, and many others had defined the contours of a general epistemological crisis in which perceptual experience had none of the primal guarantees that had once upheld its privileged relation to the foundation of knowledge. And it was as one dimension of a widespread response to that crisis that, beginning in the 1870s, visual modernism took shape.

The idea of subjective vision—the notion that the quality of our sensations depends less on the nature of the stimulus and more on the makeup and functioning of our sensory apparatus—was one of the conditions for the historical emergence of notions of autonomous vision, that is, for a severing (or liberation) of perceptual experience from a necessary and determinate relation to an exterior world. Equally important, the rapid accumulation of knowledge about the workings of a fully embodied observer made vision open to procedures of normalization, of quantification, of discipline. Once the empirical truth of vision was determined to lie in the body, the senses—and vision in particular—were able to be annexed and controlled by external techniques of manipulation and stimulation. This was the epochal achievement of the science of psychophysics in the mid-nineteenth century—above all the work of the scientist-philosopher Gustav Fechner—which rendered sensation measurable and embedded human perception in the domain of the quantifiable and the abstract. Vision thus became compatible with many other processes of modernization. The second half of the nineteenth century was a critical historical threshold, during which any significant qualitative difference between a *biosphere* and a *mechanosphere* began to evaporate. The relocation of perception into the thickness of the body was a precondition for the instrumentalizing of human vision into merely a component of new mechanic arrangements. This disintegration of an indisputable distinction between interior and exterior became a condition for the emergence of spectacular modernizing culture.

It may be unnecessary to emphasize that when I use the word "modernization" I mean a process completely detached from any notions of progress or development, one which is instead a ceaseless and self-perpetuating creation of new needs, new production, and new consumption. Perceptual modalities are thus in a constant state of transformation or, it might be said, in a state of crisis. Paradoxically, it was at this moment when the dynamic logic of capital began to undermine dramatically any stable or enduring structure of perception that this logic simultaneously imposed or attempted to impose a disciplinary regime of attentiveness. It was also in the late nineteenth century, within the human sciences and, particularly, the nascent field of scientific psychology, that the problem of *attention* became a fundamental issue. It was a problem whose centrality was directly related to the emergence of a social, urban, psychic, industrial field increasingly saturated with sensory input. Inattention, especially within the context of new forms of industrialized production, began to be seen as a danger and a serious problem, even though it was often the very modernized arrangements of labor that produced inattention. It is possible to see one crucial aspect of modernity as a continual crisis of attentiveness, to see the changing configurations of capitalism pushing attention and distraction to new limits and thresholds, with unending introduction of new products, new sources of stimulation, and streams of information, and then responding with new methods of managing and regulating perception.

Since Kant, of course, part of the epistemological dilemma of modernity has been about the human capacity for synthesis amid the fragmentation and atomization of a cognitive field. That dilemma became especially acute in the second half of the nineteenth century, along with the development of various techniques for imposing specific kinds of perceptual synthesis, from the mass diffusion of the stereoscope in the 1850s to early forms of cinema in the 1890s. Once the philosophical guarantees of any a priori cognitive unity collapsed, the problem of "reality maintenance" became a function of a contingent and merely psychological faculty of synthesis, whose failure or malfunction was linked in the late nineteenth century with psychosis and other mental pathologies. For institutional psychology in the 1880s and 1890s, part of psychic normality was the ability to synthetically bind perceptions into a functional whole, thereby warding off the threat of dissociation. But what was often labeled as a regressive or pathological disintegration of perception was in fact evidence of a fundamental shift in the relation of the subject to a visual field. In Bergson, for example, new models of synthesis involved the binding of immediate sensory perceptions with the creative forces of memory, and for Nietzsche the will to power was linked to a dynamic mastering and synthesizing of forces.

These and other thinkers were adjacent to an emergent economic system that demanded attentiveness of a subject in terms of a wide range of new productive and spectacular tasks, but which was also a system whose internal movement was continually eroding the basis of any disciplinary attentiveness. Part of the cultural logic of capitalism demands that we accept as *natural* the rapid switching of our attention from one thing to another. Capital, as accelerated exchange and circulation, necessarily produces this kind of human perceptual adaptability and becomes a regime of reciprocal attentiveness and distraction.

The problem of attention is interwoven, although not coincident, with the history of visuality in the late nineteenth century. In a wide range of institutional discourses and practices, within the arts and human sciences, attention became part of a dense network of texts and techniques around which the truth of vision was organized and structured. It is through the frame of attentiveness, a kind of inversion of Foucault's panoptic model, that the seeing body is deployed and made productive, whether as students, workers, consumers, or patients. Beginning in the 1870s but fully in the 1880s, there was an explosion of research and reflection on this issue; it dominates the influential work of Fechner, Wilhelm Wundt, Edward Bradford Titchner, Theodor Lipps, Carl Stumpf, Oswald Külpe, Ernst Mach, William James, and many others, with questions about the empirical and epistemological status of attentiveness. Also, the pathology of a supposedly normative attentiveness was an important part of the inaugural work in France of such researchers as J.-M. Charcot, Alfred Binet, Pierre Janet, and Théodule Ribot. In the 1890s, attention became a major issue for Freud and was one of the problems at the heart of his abandonment of *The Project for a Scientific Psychology* and his move to new psychical models.

Before the nineteenth century, of course, attention can be said to have been a topic of philosophical reflection, and in discussions of the historical problem of attention we often encounter the claim that the modern psychological category of attention is really a more rigorously developed notion of apperception, important in very different ways for Leibniz and Kant. But in fact what is crucial is the unmistakable historical discontinuity between the problem of attention in the second half of the nineteenth century and its place in European thought in previous centuries. Edward Bradford Titchner, who moved from Leipzig to Ithaca, New York, and who was the premier importer of German experimental psychology into America, asserted categorically in the 1890s that "the problem of attention is essentially a modern problem," although he had no sense of how the particular perceiving subject he was helping to delineate was to become a crucial component of institutional modernity.[2]

For attention was not just one of the many topics examined experimentally by late-nineteenth-century psychology. It can be argued that a certain notion of attention is in fact the fundamental condition of its knowledge. That is, most of the crucial areas of research—whether of reaction times, of sensory and perceptual sensitivity, of reflex action, or of conditioned responses—presupposed a subject whose attentiveness was the site of observation, classification, and measurement, and thus the point around which knowledge of many kinds was accumulated. It was not a question, then, of a neutral, timeless activity, such as breathing or sleeping, but rather of the emergence of a specific model of behavior which had a historical structure and was articulated in terms of socially determined norms. Anyone familiar with the history of modern psychology knows the symbolic importance of the year 1879—the year when Wilhelm Wundt established his laboratory at the University of Leipzig.[3] Irrespective of the specific nature of Wundt's intellectual project, this laboratory space and its practices became the model for the whole modern social organization of psychological experimentation around the study of an observer attentive to a wide range of artificially produced stimuli. To paraphrase Foucault, this has been one of the practical and discursive spaces within modernity in which human beings "problematize what they are."[4]

Given the centrality of attentiveness as a scientific object it must be emphasized that the 1880s and 1890s produced sprawling diversity of contradictory attempts to explain it.[5] Since then, the problem of attention has remained more or less within the center of institutional empirical research, although, throughout the twentieth century, minority positions in philosophy and the cognitive sciences have rejected it as a relevant or even meaningful problem.[6] More recently, we see its persistence within the generalized disciplinary arrangements of the social and behavioral sciences in the dubious classification of an "attention deficit disorder" as a label for unmanageable schoolchildren and others.[7]

The prominence of attention as a problem, beginning in the late 1870s, is a sign of a generalized crisis in the status of the perceiving subject. In the aftermath of the collapse of classical models of vision and of the stable, punctual subject those models presupposed, attention became the ill-defined area in which to describe how a practical or effective world of objects could come into being for a perceiver. Initially armed with the quantitative and instrumental arsenal of psychophysics, the study of attention purported to rationalize what it ultimately revealed to be unrationalizable. Clearly specific questions were asked—how does attention screen out some sensations and not others, how many events or objects can one attend to simultaneously and for how long (that is, what are attention's quantitative and physiological limits), to what extent is attention an automatic or voluntary act, to what extent does it involve motor effort or psychic energy? In early behaviorism, its importance diminished, and it became merely a quantity that could be measured externally. In most cases, though, attention implied some process of perceptual or mental organization in which a limited number of objects or stimuli are isolated from a larger background of possible attractions.

Wundt's postulation of an attention center located in the frontal cerebral lobes was particularly influential.[8] His account thus posed attention as one of the highest integrating functions within an organism whose makeup was emphatically hierarchical, and (through the notion that "ontogeny repeats phylogeny") work on attention became suffused with many of the social assumptions of evolutionary thought in the 1870s and 1880s. Perhaps more significantly, Wundt's model of attention, which he effectively equated with will, was founded on the idea that various sensory, motor, and mental processes were necessarily *inhibited* in order to achieve the restricted clarity and focus that characterized attention.[9] That inhibition (or repression) is a constitutive part of perception is an indication of a dramatic reordering of visuality, implying the new importance of models based on an economy of forces rather than on an optics of representation. That is, a normative observer is conceptualized not only in terms of the objects of attention but also in terms of what is not perceived, of the distractions, fringes, and peripheries that are excluded or shut out of a perceptual field.

What became clear, though often evaded, in work of many different kinds on attention was what a volatile concept it was. Attention always contained within itself the conditions for its own disintegration; it was haunted by the possibility of its own excess—which we all know so well whenever we try to look at any one thing for too long. In one sense attentiveness was a critical feature of a productive and socially adaptive subject, but the border that separated a socially useful attentiveness and a dangerously absorbed or diverted attention was profoundly nebulous and could be described only in terms of performative norms. Attention and distraction were not two essentially different states but existed on a single continuum, and attention was thus, as most increasingly agreed, a dynamic process, intensifying and diminishing, rising and falling, ebbing and flowing according to an indeterminate set of variables. In the interest of keeping this introduction brief, I can only mention another major part of the inaugural research and discourse on attention in the late nineteenth century—and this was the study of hypnosis. Hypnotism, for several decades, uneasily stood as an extreme model of a technology of attention. As experimentation seemed to show, the borderline between a focused normative attentiveness and a hypnotic trance was indistinct; that is, they were essentially continuous with each other, and hypnosis was often described as an intense refocusing and narrowing of attention, accompanied by inhibition of motor responses. Perhaps more importantly, research disclosed a seemingly paradoxical proximity of dreaming, sleep, and attention.

Much of the discourse of attention attempted to salvage some relatively stable notion of consciousness and some form of a distinct subject/object relation, but it tended rather to describe only a fleeting immobilization of a subject effect and an ephemeral congealing of a sensory manifold into a cohesive real world. Attention was described as that which prevents our perception from being a chaotic flood of sensations, yet research showed it to be an undependable defense against such chaos. In spite of the importance of attention in the organization and modernization of production and consumption, most studies implied that perceptual experience was labile, that it was continually undergoing change and was, finally, dissipative. Attention seemed to be about perceptual fixity and the apprehension of presence, but it was instead about duration and flux, within which objects and sensation had a mutating, provisional existence, and it was ultimately that which obliterated its objects. The institutional discourses on attention depended both on the malleability and mobility of a perceiver at the same time that they sought to make this flux useful, controllable, and socially manageable.

In terms of its historical position, then, attention is much more than a question of the gaze, of looking, of opticality. Within modernity, rather, vision was merely one layer of a body that could be captured, shaped, directed by a range of external techniques, a body that was also an evolving sensory-motor system capable of creating and dissolving forms.

I want now to continue this discussion of the new practical and discursive importance of attentiveness from a more localized point of view, through the frame of a painting by Manet. He is important here less as an emblematic figure supporting some of the most dominant accounts of modernism than as one of a number of thinkers about vision in the late 1870s working within a field whose discursive and material texture was, as I have suggested elsewhere, already being reconfigured. I will, therefore, examine certain features of the painting *In the Conservatory* (1879), in terms of its position within a social space in which attention would increasingly be set up as the guarantee of certain perceptual norms and in which attention, in a wide range of institutional discourses, would be posed as a synthetic activity, as a centripetal energy that would be the glue holding together a "real world" against various kinds of sensory or cognitive breakdown (fig. 2.1).

According to a number of critics, one of the crucial formal achievements of Manet's work in the context of early modernism was his tentative splitting apart of figural, representational facts on one hand from the facts of autonomous pictorial substance on the other, and his approaching, in his advanced canvases, a breaking point of "formlessness."[10] In 1878 and 1879, for example, in *Self-portrait with Palette, Portrait of George Moore,* and *The Reader,* he dances near the edges of this possible rupture (fig. 2.2). Painted with an openness and looseness, a kind of manual velocity, but also with a deeply confident *inattention* to the object and its coherence, such images present what Georges Bataille has called Manet's "supreme indifference."[11]

However, I've chosen to look at a quite different kind of Manet painting from the late 1870s, one that was then—and has continued to be— seen as a retreat from features of his more ambitious style. Exhibited at the Salon of 1879, it provoked some telling responses by mainstream critics. Jules-Antoine Castagnary, in the newspaper *Le Siècle,* wrote with a tone of mock surprise: "But what is this? Faces and hands more carefully drawn than usual: is Manet making concessions to the public?"[12] Other reviews noted the relative "care" or "ability" with which Manet had executed this work. And the avalanche of recent commentary on Manet over the last two decades has afforded this painting relatively little notice, in a sense perpetuating the evaluation of it as somehow conservative. It is usually classed as one of Manet's representations of fashionable contemporary life, of "la vie moderne," as an image with little of the inventiveness and formal audacity of *A Bar at the Folies-Bergères* (1881). A leading Manet scholar insists that, unlike other advanced paintings of the late 1870s, the man and woman in *In the Conservatory* do not for a moment "waver and disintegrate in the colored light." Others have pointed to "the more conservative technique," and the "more contained outlines" of the figures in contrast to Manet's other work of the same years.[13]

I would like to pursue here some of the implications of the choices Manet has made in this particular image, of what it might mean to suggest that he is holding something together, working to "contain" things, or to ward off experiences of disintegration. I do not think that it explains much

Fig. 2.1. Edouard Manet, *In the Conservatory*, 1879.

to say that the work is simply a shift back to a more conventional "naturalism," or that, stung by a string of Salon rejections in the 1870s, he modified his style in the hope of wider critical acceptance, for this does not address the very strangeness of this painting. Rather, I believe that *In the Conservatory* is, among many other things, an attempt to reconsolidate a visual field that was in many ways being disassembled, an attempt to fasten together symbolic contents that resisted immobilization.

I see the painting as a complex mapping out of the ambiguities of visual attentiveness which Manet knew so deeply and intuitively, and as a playing out of his own mixed and shifting relation to a visual field. Perhaps most importantly, I see the painting as a figuration of an essential conflict within the perceptual logic of modernity, in which two powerful tendencies are at work. One is a binding together of vision, an obsessive holding together of perception to maintain the viability of a functional real world, while the other, barely contained or sealed over, is a logic of psychic and economic exchange, of equivalence and substitution, of flux and dissolution which threatens to overwhelm the apparently stable positions and terms that Manet seems to have effortlessly arranged.

Fig. 2.2. Edouard Manet, *The Reader,* 1879.

There are many signs of this binding energy in the painting, but perhaps the most striking is the carefully painted face of the woman. As contemporary critics noted, this face seemed to be an obvious indication of a shift in Manet's practice, and in fact part of the specific character of Manet's modernism turns around the problem of what Gilles Deleuze has called "faciality."[14] In much of Manet's work, the very imprecision and amorphousness of the face become a surface that, alongside its casualness, no

longer discloses an inwardness or a self-reflection, but rather becomes a
new, unsettling terrain that one can trace into the late portraits of Cé-
zanne. But something quite different is at work in *In the Conservatory*, and
it is clearly more than just a tightening up of what has been called Manet's
"messy broken touch," "his vague and sloppy planes."[15] It is, rather, a return to a more tightly bound order of "faciality," one that resists disman-
tling and connection with anything outside the articulated hierarchy of a
socialized body. It is as if for Manet the relative integrity of the face defined (or approximated) a certain mode of conformity to a dominant reality, a conformity that so much of his work evades or bypasses.

Supporting this relatively cohesive faciality, and central to the effect of
the entire painting, is the woman's corseted, belted, braceleted, gloved,
and beringed figure, marked by all these points of compression and restraint.[16] Along with the coiled, indrawn figure of the man, these indications of bodies reined in stand for many other kinds of subduing and
constraint which go into the construction of an organized and inhibited
corporality. We can also note the way in which the flower pots and vases
stand as signs of a related enclosure and "holding in," which, as instruments of domestication, at least partially confine the proliferating growth
of vegetation surrounding the figures. Even the lathed vertical posts of the
bench are little echoes of the cinched figure of the woman, as if the wood,
like some malleable substance, is squeezed in the middle with a clamp.
(This feature also suggests the mechanical repeatability of the seated figure.) Thus this image is a holding action, a forcing back of circulating and
previously scattered components into a semblance of cohesive pictorial
unity. The result, however, is a disjunct, compressed, and space-drained
field. And the thematic of pressure, of squeezing, is curiously suggested by
Manet's title for the work, *Dans la serre*. The word *serre*, of course, means
"greenhouse," although it originally meant simply "a closed place." It is also
a form of the verb *serrer*, which means to grip, to hold tightly, to clench, to
tighten.

It was around this time—the late 1870s and early 1880s—that a remarkable overlapping of problems became evident both in some practices
of visual modernism and the empirical study of perception and cognition
and in the newly emerging study of pathologies of language and perception, especially in France and Germany. If certain areas of modernism and
the empirical sciences around 1880 were both exploring a perceptual field
newly decomposed into various abstract units of sensation and new possibilities of synthesis, contemporary research on such newly identified nervous disorders as hysteria, abulia, psychasthenia, and neurasthenia all
described various weakenings and failures of the integrity of perception
and its collapse into dissociated fragments. Alongside the discovery of the
linguistic disorders grouped under the category *aphasia*, a set of related

visual disruptions was described by the resonant term *agnosia*.[17] Agnosia was one of the primary *asymbolias,* or impairments, of a hypothetical symbolic function. Essentially, it described a purely visual awareness of an object, that is, an inability to make any conceptual or symbolic identification of an object, a failure of recognition, a condition in which visual information was experienced with a kind of primal strangeness. Using the frame of the clinical work conducted by Kurt Goldstein in the 1920s, we could define agnosia as a state in which objects within a perceptual field cease to be integrated into a practical or pragmatic plasticity with intentional or lived coordinates.

If the study of aphasia was bound up in a specifically modern reconfiguration of language, the study of agnosia and other visual disruptions produced a range of new paradigms for the explanation of human perception. For classical thought, the perceiver was generally a passive receiver of stimuli from exterior objects which formed perceptions that mirrored this exterior world. The last two decades of the nineteenth century, however, gave rise to notions of perception in which the subject, as a dynamic psycho-physical organism, actively constructed the world around it through a layered complex of sensory and cognitive processes of higher and lower cerebral centers. Beginning in the 1880s and continuing through the 1890s, various models of holistic and integrating neural processes were proposed, especially in the work of John Hughlings-Jackson and Charles Sherrington, which challenged localizing and associationist models.

As a result of his work in the 1880s, Pierre Janet postulated the existence of what he called the "reality function." He repeatedly saw patients with what seemed to be fragmented systems of sensory response which he described as a reduced capacity to adapt to reality. One of the key symptoms of this loss of a so-called reality function was a failure of a capacity for normative attentive behavior. But this failure could either be the weakening of attentiveness found in psychasthenia and abulias or its intensification noted in fixed ideas and monomanias.

Janet's work, no matter how much it has been disparaged for its "incorrectness" in relation to hysteria, is particularly valuable for its formal description of different kinds of perceptual dissociation. What is important is not Janet's often exorbitant classification of various neuroses but rather his account of common symptoms that traversed so many different kinds of patients: various forms of splitting and fragmentation of cognition and perception, what he called *désagrégation,* widely varying capacities for achieving perceptual synthesis, disjunctions between or isolation of different forms of sensory response.[18] He repeatedly recorded constellations of symptoms involving perceptual and sensory derangements in which autonomous sensations and perceptions, by virtue of their dissociation and fragmented character, acquired a new level of intensity. But if I single out

Janet, it is simply because he was one of many researchers who discovered how volatile the perceptual field can be, and how dynamic oscillations of perceptual awareness and mild forms of dissociation were part of what was considered normative behavior.

Implicit within such dynamic theories of cognition and perception was the notion that subjectivity is a provisional assembly of mobile and mutable components. Even more explicit, perhaps, was the idea that effective synthesis of a "real world" was, to a large extent, synonymous with *adaptation* to a social environment. Thus, within various studies on attention there was a consistent but never fully successful attempt to distinguish two forms of attentiveness. The first was conscious or voluntary attention, which was usually task-oriented and was often associated with higher, more evolved behavior. The second was automatic or passive attention, which for scientific psychology included the areas of habitual activity, daydreaming, reverie, and other absorbed or mildly somnambulant states. The threshold at which any of these states could shift into a socially pathological obsessiveness was never clearly defined and could only become evident with some clear failure of social performance.

Now to go back to the Manet: One of the most ambivalent but significant features of the painting is the state of the seated woman. How does one begin to characterize it or situate it historically? Clearly, within Manet's work there are many figures and faces we can affiliate with this one. Is she merely another instance of Manet's often-cited blankness, psychological emptiness, or disengagement? Perhaps. But I believe such a reading can be specified and pushed further. Jean-Jacques Courtine and Claudine Haroche, in their book *Histoire du visage,* insist that in the nineteenth century a new regime of faciality takes shape.[19] After three centuries in which the meanings of the human face were explained in terms of rhetoric or language, the face in the nineteenth century comes to occupy a precarious position by belonging to a human being both as a physiological organism and as a privatized, socialized individual subject. Courtine and Haroche see Charles Darwin's *Expression of Emotions in Man and Animals,* published in 1872, as belonging to a world no longer in communication with that of Le Brun. Darwin's work is indicative of the split status the face has acquired—the face has become simultaneously a symptom of an organism's anatomical and physiological functioning *and,* in its relative impenetrability, the mark of the success or failure of a process of self-mastery and control implicit in the social construction of a normative individual. In particular, it is within the field of mental pathology, with its specifically modern analyses of hysterias, obsessions, manias, and anxieties, that the face, with all its intrinsic motility, becomes a sign of a disquieting continuum between the somatic and the social.

With the idea of that continuum in mind, it is possible to see the woman, with face and eyes as a special key, on one level as a straightforward image of a public presentation of an impassive mastery of self (perhaps a self-mastery in response to some verbal remark or proposal by the man), which, however, coexists with being in the grip of some thoroughly ordinary involuntary or automatic behavior. And again we are allowed by Manet, who painted the face with uncharacteristic definition, to ask such specific questions.[20] Is she engaged in thought, or in vacuous absorption, or in that form of arrested attentiveness that borders on a trance?

It's hard to think of another Manet figure with this kind of inert waxwork quality. In a sense, we are shown a body whose eyes are open but do not see—that is, do not arrest, do not fix, do not in a practical way appropriate the world around them, eyes that even denote a momentary state comparable to agnosia (fig. 2.3). I would restate that it is not so much a question of vision, of a gaze, as of a broader perceptual and corporal engagement (or perhaps disengagement) with a sensory manifold. If it is possible to see the suggestion of somnambulance here, it is simply as a forgetfulness in the midst of being wakeful, the indefinite persistence of a transient daydreaming. Research in the early 1880s made clear that seemingly inconsequential and everyday states of reverie could transform themselves into autohypnosis. William James, himself a painter for a time, in his *Principles of Psychology*, which he began writing in 1878, describes how such states are inseparable from attentive behavior:

> This curious state of inhibition can at least for a few moments be produced at will by fixing the eye on vacancy . . . monotonous mechanical activities that end by being automatically carried on tend to produce it . . . the eyes are fixed on vacancy, the sounds of the world melt into confused unity, the attention becomes dispersed so that the whole body is felt, as it were, at once, and the foreground of consciousness is filled, if by anything, by a sort of solemn sense of surrender to the empty passing of time. In the dim background of our mind we know what we ought to be doing: getting up, dressing ourselves, answering the person who has spoken to us. . . . But somehow we cannot start. Every moment we expect the spell to break, for we know no reason why it should continue. But it does continue, pulse after pulse, and we float with it.[21]

It was learned that in both somnambulant and hypnotic states, sensations, perceptions, and subconscious elements could loosen themselves from a binding synthesis and become floating, detached elements, free to make new connections. And with the spatial relation between the two figures in this painting, there is a curious similarity to one of the early forms of therapeutic practice which came out of the work of Charcot, Janet, and others in the early 1880s at the hospital of Salpêtrière: a method of standing behind so-called hysteric patients and whispering to them while they appeared to be preoccupied and inattentive to their surroundings which

Fig. 2.3. Detail from *In the Conservatory*.

made it seem possible actually to communicate with a dissociated element of a fragmented subjectivity.[22]

Manet's painting is about a more generalized experience of dissociation, even while he maintains a superficially unified surface, even while he asserts the efficacy of a "reality function." Consider how Manet has painted the man's eyes (or, more accurately, how he has only alluded to them). Manet suggests here an even more equivocal attentiveness and/or distraction, in which the punctuality of vision is disrupted. There is no visual mastery, no ocular potency here. His two eyes are shown as split, a literal dissociation—one eye, seemingly open, looking beyond and perhaps slightly above the woman beneath him. Of his other eye, all we see is the lowered eyelid and eyelash. Perhaps it is looking at the woman's umbrella, her gloved hand and the loose glove it holds, the pleats of her dress, perhaps even at the ring on her finger. But whatever he sees, it is as a disunified field, with two disparate optical axes, and he sees it with an attentiveness that is continually deflected and misaligned within the compressed indoor/outdoor world of the greenhouse.[23]

So within a work depicting two apparently attentive figures, Manet discloses an attentiveness that has actually been folded into two different states of distraction within which the stability and unity of the painting begin to corrode. That surpassing or breakdown of normative attentiveness, whether as autohypnosis or some other mild, trancelike state, provides conditions for new mobile and transient syntheses, and we see in this painting a whole set of associative chains which are part of a libidinal economy that exceeds the binding logic of the work. Freud, in particular, linked an involuntary mobile attention with hypnosis and with the state that immediately precedes sleep.[24] There are the obvious and not so obvious metaphoric displacements and slippage between the cigar, the fingers, the rings on the fingers, the closed umbrella, the braceleted wrist, and the rebuslike chain of flowers that become ear, eyes, and then flowers again. Or the way the man's fingertip is curiously attenuated to a point like the huge spiky green leaves behind him, or the play between the leaves of the engulfing plant to the right of the man and the pleats of the woman's skirt. We can look at the odd displacement of the man's lower legs by the two pots of a similar color to the lower right. One could go on, but these are some of the ways in which attention, as a selective or, some might say, repressive function, drifts away from itself, scattering the cohesion of the work. And this happens amid the overall compression of the space, which seems to buckle and ripple at certain points, especially in the odd push-pull of the two vases at the lower left, with their disordered figure/ground relation. At the same time, it's possible to map out a larger trajectory in which the breakdown of a normative attention into a dispersed distraction

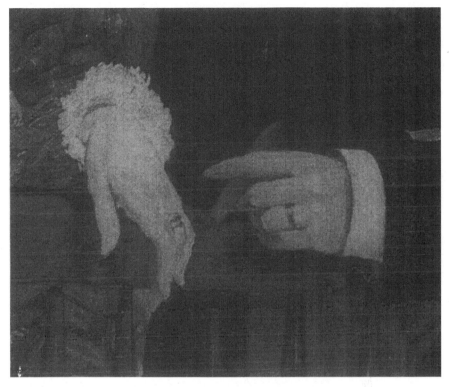

Fig. 2.4. Detail from *In the Conservatory.*

is the very condition for its reassemblage and rebinding into the repetitive laws of the unconscious.

In addition to what I have suggested so far, another obvious sign of the binding energy of the work is of course the two wedding rings, adjacent to each other near the very center of the painting.[25] Since the painting was first exhibited, there has been considerable speculation about whether Manet intended to show a married couple (and in fact his models for this work were married) or an illicit rendezvous between a man and a woman married to other partners. I would insist that this indeterminacy is a crucial part of the work. It bespeaks the split relation of Manet to his subject—it is simultaneously an image of conjugality and adultery. That is, the wedding bands and the alliance thus implied are about a field of fixed positions, of limits, of desire contained and channeled, a system in which the couple is a binding stasis (fig. 2.4). One of the original meanings of the German word *bindung* was the hooping of a cask of liquid, that is, a containing of flux, like the hooped, corseted torso of the woman which is part of this obsessive "holding-in." And one might even suggest that the structure of the work, in which the male and female are kept apart by the grid of the bench and differentiated by their two noncommunicating fields of vision, is a "blossoming" bride and bachelor enmeshed in a verdant machine of perpetual nonfulfillment.

But curiously, the French translation of Freud's *bindung* is *liaison*.[26] That is, if the liaison is what holds things together psychically, the figuration of an adulterous liaison in this painting is also what undermines that very binding. Adultery, in the context of modernization, no longer has a transgressive status but is what Tony Tanner calls "a cynicism of forms," merely another effect of a dominant system of exchange, circulation, and equivalence which Manet can only indirectly confront.[27]

The fingers that almost but do not touch is a central nonevent. They suggest a tactility that has become anesthetized or even paralyzed. It is an image of attentiveness in which there is a drift and gap between different systems of sensory response, a lessening of the mutual awareness of the different senses, say, between sight and smell.[28] It would be hard to rule out here the suggestion of an olfactory attentiveness of the kind Freud described in a letter to Wilhelm Fliess, in which he stressed that the smell of flowers is the disintegrated product of their sexual metabolism.[29] We also have the split between the woman's one gloved hand and the other, bare hand, ready to receive or initiate a caress. But the man's hand seems shaped into a pointing finger, as if to indicate a focus of attention which diverges from his already ambivalent glance, and in a direction opposite from where the umbrella directs our eye. Could he be pointing at the woman's strangely disembodied hand and overly bent wrist? A bend that is anatomically as extreme as many images of hysterical contracture? (Alfred Binet, Richard Krafft-Ebing, and others in the 1880s noted the prevalence, especially in male subjects, of a hand fetishism.) In any case, the frozen character of the scene, or what we could call its powerful system of fixations and inhibitions, coexists with another logic of *errance,* with the wandering of a sensory body that seeks pathways out of binding arrangements of all kinds. It is an unfixed eye that is always at the fold between attentiveness and distraction.

That very fold, where attentiveness produces its own dissolution, takes on concrete form in the pleats of the woman's underskirt, almost like the legless end of a mermaid beached on the greenhouse bench, and it opens onto a whole new organization of distraction, with which so much of Manet's late work is intertwined. He shows us here a rather detailed image of what is clearly a fashion of 1879, the so-called princess-style walking-out dress, with its close-fitting, hip-length jacket bodice and double skirt and tight sleeves with cuffs slightly flaring at the wrists. It is especially with the emerging commodity world of fashion that the ephemerality of attentiveness comes into play as a productive component of modernization. The display here, in which the body merely serves as an armature for the commodity, is a momentary congealing of vision, a temporary immobilization within a permanently installed economy of flux and distraction.

Manet in 1879 stands close to a turning point in the visual status of the fashion commodity—a year or so later is when Fredric Ives patents his half-tone printing process, allowing photographs to be reproduced on the same page as typography and setting up, on a mass scale, a new virtual field of the "commodity as image" and establishing new rhythms of attentiveness which will increasingly become a form of work: work as visual consumption. In this painting, we have Manet elegantly disclosing what Walter Benjamin was to articulate so bluntly in the Arcades Project; in addition to providing an image of what Benjamin called "the enthronment of merchandise," the painting illustrates Benjamin's observation that the essence of fashion "resides in its conflict with the organic. It couples the living body to the inorganic world. Against the living, fashion asserts the rights of the corpse and the sex appeal of the inorganic."[30] Thus, despite Manet's play here with the image of adorned women as a flower among flowers, or of fashion as a blossoming forth into a luminous apparition of the new, the commodity is part of the large suffocating organization of the painting. Fashion works to bind attention onto its own pseudounity, but at the same time it is the intrinsic mobility and transience of this form that undermines Manet's attempt to integrate it into the semblance of a cohesive pictorial space and that contributes to the derangement of visual attention mapped out across its surface.

Mallarmé's *La Dernière mode,* the magazine he produced in 1874, was one of the earliest and most penetrating explorations of this new terrain of objects and events. *La Dernière mode* is a kaleidoscopic decomposition and displacement of the very objects that are evoked so glitteringly. Attention in Mallarmé, as Leo Bersani has noted, always moves away from its objects, undermining any possibility of a fully realized presence.[31] The emerging world of fashion commodities and of life structured as consumption, at least for several months in the fall of 1874, revealed to Mallarmé a present impossible to seize hold of, an insubstantial world that seemed aligned with his own sublime disavowal of the immediate.

Manet in one sense gives a solidity and palpable presence to what for Mallarmé remained evanescent, but even here the fashion commodity is present as a kind of vacancy, haunted by what Guy Debord describes as its inevitable displacement from the center of acclaim and the revelation of its essential poverty.[32] Within this new system of objects, which was founded on the continual production of the new, attention, as researchers learned, was sustained and enhanced by the regular introduction of novelty. Historically, this regime of attentiveness coincides with what Nietzsche described as modern nihilism: an exhaustion of meaning, a deterioration of signs. Attention, as part of a normative account of subjectivity, comes into being only when experiences of singularity and identity are overwhelmed by equivalence and universal exchange.

Part of the precariousness of *In the Conservatory* is how it figures attentiveness not only as something constitutive of a subject within modernity but also as that which dissolves the stability and coherence of a subject position. And in a crucial sense the work, in its use of the two figures, is poised at a threshold beyond which an attentive vision would break down in a loosening of coherence and organization. Manet perhaps knew intuitively that the eye is not a fixed organ, that it is marked by polyvalence, by shifting intensities, by an indeterminate organization, and that sustained attentiveness to anything will relieve vision of its fixed character. Gilles Deleuze, writing about what he calls "the special relation between painting and hysteria," suggests that for the hysteric, objects are too present, that an excess of presence makes representation impossible, and that the painter, if not restrained, has the capacity to extricate presences from representation.[33] For Deleuze, the classical model of painting is about warding off the hysteria that is so close to its heart.

In the Conservatory, in the ways I have indicated, thus reveals Manet (for a number of possible reasons) attempting ambivalently to reclaim some of the terms of that classical suppression and restraint. But the result is something quite different from a return to an earlier model, and I have tried to suggest the range of disjunctions within Manet's synthetic activity in this work. Perhaps the painting's most notable feature to evade the state of enclosure, of being "in the grip" or "dans la serre," is the tangled mesh of green behind the figures.[34] Is this what also fills the other side of the room, a possible object of the woman's attention or distraction? Manet has applied the paint of the vegetation so thickly around the figures that it rises up in an encroaching ridge around them; the green is thus physically closer to our view than the figures themselves. This turbulent zone of color and proliferation exceeds its symbolic domestication and ceases to function as part of a figure/ground relationship. It becomes the sign of a perceptual order alien to the relations Manet has sought to freeze or stabilize around the two figures. It is a site on which attention is enfolded into its own dissolution, in which it can pass from a bound to a mobile state. It is amid the continuity between these states that vision can become unhinged from the coordinates of its social determinants. And this is what Manet's grip can only imperfectly keep in check—an attentiveness that would lose itself outside those distinctions.

In terms of the larger project of which this paper is a part, it's perhaps important to suggest some other organizations of visual attentiveness, other networks of perceptual binding and synthesis which are taking shape around this time. In Max Klinger's *Glove* cycle, which he worked on in the late 1870s, the perceptual field is held together by a very different kind of libidinal setup and a very different experience of visual ambiguity (figs. 2.5, 2.6).[35] The glove and other potential sites of fixation in *In the Conservatory* have none of the overloaded investment that the glove has in Klinger, where attentiveness overruns any normative synthesis to become exclusively determined by a singular content. What is crucial about Klinger's cycle is the way vision, although obsessively bound and focused, is at the same time dispersed into serial and metamorphic movements. Attention, even as it is ostensibly tied to the glove, deliriously opens out as a dynamic and productive process. It traces a mobile and shifting path from image to image, adjacent to that emerging social terrain on which flows of desire and the circulation of commodities will ceaselessly overlap.

In a brief historical aside in his book on cinema, Gilles Deleuze insists that the crisis of perception in the late nineteenth century coincides with the moment at which it was no longer possible to hold a certain position, and he indicates the wide range of factors which introduced more and more movement into psychic life.[36] It is especially significant that the first two images in the *Glove* cycle are about roller-skating: the observer as a newly kinetic seeing body set in motion, to glide along uncertain social and durational trajectories. Also, both the greenhouse and the skating rink were two of what Benjamin called public "dream spaces," which opened up new arenas of visual consumption and provided the possibility for previously unknown libidinal encounters and itineraries.

The future tasks of an attentive subject were also foreshadowed in 1879, when Eadweard Muybridge built his zoopraxiscope, a projection device for creating moving images which operates through a technologically induced binding-together of visual sensations (fig. 2.7). He brought it to Paris in 1881 for some celebrated demonstrations before groups of artists and scientists.[37] It is one of many elements in the automation of perception and the machine synthesis of so-called objective reality which began in the mid-nineteenth century and which continues unabated on other lines today. Despite their dissimilarities, Muybridge and Klinger are reciprocally related in terms of their temporal unfoldings of attentiveness: the former as a metric and inflexible redundancy of position, and the latter as a nomadic system of psychic transformations. But early in the twentieth century, these two poles will become overlapping elements within a generalized organization of spectacle.

Even before the actual invention of cinema in the 1890s, though, it is clear that the conditions of human perception were being reassembled

Fig. 2.5. Max Klinger, *A Glove: Action*, 1881.

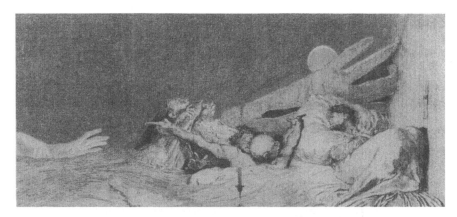

Fig. 2.6. Max Klinger, *A Glove: Anxieties,* 1881.

Fig. 2.7. Zoopraxiscope disc.

into new components. Vision, in a wide range of locations, was refigured as dynamic, temporal, and synthetic. The demise of the punctual or anchored classical observer began in the early nineteenth century, increasingly displaced by the unstable attentive subject, whose varied contours I have tried to sketch out here. It is a subject competent both to be a consumer of and an agent in the synthesis of a proliferating diversity of "reality effects," a subject who will become the object of all the industries of the image and spectacle in the twentieth century. But if the standardization and regulation of attention constitute a path into the video and cybernetic spaces of our own present, the dynamic disorder inherent in attentiveness, which Manet's work begins to disclose, embodies another path of invention, dissolution, and creative syntheses which exceeds the possibility of rationalization and control.

NOTES

1. See my *Techniques of the Observer: On Vision and Modernity in the Nineteenth Century* (Cambridge: MIT Press, 1990).

2. *Experimental Psychology* (New York: Macmillan, 1901), 1:186.

3. On Wundt and the beginnings of the psychology laboratory, see Kurt Danziger, *Constructing the Subject: Historical Origins of Psychological Research* (Cambridge: Cambridge University Press, 1990), pp. 17–33. See also Didier Deleule, "The Living Machine: Psychology as Organology," in *Incorporations*, ed. Jonathan Crary and Sanford Kwinter (New York: Zone, 1992), pp. 203–233.

4. Michel Foucault, *The Use of Pleasure*, trans. Robert Hurley (New York: Random House, 1985), p. 10.

5. A few of the very large number of works on this subject during this period are William James, *The Principles of Psychology*, vol. I (1890; reprint, New York: Dover Publications, 1950), pp. 402–458; Théodule Ribot, *La Psychologie de l'attention* (Paris: F. Alcan, 1889); Edward Bradford Titchner, *Experimental Psychology: A Manual of Laboratory Practice* (New York: Macmillan, 1901), pp. 186–328; Henry Maudsley, *The Physiology of Mind* (New York: Appleton, 1893), pp. 308–321; Oswald Külpe, *Outlines of Psychology* (orig. pub. 1893), trans. E. B. Titchner (London: Sonnenschein, 1895), pp. 423–454; Carl Stumpf, *Tonspsychologie*, vol. 2 (Leipzig: S. Hirzel, 1890), pp. 276–317; F. H. Bradley, "Is There Any Special Activity of Attention," *Mind* 11 (1886): 305–323; Angelo Mosso, *Fatigue* (orig. pub. 1891), trans. Margaret Drummond (New York: G. P. Putman), pp. 177–208; Lemon Uhl, *Attention* (Baltimore: Johns Hopkins University Press, 1890); George Trumbull Ladd, *Elements of Physiological Psychology* (New York: Scribners, 1887), pp. 480–497, 537–547; Eduard von Hartmann, *Philosophy of the Unconscious* (orig. pub. 1868), trans. William C. Coupland (New York: Harcourt Brace, 1931), pp. 105–108; G. Stanley Hall, "Reaction Time and Attention in the Hypnotic State," *Mind* 8 (April 1883): 170–182; Georg Elias Müller, *Zur Theorie der sinnlichen Aufmerksamkeit* (orig. pub. 1873) (Leipzig: A. Adelmann, n.d.); James Sully, "The Psycho-Physical Processes in Attention," *Brain* 13 (1890): 145–164; John Dewey, *Psychology* (New York: Har-

per, 1886), pp. 132–155; Henri Bergson, *Matter and Memory* (orig. pub. 1896), trans. W. S. Palmer and N. M. Paul (New York: Zone Books, 1988), pp. 98–107; Theodor Lipps, *Grundtatsachen des Seelenlebens* (Bonn: M. Cohen, 1883), pp. 128–139; L. Marillier, "Remarques sur le mécanisme de l'attention," *Revue philosophique* 27 (1889): 566–587; Charlton Bastian, "Les Processus nerveux dans l'attention et la volition," *Revue philosophique* 33 (1892): 353–384; James McKeen Cattell, "Mental Tests and Their Measurement," *Mind* 15 (1890): 373–380; Josef Clemens Kreibig, *Die Aufmerksamkeit als Willenserscheinung* (Vienna: Alfred Hölder, 1897); H. Obersteiner, "Experimental Researches on Attention," *Brain* 1 (1879): 439–453; Pierre Janet, "Etude sur un cas d'aboulie et d'idées fixes," *Revue philosophique* 31 (1891): 258–287, 382–407; Sigmund Freud, "Project for Scientific Psychology," in *The Origins of Psycho-analysis,* trans. Eric Mosbacher and James Strachey (New York: Basic Books, 1954), pp. 415–445; Edmund Husserl, *Logical Investigations,* trans. J. N. Findlay (1899–1900; reprint, New York: Humanities Press, 1970), 1:374–386.

6. See, for example, the devaluation of attention as a problem in Maurice Merleau-Ponty, *The Phenomenology of Perception,* trans. Colin Smith (New York: Routledge, 1962), pp. 26–31. Many studies since the mid-twentieth century have worked with notions of cognitive processing and channel capacity borrowed from information theory. One influential modern account of attention is Donald Broadbent's "filter theory" in his *Perception and Communication* (New York: Pergamon, 1958). Examples of recent research include Alan Allport, "Visual Attention," in *Foundations of Cognitive Science,* ed. Michael Posner (Cambridge: MIT Press, 1989), pp. 631–682, and Gerald Edelman, *Bright Air, Brilliant Fire: On the Matter of Mind* (New York: Basic Books, 1992), pp. 137–144.

7. One of the first explicitly sociological accounts of attention is Théodule Ribot, *Psychologie de l'attention* (1889), in which determinations of race, gender, nationality, and class are central to his evaluations. For Ribot, those characterized by deficient capacity for attention include children, prostitutes, savages, vagabonds, and South Americans. Ribot's book was one of the sources for Max Nordau's reflections on attention in *Degeneration* (New York: Appleton, [1892] 1895), pp. 52–57.

8. Wilhelm Wundt, *Grundzüge der physiologischen Psychologie,* 6th ed. (1874; reprint, Leipzig: Engelmann, 1908), 3:306–364; in English as *Principles of Physiological Psychology,* trans. Edward Bradford Titchner (1874; reprint, London: Sonnenschein, 1910), 1:315–320.

9. For a detailed overview of this problem in the nineteenth century, see Roger Smith, *Inhibition: History and Meaning in the Sciences of Mind and Brain* (Berkeley, Los Angeles, London: University of California Press, 1992).

10. See, for example, Jean Clay, "Ointments, Makeup, Pollen," *October* 27 (winter 1983): 3–44.

11. Georges Bataille, *Manet,* trans. Austryn Wainhouse and James Emmons (New York: Skira, n.d.), p. 82.

12. Jules-Antoine Castagnary, *Le Siècle,* 28 June 1879. Cited in George Heard Hamilton, *Manet and His Critics* (New York: Norton, 1969), p. 215.

13. Hamilton, op. cit., p. 212.

14. Gilles Deleuze, *A Thousand Plateaus,* trans. Brian Massumi (Minneapolis: University of Minnesota Press, 1987), pp. 167–191.

15. Hamilton, op. cit., pp. 165, 198.

16. See David Kunzle, *Fashion and Fetishism* (Totowa, N.J.: Rowman and Little-field, 1982), p. 31: "The lacing and unlacing of the corset were rituals which re-tained ancient levels of symbolism and the magical associations of the concepts of 'binding' and 'loosing.' In folk language, to be delivered of a child or to be deflowered, was to be 'unbound'; to unbind was to release special forms of energy. . . . The state of being tightly corsetted is a form of erotic tension and consti-tutes ipso facto a demand for erotic release, which may be deliberately controlled, prolonged, and postponed."

17. The landmark inaugural work on aphasia is Carl Wernicke, *Der aphasische Symptomencomplex* (Breslau: Cohn and Weigert, 1874). One of the first full clinical accounts of agnosia is Hermann Lissauer, "Ein Fall von Seelenblindheit nebst einem Beitrage zur Theorie derselben," *Archiv für Psychiatrie und Nervenkrankheiten* 21 (1890): 222–270. For a recent clinical and historical review of the problem, see Martha J. Farah, *Visual Agnosia* (Cambridge: MIT Press, 1990).

18. For Janet's early work on perceptual disorders and his account of "la désagrégation psychologique," see *L'Automatisme psychologique* (Paris: Félix Alcan, 1889).

19. Jean-Jacques Courtine and Claudine Haroche, *Histoire du visage* (Paris: Rivages, 1988), pp. 269–285.

20. Another approach to this work is suggested by T. J. Clark's discussion of so-cial class and the "face of fashion" in his chapter on Manet's 1882 painting *A Bar at the Folies-Bergère*, in *The Painting of Modern Life* (Princeton: Princeton University Press, 1984), pp. 253–254: "Fashion and reserve would keep one's face from *any* identity, from identity in general. The look which results is a special one: public, outward, 'blasé' in Simmel's sense, impassive, not bored, not tired, not disdainful, not quite focused on anything."

21. James, op. cit., p. 444.

22. Pierre Janet, *The Mental State of Hystericals* (orig. pub. 1893), trans. Caroline Corson (New York: Putnam, 1902), pp. 252–253. This translation should be used with caution.

23. On the organization of the gaze in Manet's multifigure paintings, see Michael Fried, "Manet in His Generation: The Face of Painting in the 1860s," *Critical Inquiry* 19 (autumn 1992): 59–61.

24. Sigmund Freud, *The Interpretation of Dreams*, trans. James Strachey (New York: Avon, 1965), p. 134.

25. Manet's ambivalence about this critical area of the painting is revealed, in part, by the anatomically anomalous form of the woman's left hand. It appears to have a thumb and only three fingers, thus putting in question the exact location (and significance) of her rings.

26. See J. Laplanche and J.-B. Pontalis, *The Language of Psycho-Analysis*, trans. Donald Nicholson-Smith (New York: Norton, 1973), pp. 50–52.

27. Tony Tanner, *Adultery in the Novel: Contract and Transgression* (Baltimore: Johns Hopkins University Press, 1979).

28. Within discussions of attention, there was considerable debate over whether one could attend to more than one sense simultaneously. See, for example, the

negative argument in Ernst Mach, *Contributions to the Analysis of Sensations* (orig. pub. 1885), trans. C. M. Williams (Chicago: Open Court, 1897), p. 112.

29. Sigmund Freud, *The Origins of Psycho-Analysis: Letters to Wilhelm Fliess, Drafts and Notes, 1887–1902,* trans. Eric Mosbacher and James Strachey (New York: Basic Books, 1954), pp. 144–145.

30. Walter Benjamin, *Reflections,* trans. Edmund Jephcott (New York: Harcourt Brace, 1978), pp. 152-153.

31. Leo Bersani, *The Death of Stéphane Mallarmé* (Cambridge: Cambridge University Press, 1982), pp. 74–75.

32. Guy Debord, *The Society of the Spectacle,* trans. Donald Nicholson-Smith (New York: Zone Books, 1994), p. 45.

33. Gilles Deleuze, *Francis Bacon: Logique de la sensation* (Paris: Editions de la différence, 1981), pp. 36–38. The paradoxical relation between representation and presence in painting is a major theme of Mallarmé's 1876 essay on Manet. If representation is to be exceeded, Mallarmé suggests, a particular kind of attentiveness must be achieved: "The eye should forget all else it has seen, and learn anew from the lesson before it. It should abstract itself from memory, seeing only that which it looks upon, and that as for the first time; and the hand should become an impersonal abstraction guided only by the will, oblivious of all previous cunning" (Stephane Mallarmé, "The Impressionists and Edouard Manet," in Penny Florence, *Mallarmé, Manet, and Redon* [Cambridge: Cambridge University Press, 1986], pp. 11–18).

34. On the structural importance of the color green in Manet's work, see Gisela Hopp, *Edouard Manet: Farbe und Bildgestalt* (Berlin: Walter de Gruyter), 1968, pp. 54–58, 116–137.

35. The first etched edition of this cycle appeared in 1881, although the ink drawings were exhibited in 1878. See Christiane Hertel, "Irony, Dream, and Kitsch: Max Klinger's *Paraphrases of the Finding of a Glove* and German Modernism," *Art Bulletin* 74 (March 1992): 91–114.

36. Gilles Deleuze, *Cinema: The Movement-Image,* trans. Hugh Tomlinson (Minneapolis: University of Minnesota Press, 1986), p. 56.

37. Muybridge spent nearly six months in Paris between September 1881 and March 1882. His first European demonstration of the zoopraxiscope was during a soirée at the home of Jules-Etienne Marey which was attended by Helmholtz and the photographer Nadar, among others. For discussions of this visit, see Robert Bartlett Haas, *Muybridge: Man in Motion* (Berkeley, Los Angeles, London: University of California Press, 1976), pp. 127–132, and Anson Rabinbach, *The Human Motor* (New York: Basic Books, 1990), pp. 100–102.

THREE

Modernity, Hyperstimulus, and the Rise of Popular Sensationalism

Ben Singer

Of the many overlapping ideas implied by the term "modernity" (and leaving aside the host of adjacent meanings denoted by "modernism"), perhaps three have dominated contemporary thought. As a moral and political concept, modernity suggests the "ideological shelterlessness" of a postsacred, postfeudal world in which all norms and values are open to question. As a cognitive concept, modernity points to the emergence of instrumental rationality as the intellectual framework through which the world is perceived and constructed. As a socioeconomic concept, modernity designates an array of technological and social changes that took shape in the last two centuries and reached a kind of critical mass near the end of the nineteenth century: rapid industrialization, urbanization, and population growth; the proliferation of new technologies and transportations; the saturation of advanced capitalism; the explosion of a mass consumer culture; and so on.

With the recent interest in the social theories of Georg Simmel, Siegfried Kracauer, and Walter Benjamin, it has become clear that we are also dealing with a fourth major definition of modernity. These theorists focused on what might be called a *neurological* conception of modernity. They insisted that modernity must also be understood in terms of a fundamentally different register of subjective experience, characterized by the physical and perceptual shocks of the modern urban environment. In a sense, this argument is an offshoot of the socioeconomic conception of modernity, but rather than simply pointing to the range of technological, demographic, and economic changes of advanced capitalism, Simmel, Kracauer, and Benjamin stressed the ways in which these changes transformed the texture of experience. Modernity implied a phenomenal world—a specifically urban one—that was markedly quicker, more chaotic, fragmented, and disorienting than in previous phases of human culture. Amid the unprecedented turbulence of the big city's traffic, noise, billboards, street signs, jostling crowds, window displays, and advertisements, the individual faced a new intensity of sensory stimulation. The metropolis subjected the individual to a barrage of impressions, shocks, and jolts. The tempo of life also became more frenzied, sped up by new forms of rapid transportation, the pressing schedules of modern capitalism, and the ever-accelerating pace of the assembly line.

Modernity, in short, was conceived of as a barrage of *stimuli*. As Simmel put it his 1903 essay "The Metropolis and Mental Life" (a crucial text for Kracauer and Benjamin), modernity involved an "intensification of nervous stimulation." Modernity transformed both the physiological and psychological foundations of subjective experience:

> The rapid crowding of changing images, the sharp discontinuity in the grasp of a single glance, and the unexpectedness of onrushing impression: These are the psychological conditions which the metropolis creates. With each crossing of the street, with the tempo and multiplicity of economic, occupational and social life, the city sets up a deep contrast with small town and rural life with reference to the sensory foundations of psychic life.[1]

Cities, of course, had always been busy, but they had never been nearly as busy as they became just before the turn of the century. The sudden increase in urban population (which in the U.S. more than quadrupled between 1870 and 1910), the escalation of commercial activity, the proliferation of signs, and the new density and complexity of street traffic (particularly with the major expansion of electric trolleys in the 1890s) made the city a much more crowded, chaotic, and stimulating environment than it had ever been in the past (fig. 3.1).[2] One need only look at early "actuality" footage of Manhattan, Berlin, London, or Paris—not to mention smaller cities such as Lyon, France, or Harrisburg, Pennsylvania—to be convinced of Simmel's assertion as an encapsulation if not of all aspects of modern experience than at least of a significant part of it.[3]

To place Kracauer and Benjamin's conceptions of modernity in context, we need to look both before and after the periods in which they formulated their ideas. On the one hand, it is apparent that their framing of modernity anticipates much of what contemporary theorists have described as the condition of *post*modernity. A definition of postmodernity stressing its "immediacies, intensities, sensory overload, disorientation, the *melée* of signs and images" overlaps greatly with the neurological conception of modernity, whether or not the overlap is complete (fig. 3.2).[4]

Looking backwards, on the other hand, one is struck by the extent to which Kracauer and Benjamin were tapping into an already widespread

Fig. 3.1. New York, Times Square, 1909.

discourse about the shock of modernity. Social observers in the decades around the turn of the century were *fixated* on the idea that modernity had brought about a radical increase in nervous stimulation and bodily peril. This preoccupation can be found in every genre and class of social representation—from essays in academic journals to aesthetic manifestos (such as Marinetti's and Leger's) to middlebrow commentaries (such as the ubiquitous discussions of neurasthenia) and cartoons in the illustrated press (both in comic magazines such as *Puck, Punch, Judge,* and *Life,* and lowbrow sensational newspapers such as New York's *World* and *Journal*).[5]

Henry Adams's description of urban life, written in 1905, was typical of this broad discourse about the sensory upheavals of modernity:

Forces grasped his [modern man's] wrists and flung him about as though he had hold of a live wire. . . . Every day Nature violently revolted, causing so-called accidents with enormous destruction of property and life, while plainly laughing at man, who helplessly groaned and shrieked and shuddered, but never for a single instant could stop. The railways alone approached the car-

Fig. 3.2. New York, Fifth Avenue and 23rd Street, ca. 1900.

nage of war; automobiles and fire-arms ravaged society, until an earthquake became almost a nervous relaxation.[6]

A New York social reformer named Michael Davis coined an apt—and surprisingly mod—term to describe the new metropolitan environment (as well as the sensational amusements it cultivated, as I discuss later); modernity, he declared in 1910, was defined by "hyperstimulus."[7]

The illustrated press offers a particularly rich trace of the culture's fixation on the sensory assaults of modernity. Comic magazines and sensational newspapers scrutinized the chaos of the modern environment with a dystopian alarmism that, in varying degrees, characterized much of the period's discourse on modern life. Many cartoons represented the new landscape of commercial solicitation as a type of horrific, aggressive stimulus (fig. 3.3). Others, portraying dense, chaotic mobs of pedestrians, keenly illustrated (fifty years in advance) Benjamin's suggestion that "fear, revulsion, and horror were the emotions which the big-city crowd aroused in those who first observed it" (fig. 3.4).[8] A 1909 illustration in *Life* magazine entitled "New York City, Is It Worth It?" represented the metropolis as a frantic onslaught of sensory shocks (fig. 3.5). Its combination of multiple spacio-temporal perspectives in a single, instantaneous view (several years before Cubism) conveys the fractured perceptual intensity of urban experience.[9]

Fig. 3.3. "How We Advertise Now," *Punch*, 1887.

Fig. 3.4. "A Quiet Sunday in London; or, The Day of Rest," *Punch*, 1886.

Fig. 3.5. "New York City: Is It Worth It?" *Life*, 1909.

A number of illustrations dealt specifically with the harsh transformation of experience from a premodern state of balance and poise to a modern crisis of discomposure and shock. A 1900 cartoon in *Life* entitled "Broadway—Past and Present," for example, contrasted a pastoral scene with a twentieth-century view of a trolley car bearing down on terrified

Fig. 3.6. "Broadway—Past and Present," *Life,* 1900.

pedestrians (fig. 3.6). In the background, billboards advertise a sensational newspaper called the *Whirl* and Sunday shows of boxing movies. The serenity of the "savage's" life in the past accentuated the true savagery of the metropolitan present. The collision between two orders of experience— premodern and modern—also figured in numerous images representing actual collisions between horse-drawn carts—the traditional mode of transportation—and their modern-day replacement, the electric trolley (fig. 3.7). Such pictures conveyed an anxiety about the perilousness of life in the modern city and also symbolized the kinds of nervous shocks and jolts to which the individual was subjected in the new urban environment.

Fig. 3.7. "Horse Smashed Cable Car Window," *New York World,* 1897.

The dominant dystopic motif around the turn of the century high-lighted the terrors of big-city traffic, particularly with respect to the hazards of the electric trolley (figs. 3.8, 3.9, 3.10). A plethora of images representing streams of injured pedestrians, piles of "massacred innocents," and perennially gleeful skeleton-figures personifying death focused on the new dangers of the technologized urban environment. Sensational newspapers had a particular fondness for "snapshot" images of pedestrian deaths. This fixation underscored the sense of a radically altered public sphere, one defined by chance, peril, and shocking impressions rather than by any traditional conception of safety, continuity, and self-controlled

IN THE WAKE OF A CABLE CAR.

Fig. 3.8. "In the Wake of a Cable Car," *Life*, 1895.

THE STANDARD

Fig. 3.9. "The Brooklyn Horror!" *The Standard*, 1895. The fine text reads: "The merciless trolley car has added another victim to its list of massacred innocents and still runs on unchecked. Thousands of citizens have protested and a united press has assailed the pitiless trolley monopoly without result. Even the Mayor is weak-kneed and weak-backed. The slaughter still goes on. What will Brooklyn do about it?"

Fig. 3.10. "Another Trolley Victim," *New York World,* 1896.

destiny. Unnatural death, needless to say, had been a source of fear in pre-modern times as well (particularly with respect to epidemic, famine, and natural disasters), but the violence, suddenness, and randomness (and, in a sense, the humiliating publicity) of accidental death in the metropolis appear to have intensified and focalized this fear. The specter of Isaac Bartle infiltrated modern consciousness. As an 1894 article in the *Newark Daily Advertiser* reported:

Isaac Bartle, a prominent citizen of New Brunswick, was instantly killed at the Market street station of the Pennsylvania Railroad this morning. His body was so horribly mangled that the remains had to be gathered up with a shovel and taken away in a basket. . . . He was ground into an unrecognizable mass under the wheels of a heavy freight engine. The engine struck Mr. Bartle in the back and dragged him several yards along the track, mangling his body in a horrible manner. Almost every bone was broken, the flesh was torn away and distributed along the track, and so completely was the body torn apart that the coins and knife in the trousers pocket were bent or broken, and the checkbook, pocketbook, and papers were torn in pieces.[10]

There is no question that descriptions such as this were motivated in large part by the fact that grotesque sensationalism sold newspapers. But they were more than simple manifestations of morbid curiosity and economic opportunism. In its meticulous attention to the physical details of accidental death, the Isaac Bartle item seems to convey a historically specific hyperconsciousness of physical vulnerability in the modern environment.[11]

The chaos of the city instilled life with a nervous edge, a palpable feeling of exposure to danger. As the *Outlook*'s editor mentioned in 1900, "The Spectator is not unduly timorous, but he confesses that in these days of haste he often gets a little nervous in the city streets lest something may happen to somebody."[12] The modern city appears to have transformed subjective experience not only in terms of its visual and aural impact but also in terms of its visceral tensions, its anxious charges. Modern experience involved a constant triggering of reflex reactions and nervous impulses, flowing through the body, as Benjamin described it, "like the energy from a battery." It is telling that illustrations of accidents almost always employed a particular presentational schema: They were obliged, of course, to show the victim at the instant of most intense shock, just before death, but along with this they almost always showed a startled bystander looking on in horror, his or her body jolted into a reflex reaction. Such illustrations thus stressed not only the dangers of big city life but also its relentless nervous shocks.

The popular fear of trolley hazards did eventually subside. One sees a dropping off of this theme in the sensational press around 1903 and 1904. But just as the public apparently was getting used to trolley traffic, another peril—the automobile—followed on its heels and assumed an equivalent position as the central motif of modernity's dystopic imagination. The 1913 illustration "When Unlicensed Chauffeurs Are Abroad," among numerous others, portrayed a state of affairs in which, as Benjamin put it, "moving through traffic involves the individual in a series of shocks and collisions" (fig. 3.11).[13] (Indeed, this image criticizes modernity on two fronts: overtly, it decries the hazards and jolts of modern traffic; implicitly, it casts aspersions on the expanded presence of women in the public sphere. The picture presents a soon-to-be stereotypical image of women as bad drivers, and at the same time, in representing only female pedestrians, expresses a common paternalistic admonition about the vulnerability of unaccompanied women in the big city.)

Aside from traffic hazards, three other motifs that pervaded turn-of-the-century newspapers suggest the depth of the popular fixation on the new dangers of modern life. The first portrayed deaths of workers mangled by factory machinery. One can get a good idea of this motif from a few sample titles and subheadings from the *Newark Daily Advertiser* in 1894: "Whirled to Instant Death: His Body Caught in Rapidly Revolving Belts and Crushed Against the Ceiling At Every Revolution," and "Horrible Death of a Street-Cleaner: His Head Twisted Almost Off by a Sweeping Machine."[14] This keen attention to graphic accidental death in the workplace, like the traffic-death stories, posed modern technology as a monstrous assault on life and limb. It stressed a hazardous dimension of modern life which, not coincidentally, was suffered most acutely by the working class that made up the sensational press's core readership.

Another motif, also focusing on modern working-class experience, concentrated on a broad variety of deaths relating to various hazards of tenement life—ranging from brutal attacks by crazed neighbors to deaths involving novel facets of tenement architecture (fig. 3.12). Newspaper stories in this genre sometimes underscored a sense that uncontrollable, almost supernatural dangers lurked everywhere in the urban environment. One item, for example, described the agonizing death of a little girl whose skull was pierced by a rusty steel rod. The account noted: "Where the rod came from, or how it received enough force to make the wound that it did is a mystery. The child was at play in the yard when the rod, propelled by an unseen force, crushed down through the branches of a cherry tree, penetrating the girl's skull. The little girl died in great agony this morning."[15] In the modern environment, death could drop from the sky, inexplicably.

Falls from great heights also preoccupied sensational newspapers. At first, this genre may seem the most "purely" sensational (that is, having little to do with anxieties about modern life). But in several respects, such illustrations overlapped with the others. All of the deaths by falling, except for suicide leaps, were workplace accidents and thus conveyed a general sense of the perils of proletarian labor. Even the suicides can be read as implicit indictments of an intolerable modern life, especially since they often involved modern modes of transportation as the immediate agents of physical obliteration (such as illustrations showing a man plunging from a building onto the tracks of an oncoming train). Some of these falls also underscored the tyranny of chance in the modern environment and

Fig. 3.11. "When Unlicensed Chauffeurs Are Abroad," *Cartoons,* 1913.

Fig. 3.12. "Child Choked By a Transom," *New York World,* 1896.

the random dangers of tenement life. A typical example is an image of a little boy about to be squashed to death by housepainters plummeting off a broken scaffolding (fig. 3.13).[16]

The portrayals of urban modernity in the illustrated press seem to fluctuate between, on the one hand, an antimodern nostalgia for a more tran-

Fig. 3.13. "A Falling Man Kills a Boy," *New York World,* 1896.

quil time, and on the other hand, a basic fascination with the horrific, the grotesque, and the extreme. The illustrated press's images were, paradoxically, both a form a social critique and, at the same time, a form of commercialized sensationalism, a part of the very phenomenon of modern hyperstimulus the images criticized. In both these aspects, the illustrated press traded in bombast. This is not surprising, since the press had an obvious commercial interest in portraying the world in a drastic light. After all, hue and cry and thrills, not uneventful quotidian realism, sold copies.

But the images in the illustrated press are historically interesting not only as instances of discourse, as examples of a particular set of critical or commercial rhetorical postures towards the modern world, but also as suggestions of a condition of cultural duress surrounding the onset of urban modernity. The illustrated press's preoccupation with the perils of modern life reflected the anxieties of a society that had not yet fully adapted to urban modernity. We have had a century to get used to modern life. At the turn of the century, however, the metropolis was still perceived as overwhelming, strange, and traumatic.

Modernity transformed the texture not only of random daily experience but also of synthetic, orchestrated experience. As the urban environment grew more and more intense, so did the sensations of commercial amusement. Around the turn of the century, an array of amusements greatly increased the emphasis placed on spectacle, sensationalism, and astonishment. On a more modest scale, these elements had always been a part of amusements geared toward working-class audiences, but the new prevalence and power of immediate, gripping sensation defined a fundamentally different epoch in popular entertainment. Modernity ushered in a commerce in sensory shocks. The "thrill" emerged as the keynote of modern diversion.

The thrill took many forms. Beginning around 1895, as we have seen, sensational newspapers began flooding their pages with high-impact illustrations of anything strange, sordid, or shocking. The Coney Island amusement complex opened in 1895, and other parks specializing in exotic sights, disaster spectacles, and thrilling mechanical rides soon proliferated across the country. These concentrations of visual and kinaesthetic sensation epitomized a distinctly modern intensity of manufactured stimulus.[17] Vaudeville, which also emerged as a major popular amusement in the 1890s, epitomized the new trend toward brief, forceful, and sensually "busy" attractions, with its random series of stunts, slapstick, song and dance routines, trained dogs, female wrestlers and the like. Gaudy burlesque shows and "dime museums" (housing sundry curiosities, freak shows, and, occasionally, short blood-and-thunder dramas) also took on greater prominence around the turn of the century, as did a variety of mechanical daredevil exhibitions, such as "The Whirlwind of Death" and "The Globe of Death," in which a car somersaulted in midair after hurling off a forty-foot ramp (fig. 3.14). The editors of *Scientific American,* who in 1905 cast a bemused eye on the expanding field of dangerous automotive stunts, aptly summarized the essential objective of all these varieties of popular sensa-

Fig. 3.14. *Scientific American*, 1905. The fine text reads: "The 'Whirlwind of Death,' an aptly named apparatus which has killed one performer and in which an automobile is made to turn a somersault before it touches the ground."

tionalism: "The guiding principle of the inventors of these acts is to give our nerves a shock more intense than any hitherto experienced."[18]

The "sensationalization" of commercial amusement was particularly pronounced in stage melodrama. Whereas Victorian melodrama had emphasized the pathos and moralizing oratory of innocent victims and their heroes, melodrama around the turn of the century became virtually synonymous with violent action, stunts, and spectacles of catastrophe and physical peril. "Sensation scenes" such as burning buildings, explosions, and shipwrecks had been an ingredient of stage melodrama at least since the early 1800s, but starting around 1890 they grew more and more realistic, ambitious, and astonishing. And whereas earlier melodramas might have had one spectacular climax, turn-of-the-century melodrama piled thrill upon thrill. "A startling change has come over the tone and spirit of melodrama," observed the British critic Archibald Haddon in 1905. "The simple, demonstrative human element no longer appeals. Touring dramas, nowadays, are not properly constituted unless every scene is a shriek, every title a yell."[19] Desmond MacCarthy, writing a few years later in the *New Statesman,* reiterated this perception: "The development of recent melodrama has been away from high moral sentiments and towards catastrophes and ingenious thrills. Noble harangues are no longer essential. . . . Mechanism [stunt effects] has almost ousted morality."[20] Theodore Kramer's 1906 play *Bertha, the Sewing Machine Girl* exemplified melodrama's new paradigm: It included a four-way race between two automobiles, a locomotive, and a bicycle, as well as a motorboat race, fire engines speeding toward a burning building, various torture scenes, and a cyclone climax in which the villain was killed by a shaft of lightning.[21] In *Edna, the Pretty Typewriter,* a 1907 melodrama by Owen Davis, the heroine jumped from the roof of a building to the top of a moving elevated train. Another scene depicted a race between real automobiles, which were placed on a treadmill while an immense panorama backdrop moved rapidly in the opposite direction. The abducted heroine leaped from the villain's clutches into the hero's car, at which point, pushed beyond its limits, it blew up in a fiery explosion.

The rise of the cinema culminated the trend toward vivid, powerful sensation. From very early on, the movies gravitated towards an "aesthetics of astonishment," in terms of both form and subject matter. The thrill was central, for example, to the early "cinema of attractions" (to use Tom Gunning's term for spectacle-centered films before the rise of narrative integration around 1906) and to powerful suspense melodramas such as Griffith's Biograph thrillers of 1908 and 1909 (*The Fatal Hour, An Awful Moment, The Lonely Villa,* among others).[22] Action serials in the early teens, such as *The Perils of Pauline* and *The Exploits of Elaine,* elaborated every form of physical peril and sensational spectacle in explosions, crashes, torture contraptions, elaborate fights, chases, and last-minute rescues and escapes.[23] It is not surprising that the modernist avant-garde, drawn to modernity's affective intensity, seized upon these serials, and upon the cinema in general, as an emblem of modern discontinuity and speed. Marinetti and other Futurists celebrated the cinema's excitement as a "jumble of objects and reality thrown together at random." For the French Surrealists, sensational serials "marked an epoch" by "announcing the upheavals of the new world." These writers recognized the mark of modernity both in the sensational subject matter of the *ciné-feuilleton* ("crimes, departures, phenomena, nothing less than the poetry of our age") and in the film medium's power to convey speed, simultaneity, visual superabundance, and visceral shock (as Eisenstein, Vertov, and other filmmaker/theorists would soon elaborate).[24]

For Kracauer, Benjamin, and their many predecessors, this broad escalation of sensational amusement was clearly a sign of the times: Sensationalism was the aesthetic counterpart to the radical transformations of space, time, and industry. Sidestepping a more strictly socioeconomic explanation,[25] they framed the commercialization of the thrill as a reflection and symptom (as well as an agent or catalyst) of neurological modernity. The increasing intensity of popular amusements, they argued, corresponded to the new texture of daily life.

Kracauer, writing in 1926, argued that amusements based on "distraction"—that is, on disconnected, busy, powerful impressions—were "meaningful . . . as a reflection of the uncontrolled anarchy of our world." "In pure externality," he observed, "the audience encounters itself. Its own reality is revealed in the fragmented sequence of splendid sense impressions. . . . Shows which aim at distraction are composed of the same mixture of externalities as the world of the urban masses."[26] The aesthetic of shallow thrill and sensory stimulation, Kracauer stated, paralleled the texture of urban, technological experience. Benjamin picked up on this concept a decade later in his 1936 Artwork Essay, and then again in his 1939 essay on Baudelaire. "The film," he asserted, "corresponds to profound changes in the apperceptive apparatus—changes that are experienced on an individual scale by the man in the street in big-city traffic, on a historical scale by every present-day citizen."[27] The medium's rapid tempo and high-impact audiovisual fragmentation paralleled the shocks and sensory intensities of modern life: "In a film, perception in the form of shocks was established as a formal principle. That which determines the rhythm of production on a conveyor belt is the basis of the rhythm of reception in the film."[28]

While Kracauer and Benjamin may have expressed this connection between popular sensationalism and urban modernity with particular acuity, the idea was already a rather familiar one. For example, a German critic named Hermann Kienzl declared in a 1911 newspaper column that movies were the prime expression of the new metropolitan experience. "The psychology of the cinematographic triumph," he proclaimed, "is metropolitan psychology. The metropolitan soul, that ever-harried soul, curious and unanchored, tumbling from fleeting impression to fleeting impression, is quite rightly the cinematographic soul."[29] In a similar but less celebratory vein, Michael Davis tied vaudeville's aesthetic to urban hyperstimulus. Vaudeville, he complained, was symptomatic of "the excitement of the city and the mental disintegration induced by the kaleidoscopic stimuli of New York life." In its vivid, disjointed, fleeting spectacle, vaudeville mirrored "the experience afforded by a street-car ride, or any active day in a crowded city."[30] This argument made its way into academic discourse as well. In a 1912 essay in the *American Journal of Sociology*, Howard Woolston (a professor at the City College of New York) stressed the connection between modern experience and the appetite for "powerful shocks" in amusement. Cataloging a series of city noises and crowd situations, Woolston noted that

> urban life is marked by its heightened stimulation. . . . Such excitement deeply stirs the nervous system. The natural result of city life is increased nervousness. The restless current in which men are immersed produces individuals who are alert, active, quick to seek new satisfactions. The recreation of city dwellers is perhaps as true an index of their characteristic reactions as can be found. The most popular amusement of large towns today is furnished by saloons, dance halls, variety theaters, and moving picture shows. Coney Island, with its "chutes" and "bumps," "loops of death" and "circular swings," "ticklers," peep shows, bars, and assorted gastronomic marvels, is a favorite resort for thousands of young New Yorkers. There is "something doing every minute." . . . All these have a tendency to stimulate a jaded attention by a succession of brief, powerful shocks that arouse the tired organism to renewed activity.[31]

These assertions of a connection between sensationalism and modernity incorporated a number of underlying and overlapping hypotheses about the psychological mechanisms by which modern hyperstimulus transposed itself into the aesthetic of popular amusement. Kracauer, Benjamin, and their predecessors all appear to have embraced a notion of the mutability of human sensation and perception. Modernity, they suggested, prompted a kind of reconditioning of the individual's sensory apparatus. The metropolis and conveyor belt, Benjamin wrote, subjected "the human sensorium to a complex kind of training." The organism shifted into a higher gear, so to speak, synchronizing to the geared-up world. This conditioning ultimately generated a "new and urgent need for stimuli," since only stimulating amusements could match the nervous energies of a sensorium calibrated to modern life.[32]

Kracauer elaborated further on this need for stimuli. Sensationalism, he suggested, functioned as a compensatory response to the impoverishment of experience in modernity. Distractions and thrills offered a momentary escape from the "formal tension . . . of enterprise," from the meaningless frenzy and tedium of alienated labor in the modern factory and bureaucratized office.[33] Simmel had made a similar argument as early as 1896; in an essay on the Berlin Trade Exhibition, he observed, "It seems as if the modern person wishes to compensate for the one-sidedness and uniformity of what they produce within the division of labour by the increasing crowding together of heterogeneous impressions, by the increasingly hasty and colourful change in emotions."[34] Kracauer's debt to Simmel (and perhaps to a wider journalistic discourse)[35] is evident here, but Kracauer was more sensitive to the argument's inherent irony: The compensatory thrills of popular amusement reproduced the very register of hyperstimulus that vitiated modern experience to begin with. Alienated labor and urban experience "demands to be compensated," Kracauer stated, "but this need can only be articulated in terms of the same surface sphere which imposed the lack in the first place. . . . The form of entertainment necessarily corresponds to that of enterprise."[36] Popular sensationalism both compensated for and mimicked the frenzied, disjointed texture of modern life.

Attempts to understand popular sensationalism as a symptom of modern life also drew on a widespread belief about the physiological consequences of nervous overstimulation. Simmel, along with a host of physicians specializing in neurasthenia (or "modern nervousness"), insisted that excessive sensory stimulus of the sort associated with the pressures of urban life had the ultimate effect of exhausting or incapacitating the senses. The idea was that human nerves were subject to physical wear and tear and became weaker, duller, and progressively less responsive when exposed to too many stimuli. "Over-excited and exhausted nerves" created a mode of "jaded" or "blasé" perception that cast the world "in an evenly flat and gray tone."[37] Stronger and stronger sensations were needed simply to break through the blunted sensorium, to make an impression and reawaken perception.[38] Popular sensationalism putatively fit into this pattern. The demand for thrills escalated as blasé perception required increasingly intense impressions. Simmel characterized the 1896 Berlin Trade Show as a manifestation of the jaded urbanite's need for increasingly vivid thrills.[39] In the same year, Maxim Gorky situated the cinema precisely within this inflationary cycle of sensory deadening and countervailing overstimulation.

His firsthand account of the first exhibition of moving pictures (by the Lumière brothers in Paris) delivered what appears to have been an already stock rhetoric about the neurological dangers of "the thirst for the strange and the new."[40]

At least one more hypothesis tried to explain the psychological mechanisms behind the "new and urgent need for stimuli." Benjamin adapted a theory laid out by Freud in *Beyond the Pleasure Principle* concerning the function of anxiety as an adaptive defense against traumatic shock. Studying victims of shell shock from World War I, Freud observed that a severe traumatic breakdown occurred only among soldiers for whom the frightful event was totally unexpected. But those who had anxiously prepared for the shock by fixating on it, by mentally rehearsing it over and over again, or, in other words, by getting used to it in small, controlled doses, did not suffer major breakdowns. In this context, Freud believed, anxiety was self-protective, since the individual could defend himself against the traumatizing potential of shock. "The more readily consciousness registers shocks," he wrote, "the less likely they are to have a traumatic effect."[41] Benjamin applied this hypothesis to the film experience: The shocks of the film medium, he suggested, functioned as a kind of preparation or immunization against the shocks of the modern environment. "The acceptance of shocks," he argued, "is facilitated by training in coping with stimuli." "The film is the art form that is in keeping with the increased threat to his life which modern man has to face. Man's need to expose himself to shock effects is his adjustment to the dangers threatening him."[42] Film, Benjamin hypothesized, provided a training in coping with the stimuli of the modern world.

In their breadth and diversity, these discourses around the subject of modernity—both the myriad representations of urban shock and the multilayered attempts to understand popular sensationalism as a symptom of modern hyperstimulus—reveal a critical fixation, a sense of anxious urgency in documenting and dissecting an awesome social transformation. At the heart of this fixation is the fact that critical observers of modernity felt the "shock of the new" firsthand. They lived in a culture that had not yet fully adjusted to the sudden transformations of experience. The premodern millennium had yet to fade into a quaint abstract concept; it was still a vital and tangible memory, one that constantly accentuated the novelty and trauma of the modern world. Ortega y Gasset aptly described this situation: "The *tempo* of modern life, the speed with which things move today, the force and energy with which everything is done, cause anguish to the man of archaic mould, and this anguish is the measure of the imbalance between his pulse-beats and the pulse-beats of the time."[43] The critical fixation on modernity and sensationalism underscores if not the anguish then at least the anxiety of a generation that could still feel such an imbalance.

NOTES

1. Georg Simmel, "The Metropolis and Mental Life," in *The Sociology of Georg Simmel,* ed. Kurt H. Wolff (New York: Free Press, 1950), p. 410.

2. The U.S. urban population more than quadrupled between 1870 and 1910, from just under ten million to over forty-two million. In other words, the urban population doubled in size every twenty years or so: Between 1880 and 1900, for example, it rose from fourteen million to thirty million. Miles of electric-trolley tracks in the North Atlantic region increased from 2,952 in 1890 to 10,175 in 1902. In the United States as a whole, coverage rose 178 percent in those years, from 8,123 to 22,589 miles of track (U.S. Bureau of the Census, *1980 Census of the Population* [Washington, D.C.: Government Printing Office, 1980], table 3; U.S. Bureau of the Census, *Special Reports, Street and Electric Railways* [Washington, D.C., 1903], p. 34).

3. A good compilation of film footage of Manhattan around 1900 can be found in episode seven of the PBS series *Heritage: Civilization and the Jews.* The series is available on video at many public libraries. The screening list of the conference "Cinema Turns 100," held under the auspices of DOMITOR in New York in 1994, includes numerous street scenes from the 1896–1902 period held by major film archives in Europe and North America.

4. Mike Featherstone, "Theories of Consumer Culture," in *Consumer Culture and Postmodernism* (London: Sage Publications, 1991), p. 24.

5. An example of an academic essay is Howard B. Woolston, "The Urban Habit of Mind," *The American Journal of Sociology* 17, no. 5 (March 1912), 602–614. Stephen Kern offers a stimulating and eclectic survey of contemporaneous literary and artistic discourses about speed, fragmentation, and modernity (such as the Cubist and Futurist manifestos) in *The Culture of Time and Space, 1880–1918* (Cambridge: Harvard University Press, 1983), especially chapter 5. On neurasthenia, see Kern (chapter 5); Tom Lutz, *American Nervousness, 1903: An Anecdotal History* (Ithaca, N.Y.: Cornell University Press, 1991); James B. Gilbert, *Work Without Salvations: America's Intellectuals and Industrial Alienation, 1880–1910* (Baltimore: Johns Hopkins University Press, 1977), pp. 31–43. George Beard's *American Nervousness* (New York, 1881) is generally considered the seminal discussion of neurasthenia.

6. Henry Adams, *The Education of Henry Adams* (1917; reprint, New York: Modern Library, 1931), pp. 494–495.

7. Michael M. Davis, *The Exploitation of Pleasure* (New York: Russell Sage Foundation, 1911), pp. 33, 36. Davis's survey was conducted in 1910.

8. It is no coincidence that social theorists began focusing on mob psychology around the turn of the century. Two key works, among many popularizations, were Gustave Le Bon, *Psychologie des foules* (1895) and Gabriel Tarde, *Opinion and the Crowd* (1901). A representative popularization is Gerald Stanley Lee, *Crowds: A Study of the Genius of Democracy and the Fear, Desires, and Expectations of the People* (London:

Methuen, 1913). Quotation from Walter Benjamin, "On Some Motifs in Baude-laire," in *Illuminations,* ed. Hannah Arendt (New York: Harcourt Brace, 1968), p. 174. All further citations of Benjamin are from this collection.

9. The *Life* illustration appeared on 6 May 1909. Picasso held the first exhi-bition of Cubist paintings at Ambroise Vollard's gallery a bit later, in the summer of 1909. Cubism did not emerge as a bona fide movement (at least not one that a mainstream illustrator in New York might catch wind of) until the period between 1911 and 1914. The famous Armory show, in which eleven hundred works of modern art were exhibited in New York (and then Chicago and Boston), and which gave this work its first real exposure in America, took place in Febru-ary 1913 (Herbert Read, *A Concise History of Modern Painting* [New York: Prae-ger, 1959], p. 117). The formal similarities between the *Life* illustration and the Cubist aesthetic suggest their common basis in the perceptual transformations of modernity.

10. Anon., "Ground to Pieces on the Rail," *Newark Daily Advertiser,* 9 May 1894.

11. A wealth of municipal-government data on the numbers of trolley and road accidents and deaths has survived. Some statistics are presented in "Highway Acci-dents in New York City During 1915," *Journal of American Statistical Association* 15 (September 1916): 318–323; Roger Lane: *Violent Death in the City: Suicide, Accident, and Murder in Nineteenth-Century Philadelphia* (Cambridge: Harvard University Press, 1979).

12. *Outlook,* 15 September 1900.

13. Benjamin, "On Some Motifs in Baudelaire," p. 175.

14. *Newark Daily Advertiser,* 18 and 29 May 1891.

15. Anon., "A Little Girl's Peculiar Death," *Newark Daily Advertiser* (26 May 1891), p. 1, columns 7 and 8.

16. Deaths by falling might also have had a particular resonance for the first-generation immigrants, many of whom came from rural agrarian cultures with no tall buildings, who read these newspaper accounts. Perhaps these images spoke to their sense of uneasiness in the strange spatial coordinates of the vertical modern metropolis.

17. John F. Kasson, *Amusing the Million: Coney Island at the Turn of the Century* (New York: Hill and Wang, 1978); Richard Snow, *Coney Island: A Postcard Journey to the City of Fire* (New York: Brightwaters Press, 1984); Andrea Stulman Dennett and Nina Warnke, "Disaster Spectacles at the Turn of the Century," *Film History* 4 (1990): 101–111.

18. "A Hundred Ways of Breaking Your Neck," *Scientific American,* 14 October 1905.

19. Archibald Haddon, "Sensational Melodrama," *Daily Express* (London), 28 August 1905. Clipping is at the Harvard Theater Collection, "Melodrama" file, Cambridge, Mass.

20. Desmond MacCarthy, "Melodrama," *The New Statesman* (London), 27 June 1914.

21. Ads and reviews for "Bertha, the Sewing Machine Girl," *Brooklyn Daily Eagle,* Sunday, September 2, 1906, p. 9; Tuesday, September 4, 1906, p. 4; Sunday, Sep-tember 23, 1906, section 3. p. 10; Sunday, October 6, 1907, section 2, p. 8 and p. 9.

22. Tom Gunning explores aspects of sensationalism in early film in "An Aesthetics of Astonishment: Early Film and the (In)credulous Spectator," *Art and Text* 34 (spring 1989): 31.

23. On sensational melodrama and the action serials, see my article "Female Power in the Serial-Queen Melodrama: The Etiology of an Anomaly," *Camera Obscura* 22 (January, 1990): 91–129, and my chapter on serials in Geoffrey Nowell-Smith, ed., *A History of the Cinema, 1895–1995* (Oxford: Oxford University Press, 1995).

24. "The Futurist Cinema," in *Marinetti: Selected Writings*, ed. R. W. Flint (New York: Farrar, Straus and Giroux, 1971), p. 131. Both Phillipe Soupault and Jean Epstein recalled the thrill of seeing *The Exploits of Elaine* in Paris in 1915. Soupault wrote in 1923, "We dashed into the movie house and realized that all was changed. Pearl White's smile appeared on the screen, that almost ferocious smile announcing the upheavals of the new world. We finally understood that the cinema was not just a mechanical toy, but the terrible and magnificent flag of life. Wide eyed, we [saw] crimes, departures, phenomena, nothing less than the poetry of our age." Jean Epstein similarly declared, "These popular, foolish (that goes without saying), penny dreadful-ish, incredible, blood-and-thunder films such as *The Exploits of Elaine* mark an epoch, a style, a civilization no longer lit by gas, thank God" (Soupault, "Cinema, U.S.A.," in *The Shadow and Its Shadow: Surrealist Writings on Cinema*, ed. Paul Hammond [London: British Film Institute, 1978], p. 32; Jean Epstein, "Le Sens 1 bis," in *Bonjour Cinema* [Paris: Editions de la Sirene, 1921], translated by Stuart Liebman in "Jean Epstein's Early Film Theory, 1920–1922" [Ph.D. diss., New York University, 1980]; an alternate, and, I think, less apt translation by Tom Milne is in *Afterimage* 10 [Autumn 1981]: 9–16, reprinted in Richard Abel, *French Film Theory and Criticism: A History/Anthology, 1907–1939* [Princeton: Princeton University Press, 1988], vol. 1).

25. A socioeconomic explanation would focus on the demographic changes of modern capitalism as a key factor in the rise of sensationalism. Clearly, the rapid growth of the urban working class in the last quarter of the nineteenth century provided a mass audience predisposed towards startling and violent spectacle, however one might want to explain this predisposition. As the journalist Rob Wagner put it in 1921, "Rough workers . . . like things that go bang." Sensational newspapers, the "mellerdrammer," action serials, burlesque—these all hinged on the new lowbrow social configuration of the amusement marketplace (Robert Wagner, "You—At the Movies," *American Magazine* 90 [December 1920]: 42-44, excerpted in *Literary Digest* 68 [26 February 1921]: 46).

26. Siegfried Kracauer, "The Cult of Distraction: On Berlin's Picture Palaces," (orig. pub. 1926), trans. Thomas Y. Levin, in *New German Critique* 40 (winter 1987): 91–96. My discussion of Kracauer and Benjamin is informed by a number of valuable essays in this issue of *New German Critique*, particularly Miriam Hansen's "Benjamin, Cinema and Experience," Heide Schlupmann's "Kracauer's Phenomenology of Film," Patrice Petro's "Discourse on Sexuality in Early German Film Theory," and Sabine Hake's "Girls and Crisis: The Other Side of Diversion."

27. Benjamin, "The Work of Art," in *Illuminations*, p. 250.

28. Benjamin, "Some Motifs in Baudelaire," p. 175.

29. Hermann Kienzl, "Theater und Kinematograph," *Der Strom* 1 (1911/1912): 219–220; quoted in Anton Kaes, "The Debate About Cinema: Charting a Controversy (1909–1929)," *New German Critique* 40 (winter 1987): 12.

30. Davis, op. cit., pp. 33, 36.

31. Woolston, op. cit., p. 602.

32. Benjamin, "Some Motifs in Baudelaire," p. 175.

33. Kracauer wrote, "The tension to which the working masses are subjected is . . . greater and more tangible [than in the provinces]—an essentially formal tension which fills their day fully without making it fulfilling. Such a lack demands to be compensated" ("Cult of Distraction," p. 93).

34. "Berliner Gewerbe-Ausstellung," *Die Zeit* (Vienna), 25 July 1896; quoted in David Frisby, *Fragments of Modernity: Theories of Modernity in the Work of Simmel, Kracauer, and Benjamin* (Cambridge: MIT Press, 1986), p. 94.

35. A British journalist named Arnold Smith expressed a similar argument in 1904, suggesting that the notion that popular sensationalism was an escape from or compensation for modern experience was something of a commonplace by the time Kracauer incorporated it. Smith writes, "The increasing mass of sensational literature which appears daily is a serious symptom of mental debility in the country at large. The cause of the demand for this fiction is not far to seek. It lies in the nerve-shattering conditions of modern life; in the ceaseless strain and worry which must be escaped from somehow, if only for an hour ("The Ethics of Sensational Fiction," *The Westminster Review* 162 [August 1904]: 190).

36. Kracauer, "Cult of Distraction," p. 93.

37. Simmel's key discussion of the blasé attitude is in "The Metropolis and Mental Life": "The blasé attitude results first from the rapidly changing and closely compressed contrasting stimulations of the nerves. A life in boundless pursuit of pleasure makes one blasé because it agitates the nerves to their strongest reactivity for such a long time that they finally cease to react at all. . . . Through the rapidity and contradictoriness of their changes, harmless impressions force such violent responses, tearing the nerves so brutally hither and thither that their last reserves of strength are spent; and if one remains in the same milieu they have no time to gather new strength. An incapacity thus emerges to react to new sensations with the appropriate energy. . . . The essence of the blasé attitude consists in the blunting of discrimination. This does not mean that the objects are not perceived, but rather that the meaning and differing values of things, and thereby the things themselves, are experienced as insubstantial. They appear to the blasé person in an evenly flat and gray tone; no one object deserves preference over any other" (Simmel, op. cit., p. 414).

38. The reader will observe that Howard Woolston invokes this theory in the last sentence of the passage quoted above.

39. Frisby, op. cit., p. 75.

40. Gorky wrote, "Say what you will, but this [the cinematograph] is a strain on the nerves. . . . Our nerves are getting weaker and weaker, are growing more and more unstrung, are reacting less and less forcefully to the simple 'impressions of daily life' and thirst more and more eagerly for new, strong, unusual, burning and strange impressions. The cinematograph gives you them—and the nerves will grow

cultivated on the one hand, and dulled on the other! The thirst for such strange, fantastic impressions as it gives will grow ever greater, and we will be increasingly less able and less desirous of grasping the everyday impressions of ordinary life. The thirst for the strange and the new can lead us far, very far" ("Gorky on the Films, 1896," in *New Theatre and Film, 1934 to 1937: An Anthology*, ed. Herbert Kline [New York: Harcourt Brace Jovanovich, 1985], pp. 227–233; a slightly different translation appears in Jay Leyda, *Kino: A History of the Russian and Soviet Film*, 3d ed. [Princeton: Princeton University Press, 1983]).

41. Sigmund Freud, "Beyond the Pleasure Principle" in *The Standard Edition of the Complete Psychological Works of Sigmund Freud* (London: Hogarth Press, 1953–1974), 18:13.

42. Benjamin's fullest discussion of Freud's theory of protective anxiety is in "Some Motifs in Baudelaire," pp. 161–163. The first quotation is taken from "On Some Motifs in Baudelaire" (p. 162); the second is from "The Work of Art" (p. 250). For a similar interpretation of this aspect of Benjamin's framework, see Susan Buck-Morss, "Aesthetic and Anaesthetics: Walter Benjamin's Artwork Essay Reconsidered," *New Formations* 20 (summer 1993): 123–143.

43. José Ortega y Gasset, *The Revolt of the Masses* (New York: W. W. Norton, 1932), p. 31. Also available in a newer translation by Anthony Kerrigan (Notre Dame, Ind.: University of Notre Dame Press, 1985).

PART TWO

Circulation and Consumer Desire

FOUR

The Poster in *Fin-de-Siècle* Paris: "That Mobile and Degenerate Art"

Marcus Verhagen

The poster had once been a crude commercial tool, a black-and-white announcement with a highly schematic image or none at all. With the emergence of the color poster in the early decades of the Third Republic, however, it developed into a sophisticated medium; by the mid-1880s, posters were being collected by aesthetes and commented on enthusiastically by art critics. Those changes were widely attributed to the efforts of a single man, the poster artist Jules Chéret, who soon became a household name. For a time, Chéret's work and the poster were virtually synonymous. In 1890 the writer Edmond de Goncourt presided over a banquet that was given in the artist's honor and called him "the first painter of the Parisian wall, the inventor of art in the poster."[1] That was high praise, particularly as the aging writer, whose pronouncements had something of the force of official decrees in literary and artistic circles of the time, was not given to commending artists out of hand. By that point, however, it was not an uncommon view.

As Chéret rose to a certain prominence in *fin-de-siècle* Paris, so did the *chérette*, as she was called—the dancing, nymphlike woman who dominated his designs. Buoyed by her mirth, she mostly appeared in a void, as in a poster of 1894 for the Eldorado, a fashionable music hall (fig. 4.1). There she was illuminated from below, like an actress standing in the glare of a series of footlights, but she dispensed with the stage, hovering restlessly against the background. Her legs were freed from carrying her weight and, daringly uncovered, they danced in the air, while a couple of clowns gazed up at her in adoration. She was a performer, and her charm was made of artifice. In her act, the contrivances of the entertainment world were compounded by those of the artist, who touched her up and accented her sexual exposure while removing her to an undefined zone above and beyond

Fig. 4.1. Jules Chéret, "Eldorado," poster, 1894.

her ordinary perimeter. Impish and provocative, the *chérette* was a figure of brazen sexual invitation, but her suspension undermined the corporeality of her presence and removed her pantomime of desire to the realm of fantasy. Apparently, she offered and transcended her body in a single movement.

In his design of 1889 for the opening of the dance hall Moulin Rouge (fig. 4.2), as in so many other posters, Chéret pictured a number of women and implicated them in some form of aerial celebration, "a vertiginous carnival," as the bohemian poet Raoul Ponchon put it.[2] Ponchon was right: the festivities in which the *chérette* participated were in some crucial sense carnivalesque. She danced about, wore masks and provocative costumes, and joined processions that meandered from one side of a poster to the other. Here, she and her friends even appeared on donkeys, age-old carnivalesque symbols of lechery. However, as she engaged it, carnival was not a time of popular revolt, in any case not of revolt against capitalist enterprise. Rather, it was an interlude of generalized amusement in which laughter gained one figure after another and so imposed a vision of mindless amusement and complicity. The *chérette* laughed with the entrepreneur, not at him. Our view of carnival will have to be altered before it can accommodate her; those conceptions of it that stress its utopian or resistant dimension are unlikely to shed any light on the effect of Chéret's imagery in *fin-de-siècle* Paris.

In her infectious good humor, the *chérette* was an emblem and a catalyst rather than a fully independent figure. Her joy reverberated in a fantastic circuit of laughter, touching the faces around her but at the same time blurring the marks of individuality. A critic of the time spoke of Chéret's women and their "masks of lyrical joy"; as he suggested, their laughter was a sign of vacuity, existing only in circulation, in the absurd spread of identical simulations of amusement.[3] Character in Chéret's work was transmuted into ambient consciousness. Another critic wrote that the artist deprived his figures of a soul. They already had one: "The soul is joy. Jules Chéret is the Great Promoter of Joy."[4] To impress on their audience the universal validity of their message, Chéret figures combined the attributes of sentience with a personal anonymity, locating their function outside the personality, in a mask, say, and in its laughter. Having no souls, they served as vectors for sentiments that were initiated elsewhere. Their joy attached to the place or event with which they were associated, in this case the Moulin Rouge: they simply relayed it to the consumer, or to the audience at which their grins were directed. Without the viewer, the scene could have no point of origin or closure. *Chérettes* anticipated the pleasures of consumption and spiced them with fantasies of seduction. In the pervasiveness and implied reciprocity of their joy, they locked those

Fig. 4.2. Jules Chéret, "Bal au Moulin Rouge," poster, 1889.

pleasures into a mad cycle of echoes and repetitions, of which the recommended attendance was at once the cause and the culmination.

Clearly, Chéret's designs conjured a vision of carnival that chimed perfectly with their function as promotional images. The *chérette*'s laughter was both an invitation to the pleasures it pretended to mimic and an assurance of their present enjoyment; with artful presumption, the artist's posters persuaded by taking for granted the accomplishment of their commercial goals and by claiming the viewer as the point of departure for the ripples of joy that suffused them.

During the last quarter of the nineteenth century, Chéret's and other color posters became an integral part of the Parisian environment. In the early 1870s, Chéret and the Choubrac brothers, Léon and Alfred, introduced technical improvements that reduced the costs of color lithography and made it doubly attractive as a means of promotion. The liberal laws of 1881 eased the state's control of the media and so paved the way for a large increase in the production and dissemination of advertisements. In 1884 the city council announced that surfaces belonging to the municipality would be available for rent. Other surfaces were created. By the turn of the century, the boulevards were studded with Morris columns (circular pasting boards); and the trams that carried passengers out to far-flung areas of the city from 1874 also sported advertisements. By 1886 Chéret alone had created almost one thousand designs.[5] With varying degrees of enthusiasm, journalists noted that posters were appearing everywhere, clamoring for attention and transforming the urban landscape with their jaunty images and glaring colors.

The poster evolved in tandem with the burgeoning entertainment industry. It was not until the mid 1890s that artists like Chéret were regularly called upon to design advertisements for foodstuffs or consumer durables; until then, they were primarily concerned with the promotion of the new leisure palaces, the café concerts, music halls, circuses, and hippodromes that offered novel, moderately priced shows to large and growing audiences in the Third Republic. Smarter establishments such as the Opéra, the Comédie-Française, and a handful of other theaters disdained the poster. Smaller ones could rarely afford it; Chéret, for instance, charged six hundred francs per poster, a sum that was completely out of proportion with the modest revenues of cafés, fairground installations, or working-class dance halls, which relied primarily on handbills and word of mouth.[6]

The large, modern venues, however, spent lavishly on advertising. They often put on a variety of attractions at once and favored spectacles with a wide appeal (operetta, acrobatics, popular song, and so on), responding quickly to changes in fashion and so attracting a large and diverse clientele. Posters were crucial to their success, informing the public of their ever-changing programs and creating an impression of luxury, often overlaid with a hint of sexual license. The new leisure establishments were built and run by men like Joseph Oller, Charles Zidler, and Hippolyte Houcke, who were speculators and managers rather than performers or artistic directors. With their professionalism and vast ambitions, they revolutionized the Parisian entertainment business. Above all, they took advertising extremely seriously, using it to poach pleasure-seekers from their competitors, high and low. As it appeared in the late nineteenth century, the poster was tailored to their requirements. It was, in other words, both a manifestation of the emergence of mass culture in France and a catalyst in the development of other mass cultural forms.

Commentators of the time were impressed by the sheer number of posters around them: Like the businesses it served, the poster apparently carried a hint of megalomania. Typically, Georges d'Avenel, a middle-of-the-road conservative and inveterate fact finder, had the exact figures to prove it. According to him, posters worth twenty-five million francs were pasted every year in France, one and a half million of them in Paris alone.[7] D'Avenel recited the figures with some admiration. Advertising, he felt, was becoming a science. It had honed different instruments for different purposes and was quick to avail itself of technological advances. As its methods grew more sophisticated, its imagery tended towards simplicity and repetition. The rise of the poster in France was an indication of renewed vitality: it augured well for French industry and commerce.

In moral and political terms, however, it was distinctly suspect. It was, wrote d'Avenel, an intrusive presence in the public scene, fostering human vanity and exciting the senses. In presenting the poster's archetypal protagonist, d'Avenel accurately described the *chérette,* stressing the sexual promise in her diaphanous clothes, casual postures, and pouting expressions; she was, he wrote, "too audacious in the deployment of her charms."[8] That, presumably, was why the monks of Saint Sulpice were told not to look at posters, an instruction d'Avenel relayed without a trace of irony. Plainly, advertising dispensed with good taste. It was like democratic government, he wrote, meaning that it had to address itself to workers as well as to the middle class. There was no question of viewing the poster as a high art.[9]

Here as elsewhere, the question of the poster's good or bad taste and the issue of its status as an art were inextricably tied to perceptions of its social valency. In likening it to the democratic process and dismissing the view that it was an art in its own right, d'Avenel was giving expression to the anxiety with which the rise of mass culture was greeted in conservative circles. Advertising, he wrote, derived from "the more intimate mingling of the classes."[10] He was clearly distressed by the breadth of the poster's address, which he saw as injecting a note of radical indeterminacy in the public domain. D'Avenel was in a bind. The positivist in him marveled at the poster's success and growing technical sophistication, while his conservatism induced him to present it as constituting an obscure challenge to the integrity of class society and, to disparage the sauciness of its imagery. A more coherent picture of the threat the poster was seen as posing to the existing cultural and social order will emerge from the examination of a variety of other texts, for and against. Unlike d'Avenel, writers of the Left had no qualms about endorsing the poster. In the anarchist press, Félix Fénéon argued in truculent *argot* (slang) that poster design was an art; it lacked the trappings of official favor, but it had a vitality that Salon painting could never match and the great merit of being visible to all. He enjoined his readers to rip advertisements from the walls where they were posted and to use them in the decoration of their living quarters.[11] In much the same vein, the socialist critic Arsène Alexandre wrote with approval that the poster, like the caricature and the illustration, had become an entirely legitimate art form.[12]

It was also celebrated by the bohemian community of Montmartre, with which many of the most successful poster artists of the time (Henri de Toulouse-Lautrec, Alfred Choubrac, Adolphe Willette, Théophile-Alexandre Steinlen) were closely affiliated. Montmartre, or *la butte* (the hillock) as its residents affectionately called it, had long been a rural outpost of the northern fringe of the capital, but in the second half of the nineteenth century it was gradually engulfed by the city below. All the same, it maintained a distinct identity, becoming a rallying point for both working-class anarchists and middle-class bohemians. At a time when slumming was the height of fashion, its cabarets, which cultivated a reputation for seditious entertainment, attracted pleasure-seekers from all over Paris. For all their avant-gardist talk of resistance to mainstream culture and society, however, the bohemians of Montmartre developed close ties with the larger entertainment concerns of the capital and had a clear stake in their success. Those concerns, likewise, had much to gain from their association with bohemia, which gave their shows the added spice of boisterous cultural dissent.

Chéret himself had the good sense to cultivate ties with the luminaries of Montmartre, specifically with Jules Roques, the editor of its foremost weekly. Roques's paper, *Le Courrier français,* devoted a whole issue to Chéret in February 1890. The editor, of course, had a vested interest in the critical validation of the poster: for one thing, most of his illustrators also designed posters, and for another, he himself pioneered another, related form of promotion, the magazine advertisement. Every week he ran a different ad for Pastilles Géraudel, a brand of cough drops, and in exchange he received generous financial backing. D'Avenel called Roques the "living genius of advertising."[13] Another writer said of *Le Courrier* that it had "the glory of being the most daring and intelligent promoter."[14] Roques and others in Montmartre had every reason to hope that the poster would be recognized as an art form in its own right.

Bohemia provided a testing ground and a pool of talent for the advertising business. In the process, it also cemented its alliance with the moguls of the entertainment industry. The most remarkable product of that alliance was the Moulin Rouge, which was located at the foot of the butte. It was run by Oller and Zidler, who hired Chéret and, later, Toulouse-Lautrec to tempt potential customers with images of can-can dancers and other lightly clad women. They consulted the artists and writers of Montmartre on the design of their building and the organization of their shows. That kind of collaboration clearly benefited both parties; by association with the bohemians of Montmartre, the entrepreneurs gave their ventures a (thin) veneer of avant-gardism, while the writers and artists themselves found a wider setting for their activities and reveled in the licentiousness they saw there. The poster stood at the intersection of bohemia and the entertainment business, playing on the provocations of the first and using them to glamorize those of the second. No wonder d'Avenel was reluctant to give it his approval.

The poster's most dedicated defender, however, was neither a radical nor a bohemian, and he was anxious to downplay its more controversial associations. Ernest Maindron curated an exhibition on the history of advertising in 1889 and wrote two books on the poster, the first appearing in 1886 and the second a decade later. Like Alexandre and Fénéon, he was keen to establish the validity of the poster as an art form. His reasoning, however, was different. Where they hinted that the canonical ordering of the arts was in itself a questionable practice, he simply tried to tinker with the canon by revising the status of the poster, to which he gave all the attributes of a fine art.

Maindron's claims, however, were extremely labored—too labored, and too numerous, to be entirely convincing. First, he insisted that the poster had a distinguished heritage, like any other fine art. He continually referred back to Daumier and other mid-century artists, whom he saw as the precursors of the poster designers of his day. Second, it had become a collector's item. He had a large collection himself and reported that there were now so many other collectors that printers were beginning to regard them as a menace.[15] Third, several exhibitions had recently been devoted to it, including, of course, the one he had organized himself. (Chéret had also had a successful one-man show in 1889.) Finally, he saw it as reviving a decorative tradition that had a well-established place in the history of art, noting "I think we can expect [from the poster] the ideal formula for a new art of fresco painting."[16] The comment may seem far-fetched, but it was in fact a popular refrain; a number of other writers made exactly the same point in pieces on Chéret.[17]

In their efforts to assimilate the poster to the fine arts, several critics also compared it to the more recent decorative tradition of rococo painting, likening Chéret, Willette, and others to such newly fashionable eighteenth-century painters as Watteau, Boucher, and Fragonard.[18] The comparison usefully provided an art-historical rationale for the prominence in the modern poster of characters from the *commedia dell' arte* (Pierrot, Colombine, and the rest), who figured prominently in rococo painting. It also had the merit of recognizing the poster's reliance on highly suggestive scenarios of courtship and seduction, while tracing them to a fully legitimate art of the past. The poster, the argument went, was instrumental in reviving *la gaieté française,* a national tradition of public festivity and humor, of which the eighteenth-century *fête galante* and its representation in rococo painting were particularly refined expressions.[19] Maindron was appealing to precisely that view when he wrote that the poster was the embodiment of "French taste."[20]

When he was not insisting on the poster's credentials as a fine art, Maindron was attesting to its edifying influence on the general public. He claimed, for instance, that it inculcated a taste for art, and, further, that it taught the illiterate to read. The arguments he cited in its defense are oddly heavy-handed; with every additional virtue, his reasoning sounds more fully predicated on the views he intended to contradict. The poster was a collector's item, a modern fresco, a learning aid, and a vehicle for *la gaieté française.* It served too many different purposes, and in his breathless search for further justifications Maindron betrayed a certain nervousness, an abiding sense of the resistance he expected to meet. It is a measure of his uneasiness that in listing the poster's various functions, he made virtually no mention of its ostensible purpose. He even suggested that its promotional function was purely incidental. "Advertising," he wrote, "is just a pretext," a way of reaching a wider audience.[21] Maindron was on uncertain ground. He tried to validate the poster by eliding its commercial goal in favor of a host of other functions, most of which were spurious or forced. It is clear from the circuitousness of his argument that the issue was still contentious; as Maindron was painfully aware, both the poster's artistic worth and its moral and social repercussions were open to debate.

Artists too defended the poster, often with a touch of humor. In a design of 1893 for the cover of *Le Mirliton,* which was edited by Aristide Bruant and named after his cabaret, Steinlen pictured a young dandy in one of the back streets of Montmartre examining a poster that Lautrec had recently designed for Bruant (fig. 4.3). The butte, home to *Le Mirliton,* was familiar territory to Steinlen, Lautrec, and Bruant, but the young

Fig. 4.3. Théophile-Alexandre Steinlen, cover for *Le Mirliton*, 9 June 1893.

man is completely out of place there; his precious mannerisms and dress strike a discordant note against the desolate background and form an absurd contrast with the dogs that sniff at each other and urinate behind him.[22] Bruant appears to laugh at him, much as he did at the middle-class patrons of his cabaret. Oblivious to his own ridicule, the young man stares back at Bruant's image and expertly assesses it, the implication being that the poster is a deserving object of study, and, further, that serious aesthetes are bound to gravitate towards Montmartre. In the process, the poster's function is downplayed; here, as elsewhere, the dandy's chief concern is style (of dress, conduct, etc.) and the effect of his gaze is to present the image as primarily a formal exercise, bracketing off or sublimating its commercial goal. Once again, advertising is pictured as a "pretext."

Humorous mutual congratulation was a popular strategy in the bohemian community; here, it was used to further the cultural claims of the poster. It may have succeeded in this, but only at a certain cost in ideological coherence. There is a sense in which the artist's humor barely manages to disguise his difficulty in imagining the poster's true audience. In defending the artistic worth of Lautrec's image, Steinlen interpellates such an unlikely figure that he effectively exposes the social indeterminacy of its address. Lautrec's advertisement is pictured as mediating uneasily between communities that were poles apart socially and politically. The poster was a result of "the more intimate mingling of the classes," wrote d'Avenel, and so it appears here; such is the price it pays for its artistic elevation.

In a design of 1897 by Henri-Gabriel Ibels, a painter and anarchist who had close ties with Lautrec and the Nabis, the poster defended itself with a little more conviction (fig. 4.4). The image was intended as an advertisement for a dealer in posters, and in it Ibels forcefully acknowledged the commercial intention that lay behind his design and that it shared with those it was commissioned to promote. Colombine, Arlequin, Pierrot, and a particularly clownlike Cassandre serve as barkers in a *parade,* a sideshow that was traditionally put on to draw passersby into fairground theaters or circuses. The figures stage a pantomime of collective persuasion: Arlequin strikes a characteristically boastful pose, while Pierrot puts on a display of servility, and Colombine provides a running commentary. They stage a brash advertisement for their own dramatic talents. Together they provide an analogy for the poster and its cunning array of visual allurements, and in the process they give it something of their own prestige. Pantomime was in vogue in the final decades of the century; it had long been considered a working-class distraction, but in the 1880s and 1890s, fashionable authors penned pieces of their own and staged them before select audiences.[23] As he became more refined, Pierrot came to serve as a stand-in for the artist or writer, acting out the hardships of an avant-gardist vocation in the poetry of Jules Laforgue, for instance, or in Willette's paintings

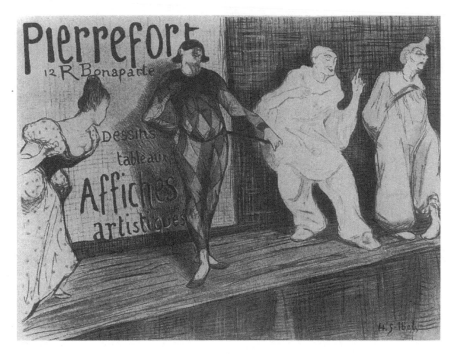

Fig. 4.4. Henri-Gabriel Ibels, "Pierrefort," poster, 1897.

and illustrations. By involving Pierrot and his companions in a promotional drama, then, Ibels was effectively suggesting that the poster had followed a similar trajectory, from popular to high culture, and that it was an art form that specifically exercised the avant-garde.

The poster had many defenders, but the case in its favor had to be argued afresh by every one of them and buttressed with references to an improvised high-art lineage or to other newly elevated cultural forms. It was not a cause that was won in advance. In most of the texts and images that appeared in the poster's defense, the opposite view can be felt as a kind of afterimage, largely determining the contours of the debate.

The case against the poster was most forcefully made by Maurice Talmeyr, a writer of commentary and fiction. Talmeyr's article on the poster appeared in *La Revue des deux mondes*, an organ of the moderate Right.[24] The article itself, however, was anything but moderate. In strident terms, the author painted the poster as an emblem, powerful and alarming, of modern industrial society: "Nothing . . . is more violent in its modernity, nothing belongs quite so insolently to the present" (p. 201). He admitted to admiring poster artists, Chéret in particular, and recognized the seduc-

tiveness of their designs. All the same, the poster was a corrupting presence in the modern environment. In the brevity of its life span, it reflected
the frenzied pace of urban life, to which it gave an edge of madness as it
assaulted city dwellers with a barrage of unsolicited messages. It fueled
every desire and ambition and so contributed to the degeneracy of the
urban population. Crowds were easily moved by it, as were women and children; impressionable as they were, they were doubly susceptible to advertising, which exposed them to a continual parade of rutting figures.[25] Talmeyr emphasized the corrosive beauty of Chéret women, adding that the
poster was fundamentally pornographic and promoted the "total abolition
of maidenly modesty" (p. 216). He also hinted darkly at another threat,
"can we not imagine the uses to which Chéret's own procedures will be
put in order to lead the way to the social paradise, the great unleashing of
the downtrodden!" The poster, Talmeyr felt, was ideally suited to serving
revolutionary causes. It was and always would be an incitement to chaos:
The poster "already destroys as pleasure does, and it will destroy like rage"
(p. 212).

In the beginning of his article, Talmeyr noted with a touch of irony that
the poster resembled a fine art in the expert attention it attracted. It had
its critics, historians, and other aficionados, he wrote, specifically citing
Maindron, and was definitely "the thrill of the day" (p. 203). He described
the poster artists of his time as "a generation of . . . masters of the billboard, creating art-works *or trying to*," the qualifying phrase apparently being the more accurate indication of his own opinion (p. 204, italics mine).
Further on, his tone changed from condescension to brazen cynicism as
he claimed that it was indeed an art; it was an art because it chimed perfectly with the moral tenor of the times. The decadence of the modern urban environment resonated in the poster, giving it the reach and power of
a fine art. In fact, it was virtually the only art that remained: "Triumphant,
exultant, brushed down, pasted, torn in a few hours and continually sapping the heart and soul with its vibrant futility, the poster is indeed the art,
and almost the only art, of this age of fever and laughter, of violence, ruin,
electricity and oblivion" (p. 216). His position on the question of the poster's artistic merit clearly underwent a decisive change midway through the
article. There was an element of sheer rhetorical bravado in the view he
put forward in the final pages, but he was also making a tactical concession.
He apparently endorsed the conclusions of Maindron and company but
subverted their intended meaning by incorporating them into an argument that was broader and altogether more damning.

The poster stood, in Talmeyr's view, as a distillation of the excesses of
contemporary society, and as such it was inextricably tied to a variety of
other recent trends and creations. It was comparable, he felt, to the Eiffel
Tower, the gramophone, and the electric light, bearing witness, as they

did, to an inventiveness that had lost its moorings in tradition and become random and unprincipled. More pertinently, he related it (repeatedly) to the modern entertainment industry, to the new café-concerts and other night spots, with their titillating entertainments. On account of the poster's omnipresence, he wrote, "the inhabitant of Paris carries with him a never-ending internal 'Moulin Rouge'" (p. 214). Talmeyr saw another parallel in the motion picture. In attempting to describe the exact nature of the poster's malignant effects, he wrote that "the inescapable result of that mobile and degenerate art is . . . a particular, mechanical form of demoralization, as if [it were effected] through the seried images of the cinematographer" (p. 210). Expanding on the popular view that city dwellers were increasingly prone to nervous debility, Talmeyr suggested that the moral fiber of the nation was being eroded by the continual ennervation that resulted from the mechanical proliferation of images.

As the antithesis of recent, "mobile and degenerate" mass cultural forms, he advanced the stone edifices of earlier ages, the castle and the cathedral. While the poster was ephemeral, pandering to the viewer's vanity and lust, the stone building was durable and communicated a respect for authority. To borrow a term from Walter Benjamin, the poster had lost the *aura* that still attached to the stone construction; it lacked the authenticity of the unique creation and hence the weight of tradition.[26] To Benjamin, the loss of the aura through mechanical reproduction was a liberating development; to Talmeyr, though, it was ominous. The poster was "the natural art of a period of unremitting individualism and egoism" (p. 209). Monumental architecture, on the other hand, humbled the individual, pressing him into the service of a higher power, social or religious. Appropriating for a moment the terms of a debate over the relative merits of line and color in painting, he even suggested that the chromatic sobriety of the stone building attested to a noble purpose, while the polychromy of the poster was an added indication of depravity:[27] "Line is the last word of the soul, color is that of sensuality" (p. 214). Accordingly, the stone building, which was, he felt, essentially linear in conception, was infused with lofty thoughts and ideals, while the poster, with its "perpetual coloristic titillation," its "indefinable colors" and "perverse tones," was "the natural tongue of the inferior stimulations" (pp. 208, 214).

In describing the poster, Talmeyr made a number of symbolic connections—with the electric light, the motion picture, and so on—but only two recurred throughout the article. First, the poster was affiliated with the prostitute. Second, it was a reminder of the celebrations of carnival.

In the poster, as in so many of the large new places of entertainment, the prostitute was on display. Whether she was dancing the can-can or looking for customers, Talmeyr wrote, she had a privileged place in its repertoire. Further, the poster was itself involved in a form of prostitution. Like a streetwalker, it accosted passersby in public, using every artifice to gain their attention; like her, it was garish and immodest. At a time when the use of makeup was still largely confined to the courtesans and kept women of the demimonde, Talmeyr described the poster as an exercise in cosmetics and its vocation as a derivative of the prostitute's: "The insolent poster . . . is equipped for war, decked out for the street, done up for the promenade or the theater, and her very nudity, when she is naked, is a contrived, painted, whitened nudity, a cosmetic nudity. She is a barnstormer and a creature who is there to 'do business'" (p. 213). The poster resembled the prostitute in the cunning orchestration of its charms and in the financial calculations that underpinned them. It captured "the giddiness of generalized prostitution" and so prefigured a society in which the decadence of late nineteenth-century Paris would be pushed to new extremes (p. 216).

A number of other writers, including some of the poster's defenders, drew the same parallel. A young woman played the part of La Réclame (The Ad) in a pantomime of 1888, a kind of hymn to prostitution by the Decadent writer Félicien Champsaur; in cloying, allegorical terms, she was pictured as conspiring in the gradual enslavement of a young woman to her suitors.[28] To Champsaur, advertising and prostitution were variations on a single theme, the joyful celebration of female beauty for commercial ends. Jean Lorrain, who was possibly the most assiduous *fin-de-siècle* chronicler of the demimonde, repeatedly described prostitutes as walking advertisements, for makeup and hair styles but, most of all, for themselves.[29] As it happens, Champsaur and Lorrain were among Chéret's most vocal admirers, and in separate articles they both insinuated that the women in his posters were themselves prostitutes.[30] D'Avenel agreed, describing the poster's archetypal protagonist as part fairy princess and part streetwalker. Like Talmeyr, he also likened the poster to a woman who was skilled in the art of applying makeup.[31] The advertisement, it appears, was animated by prostitutes, and from them it acquired the habit of continual self-display and the skills of seduction.

It was also a site of carnival. Talmeyr made the point again and again, presenting the poster and the figures that populated it as the participants in a variety of carnivalesque celebrations, from the masked ball to the parade, as well as in fairground performances and other year-round carnivalesque entertainments. According to the writer, the poster reproduced the madness and laxity of carnival, its dedication to the present—carnival, like the poster, was short-lived—and its rejection of ordinary codes of modesty and respect. He may even have seen the poster's affinity with carnival as a premonition of the insurrectionary violence he detected in it. In any case, the connection moved him to new heights of bombast: "How . . . surely we find [in the poster] the *descente de la courtille* [a once-notorious carnival procession] and the dizziness of the masked ball. . . . How all those figures of carnival and the high life . . . triumph in their very madness and ominous gaiety, under the stream of unbearable lights!" (p. 211). Carnival was the embodiment of the bawdiness and incipient chaos that Talmeyr felt he saw in the poster. It was also a time when the ethos of restraint in the public sphere, that mainstay of middle-class morality, was systematically mocked and infringed, and in that sense, too, carnival stood as a fitting parallel for the poster, which Talmeyr viewed as an aggressive intrusion in the urban landscape. The poster was an unwarranted irruption, interpellating the casual observer and undermining his reserve with intimations of familiarity and pleasure. Like carnival, it disturbed the peace.

Talmeyr's comments have a familiar ring. Various constituencies wrestled for control over public space in *fin-de-siècle* Paris, and for the most part they formulated their claims in terms of the patterns of behavior they saw as appropriate to it. In the press, the debate mostly revolved around carnival and the fair. Writers of the Right claimed that fairground performers were a nuisance; they behaved in unseemly ways, made a din, and generally obstructed ordinary Parisians in the conduct of their daily affairs.[32] Writers of the Left sided with the performers, as did Roques and others in Montmartre, arguing that the fair perpetuated *la gaieté française* and mocking the solemnity of the good bourgeois who disapproved of it.[33] In their own defense, fairground operators maintained that virtue was not always best served by the strictest dignity and seriousness.[34] The fair was opposed in the name of "public tranquility" and defended on the grounds that it upheld "the right to laugh."[35] Carnival, which was undergoing a sputtering revival, was seen in a similar light, its enthusiasts presenting it as one of the few remaining manifestations of a national tradition of merrymaking and lamenting the passivity of middle-class pleasure seekers of their time.[36]

In referring to carnival, Talmeyr was situating the poster in the context of the same debate. Unsurprisingly, he referred to the fair as well, using it to stress the poster's invasiveness: "Fairground colors . . . always violent . . . now solicit the gaze from all directions, irritating it, and truly transforming the physiognomy of the streets" (p. 204). He also mentioned "the blast of fairground music which you hear" in the poster (p. 207). In a similar vein, d'Avenel saw the poster as operating in the same fashion as the barrel-organ, an instrument that the opponents of the fair considered particularly offensive.[37] Other writers made similar comments but in a more indulgent tone. Joris-Karl Huysmans, who was among the first to voice an appreciation of the poster, saw it as loudly disrupting the oppressively somber environment of Haussmannian Paris, while his friend Lorrain spoke of it as causing a "harmonious racket."[38] Ibels addressed the same issue in his Pierrefort poster (fig. 4.4). The figures enacting the poster's function appeared on a fairground platform; they were definitely intrusive—their purpose, after all, was to hail passersby—but their intrusiveness was fundamental to their humor and art, and the same, implicitly, could be said of the poster.

To his readers, Talmeyr's references to carnival would have seemed singularly appropriate on a number of other counts. For one thing, it was widely accepted that the *chérette* was a participant in some form of carnivalesque festivity (fig. 4.2). For another, carnival owed its revival in the 1880s and 1890s largely to those communities that were most active in their support of the poster. Talmeyr acknowledged bohemia's contribution to the development of advertising with a knowing reference to cough drops (and hence to Géraudel and *Le Courrier français*).[39] He effectively cemented it by speaking of the poster as a vehicle of carnival, given that the bohemians of Montmartre often modeled their pranks and festivities on carnival, and were directly responsible for two of the more controversial carnival celebrations of the time—the *Bal des Quat-z'Arts,* the art students' annual masked ball, which was organized by Roques, and the processions of the *Vache Enragée,* which were put on by Willette and friends.[40] In their carnivalesque ventures as in other areas, the artists of Montmartre found strategic allies in the grandees of the entertainment business. Roques, for instance, used the Moulin Rouge as a venue for the *Bal des Quat-z'Arts.*[41] Even without Roques's encouragement, Zidler, the manager of the Moulin Rouge, took an interest in the renascent tradition of carnival and for a couple of years (1896–1897) oversaw the *Boeuf Gras,* the butchers' carnival parade.[42]

The poster's carnivalesque qualities, then, could be seen as pointing to Montmartre and the entertainment industry, and to the dovetailing roles they played in its rise. Talmeyr's references to carnival were also perfectly in keeping with his view of the poster as an arena for the prostitute, who was herself a figure of carnival, constantly flouting middle-class notions of decorum in her forwardness—and frequently appearing in times of festivity. She was a fixture at the masked ball, particularly the *Bal de l'Opéra.* There, according to Lorrain, she would go every year to make new conquests and rekindle old ones.[43] In the art and literature of the time, the *Bal de l'Opéra* was regularly described as a site of sexual traffic; Lautrec, for one, pictured it as a meeting place for prostitutes and their clients. As terms in Talmeyr's analysis, the carnival and the prostitute were mutually corroborating; in aligning the poster with the one and then with the other, he was locating it within a single, entirely consistent metaphorical constellation, hemming it in with analogies that gave his warnings of invasiveness and depravity an urgent, contemporaneous ring.

In fact, he was doing more than that. Carnival was a cultural memory that was rich in associations but vague, as the efforts to restore it demonstrated; it was variously seen as a working-class festival of transience and plenty (the *Boeuf Gras*), a humorous celebration of bohemian poverty and resilience (the *Vache Enragée*), an extravagant initiation rite (the *Quat-z'Arts*), and a decadent high society gathering (the *Bal de l'Opéra*). Up to a point, the term's vagueness suited Talmeyr, who used it to embrace a cluster of related dangers. Seen in conjunction with the prostitute, however, carnival came into sharper focus, suggesting one danger in particular, that of pervasive social mobility, which effectively summarized all the others.

To many *fin-de-siècle* observers, the prostitute posed an alarming threat to the integrity of the class system. As they imagined her, she was pushed to sell her favors by overwhelming social and material ambitions and often wreaked havoc in the process, ruining the men who came into contact with her. In her more successful incarnation as a courtesan or kept woman, she would go to any lengths to be seen in the right places and in the right company, to gain access to the smarter salons and loges, or to seduce an aristocrat. She was the very picture of *arrivisme,* of aggressive social climbing and conspicuous consumption, frequently demeaning the men who pursued her as they bowed to her tastes and pretensions. That is how she was presented in novels by writers like Alphonse Daudet and Hugues Rebell, both of whom were ideologically close to Talmeyr. Daudet was particularly scathing, painting Rosa, the retired courtesan in *Sapho,* as a violent old woman who had amassed a fortune in the Second Empire and then put it on display with opulent bad taste.[44] For her part, Rebell's heroine Juliette squandered the inheritances of several men before associating herself with an aging Hungarian prince. In a particularly telling passage, she and a number of other courtesans attend a ball in Montmartre, at which they are surprised to meet the working-class locals among whom they had grown up.[45] To writers like these, prostitution was a dangerous leveler of class differences. As they saw her, the prostitute was propelled and abased by her social aspirations, using her power over men of high standing to expose the porousness of a system of social stratification that had once been more rigid.

Tellingly, the *chérette,* already widely labeled a prostitute, was also pictured as a figure of social indeterminacy, generally of upward mobility. Huysmans, for instance, described Chéret's artistry in terms that deliberately echoed the more severe texts on the trespassing ways of the successful courtesan: "He takes a woman of the people with a cheeky expression, a restless nose and eyes that light up and tremble, he refines her, renders her almost distinguished, under those fineries, turns her into a soubrette of bygone days, an elegant hussy whose lapses [*écarts*] are delicate."[46] He was punning in his use of the word *écart,* which means both a gymnastic extension, as in the can-can, and a moral lapse or deviation. His account was playful but unambiguous: as he saw her, the *chérette* was a working-class tart who had acquired a certain polish and grace, even a faint otherworldliness (his talk of "a soubrette of bygone days" deliberately recalled the female figures of rococo painting). Lorrain, who often took his cue from Huysmans, saw her in a similar light, writing that she was both "duchess and street-urchin."[47] Meanwhile, Yvanhoé Rambosson claimed that the *chérette* had a modest background and disreputable acquaintances but an aristocratic bearing nonetheless.[48] Chéret's defenders cheerfully detected in his women the very transformations that so alarmed Daudet and others in the prostitute.

In their social mobility, the *chérette* and courtesan were carnivalesque; they were participants in a subversive festival of social becoming. It was to that notion of carnival that Talmeyr was referring in his comments on the poster as a masked ball or parade. Carnival, as illuminated by the prostitute, was a time of heightened exchange in goods and symbolic values, when fortunes were made or spent overnight, status was won or lost, and everything, from sex to titles of distinction, was for sale. Writers for the Left still saw carnival as a time of humorous rebellion, even a prelude to revolution, and the processions of the *Vache Enragée* in Montmartre were billed (a little implausibly) as demonstrations of resistance.[49] As it manifested itself in the poster and prostitute, however, carnival was not so much an instrument of revolt as a moment of intensified trade and, hence, a ritual enactment of the power and instability of a market economy (though vestiges of activism remained, as Talmeyr's comments on the poster's radical potential indicated). Its guiding principle was not resistance but chance; at a time when the workings of the laissez-faire system were widely perceived to be violently unpredictable, carnival served as a lurid and humorous illustration of their effects. In that guise, it could be seen as subversive in its challenge to the integrity of the middle class, but it was certainly not incompatible with capitalist enterprise.[50]

If the prostitute was one of the pivotal figures of that form of carnival, the circus operator was another. As an itinerant entertainer, he was seen as unusually exposed to the whims of fortune and the fickleness of the public. As one observer put it, in terms that were charged with economic Darwinism, "Nowhere does the struggle for life and disdain for the defeated affirm itself as brutally as in that profession."[51] The circus and fair were pictured as places of rapid but inexorable social and professional change; endless stories were told of fallen aristocrats who worked as clowns or acrobats and of working-class prodigies who achieved fame and fortune in

the circus ring. In their subjugation to the patterns of chance, circus performers provided mythical illustrations of the fluctuations to which the
economy was prone and the disrupting effect they had on class society.

The gentleman who had fallen on hard times was a prominent character in novels that were set in the world of the circus, such as *Le Train 17*
(1877), by the conservative writer Jules Clarétie, or *Le Cirque solaire* (1898),
by the Symbolist Gustave Kahn. In an absurd twinship, the gentleman-
clown served as a foil for the circus director, who was seen as a model of
resourceful entrepreneurialism and upward mobility. The director's task
was to master the forces of hazard at work in the circus or fair and to turn
them to his profit. Claretie's director, Francis Elton, describes the joys and
tribulations of the nomadic life, which is governed, as he has it, by "the
unexpected," or "*Hazard the King.*"[52] By the end, of course, he has become
a man of substantial means. Like Cramer, the director in *Le Cirque solaire,*
he is an American, America being the land of opportunity, of unbridled
commercial enterprise and the ascendancy of wealth over birth. America
was also the home of P. T. Barnum, on whom both Elton and Cramer were
transparently modeled.[53] Barnum was the personification of *américanisme,*
as it was termed, continually mounting projects of astonishing commercial
daring. He was an upstart who had the temerity to trumpet his success
and fabulous wealth. With grudging admiration, one writer wrote of his
"grandiose but tasteless venture," in the process outlining the hallmarks of
américanisme, which resembled both carnival and the poster in its economic effervescence and in the challenge it posed to ordinary notions of
distinction.[54]

Barnum was himself indelibly associated with the poster. He freely, even
gleefully admitted that the success of his shows was often due more to advertising than to their intrinsic drawing power. "Advertising is like learning," he wrote. "A little is a bad thing."[55] Long after his death in 1891, his
name was still synonymous with lavish advertising and publicity stunts.
D'Avenel opined that the United States was the "classic land of the advertisement," and in support of his claim he naturally pointed to Barnum,
writing that the circus director spent vast sums on the printing of posters.[56] In recognition of the director's megalomania, Alfred Jarry wrote his
name in capital letters, stating, "BARNUM is within our walls, by which we
mean that he would fill them to breaking-point if he were so inclined, with
his cornucopia of wonders, just as easily as he has submerged them with
his posters."[57] Upsetting attitudes of reserve was fundamental to Jarry's
theater, as he himself explained, and he apparently saw the showman as a
distant precursor.[58] Plainly, Barnum was powerfully intrusive; like the carnivalesque figure that he was, he violated middle-class notions of propriety
with something of the gusto of Jarry's outrageous dictator, Père Ubu. As
the writer imagined him, Barnum shattered the privacy of the home, and

in that, appropriately enough, he was assisted by the poster, on which he clearly left his imprint, confirming its native invasiveness and its privileged connection with the more novel and ambitious projects of the entertainment industry.

The poster was carnivalesque in the sense that it was allied to reckless entrepreneurialism, to self-made men, to *américanisme* and *arrivisme*, and, more generally, to the adulteration of established social hierarchies. The ritual boasts of the circus director, the humiliation of the impoverished aristocrat, the social striving of the prostitute: those were the images it conjured. It promoted, and was promoted by, a masquerade of ordinary social relations, in which time-honored markers of distinction were cast aside and a form of social roulette prevailed, submitting class identity to the vagaries of the marketplace. If, as was claimed, the *chérette* had modest origins but was mysteriously distinguished all the same, it was not on account of any innate quality but because she served as a standard-bearer for the poster and hence for the destabilization of class by commerce.

It was further hinted that the spectacular progress of Chéret's career was in itself an indication of growing social mobility. Thus, Lorrain drew attention to the artist's difficult beginning, pointing out that he had worked too hard as a young man to go to drawing classes but going on to write that he was a "lover of elegance and aristocracy" and finally calling him an "aristocrat of the arts."[59] The same applied to some of Chéret's closest collaborators, the men who ran the leisure establishments for which he made most of his posters.

The charge of eroding class distinctions was regularly brought against the new entertainment businesses, which were seen as sacrificing artistic integrity to the questionable tastes of an increasingly amorphous public. Raging against their offerings, Jules Barbey d'Aurevilly wrote, "Art is undergoing a daily process of *Americanization* [*s'américanise* tous les jours] in this society of beggars who are begging to be rich. . . . *Time is money*, says the American. Well, so is Art!"[60] When art shirked the austerity of the avant-garde and catered to the wider public, he thought, it demeaned itself and, in its gaudiness and *américanisme*, recalled the desperate efforts of the social climber. Other writers were more lenient but nevertheless pictured the entertainment industry as fostering greater social promiscuity. In its success and the breadth of its address, it threatened to eclipse the cultural practices that distinguished one class from another. At the same time, the owners and managers of the new venues showed that a measure of prominence could be achieved by men of enterprise, whatever their origins, and were seen as Barnums-in-the-making. Zidler's working-class background was eagerly commented on, while Houcke was noted for his "*parisianisme* with an American slant."[61] Plainly, the businesses with which the poster was most closely associated were also perceived as contributing to

the blurring of social distinctions. Apparently, it was through mass entertainment that the randomness of the market penetrated the cultural sphere,
with the poster acting as scout and ambassador for the large new concerns
and giving a preliminary warning of their effect.

To Talmeyr, carnival was a "shoving, equivocal dance" featuring "that
part of Society that is dazzling, or anxious to become so" (p. 211). It was
quite explicitly a time when dubious social claims were made, and those
claims were reiterated by the poster. Just as explicitly, the transgressions he
had in mind were due to the capricious influence of the modern economy. Hence the emphasis he placed on the poster's impermanence; in its
transitory character, it accurately reflected the unaccountable movements
of the economic system of his day. With deliberate facetiousness, Talmeyr
intimated that changes in the marketplace, once predictable, were now
brutal and unexpected:

> [Once] you had your fortune . . . in peaceful properties, which little by little
> prospered or wasted away. . . . Now you go to bed at night in a sleeping-car
> in Paris, and you have your hot chocolate the next morning in Marseille; you
> take off again and you learn, upon returning, that you are ruined! You were
> a millionaire, but in millions that never existed, and all you have left is your
> wardrobe, which you even forgot to pay for. . . . The poster is the constant
> echo of that manner of life, which it infiltrates through its reproductions
> and reproduces through its infiltration. (pp. 207–208)

The poster militated against the more lasting values of earlier times, accurately reflecting the economic convulsions of the present. That was the
meaning of Talmeyr's passage on the stone edifice; the building was durable and attested to relations of power that were rooted in the ownership of
land and barely changed with the passing of time. The poster, on the other
hand, was as ephemeral as gains made on the stock market. Talmeyr was
anxious to surround it with the aura of vague evil-doing that attached
to high finance, particularly since the Panama scandal of 1892 and 1893,
while stressing the volatile, unfathomable nature of the modern economy.

The poster, he implied, was simply the most visible symbol of the market mechanisms that were wearing away the foundations on which class society was built. D'Avenel felt that advertising rested on "the more intimate
mingling of the classes" and winced slightly at the thought. Talmeyr con-
curred but was thoroughly alarmed, imagining that the poster and other
new trends in entertainment would undermine first the cultural influence
and then the social and political authority of the privileged classes, eventually leading to the complete collapse of public morality and, possibly, to
revolution.

It should now be clear that Talmeyr's about-face on the question of the
poster's artistic status was an astute ideological maneuver. In writing that

the poster was a fine art, he was apparently agreeing with Maindron and company, but in the light of his earlier, more dismissive comments on the artistic aspirations of the commercial artist (who was making artworks "or trying to"), his position was open to doubt. He then advanced the extravagant view that the poster was virtually the only art of modern times and, in so doing, deliberately made nonsense of his own argument. He pretended to assist in the elevation of commercial art in order to confirm his original view, simultaneously accenting and invalidating the pretensions of the poster as an art form. In his article, he made illegitimate artistic claims for the poster and so rehearsed the more ominous transgressions he saw in it, which were not artistic but social. The two were in any case connected. The artistic canon was vested with the authority of the cultural establishment, which rested in turn on the sociopolitical status quo. The debate over the relative merits of different art forms was on some level a front for a wider discussion of their political repercussions. Challenges to the existing canon were generally made in a spirit of political defiance; the pieces in which Fénéon and Alexandre defended the poster, for instance, had unmistakable social undertones, both writers implying that the poster destabilized not only the canon but also the classes that had most to gain from its continuing influence. When Talmeyr echoed their view in an article that was destined for a more conservative readership, he too meant to elide the social and the artistic and to present the rise of advertising as a sign of sweeping changes in modern society.

The poster, he felt, was a mobile, usurping presence in the pantheon of the arts; it encroached on the more established art forms and so called attention to its function as an indication of social mobility. It reproduced the transgressions of the prostitute and the seesawing fortunes of the circus operator, aiding and abetting the new entertainment concerns as they marshaled the riotous forces of the market and brought them to bear on class structure. That was the view that Maindron was so anxious to dispel; in his efforts to obscure the poster's commercial purpose and to stress instead its acceptance by the ordinary arbiters of bourgeois good taste, he was at pains to assure his readers that it was entirely in harmony with the configuration of society as they knew it. In their day, however, Talmeyr was closer to the mainstream of middle-class opinion. Although he avoided Talmeyr's bluster, d'Avenel repeated many of the central points of his argument, obviously feeling that advertising was chipping away at the power of the middle class in the areas of culture and public morality. His reasons for countering the view that the poster was a fine art were much the same as Talmeyr's reasons for advancing it. For all Maindron's enthusiasm, the poster still inspired a measure of distrust. The artists and writers of Montmartre would not have embraced it as eagerly as they did if it had generally been regarded as the innocuous art form that Maindron held it to be.

Indeed, Steinlen's image of the young dandy inspecting Lautrec's poster in Montmartre played on the social deregulation that the advertisement was seen as entailing; like Talmeyr, Steinlen indirectly suggested that the poster's status as an art was in fact contingent on its power to cross and erode class barriers (fig. 4.3).

In laughing so infectiously, the *chérette* brought the public into the circle of her joy, but there was a sense in the late nineteenth century that her amusement was an indication of carnival, and that she was also laughing at her own temerity in promoting the loosening of social and artistic hierarchies. Ponchon spoke of Chéret's characters as smiling deliriously with their "piggy-bank mouths."[62] So they were.

NOTES

1. Edmond & Jules de Goncourt, *Journal* (Robert Laffont: Paris, 1989), vol. 3, p. 413 (entry for 16 April 1890). In typically fastidious style, Goncourt was careful not to write of the artist as the inventor of the art *of* the poster but of art *in* the poster so as not to imply that the poster was an art form in its own right. (Unless otherwise noted, all translations from the French are my own.)

2. Raoul Ponchon, "Maître Chéret," *Le Courrier français*, 9 February 1890, p. 2.

3. Félix Fénéon, "Quelques peintres idéistes," *Le Chat noir*, 19 September 1891.

4. Yvanhoé Rambosson, "Psychologie des Chéret," *La Plume*, 15 November 1893, p. 499.

5. Ernest Maindron, *Les Affiches illustrées* (Paris, 1886), pp. 46, 134.

6. Georges d'Avenel, "La Publicité," *Le Mécanisme de la vie moderne* (Paris, 1902), p. 176.

7. Ibid., pp. 125–127, 162.

8. Ibid., p. 178.

9. "Then claims were made for the 'high art' poster," he wrote, using inverted commas to underline his view (ibid., p. 175).

10. Ibid., p. 211.

11. Joan U. Halperin, *Félix Fénéon: Aesthete and Anarchist in Fin-de-Siècle Paris* (New Haven: Yale University Press, 1988), p. 261.

12. Arsène Alexandre, *L'Art du rire et de la caricature* (Paris, 1892), pp. 342–343.

13. D'Avenel, op. cit., p. 141.

14. Louis Morin, *Carnavals parisiens* (Paris, 1898?), p. 177.

15. Maindron was one of a fair number of avowed poster collectors; among the others were the artists Georges Seurat and Georges Auriol and the writers Camille Mauclair, Paul Bonnetain, and Léon Hennique. In describing the lodgings of the last two, Edmond de Goncourt pointed out that with a few posters by Chéret and a small collection of Japanese art objects, an apartment could be decorated in an exotic and imaginative style and at very little cost to the tenant (*Journal*, vol. 3, pp. 96, 410).

16. Ernest Maindron, *Les Affiches illustrées, 1886–1895* (Paris, 1896), p. 32.

17. Jean Lorrain spoke of "the poster, that modern fresco" (*Le Courrier français*,

9 February 1890); in the same publication, Ponchon termed Chéret's work "a vast fresco." The Symbolist writer Gustave Kahn wrote that "a poster by Chéret is a delicate fresco" ("Jules Chéret," *Art et Décoration,* 2d semester, 1902, p. 181); and Camille Mauclair described the poster as "a small, removable and perishable fresco" (*Jules Chéret* [Paris, 1930], p. 20).

18. Roger Marx, "L'Oeuvre de Chéret," *La Plume,* 15 November 1893, pp. 483–485; Léon Bloy, "Le Neveu prodigue," *Propos d'un entrepreneur en démolitions* (Paris, 1884), pp. 113–120.

19. Many of the same texts also hint that the transience of worldly passions, which was held to be the predominant theme of rococo painting, was also reflected in the very form and function of the poster, which was put up one day only to be pasted over the next. See, for instance, Maindron, *Les Affiches illustrées,* op. cit., p. 77.

20. Maindron, *Les Affiches illustrées, 1885–1895,* p. 46.

21. Ibid., p. 4.

22. The drawing seems to be establishing a parallel between the aesthete and the black dog directly behind him; in examining the image of Bruant, the young man is performing an act of inspection which finds an echo in the dog's sniffing the rear-quarters of the urinating mongrel. This reading would create an implicit connection between Bruant and the sturdy mongrel, a connection that would not be entirely inappropriate, given that the drawing appears alongside a ditty by Bruant in which the stray dogs of Paris are described as possessing the great bohemian qualities of ingenuity and independence. However, the real satisfaction that such a scenario offers (or offered at the time) is that it further belittles the dandy. For a useful discussion of Bruant's cabaret and performances, see Richard D. Sonn, *Anarchism and Cultural Politics in Fin de Siècle France* (Lincoln: University of Nebraska Press, 1989), pp. 95–114.

23. Robert Storey, *Pierrots on the Stage of Desire* (Princeton, N.J.: Princeton University Press, 1985), esp. pp. 285–297.

24. Maurice Talmeyr, "L'Age de l'affiche," *La Revue des deux mondes,* 1 September 1896, pp. 201–206. Subsequent references will appear in the text.

25. There is a strong echo here of Gustave Le Bon's thoughts on the slogan (*Psychologie des foules,* 2d ed. [Paris, 1896], pp. 90–92; see also Susanna Barrows, *Distorting Mirrors: Visions of the Crowd in Nineteenth-Century France* [New Haven: Yale University Press, 1981]).

26. Walter Benjamin, "The Work of Art in the Age of Mechanical Reproduction," in *Illuminations,* trans. Harry Zohn (New York: Schocken, 1985), pp. 217–251.

27. Jean-Pierre Guillerm has written an excellent article on late nineteenth-century views of the roles of line and color in painting, pointing out that the bold use of color was seen, in the writings of Charles Blanc, Max Nordau, and others, as degenerate, bestial, and feminine; it was likened to the sexual parading of animals, while line was seen as the preferred instrument of reason and control ("Psychopathologie du peintre," *Romantisme* [4th quarter 1989]: 74–86).

28. Félicien Champsaur, "Les ereintés de la vie," *Lulu: Pantomime en un acte* (Paris, 1888). The pantomime was twice performed at the exclusive Cirque Molier.

29. Jean Lorrain, *Une femme par jour* (Paris, 1883), pp. 83, 159–161.

30. Félicien Champsaur, "Le Roi de l'affiche," *La Plume,* 15 November 1893, pp. 480–482; Lorrain, "Chéret," pp. 5–6.

31. D'Avenel, op. cit., pp. 162, 177–178.

32. The leader of the antifair movement was the economist Fédéric Passy, author of *Les Fêtes foraines et les administrations municipales* (Paris, 1883), and his views were echoed in the press by writers such as Jean de Nivelle, a columnist for *Le Soleil.*

33. See, for instance, Jules Vallès, "Le Tableau de Paris: Les Foires," *Gil Blas,* 6, 13, 20, and 27 April 1882, and Jules Roques, "La Ligue foraine," *Le Courrier français,* 2 December 1888.

34. "Discours de Pierrot," *Le Voyageur forain,* July and August 1885.

35. "Conseil Municipal de Paris: Compte-rendu de la séance du lundi 31 octobre 1887, relative aux industriels forains," *L'Union mutuelle,* 6 November 1887.

36. Gustave Geffroy, "Le Plaisir à Paris: Les bals & le carnaval," *Le Figaro illustré,* February 1894, pp. 29–32.

37. D'Avenel, op. cit., p. 161. On the barrel-organ, see Louis Schneider, "Au jour le jour: Orgues de Barbarie," *Le Soleil,* 8 July 1898.

38. Joris-Karl Huysmans, *Certains* (Paris, 1889), p. 52; Lorrain, "Chéret," p. 6.

39. "[The poster] whispers in our ear: 'Have fun, take care of yourself, put on your carnival show, and take cough drops if you catch a cold!'" (Talmeyr, op. cit., p. 209).

40. In his *fin-de-siècle* study, Louis Morin wrote of Montmartre as spearheading the new vogue for carnival (Morin, op. cit., pp. 5–7).

41. That was in 1893, the year he was taken to court for hiring a number of artist's models to parade with next to nothing on. The verdict prompted a riot in the Quartier Latin, and both the ball and the ensuing pandemonium must have done wonders for the Moulin Rouge's reputation as a purveyor of illicit pleasures (Charles Rearick, *Pleasures of the Belle Epoque* [New Haven: Yale University Press, 1985], pp. 43–46).

42. Unsigned article, "V'la le boeuf gras," *L'Eclair,* 31 January 1896.

43. Lorrain, *Une femme,* p. 235.

44. Alponse Daudet, *Sapho* (Paris, 1884).

45. Hugues Rebell, *La Câlineuse* (1898–1899; reprint, Paris, 1978), pp. 102–106.

46. Huysmans, *Certains,* pp. 57–58.

47. Lorrain, "Chéret," p. 5.

48. Rambosson, op. cit., p. 500.

49. Eugène Fournière, "Artiste = Socialiste," *La Vache enragèe,* May–June 1897. For a more general treatment of the revolutionary power of carnival, see Jules Vallès, "La Fête," *La France,* 15 July 1882.

50. It is impossible to speak of carnival today without mentioning Mikhail Bakhtin's classic texts on the subject, *Rabelais and His World,* trans. Hélène Iswolsky (Bloomington: Indiana University Press, 1984), and *Problems of Dostoevsky's Poetics,* trans. Caryl Emerson (Minneapolis: University of Minnesota Press, 1984), esp. pp. 101–180. Compelling as it is, however, Bakhtin's view of carnival is not entirely applicable in the present context. Bakhtinian carnival is an earthy, subversive, popular mode and its primary target is officialdom; it is a period when the signs of author-

ity are parodied and bodily functions are humorously celebrated in a ritualized enactment of the survival of a given community. As it emerges from the texts I am considering here, carnival is not a time of joyful popular resistance but of uncontrolled social promiscuity. It is *selectively* subversive: The challenge it poses is not to officialdom, much less to capitalism itself (of which it is in some sense a gruesome attenuation), but to class stratification. Nor is it genuinely joyful; as Talmeyr paints it, it has a sinister, corrupting quality that is entirely foreign to Bakhtinian carnival. Talmeyr's image of carnival is, in a sense, a *phobic representation,* as Allon White and Peter Stallybrass call it (*The Politics and Poetics of Transgression* [Ithaca, N.Y.: Cornell University Press, 1986], pp. 99–108). In their brilliant reappraisal of Bakhtinian thinking, they argue (with Bakhtin) that carnival has long ceased to be a real force in popular culture, and further (and here they part ways with him), that it has survived in the form of a powerful symbolic nexus that serves as the distillation of a variety of social and sexual fears—that is to say, as a set of *phobic representations.* As they see it, the bourgeois author-cum-observer withdraws from the festive scene, which he then views as an object of both fascination and disgust. That, of course, is an accurate description of Talmeyr's stance with respect to the poster.

51. Gustave Strehly, *L'Acrobatie et les acrobates* (Paris, 1903), p. 357.

52. Jules Claretie, *Le Train 17* (Paris, 1877), p. 6.

53. Barnum's two autobiographical volumes, *The Life of P. T. Barnum, Written by Himself* (1854) and *How I Made Millions* (1889), were both translated into French. See A. H. Saxon, *P. T. Barnum: The Legend and the Man* (New York: Columbia University Press, 1989), pp. 11, 22.

54. Strehly, op. cit., p. 51.

55. Quoted in Saxon, op. cit., p. 77.

56. D'Avenel, op. cit., p. 174.

57. Alfred Jarry, "Gestes," *La Revue blanche,* February 1902, p. 67.

58. Alfred Jarry, "Questions de théâtre," *La Revue blanche,* January 1897, pp. 16–18.

59. Lorrain, "Chéret," pp. 5, 6.

60. Jules Barbey d'Aurevilly, *Théâtre contemporain, 1870–1883* (Paris, 1892), p. 218.

61. "Au jour le jour: Monsieur Zidler," *Le Soleil,* 28 February 1897; "Spectacles et concerts: Réouverture du Nouveau Cirque," *Le Figaro,* 18 September 1897.

62. Ponchon, op. cit., p. 2.

FIVE

"A New Era of Shopping": The Promotion of Women's Pleasure in London's West End, 1909–1914

Erika D. Rappaport

"Thousands of women besiege the West," announced a *Daily Express* headline on 15 March 1909. The *Standard* proclaimed this day in early spring the beginning of "Woman's Week in London."[1] What drew these women to the West End and into the astonished consciousness of dozens of journalists? This female siege was part of a grand celebration of commerce launched by the opening of Gordon Selfridge's new Oxford Street department store, the simultaneous commemoration of Harrods' sixty-year jubilee, and the annual spring sales held in nearly every West End shop. A "lady correspondent" interpreted this intense retail competition as a benefit for women since it transformed "shopping" into "a fine art." Advertising, special sales, and opening celebrations, she argued, expanded the very meaning of shopping: "From Times immemorial woman has shopped . . . [but] it is only since Monday that we have understood what the word really means."[2] Stimulating excitement for this commercial extravaganza, the *Daily Express* declared the week to be the dawn of a "new era of shopping."[3]

Despite these assertions, however, decades of economic and cultural transformation had produced this "new era."[4] The opening of Selfridge's department store and the competing celebrations in older English shops in early spring 1909 was a moment when Edwardians reflected upon the commercial, class, and gender changes that had shaped their capital city since at least the 1860s. The overwhelming competition among retailers in the years before the war produced a new way of thinking about consumption, the city, and female pleasure. In particular, Gordon Selfridge's architectural style, along with his display and marketing strategies, sparked a widespread discussion on the nature and meaning of an expanding English commercial culture. This fevered debate among journalists, retailers, advertisers, and consumers prompted a redefinition of shopping and of women's place in the urban environment.

As the "lady correspondent" had declared, shopping had long been associated with women, but the meaning of this activity was by no means stable. For much of the Victorian era, shopping had been often denigrated as a wasteful, indulgent, immoral, and possibly disorderly female pleasure.[5] Selfridge and other Edwardian entrepreneurs rewrote the meaning of this indulgence. They used publicity, particularly the print media, to turn disorder and immorality into legitimate pleasures, transforming anxieties into profits. Shopping was advanced as pleasurable and respectable precisely because of its public setting, which Edwardian business presented as a context for female self-fulfillment and independence. Selfridge addressed women not only as urban actors but also as bodies to be satisfied, indulged, excited, and repaired. Shopping, he repeatedly stated, promised women access to a sensual and social metropolitan culture.

Nothing Selfridge offered, however, was truly novel. Department stores were not the only place where women shopped, nor were they the only institution that encouraged women to participate in West End commercial culture. Since the 1860s, restaurants, hotels, the theater, museums, exhibitions, women's clubs, guidebooks, and magazines had fostered an image of the West End of London as a place of commercial enjoyment and female exploration. The expansion of public transport, the advent of the cheap press, increasing economic opportunities for middle-class and working-class women, and shifting notions about class, gender, and the economy had produced what appeared as a "new era of shopping." Nonetheless, Gordon Selfridge successfully constructed a compelling narrative about consumption, novelty and pleasure, women and the city.

In this story, Selfridge became more than the founder of a unique shop. He fashioned himself as a builder of a female, consumer-oriented public culture and placed the department store at its center. The department store came to be privileged as a generator of this urban culture, rather than the result of a slowly developing and complex phenomenon.[6] This article examines the creation of this story and explores how mass retailing and the mass media collectively used publicity to create a powerful cultural narrative.

AN AMERICAN IN LONDON

A middle-aged Wisconsin native, Harry Gordon Selfridge had actively fostered pleasurable purchasing for more than twenty-five years in the United States.[7] As the second-in-command of the Marshall Field's store in Chicago, Selfridge claimed responsibility for many of the emporium's innovations: He introduced the first restaurant and bargain basement, invited foreign royalty for personal visits, and hired a well-known window-display artist to design spectacular show windows. Selfridge also believed in advertising, writing a good deal of the early copy himself.[8] Like many of his contemporaries, Selfridge hoped that luxurious decor, architecture, amenities, and entertainments, as well as extensive publicity, would encourage patrons to reimagine the way they viewed shopping. In these commercial environments, customers were asked to see buying not as an economic act but as a social and cultural event. Admittedly, Selfridge hoped he would reap the profits from his customers' pleasure. In 1904 he left Marshall Field's to open his own store. He came to England because of a professed affinity for English culture, particularly its economic ideals, later confessing, "I can buy merchandise there and put it on my counters more cheaply than anywhere else."[9]

London presented Selfridge with both a challenge and an opportunity. By 1909 the West End was a center of commercial leisure and pleasurable consumption for middle-class and even working-class men and women. Like New York's Times Square and similar districts in European cities, the West End had become "an attraction" that was both "bounded and free . . . familiar yet exotic . . . [a] pleasure zone."[10] Even working women window-shopped and dined in the West End. They met friends and lovers at such restaurants as the Criterion and occasionally enjoyed a visit to the music hall or similar amusement.

As a component of this commercialization, London department stores typically had grown from drapers' and grocers' shops founded in the early and middle decades of the nineteenth century.[11] These stores were both a symbol of and active player in the creation of the new West End. By the 1870s and 1880s, they sold every conceivable sort of household item, clothing, materials, toys, presents, furniture, food, and drink. They also offered patrons, particularly women, comfort and entertainment in the heart of the city. By the early twentieth century, shopping was closely associated with the idea of a pleasurable and comfortable mass urban culture. The author of a 1906 shopping guide, for example, remarked that "for the woman who knows her London, there is not a more moderate and satisfactory shopping place in the world. And daily it becomes more comfortable."[12]

Despite these commercial, social, and cultural changes, a large portion of this fashionable shopping district remained dedicated to serving its traditional aristocratic and upper-middle-class market. The aristocratic image of the West End had been centuries in the making, but during the early years of the nineteenth century it became even more firmly fixed when the Prince Regent fashioned a wide avenue to accommodate a public aristocratic culture of display and consumption.[13] By the 1850s, Regent Street was well known as a fashionable promenade, the "only spot," according to the Frenchman Frances Wey, "outside the park, where Society people are certain to meet." Its shops, which displayed "all the tempting treasures of the luxury trades,"[14] provided a glittering backdrop for upper-class society to flirt, stroll, and gossip. This aristocratic image strongly influenced the nature and perception of West End commercial culture into the Edwardian era. Bond Street, the Burlington Arcade, and the surrounding streets and squares largely served a small, elite clientele, while larger thoroughfares, such as Oxford Street, had a reputation as a middle-class marketplace.[15]

As late as 1909, only a few London stores approximated the size, services, and sensationalism of Marshall Field's or the Bon Marché in Paris.[16] Social, cultural, economic, and political forces had preserved the small scale and aristocratic tone of many West End shops.[17] Architecture, interior design, salesmanship, and advertising reflected a notion of a fixed and class-specific rather than a mass market. In the eighteenth century, English retailers were known for indulging in extremely elaborate and sophisticated forms of display.[18] By the twentieth century, these same techniques were criticized for being "backward"[19] and making shopping sometimes more painful than pleasurable. Rather than present a "unified whole," wrote Selfridge, West End stores were really an "agglomeration of shops" that were "formless and inefficient." He assumed that "subdued and disciplined" interiors and employees discouraged browsing and fantasizing about goods. Selfridge remembered that when he had attempted to just look around a London shop, the shopwalker abruptly told him to "'op it."[20]

Gordon Selfridge may have quietly left this shop, but he very loudly joined the West End business community. In less than a year, he constructed what was to be the largest, most luxurious, and most publicized store in London. After winning a struggle with the local city authorities over the proposed building's size and design, Selfridge used an innovative steel-frame structure and elaborate stonework to create a monument to mass consumption.[21] The Oxford Street emporium towered over its neighbors with eight floors, six acres of floor space, nine passenger lifts, and one hundred departments.[22] Eighty feet high, with huge stone columns and twenty-one of the largest plate glass windows in the world, Selfridge's[23] struck even the most critical Londoner as an imposing visual spectacle.

The interior, like the exterior, was considered an architectural masterpiece. The selling space had wide aisles, electric lighting, crystal chandeliers, and a striking color scheme in which white walls contrasted with thick green carpets. Although not everyone agreed with the reporter who described the interior as a scene of "unexampled perfection,"[24] architectural circles generally bestowed high praise on this ambitious new venture. While doing so, they also salvaged English reputations by portraying the store as a merger of the best of old and new, as modern American construction covered with an "elegantly English" exterior.[25]

Selfridge's embellishment of the store's physical structure turned its opening into a media event. The store's show windows, covered with large silk curtains, created a theatrical atmosphere. "Most impressive of all," one reporter claimed, "were the lights and shadows behind the drawn curtains of the great range of windows suggesting that a wonderful play was being arranged."[26] The sound of bugles announced the store's opening at exactly 9:00 A.M. on 15 March 1909. Employees drew back the curtains and revealed a sight so entertaining that one reporter described the window-gazing crowd as spectators of "a tableau in some drama of fashion." Instead of the traditional display of goods, each window "had a painted background . . . depicting a scene such as Watteau would have loved, and where ladies of the old French court would have wandered."[27] Nearly all descriptions of the opening emphasized the "new sensation" created by such "lofty" windows with "delicately painted" backgrounds.[28] Selfridge's window dressers used theatrical techniques to create tableaux that invested ordinary goods with cultural and social meanings, meanings filtered through and interpreted by a sympathetic media.

While there were numerous well-known and well-trained English window dressers, the press credited the American store with the production of a new visual landscape in which the street had been turned into a theater and the crowd had become an audience of a dramatic fashion show. Indeed, while reporting on the opening, the press created many of the meanings associated with shop windows and shopping in general. Readers unable or unwilling to venture to the West End could vicariously participate in this commercial spectacle by reading about it in dozens of journals, magazines, and newspapers.

The reporting on Selfridge's opening further tightened the relationship between mass retailing and mass journalism. Although long in its development, this partnership sold Selfridge's store by promoting a new notion of women, their pleasures, and the city. In representing the store as visual spectacle, the press produced Edwardian commercial culture in partnership with men such as Gordon Selfridge. Even while criticizing the new "monster shops," the press repeatedly figured consumption as a female, public, and sensual entertainment. Countless English writers thus joined a maverick American entrepreneur to create an international culture of pleasure in London's West End.

BUYING THE CROWD

By using advertising and the press in a new fashion, Gordon Selfridge transformed London's commercial history. Victorian and Edwardian shops had advertised sparingly, with simple columns of text announcing a special sale or promotion. They tended to avoid new printing technologies which produced better and cheaper illustrations.[29] Many ignored the press altogether,[30] relying instead on short circulars or fifteen-hundred-page catalogs.[31] Edwardian advertising managers of the newer and cheaper papers had tried to dismantle this prejudice against advertising by courting the big shops' custom.[32] Yet, an advertising expert despairingly complained in 1904 that no department store in London "is enterprising enough to emulate Mr. John Wanamaker [in Philadelphia], who published day by day usually a whole page (which he calls his editorial talk) devoted to chronicling the news of the store." This expert was convinced that "the first big house which did adopt this principle would probably be crowded day by day and the others would be compelled to follow."[33]

Gordon Selfridge brought these Wanamaker-style publicity techniques to London; and, in doing so, he became the first London store-owner to gain nearly full media support.[34] Selfridge harnessed tremendous capital, as much as thirty-two thousand pounds prior to opening, and personal influence to ensure media cooperation.[35] Before opening day, he wined and dined reporters and escorted them through his emporium. He regularly entertained editors and allowed journalists free use of telephones and other store services. For the opening advertising campaign, which lasted a week, Selfridge filled ninety-seven pages of the daily and weekly press with richly illustrated advertisements drawn by some of the best-known British graphic artists.[36] At least since the 1890s, graphic artists had made a comfortable living working for both the illustrated press and poster industries.[37] Indeed, many of Selfridge's artists were also currently selling London's attractions for the Underground's poster campaign, which had been launched in 1908.[38] However, Selfridge was the first retailer to adopt such graphically compelling advertisements on such a grand scale. After the opening, the main promotional themes resurfaced in "news articles" about the store in scores of English and foreign newspapers, journals, fashion magazines, and trade papers.[39]

In these promotions, Selfridge deliberately attempted to erase any distinction between the advertising and editorial sections of newspapers. He did so most effectively by writing a "daily column" that appeared in news sections under the pen name "Callisthenes."[40] This column explained and glorified commercial culture. Topics ranged from the "principles" of modern day shopkeeping and the importance of consumption in the evolution of commerce to how to enjoy a shopping expedition or hold a department store luncheon party. Like other advertisements, the column told readers what to buy, how and where to shop, and how to think about this activity.

Critics, of course, recognized that by advertising so extensively Selfridge was buying the allegiance of the press. One journalist, for example, complained that "simultaneously with the appearance of huge and profitable advertisements in their columns the newspapers burst forth into rapturous laudations of Mr. Selfridge. Few of them, kind friends, have ever broken into laudations over you or me. But, then, we don't advertise."[41] The *Shoe and Leather Record* similarly complained that Selfridge "bought his crowd" by "buying" the newspaper press with his advertisements.[42] These critics correctly perceived that Selfridge's advertising was reinforced by the "rapturous laudations" in the press. Even while protesting, however, they implied that Selfridge's tactics worked: by buying the press, one could buy a crowd. Thus, they too reinforced the faith in advertising's appeal.

Unpaid and paid publicity collectively promoted Selfridge's as a "sight" and shopping as a female entertainment. Along with being asked to buy commodities, shoppers were requested to travel to the city and become part of the urban crowd—essentially, to experience the store as a public place. Indeed, the department store became newsworthy not because of the commodities it sold but because of its definition as a social and cultural institution for women.

The form and message of this campaign were in part an expression of a larger cultural transformation, the construction of consumers as spectators.[43] As Stuart Culver, William Leach, and others have argued, by the 1890s professional advertisers had placed their faith in the persuasive force of "eye appeal."[44] English advertisers and retailers, particularly those interested in appealing to the female consumer, also believed in the psychological force of images. They perceived the theater, and later the cinema, as the model of how to turn images into consumer desire. An article in the *Retail Trader* in 1910, for example, compared the window dresser to a stage manager:

> Just as the stage manager of a new play rehearses and tries and retries and fusses until he has exactly the right lights and shades and shadows and appeals to his audience, so the merchant goes to work, analyzing his line and his audience, until he hits on the right scheme that brings the public flocking to his doors.[45]

Trade journals emphasized women's supposed aesthetic sense, love of music,[46] and enjoyment of "attractive" illustrations,[47] "artistic" packaging, and "dainty surroundings."[48] One "specialist" summarized, "We are beginning to see that people are influenced more through the eye than any other organ of the body."[49] Gordon Selfridge, then, was part of a larger business culture that sought to appeal to consumers as spectators. Yet, he was not solely interested in appealing to the eye, nor did he emphasize the visual pleasures of shopping over other sensual pleasures. Selfridge publicity defined and redefined an almost inconceivable range of pleasures associated with consumption.

"A TIME OF PROFIT, RECREATION, AND ENJOYMENT"

Gordon Selfridge marketed his new store by promoting shopping as a delightful and respectable middle-class female pastime. Journalists then transformed this advertising message into accepted fact by writing about both Selfridge's new store and West End commercial culture in general. Selfridge's message flawlessly spread from the advertising to the news sections of even such unlikely journals as the *Church Daily Newspaper.* In writing about the store's opening, this paper's reporter loudly proclaimed that, at Selfridge's, "Shopping" had become "an Amusement."[50] Whether imagined as an absolute need, a luxurious treat, a housewife's duty, a social activity, or a feminist demand, shopping was always a pleasure.

Selfridge's central strategy was to undermine the pleasures of preexisting urban commercial culture in order to heighten the excitement and enjoyment of his new enterprise. His first advertisements, therefore, asserted that Selfridge's had transformed shopping from labor into leisure. A typical advertisement loudly proclaimed that the emporium influenced the "shopping habit of the public." For "previous to its opening . . . shopping was merely part of the day's WORK . . . to-day, shopping—at Selfridge's . . . is an important part of the day's PLEASURE, a time of PROFIT, RECREATION, and ENJOYMENT, that no Lady who has once experienced it will willingly forgo."[51] Another emphasized that "not until Selfridge's opened had English ladies understood the full meaning of 'shopping made easy.' Never had it been quite such a delightful pastime."[52]

Other advertisements and articles emphasized this transformation of shopping from work into pleasure by endlessly defining and elaborating upon those pleasures. In addition to the visual enjoyment of the advertisements and the store's window and interior decoration, countless promotions presented shopping at the core of a new publicly oriented social life, which included men and women and people of diverse classes. Selfridge and his commentators collectively promoted shopping by legitimating and defining a consumer-based, heterosocial urban culture. The romantic possibilities of shopping, for example, were subtly encoded in the imagery of the opening day advertisement. In "Herald Announcing the Opening" (fig. 5.1), Bernard Partridge illustrated the department store as a medieval prince on a faithful steed; the powerful muscles and overwhelming size of the animal underscore the appeal of the handsome herald, who looms large in the foreground as he rides into the countryside to summon ladies and their spending power to the urban center. Despite this romantic image, the underlying economy of the buyer-seller relationship is identified in the combination of a pound and dollar sign, the store's symbol, emblazoned on the herald's breastplate. Yet the illustration also obscures the "foreign" background of the owner and his methods by linking the new

Fig. 5.1. Bernard Partridge, "Herald Announcing the Opening," 15 March 1909.
(Reproduced courtesy of Selfridge's Department Store Archives.)

venture to a representation of ancient English "tradition" and currently popular images of empire.[53]

Novelty and tradition, sensuality and consumption were thus bound together in a pastiche of medieval and Edwardian romantic imagery.[54] A second cartoon, "Leisurely Shopping," emphasized modernity and the romance of consumption by representing a fashionably dressed couple enjoying tea together (fig. 5.2). The attractive couple seems interested less in each other than in the viewer, who is invited to enjoy looking at the couple. Man or woman, the reader becomes both object and subject of the couple's gaze. The pleasures of shopping are encoded in the sexual exchange of the couple and in the voyeuristic pleasures of the reader. In contrast to this somewhat provocative drawing, the written text only indirectly encourages a sexual interplay. "Shopping at Selfridge's," it claims, is "A Pleasure—A Pastime—A Recreation . . . something more than merely shopping."[55] The advertisement constructed heterosexual and consumer desire in relation to each other and linked both to a public culture of looking and display.[56]

T. Friedelson united consumption with heterosocial culture by promoting window-shopping as visual pleasure. In "Selfridge's by Night," Friedelson illustrated a fashionable crowd streaming out of motorcars and carriages to gaze at the store's brightly lit windows (fig. 5.3). The illustration and accompanying text implied that window shopping was an exciting but respectable evening entertainment. "By Night as well as Day Selfridge's will be a centre of attraction," the copy boasted. The "brilliantly lit" and "frequently re-dressed" windows promised "to give pleasure to the artistic sense of every passer-by, and to make the 'Window Shows at Selfridge's in Oxford Street' worth a considerable detour to see."[57] This picture of evening street life both promoted shopping and suppressed the better-known image of the West End after dark.[58]

Indeed, Edwardian business owners and advertisers actively assaulted the reigning portrayal of the urban center as host to prostitution, gambling, and other illicit activities. Like the managers of West End restaurants, hotels, and theaters, Selfridge rebuilt the city's image as a modern, heterosocial, commercial pleasure center.[59] These advertisements were part of the process, identified by Peter Bailey, by which capitalist managers promoted a new form of open, licit sexuality.[60] A distinct form of modernity was constructed from this limited and controlled form of sexuality.

Store advertisements and feature articles situated the department store and shopping, then, in a larger context of commercialized leisure. Copywriters and journalists drew upon a metaphorical repertoire from both urban high and low culture.[61] They described the store and the West End as a carnival, a fair, a public festival, a tourist sight, a women's club, and a pantomime. In interviews Gordon Selfridge even claimed that his

Fig. 5.2. Stanley Davis, "Leisurely Shopping," 19 March 1909. (Reproduced courtesy of Selfridge's Department Store Archives.)

BY Night as well as Day Selfridge's will be a centre of attraction. Contrary to the usual custom after closing time, our windows will not be obscured by blinds, but brilliantly lit up every Evening until Midnight.

These twenty-one windows, twelve of which are fronted with the largest sheets of plate glass in the world, will be frequently re-dressed, and will present a constant pageant of prevailing Fashion. We hope by beautiful setting and study of harmonious colouring to give pleasure to the artistic sense of every passer-by, and to make the "Window Shows at Selfridge's in Oxford Street" worth a considerable detour to see.

Fig. 5.3. T. Friedelson, "Selfridge's By Night," 20 March 1909. (Reproduced courtesy of Selfridge's Department Store Archives.)

emporium recaptured the sociability of the early modern marketplace with its mixed-class and mixed-sex culture.[62] In 1913, for example, Selfridge discussed his store as a modern reincarnation of "the great Fairs" which flourished before "small shops began to do business behind thick walls and closed doors." With his own romantic vision of the history of commerce, he continued:

> We have lately emerged from a period when merchandising and merrymaking were kept strictly separate . . . 'Business was Business.' . . . But to-day . . . Stores—the modern form of market—are gaining something of the atmosphere of the old-time fair at its best; that is, before it became boisterous and degenerate. The sociability of Selfridge's is the sociability of the fair. It draws its visitors from far and near . . . to sell to them or merely to amuse and interest them.[63]

Selfridge argued that mass retailing reunited elite and popular culture, which he saw as having been separated during the Victorian era. He further implied that this separation had limited the pleasures of English shopping and urban culture during the Victorian era.

Selfridge's advertising also compared modern shopping to foreign or previously unrespectable forms of urban leisure. A typical promotion stated that the store served the same social function as a Continental café. "Abroad, it is the cafés," the ad suggested, "which are the familiar, lovable places where the populace resort . . . to meet their friends, to watch the world and his wife, to take a cup of coffee, or drink a glass of lager or absinthe." However, "in London . . . it is the Big Stores which are beginning to play the part of the charming foreign café; and . . . it was Selfridge's who deliberately began to create the necessary atmosphere."[64] Department stores then offered middle-class women a simulacrum of social spaces they had rarely entered and which until recently had been tinged with associations of the sexual marketplace.

Gordon Selfridge went further, however, and encouraged bourgeois women to experience city life in the role of the traditionally, but no longer exclusively, masculine character of the flâneur.[65] Walking alone through the city, this figure has been assumed to represent a masculine perspective on the city and modernity. However, this urban explorer had actually been figured as a woman in novels, guidebooks, magazines, and newspapers since at least the mid-nineteenth century.[66] Like these other texts, Selfridge positioned the shopper as a flâneuse whose urban ramble ended at his door. "What a wonderful street is Oxford-street," claimed one ad, for "it compels the biggest crowds of any street in London." "When people come here," it announced, "they feel they are in the centre of things . . . : Oxford Street is the most important highway of commerce in the world."[67] "An Ode to London in the Spring, Or, The Gentle Art of Advertisement" took up this theme by privileging the pleasures of an urban walk over those of a country stroll:

> Although the country lanes are sweet
> And though the blossom bloss,
> Yet what are these to Regent Street
> Or even Charing Cross?
> So catch a train, and thank your stars
> That there are trains to catch
> And make your way this very day
> To London, with dispatch.[68]

The excitement of looking at and being with strangers became enjoyable and respectable because the commercial West End was peopled with elite society rather than a dangerous mob. The shopper could become a queen,[69] or at least a queen of this elite crowd. In Lewis Baumer's advertisement entitled "At Home," middle-class shoppers were invited to a Society gathering of fur-wrapped and elegantly coiffed ladies. However, the picture and caption played on the two meanings of being at home. The illustration represented the formal ritualized sense of the term as a Society event, while the caption reminded readers of the comfortable domestic connotation of feeling "at home."[70] Other ads portrayed Selfridge's as a formal "event" in the Season's calendar. "Shopping" at Selfridge's, the text read, "has all the appearance of a Society gathering. . . . It holds a recognised position on the programme of events, and is responsible sartorially for much of the success of each function that takes place."[71]

Gordon Selfridge designed and publicized the department store as a blend of elite and mass culture. Compared to the private world of Ascot, the store also mirrored the public culture of the amusement park. In July 1909, for example, Selfridge displayed the Bleriot airplane, the first to fly between France and England, on the roof of his store. Despite his competitors' accusation that he was engaging in a cheap American publicity stunt, huge crowds rushed to his rooftop.[72] The *Daily Telegraph* reported that "the public interest in the monoplane yesterday was immense. Throughout the entire day, without cessation or diminution, a constant stream of visitors passed into Selfridge's and circled round the historic implement."[73] The stunt proved so successful that Selfridge eventually opened a rifle range, putting green, and skating rink on the top of the store.

In addition to these sensational entertainments, Selfridge's offered a range of services and amenities to create the feeling of both a homey environment and an escape from dull household routine. Indeed, while dozens of ads and articles promoted a heterosocial urban culture, others portrayed shopping and the city as an exclusively female social experience. These ads tended to emphasize such bodily comforts as eating and lounging more than the visual pleasures of shopping. However, many intertwined a variety of sensual experiences into one desirable consumer experience.

Since the 1870s, tea shops, women's clubs, restaurants, and hotels, as well as confectioners and department stores, served as places for women who were alone in the city to refresh themselves.[74] However, Gordon Selfridge marketed his store as the first and only provider of such services. Indeed, in a quasi-feminist tone stripped of any overtly political message, he painted his shop as the ideal female "rendez-vous" or public meeting place. In the Callisthenes column entitled "Where Shall We Meet," the store became a haven for shoppers stranded in an unfriendly and supposedly inhospitable city. Before Selfridge's, the ad claimed, women had to resort to "a cold and draughty waiting-room at a railway station" or perhaps "a bleak, dusty, congested traffic-centre, such as Oxford Street." This supposed lack of an "ideal rendez-vous in London" was "called another of woman's wrongs." While "the City man had a number of favoured resorts . . . the poor ladies 'out shopping' have been at a single disadvantage."[75] By building a "private" place in public, Selfridge later told one of his executives, "I helped to emancipate women. . . . I came along just at the time when they wanted to step out on their own."[76] This businessman wanted to profit from the limited changes in women's activities already underway. He did not want to alter gender norms dramatically.

Countless ads described Selfridge's as both a public and private place, as an institution that catered to individual and social needs and desires. The vast restaurant, which served between two and three thousand patrons a day, was advertised as the largest and best in London.[77] Ads cheered its "excellent" food at "popular prices"[78] and argued that few luncheon and tea rooms in London were thought to have finer decor.[79] After lunch, patrons were encouraged to rest in the library and reading and writing rooms. French, German, American, and Colonial reception rooms welcomed foreigners and allowed English shoppers to travel to foreign lands. The German shopper, for example, could relax in a dark-oak reception room decorated with old tapestries and designed to be a replica of a "sitting room in the Fatherland."[80] A fatigued or ill shopper had the choice between a first aid room that "looked very dainty and inviting"[81] and a "rest cure" in the Silence Room. Here, talking was forbidden, allowing customers to "retire from the whirl of bargains and build up energy."[82] Double windows excluded "street noises," while soft lights and chairs with deep cushions enabled shoppers "to find peace and recuperation."[83]

While a shopper rested, "skilled needlewomen" and a maid were always available "in case of any little accident to a button or hook-and-eye which might have occurred during the rough and tumble of a day's shopping."[84] With such free services, shopping was likened to a "rest cure" that reduced rather than increased anxiety. Underlying this nurturing image, however, lay the more traditional views of the city as dangerous and dirty and of the female body as weak and in need of comfort and protection. Although Selfridge encouraged women to enter the city, like a good Edwardian patriarch, he also claimed to protect them once they were there.

Selfridge promised these women more than comfort, however. He offered them a space for legitimate indulgence. Modern shopping was more than just buying, but it was also more than "just looking."[85] Shopping, as William Leach has put it, was a visual culture of "color, glass and light,"[86] but it was also a bodily culture stimulating all the senses. Its decor and displays allowed one to feast one's eye and enjoy the feel of fine fabric. Its restaurants and services told shoppers to "treat" themselves to "delicious" luxuries. Even a visit to the Selfridge Bargain Basement could become a sensual wonderland for the frugal shopper. "What a shining feast for the eyes are the ribbon tables; what filmy piles of blouses are here . . . what a forest of silken and velvet flowers; what delicious scents are wafted to us from that mound of tinted soaps."[87] Materials provided "feasts" for the eyes, and colors and scents were "delicious," as if oral, tactile, and visual pleasures defined and amplified one another. All appetites were united in a single desiring body.

Emphasizing the exciting indulgence of Selfridge shopping, a large proportion of early ads focused on individual, and immediately gratifying, forms of consumption. Shoppers were enticed with bonbons and sweetmeats packaged in replicas of famous Italian monuments, buildings, and statues.[88] Sweets became "wonderfully nourishing," a "benefit," even a "necessity" that "makes an appetising and delicious appeal to every visitor in the Store."[89] The American-style soda fountain, a unique temptation, proved a strong selling point and the center of Selfridge's oral appeal. Luxurious ingestion almost became the heart of the consumer experience. A typical ad showed how the soda fountain transformed women who "hated shopping" into avid practitioners of the art. Two "large iced strawberries" could thoroughly reform women who had found shopping "frightfully boring," "a most decadent development," and a "hotbed of frivolous, senseless adornment."[90]

In order to contain the potentially radical message of women indulging in public pleasures, Selfridge's sometimes was imagined as a glorified bourgeois household. The department store became a huge bourgeois home, sustaining family life in the heart of the city. After defining "afternoon tea" as "the chief ritual to the household gods," an "unrivalled and unassailable" custom that was "one of the mainstays of family life," an advertisement reminded shoppers that "even when away from home, the solace of afternoon tea cannot be dispensed with."[91] This ad both created new and used preexisting domestic associations of afternoon tea with family, stability, and tradition in order to connect a new American-owned store with notions of bourgeois Englishness, to make local customers feel at home and visiting tourists feel English. Sensual pleasures were given moral validity when placed within the language of domesticity.

Selfridge's thereby became a home away from home, offering its customers space for what had been considered private forms of socializing. One journalist reported that women were even inviting their friends to formal shopping parties. This reporter claimed that these "parties are a new thing, which have sprung into existence to meet a new need. . . . The parties are small, select, numerous, and earnest."[92] They included buying but emphasized dining and browsing with friends. A common activity for nearly forty years, public dining was marketed by Selfridge as new, modern, and fun, as an updated image of Victorian women's culture.[93] Here, female friendship, like "the family," became a vehicle for legitimizing consumption.

Both paid and unpaid media publicity walked a tightrope between praising and denigrating the home and often did both at once. Indeed, Gordon Selfridge believed that women were responsive to his store's "sensuous appeal of beauty" because they had "little opportunity of escaping the deadening routine of homelife."[96] "Women needed Selfridge's," according to one ad, "to break the monotony that had invaded and made dull a daily round." Selfridge's provided "the variety which is the spice of life."[95] "I was lonely," complained one housewife,

> so I went to Selfridge's . . . one of the biggest and brightest places I could think of. I wanted crowds . . . a happy place . . . "home" in the open . . . caught up in a whirl of these jolly human, little businesses; made part of the crowd; all sense of isolation swept away.[96]

The store could be both "'home' in the open" and contrasted with bourgeois home life, which in these ads denied rather than gave women pleasure. "I have a friend, and I want to meet her. Where shall the meeting-place be?" asked one character. "At my home? I don't think so: women spend so much time among their own all too familiar chintzes." This consumer "wanted a place with music, where there were plenty of things to see, and a companionable sense of crowds."[97]

In typically paradoxical style, other ads reminded women of the pleasures of being alone, especially when actually buying. "The absence of the orthodox shop-walker with the eternal and bothering 'what can I do for you, madame?' produces a restful effect" because "you will be allowed to stroll about just wherever you like without ever once being pestered."[98] The social life of shopping, then, was not imagined to be pleasurable when it included individuals from across the counter, when it implied interaction with a shop assistant or store manager. The author of the "Five

O'Clock Tea Talk" column in *T. P.'s Weekly* argued that it was the absence of this "hovering employee" which was the key to the "new sensation" of shopping at Selfridge's. "Safe from the tyranny of the shopwalker," the editor noted, "shopping becomes what shopping should be—a matter for individual speculation, for individual choice, and for individual satisfaction."[99] This author, like many, seemed convinced that Selfridge's offered something new to the shopping public. Whether it was individual speculation, the companionable sense of crowds, ice cream, or an evening's entertainment, the media bought and resold the story that West End shopping became more pleasurable after 15 March 1909.

This story was difficult to challenge. Although London shopkeepers and businessmen predicted that Selfridge's methods would not take hold on English soil, the *Drapery Times* admitted that London was flooded as a result of its opening and of its spectacular methods. However, the paper questioned "the possible weakness of inviting people to walk round without being asked to purchase." The journal worried that the crowds might not be a mass of customers but an interference with "those people who go to make purchases." The tempers of legitimate customers would be tried when they did not "get the attention which they want." Did a mass audience equal mass consumption? Perhaps not, but the above author admitted that, as much as he disliked Selfridge's methods, "an alternative form of attracting potential customers is difficult to alight upon."[100]

Established shops reluctantly increased their advertising budgets,[101] spruced up their windows, and rebuilt and redesigned their interiors.[102] However, only Harrod's truly rivaled Selfridge's spectacle.[103] Desperately searching for a reason to celebrate shopping and reach a broader market, Harrod's found an anniversary that precisely coincided with Selfridge's opening. It fervently advertised and celebrated the event by transforming the furniture department into a concert hall decorated with purple and white muslin and garlands of crimson rambler roses. Shoppers enjoyed the music of the London Symphony Orchestra, a famous Spanish opera singer, and other well-known performers.[104] According to a sympathetic reporter, at Harrod's "shopping was a pleasure and nervous headaches or aching feet were conspicuously absent."[105]

Trade competition in the context of the wealthy West End had erupted not into a price war but into a battle over the nature and place of women's consumer pleasures. With each store highlighting the elegance and comfort of its own showrooms, they transformed the whole of the West End into a female, commercial playground. Praising this development, the *British Congregationalist* wrote simply that "shopping becomes amusing and fascinating when it involves a visit to the West End."[106] Thus, Selfridge's, an enthusiastic press, and other English retailers collectively represented the West End as an environment of pleasurable consumption. Despite its mentor's monumental efforts, Selfridge's was never imagined as the sole source of pleasurable consumption. Even quite supportive reporters often described the store as only one of the many West End shops serving women goods and pleasures:

> London's greatest shopping week began yesterday. . . . Selfridge's had flung open its doors. Harrod's was celebrating its sixtieth year of success, and every West End firm vied with one another to dazzle and entertain its customers. Oxford-street, Regent-street, and Brompton-road were crowded with eager shoppers. Never before has it been possible for the twentieth-century woman to indulge in such an orgy of shopping.[107]

Advertising, news reports, publicity stunts, and social commentary promoted Selfridge's and the West End as a public sphere of female pleasure. Despite a considerable masculine presence on the streets, London was imagined as completely given over to women and consumption; indeed, the city seemed to have become a female space. One paper suggested that "the West End was given over to women," whose "laughter and the rustle of silken skirts enlivened the sound of buses crawling through the slush of the streets."[108] The city seemed invaded by an "army in furs and feather."[109] Although retailers' reports no doubt exaggerated the numbers of shoppers, there were possibly several million women visiting London in the third week of March 1909. Selfridge estimated that his store accommodated over a million visitors during its opening week.[110] How many could afford or even wanted to buy anything cannot be known. Nonetheless, during this week the West End appeared to offer something for everyone.[111]

In 1910 a Mrs. Stafford of Museum Cottage, Oxford, received a postcard from "Nannie."[112] On the back of a picture of a London hotel, a short note read: "Shall leave London tomorrow at 1.45, arrive at Oxford at 3. Am just off to Selfridges to tea with Annie Coleman. Had a P.C. [postcard] from Aunty. Much Love, Nannie."[113] By 1910 the store was already a household word for a network of women. This postcard advertises a whole matrix of urban, commercial activities, including a system of public transport, a hotel, and a department store. Along with expensive ad campaigns, postcards, letters, and gossip also contributed to the imaginary creation of the West End. "Nannie" both experienced and promoted women's pleasure in London's West End.[114]

Despite the fact that men often shopped, shopping was represented as a uniquely feminine and urban pleasure. In Edwardian England, middle-class and lower-class women were invited to enjoy themselves in the heart of the metropolis. This promotion of shopping as feminine pleasure also served to construct the very notion of the West End as a female arena. The pleasure of shopping in the West End remained limited to particular areas and circumscribed by political, economic, and social constraints on women's full participation in public life. However, new images of femininity which highlighted the centrality of women in urban life were integral to the development and success of mass consumer culture in early twentieth-century England. Definitions of public and private, male and female, were necessarily renegotiated as women literally and metaphorically besieged the West End, occupying a central position in the economic and cultural life of the city.

NOTES

An earlier version of this article was presented at the Rutgers Center for Historical Analysis in December 1991. I am grateful to all the participants for their suggestions and comments. I also owe special thanks to Victoria de Grazia, John Gillis, Bonnie Smith, Cora Kaplan, Judy Walkowitz, Leo Charney, Vanessa Schwartz, and Jordan Witt for all their criticism and support.

1. *Daily Express*, 15 March 1909; *Standard*, 16 March 1909. Many of the newspaper references in this article were collected in scrapbooks housed at the Selfridges Department Store Archive and do not have page numbers.

2. *Standard*, 18 March 1909.

3. *Daily Express*, 15 March 1909.

4. For a broader discussion of this development, see Erika Rappaport, "The West End and Women's Pleasure: Gender and Commercial Culture in London, 1860–1914" (Ph.D. diss., Rutgers University, 1993). See, for example, William Leach, "Transformations in a Culture of Consumption: Women and Department Stores, 1890–1925," *Journal of American History* 71 (September 1984); 319–342; Elizabeth Wilson, *Adorned in Dreams: Fashion and Modernity* (London: Virago, 1985); idem, *The Sphinx in the City: Urban Life, the Control of Disorder and Women* (Berkeley, Los Angeles, London: University of California Press, 1991); Rachel Bowlby, *Just Looking: Consumer Culture in Dreiser, Gissing, and Zola* (New York and London: Methuen, 1985).

5. Erika Rappaport, "'A Husband and His Wife's Dresses': Consumer Credit and the Debtor Family in England, 1864–1914," in *The Sex of Things: Gender and Consumption in Historical Perspective*, ed. Victoria de Grazia and Ellen Furlough (Berkeley, Los Angeles, London: University of California Press, forthcoming).

6. This is most pronounced in business histories, such as Gordon Honeycombe, *Selfridges: Seventy-Five Years: The Story of the Store* (London: Park Lane Press, 1984); Reginald Pound, *Selfridge: A Biography* (London: Heinemann, 1960); Alfred H. Williams, *No Name on the Door: A Memoir of Gordon Selfridge* (London: W. H. Allen, 1956); Richard S. Lambert, *The Universal Provider: A Study of William Whiteley and the Rise of the London Department Store* (London: George G. Harrap, 1938); Michael Moss and Alison Turton, *A Legend of Retailing: The House of Fraser* (London: Weidenfeld and Nicholson, 1989).

7. Lloyd Wendt and Herman Kogan, *Give the Lady What She Wants! The Story of Marshall Field and Company* (Chicago: Rand McNally, 1952), pp. 201–215. For the

most detailed analysis of the role of the department store as an American cultural institution, see William Leach, *Land of Desire: Merchants, Power, and the Rise of a New American Culture* (New York: Pantheon Books, 1993); Susan Porter Benson, *Counter Cultures: Saleswomen, Managers, and Customers in American Department Stores* (Urbana and New York: University of Illinois Press, 1986); Elaine S. Abelson, *When Ladies Go A-Thieving: Middle-Class Shoplifters and the Victorian Department Store* (Oxford and New York: Oxford University Press, 1989). For a broader discussion of the cultural history of promotion in America, see Neil Harris, *Cultural Excursions: Marketing Appetites and Cultural Tastes in Modern America* (Chicago and London: University of Chicago Press, 1990); Susan Strasser, *Satisfaction Guaranteed: The Making of the American Mass Market* (New York: Pantheon, 1989); Simon J. Bronner, ed., *Consuming Visions: Accumulation and Display of Goods in America, 1880–1920* (New York: W. W. Norton, 1989).

8. Robert Hendrickson, *The Grand Emporiums: The Illustrated History of America's Great Department Stores* (New York: Stein and Day, 1979), pp. 86–87.

9. Pound, op. cit., p. 32.

10. Jean Christophe Agnew, "Times Square: Secularization and Sacralization," in *Inventing Times Square: Commerce and Culture at the Crossroads of the World,* ed. William Taylor (New York: Russell Sage Foundation, 1991), p. 2.

11. James B. Jefferys, *Retail Trading in Great Britain, 1850–1950* (Cambridge: Cambridge University Press, 1954), p. 326. H. Pasdermadjian, *The Department Store: Its Origins, Evolution, and Economics* (London: Newman Books, 1954); David Chaney, "The Department Store as a Cultural Form," *Theory, Culture, and Society* 1 (1983): 22–31; Michael Winstanley, *The Shopkeeper's World, 1830–1914* (Manchester: Manchester University Press, 1983). For a more general history of English retailing, see Alison Adburgham, *Shops and Shopping, 1800–1914: Where and in What Manner the Well-Dressed Englishwoman Bought her Clothes,* 2d ed. (London: Barrie and Jenkins, 1989); Dorothy Davis, *Fairs, Shops, and Supermarkets: A History of English Shopping* (Toronto: University of Toronto Press, 1966); Molly Harrison, *People and Shopping: A Social Background* (London: Ernest Benn, 1975); David Alexander, *Retailing in England During the Industrial Revolution* (London: The Athlone Press, 1970).

12. *Olivia's Shopping and How She Does It: A Prejudiced Guide to the London Shops* (London: Gay and Bird, 1906), p. 9.

13. Hermione Hobhouse, *A History of Regent Street* (London: Macdonald and Jane's and Queen Ann Press, 1975).

14. Frances Wey, *A Frenchman Sees the English in the 'Fifties,* trans. Valerie Pirie (1856; reprint, London: Sidgewick & Jackson, 1935), p. 72.

15. F. J. Fisher, "The Development of London as a Centre of Conspicuous Consumption in the Sixteenth and Seventeenth Centuries," in *Essays in Economic History,* vol. 2, ed. E. M. Carus-Wilson (London: Edward Arnold, 1962), pp. 197–207; Peter Earle, *The Making of the English Middle Class: Business, Society and Family Life in London, 1660–1730* (Berkeley, Los Angeles, London: University of California Press, 1989); Gareth Shaw, "The Role of Retailing in the Urban Economy," in *The Structure of Nineteenth-Century Cities,* ed. James H. Jonnson and Colin G. Pooley (London: Croom Helm and St. Martin's Press, 1982), pp. 171–194; P. J.

Atkins, "The Spatial Configuration of Class Solidarity in London's West End, 1792–1939," *Urban History Yearbook* (1990): 36–65.

16. Bowlby, op. cit., p. 8. For an analysis of the culture of the French department store, see Michael Miller, *The Bon Marché: Bourgeois Culture and the Department Store, 1869–1920* (Princeton: Princeton University Press, 1981); Rosalind Williams, *Dream Worlds: Mass Consumption in Late Nineteenth-Century France* (Berkeley, Los Angeles, London: University of California Press, 1982).

17. Rappaport, "West End and Women's Pleasure," pp. 287–292.

18. Neil McKendrick, John Brewer, and J. H. Plumb, eds., *The Birth of a Consumer Society: The Commercialization of Eighteenth-Century England* (Bloomington: Indiana University Press, 1982); Colin Campbell, *The Romantic Ethic and the Spirit of Modern Consumerism* (Oxford: Basil Blackwell, 1987); Hoh-Cheung and Lorna Mui, *Shops and Shopkeeping in Eighteenth-Century England* (Kingston and Montreal: McGill-Queen's University Press and Routledge, 1989); Lorna Weatherill, *Consumer Behavior and Material Culture in Britain, 1660–1760* (London and New York: Routledge, 1988). See also the recent collection of essays, *Consumption and the World of Goods*, ed. John Brewer and Roy Porter (London and New York: Routledge, 1993).

19. Quoted in Williams, op. cit., p. 80. This was a particularly strong theme in business journals at the time. See, for example, *The Magazine of Commerce* 4 (February 1904): 120.

20. Pound, op. cit., p. 29.

21. Jeanne Lawrence, "Steel Frame Architecture Versus the London Building Regulations: Selfridges, The Ritz, and American Technology," *Construction History* 6 (1990): 23–46.

22. Honeycombe, op. cit., p. 9.

23. The store's name is now Selfridges, without an apostrophe. However, at the time it opened, the name included the apostrophe.

24. *Daily Express*, 16 March 1909. For criticism, see *The Builder*, 20 March 1909.

25. *Black and White*, 20 March 1909.

26. *Daily Chronicle*, 15 March 1909.

27. *Daily Chronicle*, 16 March 1909.

28. *Christian World*, 18 March 1909.

29. Only a few examples of full-page illustrated advertisements exist before this point. An example of one, however, was the special 1897 Jubilee promotion, which Harrod's placed in the special addition of the daily papers.

30. T. R. Nevett, *Advertising in Britain: A History* (London: Heinemann, 1982), p. 74.

31. E. S. Turner, *The Shocking History of Advertising!* (New York: E. P. Dutton & Co., 1953), p. 198. For an example, see Alison Adburgham, ed., *Yesterday's Shopping: The Army and Navy Store's Catalogue, 1907*, facs. ed. (Devon, England: David and Charles Reprints, 1969). Many catalogs did not match this example, however. Edward Maxwell wrote in 1904 that most were "marvels of typographical imperfection. . . . They cry Cheap! Cheap! Cheap!" See "A Matter-of-Fact Talk on Advertising," *The Magazine of Commerce* 4 (February 1904): 120.

32. Turner, op. cit., p. 198.

33. Maxwell, op. cit., p. 117.

34. On the alliance between American newspapers and department stores, see Michael Schudson, *Advertising, The Uneasy Persuasion: Its Dubious Impact on American Society* (New York: Basic Books, 1984), p. 4.

35. A typical budget was about five hundred pounds a month. Nevett, op. cit., p. 74.

36. Each artist signed their drawings, and their names were republished when the designs were bound into a souvenir booklet. The artists were Lewis Baumer, R. Anning Bell, Walter Crane, John Campbell, Stanley R. Davis, J. T. Friedenson, E. Grasset, H. A. Hogg, Garth Jones, Will Lendon, Ellis Martin, John Mills, Harold Nelson, Bernard Partridge, Fred Pegram, F. V. Poole, Tony Sarge, E. J. Sullivan, S. E. Scott, Linley Sambourne, Fred Taylor, Howard Van Dusen, Frank Wiles, J. F. Woolrich. The list also included two women, Miss B. Ascough and Miss S. B. Pearse, who did the two cartoons promoting "Children's Day."

37. Harris, op. cit., p. 351–355. Thomas Richards argues that Victorian advertisers had been the leading figures in the creation of commodity culture since at least the Great Exhibition in 1851. See Thomas Richards, *The Commodity Culture of Victorian England: Advertising and Spectacle, 1851–1914* (Stanford: Stanford University Press, 1990).

38. Oliver Green, *Underground Art* (London: Studio Vista, 1990); Christian Barmen, *The Man Who Built London Transport: A Biography of Frank Pick* (London: David and Charles, 1979).

39. Some of the many papers in which notices of the new store appeared are *Barrow News, Belfast Evening Telegraph, Bolton Evening News, Bolton Journal, Bristol Times, Burton Daily Mail, Cork Constitution, Cork Examiner, Coventry Herald, Derby Daily Telegraph, Dublin Express, Dundee Courier, East Anglian Daily Times, Leicester Chronicle, Manchester Guardian, Midland Counties Express,* and *Nottingham Echo.* The foreign papers included *African World, Egyptian Morning News, Gold Coast Leader, Indian Engineering, Toronto Evening Telegram, Transvaal Critic, Brisbane Telegraph,* and numerous German, French, and American papers, as well as other English-language Commonwealth papers. Papers from different Christian faiths, such as *Catholic Weekly, Christian Commonwealth, Christian World, Church Daily Newspaper,* and *British Congregationalist,* praised the new shop and the pleasures of shopping, as did the *Jewish Chronicle, British Journal of Nursing, Car,* and *Co-Operative News.*

40. Although readers thought Callisthenes was a composite of many English authors, it was a pseudonym for Selfridge and the employees whose copy he revised.

41. *London Opinion,* 27 March 1909.

42. *Shoe and Leather Record,* 19 March 1909.

43. For the particular history of this transition in England, see Rappaport, "West End and Women's Pleasure," pp. 211–274, 346–389. See also Anne Friedberg, *Window Shopping: Cinema and the Postmodern* (Berkeley, Los Angeles, London: University of California Press, 1993).

44. Leach, *Land of Desire,* p. 43; Stuart Culver, "What Manikins Want: *The Wonderful World of Oz* and *The Art of Decorating Dry Goods Windows,*" *Representations* 21 (winter 1988): 97–116, 106.

45. "The Show Window," *Retail Trader* (25 October 1910): 18.

46. Maxwell, op. cit., p. 118.

47. Berthe Fortesque Harrison, "Advertising From the Woman's Point of View," *Modern Business* 2 (December 1908): 511.

48. R. Strauss, "Original Retailers: Mr. W. B. Fuller," *Modern Business* 3 (June 1909): 452.

49. "The Reign of the Artistic," *Success Magazine,* reprinted in *Retail Trader* (19 May 1910): 16.

50. *Church Daily Newspaper,* 19 March 1909.

51. *Daily Telegraph,* 11 April 1910.

52. *Daily Chronicle,* 17 March 1909.

53. Mark Girouard, *The Return to Camelot: Chivalry and the English Gentleman* (New Haven and London: Yale University Press, 1981).

54. Foreshadowing the techniques described as capitalist realism in Schudson, op. cit., pp. 214–215.

55. *Daily News, Telegraph,* and *Westminster Gazette,* 19 March 1909.

56. Indeed, all of Selfridge's advertising assumes that any consumer has what Lawrence Birken has termed the "polymorphous potential to desire everything" (Lawrence Birken, *Consuming Desire: Sexual Science and the Emergence of a Culture of Abundance, 1871–1914* [Ithaca and London: Cornell University Press, 1988], p. 50).

57. *Daily Chronicle,* 20 March 1909.

58. Judith R. Walkowitz, *City of Dreadful Delight: Narratives of Sexual Danger in Late-Victorian London* (Chicago: University of Chicago Press, 1992); Wilson, op. cit., pp. 3–46; Tracy C. Davis, *Actresses as Working Women: Their Social Identity in Victorian Culture* (London and New York: Routledge, 1991), pp. 137–150.

59. Rappaport, "West End and Women's Pleasure," pp. 197–210.

60. Peter Bailey, "Parasexuality and Glamour: The Victorian Barmaid as Cultural Prototype," *Gender and History* 2 (summer 1990): 148-172.

61. For parallel examples, see Lauren Rabinovitz, "Temptations of Pleasure: Nickelodeons, Amusement Parks, and the Sights of Female Sexuality," *Camera Obscura* 23 (May 1990): 72–89; Tony Bennett, "A Thousand and One Troubles: Blackpool Pleasure Beach," in *Formations and Pleasure,* ed. Frederic Jameson (London: Routledge and Kegan Paul, 1983), pp. 138–155.

62. On the interplay between the market and visual entertainment in the early modern period, see Jean-Christophe Agnew, *Worlds Apart: The Market and the Theater in Anglo-American Thought, 1550–1750* (Cambridge: Cambridge University Press, 1986).

63. *Hardware Trade Journal,* 3 March 1913.

64. *Evening Standard,* 22 January 1912.

65. Several cultural critics have suggested that, as the object of the flâneur's gaze, women cannot occupy the same role. See Janet Wolff, "The Invisible Flâneuse: Women and the Literature of Modernity," *Theory, Culture, and Society* 2, no. 3 (1985): 37–46; Griselda Pollock, *Vision and Difference: Femininity, Feminism and Histories of Art* (London and New York: Routledge, 1988), pp. 50–90; Andreas Huyssen, "Mass Culture as Woman, Modernism's Other," in *Studies in Entertainment: Critical Approaches to Mass Culture,* ed. Tania Modleski (Bloomington: Indiana

University Press), pp. 188–205; Susan Buck-Morss, "The Flâneur, The Sandwichman, and the Whore: The Politics of Loitering," *New German Critique* 39 (fall 1986): 99–140.

66. See, for example, Charlotte Brontë, *Villette* (1853; reprint, London: Penguin Books, 1979), p. 109; Rappaport, "West End and Women's Pleasure," pp. 211–274; Walkowitz, op. cit., pp. 46–48; Elizabeth Wilson, "The Invisible Flâneur," *New Left Review* 191 (January–February 1992): 90–110.

67. *Evening Standard,* 11 December 1915.

68. Ibid., May 1912 (specific date not available).

69. See Richards, op. cit., pp. 73–118.

70. *Standard,* 20 March 1909.

71. *Evening Standard* and *Pall Mall Gazette,* 13 May 1912.

72. Honeycombe, op. cit., p. 39.

73. *Daily Telegraph,* 27 July 1909.

74. Robert Thorne, "Places of Refreshment in the Nineteenth-Century City," in *Buildings and Society: Essays on the Social Development of the Built Environment,* ed. Anthony D. King (London: Routledge and Kegan Paul, 1980), pp. 228–253.

75. *Evening Standard,* 23 March 1911.

76. Williams, op. cit., p. 55.

77. *Daily Chronicle,* 22 March 1909.

78. *Church Daily Newspaper,* 19 March 1909.

79. *Morning Leader,* 17 March 1909.

80. *Daily News,* 22 March 1909.

81. *British Journal of Nursing,* 20 March 1909.

82. *Evening Standard,* 11 March 1909.

83. *Daily Mail,* 12 March 1909.

84. Ibid.

85. On the relation between looking and shopping, see Bowlby, op. cit., pp. 32–34.

86. Leach, *Land of Desire,* pp. 39–70.

87. *Evening Standard,* 11 November 1915.

88. *Morning Post,* 30 October 1915.

89. *Pall Mall Gazette,* 6 November 1916.

90. *Evening Standard* and *Pall Mall Gazette,* 20 June 1912.

91. *Standard,* 10 April 1911.

92. *Daily Mail,* 15 March 1909.

93. Susan Porter Benson has argued that "women shared both knowledge and the experience of consumption in their kin and friendship networks" (Benson, op. cit., p. 5). Businessmen recognized and used this culture in a variety of different ways.

94. Williams, op. cit., p. 96.

95. *Evening Standard,* 21 April 1911.

96. Ibid., 16 July 1912.

97. Ibid., 23 November 1915.

98. *Morning Leader,* 17 March 1909.

99. *T. P.'s Weekly,* 2 April 1909.

100. *Drapery Times,* 27 March 1909.

101. Messrs. Dickins and Jones Minute Book of Board Meetings, 1909–1914, General Board Meeting Minutes, March 10, 1910, House of Fraser Archives, HF/10/1/3, the Archives and Business Record Centre, Glasgow University, Glasgow.

102. *Times* (London), 15 March 1909.

103. Honeycombe, op. cit., p. 14.

104. *Daily Express,* 17 March 1909.

105. Ibid., 16 March 1909.

106. *British Congregationalist,* 16 April 1909.

107. *Daily Express,* 16 March 1909.

108. Ibid.

109. *Daily Graphic,* 15 March 1909.

110. *Daily Chronicle,* 22 March 1909.

111. *Daily Express,* 15 March 1909.

112. It is unclear whether "Nannie" was the former nanny of Mrs. Stafford, given how she signs the postcard.

113. Noble Collection, Box C23.3, 1910, Print Room Guildhall Library, London.

114. However, this should not be read as a story of manipulation or seduction of passive female consumers by big business. As the sociologist Colin Campbell has noted, "Advertisements (and other product-promoting material) only constitutes one part of the total set of cultural influences at work upon consumers" (Campbell, op. cit., p. 47).

SIX

Disseminations of Modernity: Representation and Consumer Desire in Early Mail-Order Catalogs

Alexandra Keller

Sunday School Teacher: Where do the Ten Commandments come from?
Rural Idaho Student: From Sears, Roebuck, where else?[1]

Mail-order catalogs function as a central emblem of modernity in ways strikingly similar to cinema. Unlike cinema, however, catalogs are a uniquely American icon. In their formative years from 1895 to 1906, mail-order catalogs, like the preliminary cinema of the turn of the century, went through major changes on their way to a codification of spectator address and construction, as well as audience consolidation. By 1930 mail-order catalogs had long since settled into "classical" vocabularies of communication, rituals of reception, and processes of circulation even more firmly than had cinema. The early period, however, burgeoned with chaos and change, trial and error. Conventions of discourse developed, as in cinema, as the viewing, reading, and consuming subject was introduced to and moved through mail-order discourse. This essay will focus on Sears, Roebuck and Company catalogs—the recently deceased exemplar of the form—during the hairpin turn of the century: that is, those catalogs issued between 1899 and 1906, especially the 1902 edition, in which so many aspects of structure and address which became part of the classical vocabulary first made themselves apparent.

Materially, mail-order catalogs and cinema functioned as related markers of their episteme, not least because they equally depend on and manifest both mechanical reproduction and mass dissemination. As Walter Benjamin argued in relation to art, before the age of mechanical reproduction, "the presence of the original [was] the prerequisite to the concept of authenticity," whereas in this new age "the work of art reproduced becomes the work of art designed for reproducibility."[2] Herein lies the link between cinema and mail-order catalogs. The catalog, like the film, has no auratic original. Film is, in this sense, a representation of itself—something consumed without a material trace. True, a filmic representation of Lillian Gish does in many ways stand in for a real Lillian Gish, but film spectators do not treat her image as a momentary replacement for the actual woman whom they will soon come physically to possess as if she were a shirtwaist or a watch fob.

Early mail-order catalogs, however, embodied a Janus-faced representational system. Viewed one way, they stood in for the absent consumer good, sustaining desire through representation of the absent object. As Freud suggests in his description of the "fort-da" game, by repeatedly hiding and finding a small bobbin his grandson simultaneously articulated the anxieties of momentary nonpossession and attempted to master and annihilate those losses. That is, catalogs placed themselves through representation at the intersection of desire and lack. Viewed another way, however, as I will suggest, the catalogs' contextualization in rural rather than urban America allowed them to become used and valorized as literature and entertainment. The catalog could simultaneously function as a marketplace—a mall between two covers—and pass itself off as noncommercial, something that, like cinema, claimed to exist largely for entertainment, edification, and fantasy. Its cover was even more complete than cinema's in one obvious way. There was no ticket to buy; the catalog cost nothing to receive, and it sometimes came to consumers whether they wanted it or not.

These early catalogs, therefore, forced even more direct subject modulations than cinema: The "subject" at issue as the "reader" of catalogs was first constructed as a "spectator" who would then become a "consumer," and it is in part this unique pattern of interpellation which makes mail-order catalogs such a compelling turn-of-the-century phenomenon. For through these modulations, the catalog effected a kind of rural flânerie for those who browsed its pages. Initially this seems a contradiction: The flâneur, as he wanders through the city perusing its spectacles and enjoying its parks and cafés, is a kinetic subject, constantly in motion.[3] Yet there is a certain inverted flânerie to be ascribed to both early filmgoing and catalog reading: The subject remains still while the object of inquiry is kinetic. In cinema, of course, this movement is literal, as images play across a screen. Catalogs, however, in the way that they assembled thousands of items for hundreds of purposes categorized for easy negotiation and selection, promoted an unprecedented movement of sorts in the rural subject. The world as brought into the rural home by the mail-order catalog was an abundant and crowded place, jammed with goods, the representation of a marketplace whose fleshly embodiment would be equally jammed with vendors, consumers, and gawkers. It is in relation to the crowd that the flâneur is defined, whether as a figure in privileged concealment or adjacency, or in critical opposition to it.[4] In moving through the catalog, the rural subject not only constantly shifted among subject positions but also wandered through the invisible streets of the metropolis that Sears, Roe-buck had created. And though the Sears catalog always claimed to address rural subjects on their terms, its very structure and purpose make it as an instantiation of the urbanization of that rural subject.

In bringing the city to the country and the department store to the shopper, Sears brought the outside world into the home. Thus viewed, early cinema and mail-order catalogs reveal themselves to be equally in-strumental in reconfiguring notions of public and private space, notions which had long been articulated in terms of gender division. Indeed, one sign of early cinema's codification both as narrative system and exemplar of public event was the construction of the female spectator as turning on the commodification of desire.[5] The cinema provided one of few accept-able spaces for women in the public sphere, and since the private, domes-tic sphere had long been configured as, indeed, exemplifying the feminine, women's presence could not help but bring a sense of the private into these public spaces. If the city and its markets and squares and theaters of all kinds propelled women into the public as never before, women were nevertheless required to do double duty. Their new status as public fig-ures, ratified by both the marketplace and increasing progressive political and social activity, did not relieve them from their responsibilities in and to—*and identification with*—the home, the maintenance of which required an average of twenty-seven hours per week.[6] Likewise, the blurring of pub-lic and private spheres that was intrinsic to mail-order catalogs inverted the "private spectacle" of cinematic spectatorship, in which an assembly of people nevertheless view any film individually.

Mail-order catalogs brought the usually public activity of commodity con-sumption into the home. The private sphere was thereby somewhat publi-cized, made—if not actually public—something parallel to public, some-thing which, at any rate, was emphatically no longer seemingly private. It also, *for this very reason,* sought to reinforce, through representation of and address to both men and women, the very notions that mass culture and mass consumption threatened to destabilize. That is, these early Sears catalogs strove to textualize, and therefore to cement in place, traditional patterns of gender spatialization—public space for men and private space for women.

At the turn of the century, women were taking to the public sphere in record numbers, constituting the vast majority of consumers—85 percent by 1915.[7] In the Sears catalogs, especially with items of apparel and med-icine, the question of how to represent women was indivisible from the feeling that their increasingly public and active presence made them dan-gerous, and that their images, therefore, needed to be controlled in a way that those of men did not. It was as if there were a risk of the female con-sumer becoming "Consumption" itself if her image were too variable or given too much leeway. Recalling that ordering from a catalog requires an element of activity not extant in rituals of absorbing cinema, we will embark on a brief tour of mail-order procedures and history before broaching specific issues of gender construction and subject address vis-à-vis mass reproduction and dissemination and questions of public versus private space.

Mail-order catalogs proliferated between 1895 and 1925, and though the Sears catalog blazed new trails in the industry, it was by no means the first of its kind. In many ways it imitated its giant predecessor and greatest competitor, Montgomery Ward, most notably in its address exclusively to a rural constituency and its professed function as an eliminator of middlemen. But it was unique not least because Richard Warren Sears wrote virtually all the copy for each item in his catalogs and oversaw the layout of every edition until his retirement in 1908. That is, there was a single— and singular—author operating in a way to which most catalogs only pretended.[8] The vital statistics of Richard Sears's "Wishbook" (whose title alone put it in play in the arena of consumer desire) reflected its importance: At its most powerful, it weighed six pounds, ran to fifteen hundred pages, listed one hundred thousand products, and reached the homes of twenty million Americans.[9] Sears was, as David McCullough has put it, "the most widely read man in America."[10]

Before looking at the Sears catalogs in detail, it is worth reiterating one fundamental difference between them and contemporaneous cinema: While the latter was a decidedly urban phenomenon, the Sears catalog never would have existed without a rural population, whose purchasing power—largely because of rising agricultural prices and soaring property values—grew apace with its numbers. So, although aspects of mechanical reproduction dovetail snugly with those of cinema, methods and motivations of dissemination differ, due largely to three historical factors, each of which warrants brief discussion: the invention of time zones, the situation of Sears's headquarters in Chicago, and the passage of the Rural Free Delivery Act (RFD).

The mail-order catalog as an emblem of modernity was even more exclusive to the United States than the train, that more obvious symbol of the struggle between speedy progress and rapid exploitation.[11] In the case of Richard Sears, however, those two icons intersect uniquely. Nineteen-year-old Richard Sears started his company selling watches from his post as a railroad station agent in the small village of North Redwood, Minnesota. His boyhood dream of being a railway man and the lucrative accident of vending a case of abandoned pocket timepieces came together in a particularly fitting allegory of modernity itself. Sears's entrance into the business could not have been more fortuitous; his timing was perfect. By 1888 farmers across America were buying Sears watches not because they were a luxury finally made affordable but because they had suddenly become a necessity: At the insistence of the Chicago railroad companies, the United States had been divided into time zones on 18 November 1883, requiring small villages and large cities alike to conform to "railroad standard time." Prior to that moment, people set their clocks by the sun, and times were standardized only according to individual railroad lines, creating not four vertically oriented regions but more than one hundred overlapping time zones.

In addition to the official rationale for the change, which was to streamline the train schedules,[12] the use of time zones effectively homogenized each region's perception of *what time looked like*. All across the country, from New York to Chicago to San Francisco (and every tiny farming community in between), 3:30 P.M. looked more or less the same. Moreover, time's ability to be reproduced across the country in this manner commodified it. This effect of uniformity and infinite repeatability of commodity has an obvious resonance vis-à-vis mass reproduction—any copy of a given film, any item from a Sears catalog will be homogeneous with the next of its kind. This extremely broad pattern of homogenization provided an essential foundation on which were built subsequent homogenizing discourses and strategies, such as the capability for mass mailing, on which Sears heavily relied.

Four years after the invention of railroad standard time, Sears moved his operation from Minneapolis to Chicago. Chicago in 1887 was the most modern metropolis in the world. The city had burned to the ground in 1871, and Henry Louis Sullivan, Frank Lloyd Wright, and other revolutionary architects were rebuilding it with skyscrapers and other emblems of the modern moment. The city cable cars circulated everywhere carrying "modern" citizens reading one of the many daily newspapers, possibly on their way to a job in one of the steel mills, meat-packing plants, shipyards, or railroads, where they would certainly encounter the use of electricity.[13]

From this center of modernity, Sears sent out his catalogs to potential agrarian consumers who, though highly suspicious of city ways, were experiencing a parallel age of prosperity, as this thumbnail sketch written in 1931 indicates:

> The farmer, who had lived since the Panic of 1893 on the ragged edge of financial insolvency, looked forward with renewed hope; between 1900 and 1910 the prices of agricultural products increased . . . while the value of farm property doubled. . . . The typical farm now had its frame house and commodious barns, and the agricultural West, which for three decades had seethed with unrest, showed by its well-kept buildings, its new equipment and improved roads that a new era had come.
>
> There were few well-established farmers who could not afford spring buggies, upholstered furniture, a telephone and even a piano.[14]

Aimed primarily at the millions of rural farming families scattered throughout the plains and heartland of America, the Sears catalog sought to exploit recent technology for the dissemination of information without intimidating its unsophisticated clientele. To this end, as we shall see momentarily, Richard Sears established a rhetoric of inclusive regimentation which, while making customers comfortable in the ordering process, also prevented them from articulating desires beyond the parameters set out by the catalog itself.

The third essential factor in the development of catalogs was the passage of the Rural Free Delivery Act in 1896. Instead of having to go to the nearest general store to pick up the mail, farmers could now have it brought directly to them free of charge. This shift introduced potentially daily contact with a rural postal carrier, who would also do small favors, such as watering gardens and livestock, or even slightly larger favors, as one farmer requested in this note left on his front porch:

Mailman:

I didn't have any change this morning, so would you sell this half a dozen eggs to get a stamp for this letter? And what change is left, bring me about six postcards and the rest in three-cent stamps.[15]

RFD changed the farmer's relationship to acquiring information from one which required extensive volition (hitching up a horse and wagon and driving dozens of miles) to one which did not even require actual presence. By the turn of the century, RFD had brought the catalog to farmers across the nation.

But the passive reception involved in receiving a catalog was not duplicated in the process of ordering an item. In addition to the significant amount of time involved in mailing cash or a money order to Chicago, the consumer was obliged to wait for the merchandise to arrive by freight train, which could take weeks, and occasionally took even longer. Sears, Roebuck and Co. guaranteed a twenty-four-hour turnaround time from the moment the order arrived at the Sears warehouse to the time it left, but once it hit the rails the company could do no more about assuring immediate access to the commodity.

Moreover, freight rates were often prohibitively expensive; in the 1902 catalog, for example, Sears printed a caveat to his readers, staunchly refusing to ship any "unprofitable orders" (p. 5). In fact, in the 1902 edition there were fourteen pages of instructions, including extensive freight tables and even a full-page reference from the Metropolitan Bank of Chicago assuring the company's solvency. There were two dozen additional separate headings.[16]

That such explicit information was needed seemed to turn on the necessity of making consumers fluent in the ordering process. Early on, Sears did not have a clear and detailed picture of his consumers, whom he nevertheless addressed as "kind friend," and whose portraits he could only have painted in the broadest strokes: "farmer," "consumer," "literate," and so on. While cinema had certain ritual precursors in theater—buying tickets, being seated, mingling at intermission—Sears needed to provide his reader-spectator-consumer subjects with more detailed training.

The 1902 catalog's "how to" text is rife with interdictions and caveats. The reader is instructed in witheringly stiff terms to fill out the order form *exactly* according to the model provided. Of the fifteen paragraphs in the "how to order" section, five start with "always" and four start with "be sure" (p. 3). The section labeled "About Substitution" commences, "We are bitterly opposed to substituting." Moreover, a prohibition was also set along personal lines. An extensive section discourages "unnecessary correspondence," which is to say almost anything that did not include an order form: Although at the time the company employed more than one hundred stenographers to handle customer mail, Sears assured his readers that "it is very seldom necessary to write to us," noting that "our old customers rarely have occasion to write us" and reiterating that "letters concerning shipments can often be avoided" (p. 6). All this was in a catalog which arrived with a cover letter beginning "Kind Friend."

So the discourse of 1902 which dissuaded expressions of individuality stemmed from the catalog's inability to be precise about whom it was addressing. The extent to which a feeling of warmth made any inroads into the catalog text had to do with diminishing the receiver's feeling of isolation. Prefacing the freight tables was this assurance: "No matter how far away you may live, we can still save you money. . . . DISTANCE IS NO DRAWBACK" (p. 7). By 1906, however, the picture had obviously elucidated itself; either consumers wrote in more often and more personally or changes in migration and settlement patterns were simply more evident. The introductory text had not only shrunk somewhat but had also adopted a distinctly ameliorative stance, addressing the reader in a relaxed tone, with a view to individuality and constituency. Sears was actively addressing—and building—his audience.

The earlier ordering pages of the catalogs had presented the potential consumers with an either/or dilemma: either they could accommodate themselves to the instructions and thereby succeed in voicing their desires or they couldn't. The consumer was certainly constructed imitatively as male: The sample order form was filled out by a Mr. William Johnson of Cherry County, Nebraska (p. 13). And in 1902, if he couldn't say what he wanted, he couldn't get what he wanted. Yet on the first page of the spring 1906 edition alone, we see a number of radical changes that seek to remove all impediments to consumer power.

First of all, the big book was now free to any home. The potential consumer was constructed as a star performer, with the ever-attendant Sears feeding the lines. "Write a letter or a postal card and say SEND ME YOUR BIG CATALOG and it will be sent to you immediately, free by mail, postpaid." And instead of prefacing the consumers' guide with the bold headline "Our only terms are cash with order," as he had in the past, the lead had been rewritten in decidedly unintimidating terms: "Simple rules for ordering." And, as if he felt guilty that he was imposing rules at all, Sears proceeded to invite the consumer, if necessary, to break almost all of them.

If a farmer didn't have an order blank, he could "use any plain paper." "Tell us in your own way what you want," Sears urged,

> don't be afraid you will make a mistake. We receive hundreds of orders every day from young and old who never before sent away for goods. We are accustomed to handling all kinds of orders. Tell us what you want in your own way, written in any language, no matter whether good or poor writing, and the goods will promptly be sent to you. We have translators to read and write all languages.

And sure enough, the orders flooded in, sometimes in a scrawl so illegible that the order fillers' improvisational skills were sorely tested, and often in languages other than English.[17] And no wonder. The most striking component of the 1906 edition was the replication of the English instructions in both Swedish and German, the better to serve and attract the region's two major non-English-speaking immigrant groups.

This particular phase in catalog history marks its affinity with preliminary cinema precisely in its apparent difference from it, particularly in relation to the rituals and processes endemic to watching film for an immigrant audience. The cinema provided a place and a reason for the convocation of different immigrant groups, and it assimilated them all as Americans in the dark. It was part of "the emergence of a new culture of consumption which blurred all class and ethnic divisions in an illusive community of abundance."[18] In the private confines of the home, the immigrant maintained a national and class identity. In the public sphere of the cinema, difference was marked even as it was obscured: As they came together to become American, immigrants could see who else aspired to fluency in the reading of intertitles and all it implied. Moreover, cinema and consumer culture converged, such that "spectatorship became the commodity form of reception."[19] Film viewers became interpellated into commodity fetishism, even though, properly speaking, they could not possess what they had bought, save in the trace of a ticket stub.

But in the solitude of the rural heartland, immigrants far less frequently came together with their own folk, let alone with anyone else. The prolific dissemination of images and commodities from Chicago (and the equally intense consumer reply from the country) makes it easy to forget the rapidity with which the same geographical space to which Sears sent his catalogs had only very recently made the transition from frontier territory to ratified statehood. Sears started his company in 1886, four years *before* the 1890 United States census officially pronounced the frontier closed. Three years after the census, Frederick Jackson Turner first presented his famous frontier thesis (an apparently progressive attempt at defining the American identity in relation to the newly colonized West) at the 1893 World's Columbian Exposition in Chicago.[20] In between, during the period from 1889 to 1893, the Oklahoma Land Runs, in which tens of thousands of people actually gathered at a starting line and physically raced to stake homestead claims, emblematized the swift rate at which frontier land could become settled farmland. During these frenzied races, towns sometimes went up literally overnight.[21] Nevertheless, by the time the Sears catalog was fully covering the nation (about 1899), the rubber band of western expansion had been stretched as far as it would go, and the same immigrants who flocked west in the 1890s (a similar number had settled in urban areas during each preceding decade) were already moving back towards the cities, creating increasingly sparse populations in rural areas.[22]

So the "natural" congregation of spectators who subordinated their differences to the equalizers of image, story, and intertitle at the urban cinema did not occur on the plains. There were few opportunities in the normal course of agrarian life to melt into the melting pot. One such forum, however, was the Sears catalog. Translated instructions did indeed offer the consumer what, in cinematic terms, might be the equivalent of intertitles and vaudeville acts in a native tongue. Conversely, however, the placement of many different languages on one page removed the consumer from quotidian isolation. To the Swedes and Germans addressed in 1906, it was a sign that, although English predominated as status quo and as goal (all the more so for being placed in full-page width above the other two languages), they were not alone in their otherness. This multilingual presentation may have been intended to increase profits, but it doubled as a sign of life, a chronicling of who else was out there, while working within the confines of the relative isolation of the farmer on the plains. Moreover, this page of the catalog performed its two-tiered assimilation of the immigrant as American precisely in the form of consumerism—by this point the appropriate icon of America and American life. Consumerism made the immigrant American.

Furthermore, the mail-order catalog made manifest the predication of commodification on technological reproduction as it specifically muddied the boundaries between private and public space. The home was a private space, but those homes that received and used catalogs were impelled into the public sphere. The catalog as a form of public sphere was specifically tied to commodification—it reached into the homes of isolated subjects, and, by inspiring an articulation of desire, made them consumers. Insofar as they were represented metonymically by their order forms, they were pulled into a broader arena of consumption.

This expanded rural consumption inevitably rubbed up against the urban framework that incited it, and Sears had to negotiate very carefully between rural aspirations to urbanity and country suspicions of city ways. At the time of the 1893 exposition, Sears had already been headquartered in Chicago for five years; had he attended it, he would have been more aware than most of the cautious way in which visitors from outlying regions inspected the various installations and shows. Surviving comment books from individual state pavilions reflect a deep ambivalence toward the city. On the one hand, rural visitors wrote with pride about the displays; on the other, they registered the sentiment that more should have been done to express state identities in the urban, even global context defining the 1893 fair: "The fair reminded people of something not always so obvious back home: the place in which they lived was a hinterland, whose cultural worth would be measured by the metropolitan vision that [Chicago] so clearly exemplified."[23]

Just as the ordering instructions became increasingly user-friendly, so Sears offered the farmer a warm voice to guide him through the avenues of the catalog city, never letting him forget that the voice (unlike others the farmer might have encountered in Chicago) was real and genuine. For Richard Sears wrote virtually all the copy and personally supervised almost every page of catalog design. Partially because of this univocality, his catalog served to homogenize America, insofar as rural farmers could, through the catalog, trust Sears to help them compensate for a long- and deeply held feeling of inferiority by buying what the townfolk bought. But if Sears was the absolute author of the catalog, he had a technique for catechizing consumers into his side of the discourse, giving them an illusory feeling of authorship and its concomitant (and concomitantly illusory) empowerment. The catalogs always articulated a deep respect for consumers' rural pragmatism, ingenuity, and spirit of economy. Developing an "A-list" based on what and how much each family purchased, Sears would send certain people additional catalogs, with instructions to distribute them among likely buyers. They would be rewarded for their efforts; depending on the returns, these distributors could earn merchandise as significant as a piano. With these incentives, Sears had access to a picture of the American farmer which was in certain respects far more complete and accurate than the image that the United States government could obtain through census-taking and tax returns. The government could know how much each person had and how the money came in. Sears knew what each person desired and where the money went.

The A-list (also known as "Iowaization" after the first state in which it was implemented) solidified into commonplace ritual the new patterns in the flow of capital which the catalog itself had initiated. Sears's A-list availed itself of standing kin and social relations in rural communities, and in some ways it actually helped to cement them. But it also severely undermined the communal nature of the country general store, to which farmers previously had had no choice but to make weekly, monthly, or seasonal trips to stock up on supplies. Sears catalogs themselves never completely, or even fundamentally, replaced the general store, though the latter always expressed its animosity toward the former, even when it eventually capitulated and became agents for A-list bulk deliveries. Yet because Sears required cash up front, it did ossify the previously flexible economic structures, significantly curtailing more community-oriented systems of payment like barter and credit.

This intersection of social control and the catalog would be strengthened by 1913, when Sears had help once again from the conjoining of legislative and technical discourses. The Parcel Post Act of 1913 not only made it possible to reduce the cost of sending things by rail and mail but it also, like the RFD Act and the campaign to "electrify" the countryside throughout the first fifteen years of the century, brought huge numbers of rural communities under the control of a highly centralized discourse of power. One could only hide if one suppressed one's consumer desire: the moment a farmer placed an order with Sears, he could be located, he could be found.

Sears also covered his bases by advertising in magazines commonly and diligently read by agrarian readers: *American Woman, Youth's Companion, American Fireside, Fireside Companion, Fireside Visitor, Harper's, Hearth and Home, Home Monthly,* and *People's Literary Companion.* Many of these titles give an indication of their additional function. As the anthropomorphized "companion" or "visitor," they helped to ease the isolation brought on by the vast distance among farms. (When not being used, the Sears catalog took its place on the shelf beside them.) The catalog itself was discursive on a similarly personal level; when it was not used to order items, it was read aloud as literature to everyone from sick children to women sewing by the fire. For more highbrow magazines like *Ladies Home Journal,* however, the ads were too hyperbolic and garish to run.[24]

Nonetheless, Sears made his catalog seem a natural occurrence, something that could camouflage itself as having nothing to do with commerce, by inverting its position with these journals of popular literature. Sears ads were embedded in the course of these collections, and entries for books were likewise lodged in the Sears catalog, making them seem part of the same flow of reading material into the home. This is a doubly remarkable turn: First, it allowed Sears significant control over the reading tastes of the American farmer; second, it enhanced the catalog's ability to sell without appearing to be selling—to cloak one discursive apparatus in the accoutrements of another.

Despite the startlingly high levels of literacy in rural, as opposed to urban, America, some families still held an extremely limited reading list.[25] At the very least, however, every farmhouse had a Bible, a Montgomery Ward catalog, and a Sears catalog. Bibles tended to be kept on specially made stands or safely stored in cupboards, but the Montgomery Ward and Sears catalogs would be displayed on the sitting room table, and the former was always bigger than the latter. Seemingly a contradiction to Richard Sears's inclination to hyperbole and superlative, it was actually a typically canny maneuver: by being smaller, the Sears catalog would always be stacked on top.[26]

The Sears book department was preceded by the "Department of Public Entertainment Outfits and Supplies," in which we can find the material convergence of cinema and catalog. The key word here is, of course, "public." Even though the catalog addressed itself to private individuals, it occasionally did so in order to incite their modulation into public personages—in this case public exhibitors of films. At the turn of the century, film was not yet perceived as at all connected with the home or with private life, and the majority of films reflected this, concentrating mainly on public spaces (Lumière's *Train Entering a Station* [1895], Porter's *Great Train Robbery* and *Romance of the Rail* [1903]), even if, as in *What Happened in the Tunnel* (1903), what transpired was of a very private nature. Edison's kinetoscope had been exhibited at the 1893 exposition. It was also possible to view films at seasonal and annual regional and county fairs, events which not only celebrated rural life and custom but also featured the latest in urban entertainment.[27] Beyond these venues, however, rural access to cinema was far more haphazard, and the Sears catalog became a reliable resource, although, compared to city fare, the number and scope of available films remained limited.

Sears not only carried the 1901 "improved version" of Edison's kinetoscope as well as an exhibition outfit similar to Hale's Tours but he also intensified the push toward identification by urging his customers to get a piece of his own aura, to partake in his success in the American Dream, by going into business as presenters of Hale's Tours and short films on Edison's new kinetoscope machine. Taking the dissemination of power and control toward consumption to a new limit, Sears encouraged them to emulate his own catalog by buying extra equipment and farming it out at a profit. Cinema, it seemed to Sears, was an ideal venue and material through which to expand and diversify the farmer's position in the complex of capital.

Of course, Sears also sold the necessary films and slides, and an examination of that section of the catalog gives us an interesting indication of the pace at which subjects of information and entertainment circulated throughout nonurban America. Editions of the first few years of the twentieth century list the following titles: "Pan-American Exposition"; "The Philippines and Our New Possessions"; "The Passing of the Indian"; "Assassination of President McKinley"; "Around the World in Eighty Minutes"; "Life Under a Circus Tent"; and "The Chicago Stockyards, or from Hoof to Market." All of these films are urban, national, or even global in scope and focus, as well as documentary in nature. The rural subject's attention was thus urged to look past his own community, as cinema, a new technology, articulated current events, recent history, and phenomena thousands of miles away. For the rural subject, then, cinema and the modern world beyond the homestead *defined each other*, and they did so through the Sears catalog.

Like the process of disseminating the catalog and the goods, the process of ordering (which was the process of inculcating the subject into the Sears discourse itself) changed over time. The earlier catalogs were highly discursive, with many star items described not only in great detail but also with a high level of narrativity. Because things largely went by freight, the lag time between placing an order (always through the mail) and receiving the goods (usually by driving into town with the horse and wagon and picking it up at the train station) was significant, certainly a question of weeks and often, in more isolated areas, of months. Indeed, by 1902 Sears had abandoned his motto and battle cry of "Send No Money." By the time the slow freight trains bringing ordered items finally arrived, many people had lost their desire and sent the items back without paying, creating a severe financial burden on Sears. Yet the crisis of the dissipation of desire also had solutions on the level of narrativity, about which more momentarily. So the rhetoric of selling the item also had to function as a rhetoric for sustaining desire. What was required was a blend of sales pitch and short story which could be read aloud repeatedly to rekindle the flame of desire, even when the only tangible ember might be in the form of a money order receipt filed months ago. In the city, where goods were manufactured and sold in greater proximity to where they would be used, the rhetoric, as well as the use of huge quantities of bright colors, explicitly concentrated on "the intensification of desire."[28] In either case, however, desire was conceived as something both quantifiable and malleable, capable of being shaped and molded by the contingencies of transport and capital. In the city, desire burned bright and fast, but in the country the flame needed to be fanned gently and constantly so that it might burn low and long.

Consider the excess of narration in the Vin Vitae entry, which held a prominent place in the patent-medicine section for many years. Although the entire layout takes up only a page, it manages to function very efficiently as an epic. The extensive text is balanced by two images, which, read left to right, tell the story of an exhausted man revivified for a mere sixty-nine cents. Prodded by the gentle angel-muse of consumerism and of life itself, he seems at left to be filling out an order blank for this "wine of life," the Latinized title of which made it seem more scientific and, therefore, more medically sound. Traveling through the inter-image text that chronicles his ailments, he is transformed at the other side into a lion-taming Adonis. The formula having worked brilliantly for him, he might well be inspired to assemble his wife and children and urge them, as does the lower text, to partake as well. The fantasy (and) chain of causality that has been established is made airtight by the self-sufficiency and endless loop of the narrative, which concludes with a claim for constant demand that leads the reader right back to the image on the bottle.[29]

Such perpetual narratives emphasize the way that the catalog, to the extent that it stood in for things that were not present but whose presence was impending, presented itself as an arena for fetishization. Catalogs subsequent to those discussed here exhibit a decline in narrativity, since, with the onset of the Parcel Post system in 1913 and other technologies, desire needed to be sustained for shorter and shorter periods of time. But even by 1915, Sears had a reflexive modernity creed prefacing its book, extolling the virtues of saving time and money through mass communication and state-of-the-art technology:

> You may drive to town to get the price of wheat, or use the telephone—the MODERN way.
>
> You may write a letter to accept a price for a hundred acres of land and find the offer withdrawn before your letter arrives, or wire your acceptance and clinch the sale at once—the MODERN way.
>
> You may depend on hand power and find the day too short to do your work, or get a gasoline engine, do your work better and have time to spare—the MODERN way.
>
> You may GO to an average store, spend valuable time and select from a limited stock at retail prices, or have our Big Store of World Wide Stocks at Economy Prices COME to you in this catalog—the Modern Way.
>
> No matter where you live, rain or shine, you can with this catalog do your

shopping from your easy chair. Consult its pages as your needs arise and you will experience the comfort and economy in buying that have made this Big Store the supply house of so many million homes—buy the MODERN way.

What lay behind this creed, as well as behind earlier editions' epic instructions for placing an order, was the presentation of the tens of thousands of items to request between those tiny lines on the order form. In 1902 the first section of the catalog was the Sears grocery line, which, though intended to function as a loss leader, actually served as a profit line because rural farmers would order dry goods in huge quantities in anticipation of long periods of isolation during winter months. In fact, the unanticipated success of the grocery line points up the hit-or-miss nature of so much of the early process. Following dry goods was a section devoted to watches, a sign that Richard Sears the author still thought of his company in terms of its roots.

The next prominent section also provides the first marked constructions of gendered address in the catalog. Until the passage of the Pure Food and Drug Act of 1906, there were no laws to legislate the contents of pharmacological products. Despite this lack of regulation, the Sears patent medicine pages frequently took the place of a physician's care and diagnosis, since many rural families did not have a doctor nearby. Although these "medicines" could be equally inappropriate, and even abusive, to both men and women, a woman's place as caregiver often put her at both the giving and receiving ends of formulas that sometimes did more than simply fail to work. One particularly poignant example was an entry for "Mrs. Winslow's Soothing Syrup." The accompanying image is of a mother as administering angel, treating her teething infant to a few precious drops. Unfortunately, there could be a sinister subtext: The drops contained considerable quantities of opium, leading occasionally to obvious and disastrous consequences, and women unknowingly became the conduit for their own children's addiction.

Another patent medicine, Dr. Hammond's Nerve and Brain Pills, touted as "a boon for weak men," was the lone entry on the subject of inherently male physiological difficulties. Women's bodies, however, were relentlessly presented in these pages as weak. "Dr. Worden's Female Pills," for instance, claimed to cure "all diseases arising from a poor and wasted condition." Yet some of the problems it cited, such as "lack of ambition," "feebleness of will," and "early decay," were hardly medical.

Following the European trend in which bourgeois women ingested cobalt and arsenic to acquire the pale and ashen look dictated by the cult of the invalid, Sears also suggested that a frail female body was a more feminine one.[30] Dr. Rose's Arsenic Complexion Wafers similarly promised farm women "a transparency and pellucid clearness of complexion." "Ladies," it extolled, "you can be beautiful. No matter who you are, what your disfigurements may be, you can make yourself as handsome as any lady in the land."

Not surprisingly, there was a distinct contrast between the real, daily lives of rural women and what the Sears pharmacological discourse constructed them to be. The rural life was, perhaps, more trying for women than for men; agricultural technology far surpassed domestic innovations, including those involving the most basic needs. With no running water, much of every day was spent transporting water in large, hand-held buckets from wells or pumps. Washday was a chore that truly took up all daylight hours. Given the strenuousness of quotidian rural life, to take Dr. Rose's wafers would have been itself a leisure rather than a therapeutic activity.

Similarly, the catalog stocked items that signaled the entrance of the post-industrial revolution into the home on terms of strict reification, insofar as people could be replaced by things and technological discourse could replace social discourse. Many of the products made life easier for the homemaker, while also, ironically, further entrenching her in a loop of solitude. One woman wrote to Sears praising her new stove, claiming with exuberance that she had brought a couch into the kitchen so that she could sleep near it and "had not moved from it, night or day," since she bought it.[31] So much for freedom. Similarly, Sears sold a sewing machine at a price significantly lower than anyone else in the country and by 1902 was selling one sewing machine every minute. But, as the social historian Annette Atkins notes, women paid a social price for this newfound ease.[32] Before the widespread distribution of the sewing machine, rural housewives employed seamstresses for periods of one to ten days to help them make undergarments and outergarments for their families. With the permanent placement of the sewing machine, the occasional—if sporadic— presence of another woman in the house disappeared entirely, depriving the homemaker of the social aspect of this chore.

An eerie coincidence points up the vast range of goods Sears stocked and sold. The last page of the baby carriage department directly faced the memorial department, subliminally assuring the consumer that the catalog could satisfy all needs from the cradle to the grave. But the beginning of the twentieth century heralded the start of a new age at Sears, when wearing apparel would take increasing prominence in its pages and its profits. Concomitantly, so would hierarchies of power and gender in the various representations of women, men, babies, and children.

Most correspondence received at Sears and Roebuck's Chicago headquarters was from adults, but occasionally children would write as well, urging a change in the catalog's agenda for purposes of their own:

Dear Sears and Roebuck:

Please put feet on your ladies in the catalog, so they'll make nicer paper dolls. We can barely find ladies with feet to finish our families. We are 11 years old. Please do not put prices on their legs. Please give this to Mr. Sears. Thank you.[33]

Embedded in this piece of juvenile correspondence is the crux of the problem of the gendered address developing in the catalogs. On the one hand, we have only to recall the semi-illicit scopophilic pleasures of the exposed and cradled ankle of Edison's *Gay Shoe Clerk* (1903) to understand why the ladies had no feet. But women's complex roles as "family finishers," as well as starters and managers, is another matter. A gendered address is discernible in these texts at the end of the nineteenth century, but by the pivotal 1902 catalog, the struggle was already underway with the notion of women not only as consumer powers but as *loci* of desire.

For there was an inherent and apparently unresolvable conflict in the presentation of women's actual bodies in the public spheres of America and their representation in the public privacy of the catalog. The presentation of women's bodies in the public sphere during the turn of the century was predicated on a particular paradigm of modesty. Upper bodies could be tantalizingly displayed, with shoulders bared, décolletage revealed, backs slightly visible, and so forth. Yet from the heavily corseted wasp waist down to the ground, no part of a woman could be visible. So persistent was this morally driven aesthetic that it overruled more practical concerns: rural women wore a looser version of the tightly laced hand-span corset while working in the fields. Indeed, most women dressed as if they had no lower limbs at all, effecting the impression that their visible body parts were mounted on pedestals like statues and were propelled by some unseen engine beneath their skirts.

Concomitantly, a woman's entire body could not be tastefully displayed in the catalog. So in order to sell shoes, only the shoe itself could be shown, likewise underclothing intended for wear below the corset level. Even corsets were illustrated with only a drawing of a woman's upper body; the picture ended where the corset did (fig. 6.1). Such modest predicates for codes of representation necessitated the increasing and incessant fragmentation of women's bodies.[34] The subject of the catalog entries—a woman's body—was destroyed, and the female subject that Sears addressed was likewise made to fragment herself. That is, to put herself in sync with what was presented on paper, she had to take herself apart, to perceive herself in pieces, page by catalog page, item by item, gradually putting herself back together as she ordered goods. It would seem that occasionally the metaphorical self-destruction effected by these images found a literal echo—if we are in fact to believe anything we read in the medicine pages.

No. 31R454
$6.75

No. 31R455
$6.95

No. 31R446
$2.98

No. 31R448
$3.95

No. 31R449
$4.95

No. 31R467
$4.95

No. 31R453
$4.95

No. 31R450
$4.75

No. 31R457
$3.75

LADIES' SILK WAISTS.

When ordering please state bust measurement, length of waist in back, inside sleeve length and the color you desire.

If you want any other color than listed in catalogue we shall be pleased to make it for 20 per cent above the regular price. If you fail to allow 20 per cent for extra sizes we will make the garment and charge the difference. Sizes measuring over 42 inches bust, 18 inches sleeve and 19½ inches length of waist are considered specials. It takes about two weeks to make specials.

Average postage on silk waists, 18 cents.   FOR VERY STYLISH CORSET COVERS, SEE PAGES 1065 AND 1066.

No. 31R446 STYLISH WAIST. Made of taffeta silk; the entire front is tucked and trimmed with hemstitched straps, each strap finished with a buckle; nice standing collar, wide cuffs; three rows of tucking in the back; this waist buttons in front. Colors, black, turquoise blue or pink. Price **$2.98**

No. 31R447 EXCEPTIONAL GOOD VALUE IN LADIES' WAIST. Made of black taffeta; the very newest Norfolk style; strap trimmings in front forming a pointed yoke, and finished with tucking from point of yoke to waist; three straps in back from shoulder to waist; high standing collar; waist is lined throughout with cambric. Price **$3.75**

No. 31R448 VERY ATTRACTIVE LADIES' WAIST. Made of taffeta silk; yoke ... on both sides, silk embroidery on both sides of the waist; nice standing collar, stitched cuffs; tucks in back from shoulder to waist; lined throughout with cambric; this waist buttons in back. Colors, black with black yoke and black embroidery; rose or lavender with fresh ... collar, and white embroidery. Price **$3.95**

No. 31R449 VERY GOOD VALUE LADIES' WAIST. Made of a good quality of taffeta silk; entire front is tucked and trimmed with straps of taffeta silk, each strap attached ... general effect, high standing collar, trimmed in a similar manner; broad cuffs and several rows of tucking on the sleeves, five rows of tucking in back of waist; lined throughout with cambric; this waist buttons in front. Colors, black, turquoise blue or pink. Price **$4.95**

No. 31R450 LADIES' WAIST. Made of fine taffeta silk. The entire front is covered with tucking, with slit openings in the plastron; high standing in the back with puffs, rows of tucking, ... cuffs and full sleeves. This waist is made to button in the back; silk button trimmings in the back of waist; lined throughout with a good quality of cambric. Colors, black with black embroidery. Price **$4.75**

No. 31R453 LADIES' WAIST. Made of very fine peau de soie. This waist is strictly tailor made; dress waist on each side in front, finished with hemstitching and four rows of tucks in back; high standing collar with small flaps and narrow cuffs, full sleeves. The material ... silk on the back. Colors, black or navy blue; price **$4.75**

No. 31R467 LADIES' FANCY WAIST. Made of good quality taffeta silk; the yoke in front, ... attached in the back with narrow lace... straps of taffeta silk; full sleeves, narrow cuffs, high standing collar; ... from the yoke down and to the side of the yoke and gives a blouse effect; the yoke, the waist free of any ... and several rows of tucking in back, this is tucked several times; lined throughout with a good quality of cambric, this waist buttons in the front. Colors, black, pink or green. Price **$4.95**

No. 31R455 LADIES' WAIST. Made of a very fine quality of taffeta silk; entire front is tucked with a new tucked effect all over, fancy embroidery trims yoke down, all straps of taffeta silk, waist in front, plain standing collar trimmed with two rows of ...; wide cuffs, full sleeves; this waist is made to button in the back; fancy button trimmings in back of waist; lined throughout with a good quality of cambric. Colors, black with black embroidery, red with ... **$4.95**

No. 31R454 LADIES' WAIST. Made of a very fine quality of taffeta silk; ... front is tucked all over, sewed embroidered with silk from where the rows meet in the back; ... instead of buttons on each side mid way, with a standing collar flaps on both sides; soft rows of tucking in front, on the bishop sleeves, and to back; facing cuffs embroidered silk ... Colors, turquoise blue ... Price **$6.75**

No. 31R455 LADIES' WAIST. Very fine taffeta silk; the entire front is made of waist, taffeta silk tucked all over, high standing collar neatly trimmed with taffeta silk strip, ... made of waist in front; front of waist is trimmed with pointed silk straps and applique of white, ... collar of waist, fancy sleeves tucked and ruched, four rows of tucks in back row and the collar of waist; this waist buttons in front. Colors, all black, turquoise blue with white or pink with white front and trimmings. Price **$6.95**

All waists button in front with exception of No. 31R450 and No. 31R455.

Fig. 6.1. A woman's entire body was seldom displayed in one discrete image. In this case, women's shirts were sold with an image that ended where the item for sale did—at the waist.

One can also regard the problem of gender representation in relation to the order of presentation in the catalog. Sears divided the genders, chivalrously presenting ladies first, starting with babies and moving in chronological order. The men's section, on the other hand, began with made-to-measure suits and moved *backwards* through boyswear. In each case, the image—always a full male body from head to toe—and its accompanying text were allowed discrete space. Many entries were even framed as if they were commissioned portraits (fig. 6.2).

Women, on the other hand, were always depicted in large numbers, with photographic heads sitting uneasily and often grotesquely atop hand-drawn bodies or fragments of bodies. But the crowds in which they were assembled had no diegetic significance. There were no eyeline matches to indicate communication between figures, so there could be no inference of a presence within. The representations were empty, with no promise of being filled. Earlier in this section, babies and toddlers of both genders were grouped together in the women's section in crowded compositions (fig. 6.3). But roughly at the age when sexuality becomes socialized at the level of the division of labor, boys were given their own portraits, while girls and women remained represented as if in arrested development (fig. 6.4). "Boys" in 1902 constituted males starting at age three. Sexually retarded, women were stuck in the crowd like babies.

This depiction of women in masses rehearses a common trope of closely identifying women in modernity with mass culture. This equation reinforced "the notion which gained ground in the 19th century that mass culture is somehow associated with woman while real, authentic culture remains the prerogative of men."[35] That is, mass culture was subordinate, inferior, dangerous, needing to be contained and controlled but, paradoxically, ungovernable and, essentially, unknowable. Men were represented as entities separated from each other by a space each commanded. They may have been types, but that did not preclude their individuality. Men were seen as *representable* in a way that women were not, as if there were a danger in displaying the whole discrete female body, as if the female body were a Pandora's box.

In fact, there were at certain moments concerted efforts to evoke various discourses of male power through consumption by placing the heads of actors, politicians, and other celebrities on drawings for men's apparel. In 1899 Teddy Roosevelt and his Rough Riders were the photographic facial images carefully grafted onto the bodies of stout men's suits. No such contemporaneous promotion occurred on women's clothing. Indeed, a woman's representation based on an actual contemporary figure did not occur until well into the 1920s, when Gloria Swanson, Clara Bow, and Joan Crawford all posed either for pieces designed for them or for items that somehow evoked roles they had played.[36]

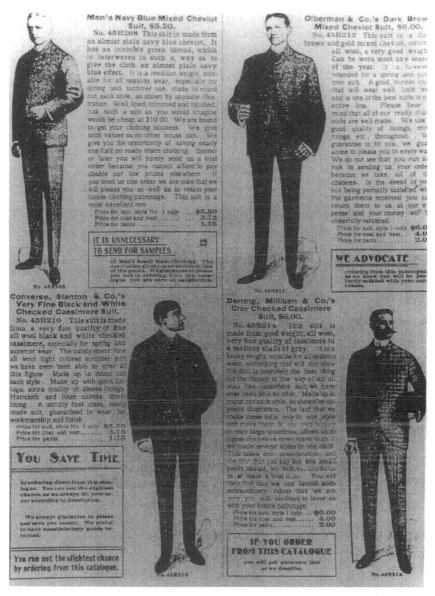

Fig. 6.2. While women's images were often fragmented, men's clothing was typically illustrated on whole bodies occupying autonomous space.

Fig. 6.3. Girls' images, like those of women and babies, were displayed in overlapping, collagelike masses.

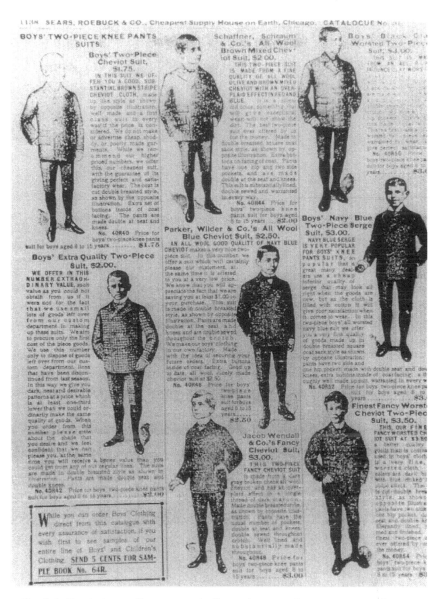

Fig. 6.4. Depictions of boys were similar to images of men—separate from each other and individually connected to a specific text.

Fig. 6.5. Images achieved a level of narrativity independent of text at the same time that urban populations exceeded rural ones. At that time, these images began to implement figures of women as figures of desire rather than strictly as models of goods for sale.

Throughout the 1920s, men too were portrayed in a mass, even as representations of women began, by dint of the star power of Swanson, Bow, and Crawford, to become untangled. These masses, however, were of a completely different nature, one which is clearly a representational response to the massive demographic shift of Americans into urban areas as well as a product of innovations in technologies of photographic reproduction. In these compositions, there was legible, intentional, and narrative body contact, with a more complete system of looks and gazes, as if this company of car coat–clad lads were a fraternity on holiday, whereas the women continued to appear as if they had been randomly pasted, one overlapping the next, like a collage. It seems quite significant in relation to this supposed brotherhood of and in representation that women started to appear in the men's section as a central focus of desire. A full seven years before the release of Fritz Lang's *Metropolis,* the fall 1920 edition of the Sears book had a scene in which four young men eye a woman in her convertible; it is impossible to tell which they are ogling more (fig. 6.5). Lang's compelling presentation of the combined threat of female sexuality and rampant technology finds an eerie prologue here.[37] For we see more than just a vamp and a machine. We see a vamp *in* a machine, and because fragmenting the female body remains a common trope, the possibility exists that the young lady in question is actually welded to her car: the vamp *is* the machine.

This vamp-machine signals the moment when urban populations exceed rural ones, and the Sears catalog reflects that. But even in its early years, it always presented itself as something that emanated from a great urban center, though it existed for a rural constituency. Its dissemination from Chicago, the great nineteenth-century entrepôt and gateway to the West, remade the American consumer landscape, and "even more than ordinary cartography, it offered its readers a map of capital."[38] Catalogs, then, rely as heavily as cinema on mechanical reproduction, mass dissemination, and the reproduction of absent objects, and through them we can see the formation of the modern rural American as clearly as through cinema we may discover the modern urban subject.

NOTES

1. Viola I. Paradise, "By Mail," *Scribner's* 4 (April 1921): 480.

2. Walter Benjamin, "The Work of Art in the Age of Mechanical Reproduction," in *Illuminations: Essays and Reflections,* ed. Hannah Arendt, trans. Harry Zohn (New York: Schocken Books, 1969), p. 220.

3. Painted representations of the period bear this out, especially those of the Impressionists: Manet's and Degas's canvases, particularly, are full of people whose images have been cut off by the edge of the frame, as if either they or the painter

were unable to fix a gaze or keep a body still long enough to paint it. Or, perhaps, as a precursor to cinema, the limits of the canvas were mutable, themselves distracted nearly to the point of kineticism.

4. "It is an immense joy [for the flâneur] to make his domicile amongst numbers, amidst fluctuation and movement, amidst the fugitive and infinite" (Charles Baudelaire, "The Painter of Modern Life," in *My Heart Laid Bare and Other Prose Writings* [London: Soho Book Company, 1986], p. 34). See also Baudelaire, *Paris Spleen*, trans. Louise Varèse (New York: New Directions, 1947). In discussing this very theme in Baudelaire's work, Benjamin states that "Baudelaire saw fit to equate the man of the crowd . . . with the flâneur. It is hard to accept this view. The man of the crowd is no flâneur. . . . There was the pedestrian who would let himself be jostled by the crowd, but there was also the flâneur who demanded elbow room and was unwilling to forgo the life of a gentleman of leisure" (Benjamin, "On Some Motifs in Baudelaire," in *Illuminations*, p. 172).

5. Miriam Hansen, "Early Cinema: Whose Public Sphere?" *New German Critique* 29 (spring/summer 1983): 155–159; idem, "Adventures of Goldilocks: Spectatorship, Consumerism and Public Life," *Camera Obscura* 22 (January 1990): 55–56.

6. Ellen Richards, *The Cost of Cleanness* (New York, 1908), pp. 8–10, cited in Thomas J. Schlereth, *Victorian America: Transformations in Everyday Life, 1876–1915* (New York: Harper Collins, 1991), p. 131. For a contemporary feminist perspective which nevertheless maintains a focus on the home, see Catharine Beecher and Harriet Beecher-Stow, *The American Women's Home, or Principles of Domestic Science* (1869; reprint, Hartford, Conn.: Stow-Day Foundation, 1975).

7. William Leach, "Transformations in a Culture of Consumption: Women and Department Stores, 1890–1925," *Journal of American History* 71 (September 1984): 333.

8. That "authentic" authorship finds its contemporary successors in catalogs such as J. Peterman, whose highly narrative and personalized copy is claimed to emanate from J. Peterman himself.

9. In its gargantuan proportions the Sears catalog was not alone. At the turn of the century the Montgomery Ward catalog was 1,200 pages long, listed seventy thousand items, displayed seventeen thousand illustrations, and sent thirteen thousand packages daily. For more on Montgomery Ward, see William Cronon, *Nature's Metropolis: Chicago and the Great West* (New York: W. W. Norton, 1991), especially pp. 335–340.

10. The documentary "Mr. Sears' Catalog" aired on the PBS series "The American Experience" in 1989.

11. For accounts of the significance of trains in the cinema, see Lynne Kirby, "Male Hysteria and Early Cinema," *Camera Obscura* 17 (May 1988): 112–131; idem, "The Railroad and the Cinema, 1895–1929: Technologies, Institutions and Aesthetics" (Ph.D. diss. University of California, Los Angeles, 1989); Mary Ann Doane, "'When the direction of the force acting on the body is changed': The Moving Image," *Wide Angle* 7, nos. 1–2 (1985): 42–57. See also Barbara Novak, *Nature and Culture: American Landscape and Painting, 1825–1875* (New York: Oxford University Press, 1980), and Wolfgang Schivelbush, *The Railway Journey*, trans. Anselm Hollo (New York: Urizen, 1979).

12. William Cronon notes some extremely urgent reasons for using time zones: Two trains operating under different times could nevertheless find themselves heading in opposite directions towards the same point on the same track at the same moment (Cronon, op. cit., p. 79).

13. Chicago's claim to being the most modern city in the world was in a sense clinched by cinema itself; other urban locales could say what they wanted about their own up-to-the-minute status, but Chicago could show much of its rebuilding on film. Other cities were merely chronicling development with cinema; Chicago was filming its own rebirth.

14. Harold U. Faulkner, quoted in Boris Emmet and John Jeuck, *Catalogs and Counters: A History of Sears, Roebuck and Company* (Chicago: University of Chicago Press, 1950), p. 191.

15. In "Mr. Sears' Catalog."

16. By 1930 all limits and directives were confined to the slim order form in the middle of the book.

17. Emmet and Jeuck, op. cit., p. 86.

18. Hansen, "Adventures of Goldilocks," p. 52.

19. Ibid., p. 56.

20. Frederick Jackson Turner, "The Significance of the Frontier in American History," *Annual Report of the American Historical Association for the Year 1893* (Washington, D.C., 1894), reprinted in Turner, *The Frontier in American History* (New York: Henry Holt, 1920).

21. Schlereth, op. cit., pp. 14–15.

22. Ibid., 8–18; Fred Shannon, *The Farmer's Last Frontier, 1865–1900* (New York: Holt, Rinehart & Winston, 1966), pp. 355–358; Cronon, op. cit., pp. 364–369; *Historical Statistics of the United States*, I, Series C25–75, pp. 93–95.

23. Cronon, op. cit., p. 343.

24. Emmet and Jeuck, op. cit., p. 89.

25. Congress passed laws requiring literacy as a prerequisite for entry into the United States in 1893, 1903, and 1915, although each was vetoed by the president. Clearly such legislation was exclusionary, even racist. That it got as far as it did, however, seems to suggest that literacy was a ratifying American trait. Even if many Americans couldn't read, the country as a whole apparently wanted to be *perceived* as literate. It is at this level that mail-order catalogs and cinema are furthest removed from each other, since catalogs rely entirely on a literate user, whereas contemporaneous cinema, in which even intertitles were not needed, did not.

26. A fictional account of mail-order catalogs tells a story that makes the same point about Sears as a "farmer's bible." In Edna Ferber's novel *Fanny Herself* (1917), a Wisconsin woman says, "There's a Haynes-Cooper catalog in every farmer's kitchen. The Bible's in the parlor, but they keep the H.C. book in the room where they live." Quoted in Schlereth, op. cit., p. 153.

27. Schlereth, op. cit., p. 233.

28. Leach, "Women and Department Stores," p. 323.

29. This hermetically sealed narrative loop has come down to us in the form of infomercials, where the ad itself is structured as a thirty-minute program within

which there are ads where one would expect to find ads—but only for the same product the infomercial itself is advertising.

30. Bram Dijkstra, *Idols of Perversity: Fantasies of Feminine Evil in Fin-de-Siècle Culture* (New York: Oxford University Press, 1986).

31. In "Mr. Sears' Catalog."

32. Ibid.

33. Ibid.

34. Tom Gunning's well-known argument that it is the avant-garde film rather than the narrative mainstream which has maintained early film's politics of attraction vis-à-vis cinematic spectatorship ("The Cinema of Attraction: Early Film, Its Spectator, and the Avant-garde," *Wide Angle* 8, nos. 3–4, pp. 63–70), finds an interesting resonance with the fragmentation of women's images in these early catalogs. The avant-garde filmmaker Harry Smith, known for his use of cut-out images (see especially *Heaven and Earth Magic* [1950–1960] and his series *Early Abstractions* [from the 1940s]), actually derived many of them from turn-of-the-century Sears catalogs. Significantly, Smith goes even further in a gendered treatment of his cut-outs. The male figures already having been cut out, Smith tends to leave their bodies intact. The female figures, on the other hand, he cuts up into even smaller subdivisions.

35. Andreas Huyssen, "Mass Culture as Woman: Modernism's Other," in Huyssen, *After the Great Divide: Modernism, Mass Culture, Postmodernism* (Bloomington: Indiana University Press, 1986), p. 47.

36. By that time the Sears company was even producing its own films, although they were mainly of interest to farmers, with titles such as *Under the 4-H Flag, The Green Hand,* and *The Golden Egg.* This domestic focus is the opposite of the worldly scope Sears had when it was selling Edison's films twenty years before.

37. Andreas Huyssen, "The Vamp and the Machine: Fritz Lang's *Metropolis*," in Huyssen, op. cit., pp. 68–70.

38. Cronon, op. cit., p. 339.

SEVEN

The Perils of Pathé, or the Americanization of Early American Cinema[1]

Richard Abel

The subject framing this essay is the relationship between modernity, or the development of "modern consumer society," and what Homi Bhabha has called "the ideological ambivalence" of the "nation-space."[2] One can hardly find a better site for investigating that relationship than the emergence of mass culture and, more specifically, the moment of the cinema's industrialization soon after the turn of the last century. For it was then that the cinema as a specific instance of modernity—a new technology of perception, reproduction, and representation; a new cultural commodity of mass production and consumption; a new space of social congregation within the public sphere—was inscribed within the discourses of imperialism and nationalism and their conflicted claims, respectively, of economic and cultural supremacy. Here imperialism is understood, following Eric Hobsbawm, as the aggregate of rival capitalist economies, divided into national blocs in Western Europe and North America, which, fueled by the demand for profitable investments and markets for products, had embarked on a binge of global expansion by the end of the nineteenth century.[3] That there were "national economies" depended on the existence of "nation-states," as Hobsbawm puts it, that is, macrostructures of interconnected social institutions in which those of education and culture (including the press) had assumed particular importance in constructing a national sense of "collective identity."[4] Such institutions were the principal locus for a discursive conception of the nation "as a system of cultural signification . . . [or] representation of social life," to invoke Homi Bhabha again,[5] whose ideological parameters increasingly were being defined not only in terms of language and ethnicity but in terms of the foreign "other."

As one of the more contested sites of cinema's industrialization, the

United States provides a compelling instance of early cinema's inscription within those discourses. Here the foreign "other" was Pathé-Frères, a French firm headquartered in Paris (its trademark a red rooster), the company that clearly led the way in industrializing the cinema worldwide. Pathé's leadership was evident in its pioneering system of mass production and mass distribution (with dozens of agencies selling its products across the globe), all instituted between 1904 and 1906.[6] The largest market for Pathé's products by 1906, however, was not France or even Europe but the United States, particularly with the astonishing growth of the nickelodeon, a storefront theater usually seating no more than several hundred. This new venue of exhibition was devoted exclusively to films, with programs often running no more than fifteen or twenty minutes, throughout the day and into the night, and it claimed a new mass audience of weekly "movie-goers," many of them women and children.[7] Coinciding with this transformation of the American cinema market, moreover, was a massive wave of new immigration into the country, which reached record numbers in 1907.[8] As those immigrants (most of them working-class) came to be seen as a sizable portion of the cinema audience, the nickelodeon seemed to offer, to cite Miriam Hansen and Roy Rosenzweig, the possibility of an "oppositional" or "alternative" public sphere, in contrast to the increasingly dominant "industrial-commercial public sphere" of mass consumer culture.[9] This produced a specific crisis of anxiety over the American "experience of modernity,"[10] I would argue, in terms of defining and controlling the economic and ideological power of the cinema. At issue was whether or not, as a "foreign" company selling "foreign" commodities—specifically, its trademark "red rooster" films—Pathé could be "assimilated" within the developing American cinema industry, and whether or not it should take part in circulating ever more significant representations of social life and behavior.[11] More generally, the question was how, with a "foreign" body like Pathé at or near its "center," could the American cinema be truly "American"? How could American society claim to have a distinct "national" identity or even, to appropriate Ernest Renan, a superior sense of "moral consciousness"?[12]

THE FRENCH ROOSTER RULES THE ROOST

Pathé's considerable power within the developing American cinema industry hardly went unnoticed at the time. The company itself asserted that, among its many accomplishments, no other firm had done as much to promote or "boom" the film business in the United States, and that assertion is borne out in the pages of *Views and Films Index,* the industry's first weekly trade journal, which the French company, along with Vitagraph, helped to launch in April 1906.[13] *Moving Picture World,* a rival weekly that eventually became the most influential trade journal in the United States, also accepted Pathé's crucial importance in spurring the American market's growth.[14] Even the Edison Manufacturing Company, Pathé's chief competitor/partner, and the only American firm determined to assert some measure of control over the industry, acknowledged Pathé's dominant position.[15] Among the many pages of testimony given by Frank Dyer, Edison's former vice president, in the famous antitrust case against the Motion Picture Patents Company (MPPC) is the following exchange:

Q. At that time, what was the most popular brand of film being exhibited in this country? In January and February, 1908?
A. I think the Pathé pictures were the most popular of them, although the Biograph pictures came into vogue shortly afterwards, and have always been popular.
Q. Then, had Pathé at that time established, so to speak, a standard of good quality?
A. Yes, sir. The Pathé pictures were the highest standard known in the art at that time. They were pre-eminent.[16]

At another point, Dyer even claimed that, in 1908, Pathé's "red rooster" films made up 60 percent of the total film product then in circulation in the United States.[17] Although Dyer's figure may at first seem inflated, there is no doubt that Pathé was the leading supplier of films during the early years of the American cinema industry, especially between 1905 and 1909, the so-called nickelodeon era.[18]

Pathé's "preeminence" can be gathered from the extent of the French company's penetration of the American market by 1906, the initial year of the nickelodeon's real "boom." That fall, in an editorial, *Billboard* called attention to the rapid "growth of the film business" by describing the principal venues of moving picture exhibition.[19] First of all, nearly "every up-to-date vaudeville theatre" across the country, from Keith's "high-class" theatres to smaller "family" houses, "include[d] moving pictures as part of the performance." Then, there were "hundreds of traveling shows," from national or regional figures like Lyman Howe to small companies touring only one or two states, "that set up in halls or small opera houses" and projected films—for a day or two, or even a week. The newest, and by then the most important, venue went under various names—nickelodeon, electric theater, theatorium—and could be found in "every town of sufficient size to support it" and as "a feature concession" in many amusement parks. By the summer of 1906, according to reports in *Billboard* and *Views and Films Index*, there were thirty nickelodeons in and around the parks on Coney Island and at least ten on the Atlantic City boardwalk.[20] By that fall, there were probably a hundred in both Chicago and New York, at least forty in Pittsburgh and Philadelphia, and perhaps fifteen in Cleveland.[21] Partly fueled by Harry Davis—whose Nickelodeon probably started it all in

Pittsburgh, back in June 1905,[22] and whose Bijou Dreams now stretched from Philadelphia, New York, Rochester, and Buffalo, to Cleveland, Toledo, Dayton, Detroit, and Grand Rapids—moving picture theaters were everywhere from cities like Birmingham, Kansas City, and Des Moines to small towns like Charleroi, Pennsylvania, and Pine Bluff, Arkansas.[23]

That Pathé often supplied the majority of films for all of these venues is suggested by surviving documents, some of which listed programs of specific film titles. According to its weekly managers' reports, especially from the theaters in New York and Boston, for instance, the Keith vaudeville circuit (the best and largest in the country) relied heavily on Pathé's "red rooster" titles to fill its popular programs.[24] Based on its newspaper ads, the Bijou, a "family" house in Des Moines, also rented Pathé films more frequently than it did others; and when the Bijou became the Nickeldom, in May 1906, it continued that pattern.[25] That same month, the Mueller Brothers, proprietors of four moving-picture shows on Coney Island, reported that their clientele, who loved melodramas and comedies, clearly preferred Pathé films.[26] Finally, according to the *New York Clipper*, Boston's first nickelodeon, the Theatre Comique, from its opening in September 1906, consistently showed one or two Pathé subjects on its weekly two-reel, or half-hour, programs; from December through February, it used "red rooster" titles almost to the exclusion of all others.[27]

That Pathé was able to dominate the American market by 1906, especially the nickelodeons, was due to an exceptional production and distribution capacity (fig. 7.1). In contrast to American companies such as Edison, Biograph, and Vitagraph (none of which had more than a single studio for shooting interior scenes), Pathé had three studio facilities (two of which had double stages) on the outskirts of Paris.[28] Moreover, it already had shifted to something like a factory system of production, with "director units" headed by Ferdinand Zecca, Lucien Nonguet, Gaston Velle, Georges Hatot, Albert Capellani, and Louis Gasnier all working more or less simultaneously. Unlike the American companies, which managed to complete just one film every week or two, by the summer of 1906, Pathé was releasing from three to six films per week and printing eighty thousand feet of positive film stock per day.[29] That fall, the company raised those figures to an average of six subjects per week and one hundred thousand feet of positive film stock per day.[30] By then, Pathé had advance orders for seventy-five prints of each new film title it placed on the American market.[31] Finally, unlike the American companies, which tended to produce a limited number of relatively lengthy "headliner" films, Pathé could offer a wide range of film lengths, from one hundred to more than one thousand feet, and in a variety of genres. Such a production strategy was perfectly suited for the nickelodeons, which demanded variety and novelty as well as increasingly frequent changes in their programs. The

Fig. 7.1. Pathé-Frères poster for the Omnia Pathé cinema, ca. 1907.

French company also was well situated to disseminate its "red rooster" films on the American market. Not only had it opened a second sales office in Chicago, one year after opening a New York office (in August 1904),[32] but it had also supplied the principal sales agents and rental exchanges which either, like Kleine Optical and Eugene Cline, tended to serve "family" vaudeville houses in the Midwest or, like Miles Brothers, serviced the big city amusement parks.[33] And Pathé films constituted the primary stock of two new major suppliers for the nickelodeons, Wm. H. Swanson and Carl Laemmle, both of whom established rental services in September 1906 in Chicago, the uncontested center of the American market.[34]

By early 1907, *Views and Films Index* put the number of "electric theatres" in the United States at approximately five thousand, with the *New York Dramatic Mirror* estimating there were five hundred in the greater New York area alone.[35] Throughout the year, in newspapers, trade weeklies, and monthly magazines, articles devoted to the "nickel craze" consistently mentioned that the films shown in the nickelodeons were primarily French (meaning Pathé's) and that they were preferred to all others.[36] That spring, in Chicago, for instance, those who defended the nickelodeons against a series of attacks by the *Chicago Tribune* invoked Pathé titles specifically as models of the "clean and wholesome" subjects best suited for their audiences.[37] In a letter blasting the *Tribune*'s charges, George Kleine singled out the company's newly released *Passion Play* and *Cinderella* as not only popular but also respectable and instructive.[38] Moreover, according to Kleine, nickelodeon owners throughout the country praised Pathé's films as the best, and two of the largest Chicago rental exchanges, Swanson and Laemmle, seconded that praise in letters that Pathé itself used as testimonials in its ads, for they attributed the success of their business to the quality of the "red rooster" films they bought and rented in such volume.[39] In fact, Carl Laemmle claimed that many of his customers wanted "Pathé films or none" at all.[40] That summer, when the "nickel craze" reached Des Moines, no less than three new theaters used Pathé films to kick off their opening programs. The Radium and the Dreamland, respectively, listed Pathé's *Two Sisters* and *Police Dogs* prominently in their initial ads, while the Lyric advertised the latest French films "right off the reel from foreign shores."[41] Later that same summer, in surveying New York nickelodeons for *Harpers Weekly,* Barton Currie concluded that "the French seemed to be the masters in this new field" of "innocent entertainment," noting that "thousands of dwellers along the Bowery [were] learning to roar at French buffoonery."[42]

In its predictions for a record-breaking 1907–1908 season, *Views and Films Index* wrote of "a scramble" among agencies to book "foreign productions." Even if this has the ring of a promotional tactic, it seems borne out by Pathé's experience that fall. In October, the New York office manager, J. A. Berst, told *Billboard* that the company's volume of business had doubled over the previous four months. Within weeks, Berst was publishing a "Weekly Bulletin" of information on the company's new releases and offering it directly to nickelodeon managers. By December, Pathé's ads were boasting that its six factories were turning out an incredible "230,000 feet of films daily," more than double that of the previous year. That same month, in *Views and Films Index*, the company reproduced a letter from Eastman Kodak to Charles Pathé, confirming that, in order to print such a high volume of product, he had placed an order, in October, for fifty million feet of positive film stock. There were other signs, however, of the broad circulation of "red rooster" films. *Moving Picture World*, for instance, reported that most of the Chicago rental exchanges "contract[ed] with French manufacturers for their films," and the newly established Standard Film Exchange supported this, in *Show World*, by specifically recommending the Pathé films it purchased each week. And Pathé's biggest seller, as E. H. Montague, the company's Chicago manager, first suggested, turned out to be *Passion Play*, the four reels of which took a whole hour to project.[43] In September, for instance, the Des Moines Lyric held the film over for an extra week; in November, the New Orleans Wonderland reported that it had been running the Pathé film for six weeks, at fifteen shows per day.[44] In December, the Theatre Royale in Detroit, which had opened with *Passion Play* in August, even claimed that over the course of thirteen weeks "nearly 250,000" people had seen it.[45]

Despite the emergence of such new producers as Essanay and Kalem and the increasing output of Vitagraph, Selig, and Lubin, the "strange, magnetic fascination" for Pathé films continued unabated into 1908, confirming *Views and Films Index*'s claim that the "success of your show depends exclusively on the number of Pathé-Frères films you receive."[46] In February, Swanson and Laemmle stressed the huge size of their orders for new "red rooster" films; about the same time, Greater New York Film Rental, founded by William Fox, was buying "a good many thousand dollars of films from Pathé Frères" and "show[ing] preference to [the] company."[47] In Des Moines, French films dominated both nickelodeon and vaudeville programs from December through May, and the Lyric took the unusual step, in its ads, of describing Pathé as "the world's most wonderful filmmakers."[48] Perhaps more conclusively, Joseph McCoy demonstrated the French company's popularity in a June 1908 survey for the Edison company of the films projected in New York–area nickelodeons. Of the 515 film titles that he viewed over the course of a month, more than a third came from Pathé.[49] That fall, in a summary of American and foreign manufacturers, the *New York Dramatic Mirror* concluded that the French company was still the world's "largest producer of moving picture films," which were "famous for their good photographic quality, superior pantomime, ingenious trick effects, beautiful colored results, and the clear, lucid manner of telling a picture story."[50] On a more personal note, cinema historian Edward Wagenknecht recalls that "all the films shown" at his neighborhood nickelodeon in Chicago at that time "were French Pathé" and that he "loved the titles and subtitles . . . [which were] always tinted red, with enormous lettering, and [had] the famous Pathé roosters at the bottom of each."[51] And it was that year that Pathé reached the point of "issuing from eight to twelve new films every week," which amounted to five reels in all, and of selling, on average, two hundred copies of each "red rooster" title released in the United States.[52]

FENCING THE ROOSTER IN

Pathé's role in stimulating and then exploiting the nickelodeon boom of 1906–1907 sharply defined the issue of who would exercise control over the cinema business in the United States, and how. Once one frames that struggle for control in terms of "American interests" versus "foreign interests," as such were perceived at the time, especially during the period from 1907 to 1909, the "foreign body" of "red rooster" films looms large indeed. There is perhaps no better evidence of Pathé's economic threat than a letter from George Eastman, head of Eastman Kodak, which at the time supplied 90 percent of the negative film stock used throughout the world.[53] According to Eastman's figures, the French company was selling on the American market between thirty and forty million feet of positive film stock per year by the fall of 1907, nearly twice as much as all the American companies combined.

As early as 1906, Pathé had drawn up plans to build factories for printing positive film stock in those countries where it was distributing the highest volume of films.[54] Such factories would reduce the high costs that the company already was paying for transportation and import duties, especially in the United States. In the spring of 1907, Pathé was preparing to construct such a facility in Bound Brook, New Jersey, based not only on its ever-expanding business but also on its understanding that a March 1907 court decision upholding the Edison camera patent (against Biograph) did not apply to perforated film.[55] Alarmed by the French company's move to embed itself more firmly in the American market, Edison set up negotiations with Pathé in April, threatening the company with litigation but also sweetening that threat with a "generous" proposition.[56] To counter the Bound Brook factory plans, Edison made what at first seemed a lucrative proposal, offering to print Pathé's positive film stock (from the shipped negative) at its own facilities and to serve as the principal sales agent of that film stock in the United States. Tempted by the offer, the French company responded favorably, assuming that Edison would print the sum total of its weekly negative output and that, in turn, it might gain exclusive rights to sell Edison films in Europe. However, it was more than a month before the Edison company finally replied, refusing to take Pathé's entire list of weekly subjects and demanding the right to select which

French films would be released on the American market.[57] After that, the deal quickly collapsed, and Pathé accused Edison of costing it a good deal of lost revenues.[58]

The result of Edison's delaying tactic was to stall the French company at a critical point in its expansion. Construction could not begin on the Bound Brook factory until early that summer, and Charles Pathé himself hurried across the ocean to join Berst for the factory's groundbreaking as well as for Pathé Cinematograph's incorporation as an American company.[59] Despite the company's record-setting business that fall, Berst remained uneasy because of the persistent "unsettled conditions" created by the proliferating nickelodeons and rental exchanges. The practice of duping film prints continued to the extent, for instance, that Kalem's Francis Marion warned that it could drive manufacturers like Pathé into the rental business.[60] And Pathé's recent decision to stop selling films in France and to establish its own rental system and exhibition circuit there raised fears that it was about to do the same in the United States.[61] Another practice that worried Berst as well as others was the subrenting of films without proper authorization. In order to curb these practices, in October Berst sent out new contracts to the exchanges and exhibitors which set forth tighter restrictions on reselling, duping, and "bicycling" prints (that is, sharing them "illegally" with other exhibitors) and encouraged customers to take all of the company's weekly releases *en bloc* rather than select several titles from among them.[62] As reported by *Show World, Moving Picture World,* and *Billboard,* representatives of the leading rental exchanges convened in Pittsburgh in November and, one month later, in Chicago, to remedy these and other problems.[63] Their solution was the United Film Service Protection Association (UFSPA), which promised to combine all sectors of the industry into a single national "regulatory" organization.

Behind the scenes, however, Edison was maneuvering to gain control of the new association. Emboldened by a Chicago court decision in October which upheld one of its patent suits against Selig and by the evidence accumulating in its case against Vitagraph—both of which strengthened its legal position—Edison set out to negotiate a licensing agreement with the other manufacturers that would let them, for an annual fee, exploit its patents.[64] Its purpose, besides the obvious one of self-interest, was to shift the industry's profits away from the renters and exhibitors and increasingly towards the manufacturers. Again Edison set up negotiations with Pathé, assuming that once the world's leading film producer fell in line, along with Vitagraph, the others would as well. Although its threat of litigation still loomed large, Edison now focused on assuring the French company that its licensing agreement would disallow or discourage "foreign imports" other than those from Pathé itself. It was this assurance,

Berst later testified, which persuaded Pathé to accept Edison's plan, as well as its insistence on paying only half the fee percentage the other manufacturers did.[65] The Edison licensing group then began securing contracts with members of the UFSPA, transforming it into the Film Service Association (FSA) and, in the process, excluding from its ranks the man who had brokered the original organization, George Kleine, the only other major dealer in "foreign imports."[66] In that it "shut out the importation of foreign stuff . . . not suitable or good enough for the American market,"[67] the FSA seemed to secure Pathé's position not only as the largest film supplier for that market but also as the only significant foreign producer, a position which could only have supported the French company's own strategies of dominance within Europe.[68] Moreover, as Martin Norden has pointed out, the Edison agreement permitted Pathé to begin manufacturing its cameras and projectors at the Bound Brook facility when it finally opened in late 1907 and began processing the fifty million feet of negative it had ordered from Eastman Kodak.[69]

However, not long after Biograph, together with Kleine, set up its own rival licensing group in February 1908 to serve the foreign companies and importers excluded from the FSA, Pathé began to sense that its operations were being blocked, its "red rooster" films fenced in.[70] First of all, Biograph promised to offer "a regular weekly supply of from 12 to 20 reels of splendid new subjects" and soon had commitments from a sufficient number of rental exchanges and exhibitors' associations, especially in Chicago, to sustain what was being dubbed the "Independent Movement."[71] Then, not only did Biograph refer to the FSA as the "Edison-Pathé combination" but Kleine, often called the leader of the new "Independents," also pointedly blamed Pathé more than Edison for the FSA's exclusionary strategy and for the ensuing "film war."[72] As if that were not enough, according to Georges Sadoul, with the revenue from the FSA licensees (which, at its peak, included one hundred and fifty rental exchanges as well as the eight manufacturers), Edison's gross profits equaled and then exceeded those of Pathé for the first time in years.[73] Even as it continued to amass high revenues on the American market, the French company found itself being outflanked by rivals both within and without the FSA. Early in the summer of 1908, as a means of regaining some measure of control, Berst floated an idea that Pathé had used successfully before: If the FSA producers were to cut prices on their positive film stock, the "Independents" would be unable to compete with them for long.[74] When that failed to win approval, the French company considered something more drastic. Now Charles Pathé himself came to the United States once again to explore the viability of establishing a circuit of film rental exchanges modeled on the system he had recently put in place in France, a system that, in its exploratory stages, may well have included Vitagraph along with the "Independents."[75]

That Pathé finally decided against making this move, or felt unable to do so, is revealing. The recession and monetary crisis threatening the United States economy at the time may have played a role in the decision, but the company's revenues, according to its own internal reports, seem not to have been much affected by that threat.[76] More to the point, Berst later admitted that Pathé found itself overextended in its investment and could not afford to set up the kind of rental exchange system that such a huge country as the United States would require.[77] Perhaps most crucially, the French company's internal records reveal that Charles Pathé and his directors were all too aware that, despite the best efforts of Berst in New York and Ivor Montague in Chicago, "they continued to be considered . . . foreigners."[78] Pathé was no more able to exert a leadership role in the American cinema industry now than either it or *Views and Films Index* had been two years earlier at the start of the nickelodeon boom.[79] In late September 1908, the *New York Dramatic Mirror* made a cryptic reference to one of the first signs of the French company's retreat. Whereas Vitagraph and Edison were increasing their output, respectively, to three and two reels per week, Pathé's output "of new subjects" was being cut "to four reels per week as against the five reels" released previously that year.[80]

Throughout the spring and summer of 1908, the rivalry between the two licensing groups led to much less stability in the industry than either Edison or Biograph had imagined. The FSA set up a regularized schedule of weekly releases in order to encourage stability, but soon there were complaints that it was too inflexible and that rental prices were too high, which increased the operating costs especially for nickelodeon owners.[81] Then, in July, the FSA pegged its pricing system to a film's release date, making those shown on the very first day of their release, as Eileen Bowser has written, the only "truly 'fresh' and valuable" commodities.[82] Among the trade press weeklies, only *Views and Films Index* strongly endorsed the FSA, earning it the reputation of being a mouthpiece for "Edison and its allied interests."[83] *Show World, Billboard,* and the *New York Clipper,* by contrast, all actively supported the "Independents," and *Moving Picture World* was hard-pressed to maintain the neutrality of its professed "independence."[84] Finally, as Charles Musser has documented, for the first time exhibitors were complaining, at least in New York, about a dearth of subjects.[85] By July, consequently, Edison was negotiating with both Biograph and Kleine to merge the rival groups into a single patent association—and Pathé's absence from those discussions clearly signaled its waning influence.[86] By September the Motion Picture Patents Company (MPPC) was all but in place, and now it was Eastman and Pathé, after a brief flurry of publicity over its proposed rental exchanges, who delayed the MPPC's official institution until December.[87] That the MPPC provisions limited foreign imports even more than before surely addressed one of Pathé's demands, but the provisions also restricted each licensed producer to a maximum of four thousand feet (or four reels) of new positive film stock per week.[88] That restriction contractually bound the company to the concession it already had made in September, and the weekly maximum of four thousand feet was considerably less than its full production capacity.

In the struggle to ensure that "American interests" rather than "foreign interests" controlled the American cinema industry, the formation of the FSA and then the MPPC played a significant role by curbing Pathé's considerable, if far from invulnerable, economic power at a crucial stage in that industry's development (fig. 7.2).

CLIPPING THE ROOSTER'S WINGS

Yet the struggle for control of the American cinema industry was hardly confined to the production and circulation of films as "fresh" and valuable commodities. It also encompassed their venues of exhibition and, especially, their reception and the efforts to mediate that reception. Evidence of this struggle is unmistakable in the trade journals, newspapers, and magazines. It is expressed perhaps most openly in an October 1908 article on the nickelodeon in *World Today*, in which the writer notes that "competition has lately become very keen between French and American manufacturers" but frames that competition in terms of taste and morality—associating the French with "bad taste" and immorality.[89] This kind of moral discourse appears repeatedly throughout the previous year and is often invoked to describe Pathé films in circulation. The reviews in *Variety*, which primarily addressed the vaudeville circuit, are especially striking: *The Female Spy* (December 1907) is "chaotic" and "disagreeable"; *Avenged by the Sea* (March 1908) is so "gruesome and morbid" that it "should not be on the market"; *A Christmas Eve Tragedy* (April 1908) (fig. 7.3) is "as well conceived for children as an interior view of a slaughter house would be" and reprehensible enough to justify censorship.[90] This attitude toward Pathé films can be found even earlier, however, in the spring of 1907, specifically in the correspondence conveying Edison's refusal to negotiate further with the French company, a refusal couched self-servingly in terms of moral objections to Pathé's subjects.[91] Furthermore, it is important enough that, when he visited the United States in May 1908 in order to assess the FSA's operations, Charles Pathé himself responded implicitly to such criticism by insisting that he would personally select the films his company released in the American market.[92] Indeed, as late as June 1909, the American correspondent for the British trade journal *Bioscope* went so far as to unmask this moralistic attitude toward Pathé films as symptomatic of something else entirely: "The quality of the Pathé picture is far and away ahead of that of its competition. . . . The public like Pathé pictures. . . .

Fig. 7.2. Cartoon in *Pathé Weekly Bulletin*, 20 April 1908.

Fig. 7.3. French poster for *Christmas Eve Tragedy,* 1908.

From this state of affairs there has arisen a condition of mind which one can only call Pathé-mentia."[93]

All this controversy suggests that, in the United States, Pathé was situated near the center of a debate over early cinema's status as a modern form of mass culture and, more importantly, over its ideological function as "a new social force" within an increasingly contested public sphere.[94] In one sense, the conflicted discourse about Pathé reveals how the company and its products served a double role in "legitimating" the cinema in the United States.[95] Initially, that role was to align certain positively perceived attributes of French culture with the "American" cinema. This can be seen in Pathé's own appeal, in its early advertisements, to the acknowledged high quality of French technology, demonstrated elsewhere by the photography industry (where the Lumière name was held in high regard) and the new automobile industry but also emblematized by such engineering marvels as the Eiffel Tower and the Gallery of Machines at the 1889 Paris Exposition.[96] Exhibitors, journalists, and others, however, also consistently celebrated the cinema by invoking the marvels of Pathé's "high quality"— from its unique stencil-color process to the "flickerless images" produced by the superbly crafted apparatuses of its laboratories.[97] That technology continued to be praised as late as 1909 and 1910, when a new version of the Pathé projector came on the market and was soon being installed not only in nickelodeons and the best new New York cinemas but also on ships of the United States Navy.[98] Pathé subjects also allowed vaudeville and nickelodeon exhibitors to treat their programs like a new, but inexpensive and continually renewed, version of the European theatrical tour, a significant form of French (as well as British) cultural influence in the late nineteenth century.[99] And one of the more famous of those tours just happened to coincide with Pathé's rise to power in the American market—the "Farewell America Tour" of Sarah Bernhardt from 1905 to 1906.[100] Finally, Pathé's "red rooster" films may well have benefited from the turn-of-the century belief "that the magical link to everything Parisian was a near guarantee" of sales, especially for department stores, through the mass market introduction of "Paris" fashion shows in stores like Wanamakers in Philadelphia.[101]

Just as often, however, and more frequently from 1907 on, writers in the trade press as well as exhibitors eschewed such "legitimating" appeals to play on another conception of French culture as risqué, deviant, and decidedly different from American culture—especially in its display of sexuality, sensational violence, and distasteful comic business. Here, the French *grand guignol* melodramas offer a telling instance of that shift.[102] During the nickelodeon boom, Pathé versions of such melodramas seem to have been not only accepted but also quite popular.[103] This was clearly the case in Des Moines, where a dramatic critic in March 1907 cited "the tense one-act drama[—]short character plays, vivid pathetic flashes from human life, a whirl of comedy[—]which claims prominent attention on the French stage" (a reference to the Grand Guignol theater in Paris) as a model for vaudeville programs in the city.[104] One month later, when the Colonial Theatre opened there with an entire program of Pathé titles, it ran *The Female Spy* (which *Variety* would later condemn) as a prominent feature.[105] The same film ran two weeks later at the Nickeldom, whose programs the *Des Moines Register and Leader* was then praising for their well-chosen variety, which included "scenes from foreign countries, unique adventures on land and water, and skillfully posed grotesque pictures."[106] That summer, according to the manager of the Theatre Film Service, the demand for sensational melodramas began to wane throughout the country, or, rather, he and other renters began to participate in their denigration, probably in response to recent attacks on Chicago nickelodeons.[107] In articles and interviews, the French tradition of grand guignol melodrama now was presented as sharply different from the American tradition of "ethical melodrama" and its "bright, happy denouements,"[108] or what William Leach, paraphrasing the department store magnate John Wanamaker, describes as the American "quest for pleasure, security, comfort, and material well-being."[109] Perhaps Carl Laemmle put it most succinctly: "Let's cater more to the happy side of life. There's enough of the seamy side without exposing it to further view."[110]

This illicit or "low-other" conception of French culture grew increasingly persistent over the next year or so. And it ranged across the spectrum of French films, encompassing much more than the sensational and the grotesque (fig. 7.4). One summer day in 1907, for example, a New York nickelodeon advertised its program as "FRESH FROM PARIS, *Very Naughty*."[111] In a similar vein, *Variety* repeatedly vilified Pathé's films well into 1909—as in its disgust at an early Max Linder comedy, *The Servant's Good Joke,* which exploited the effects of a salad deliberately dressed with castor oil.[112] Ironically, the language of approbation which the FSA (including Pathé) invoked to exclude that unwanted "foreign stuff" from the American market shifted to target and tar the French company itself.[113] The process accelerated as demands grew, especially among Progressive moralists, for a greater measure of control over this new arena of the "cheap" and the "low"—whether or not they agreed with economist Simon Patten's view of the nickelodeon as a source of regeneration for the masses—and for the construction of cinemas that would be as spacious and elegant as "legitimate" theaters and, therefore, would be more suitable for the "better classes."[114] In other words, as the nickelodeon boom increasingly came to be inscribed within the rhetoric of moral reform and uplift (with its "imperialist" notions of responsibility for "others less fortunate") and described as a "detour . . . through the lower regions of the en-

Fig. 7.4. Editorial cartoon in the *Des Moines Register and Leader,* 18 February 1909.

tertainment market,"[115] Pathé found itself more and more circumscribed in public discourse as representative of much that was "low" and "illegitimate" about the cinema.

   As the demands for social control of the cinema converged with those for economic control, the need to deal with "Pathé-mentia," otherwise translated into Pathé "illegitimacy," took on greater urgency. This is perhaps no more evident than in the actions of the National Board of Censorship, at least for the first year or so after its formation in March 1909.[116] According to documents housed at the Edison National Historical Site, throughout 1909 and 1910, Pathé films were either rejected or returned for alteration much more frequently than were the films of American producers. In May 1909, for instance, the board "condemned" two Pathé titles it had asked to be altered *(Le Parapluie d'Anatole* and *Le Boucher de Meudon)*, but accepted Biograph's *Two Memories* after changes were made.[117] One month later, no less than six of thirteen Pathé titles were rejected or recommended for alteration.[118] As late as February 1910, the board found Alfred Machin's *Moulin maudit* so offensive that, in order to eliminate its adultery, murder, and suicide, it ordered Pathé simply to lop off the second half of the film.[119] An October 1910 article in *World Today* unequivocally supports this evidence: "In the early days of the censors about one in every ten French pictures had to be condemned."[120] So does H. N. Marvin's testimony in the antitrust court case against the MPPC, in which he specifically referred to the great number of "indecent and obscene . . . pictures imported from foreign countries" as a principal reason for the board's formation.[121] In effect, the board's early work neatly complemented that of the FSA and the MPPC, not only in curbing Pathé's economic power but also in curtailing what was seen as an undesirable, immoral, "foreign" influence.

"AMERICANIZATION" AND THE "RED ROOSTER" SCARE

What made Pathé's influence especially undesirable at that particular historical moment, I would argue, was a conjunction of concerns about who went to the cinema and about what and who was being constructed as "American." Those concerns intensified, of course, as the "cheap amusement" of the "5¢ theaters" increasingly turned into "a permanent feature of municipal life."[122] In the spring of 1907, for instance, Kleine estimated that one hundred thousand people were attending the cinema daily in Chicago.[123] One year later, according to a four-month survey, the Woman's Municipal League and People's Institute reported that, in New York City, the nickelodeons "entertained from three to four hundred thousand people daily"—confirming J. Austin Fynes's earlier estimate of three million per week.[124] By then, more and more writers had come to see the nickelodeon as a new neighborhood "social center," a "veritable chautauqua for the masses," and "perhaps the beginning of a true theater of the people."[125]

Of all those who constituted the nickelodeon's mass audience (and variations existed from one region or city to another), there were two groups that especially attracted attention in the press. One was the disproportionally large number of recent immigrants, concentrated in metropolitan centers such as New York, Chicago, and Philadelphia.[126] Turn-of-the-century immigration was perceived as a tidal wave, peaking at nearly one million in 1907, with most of the new arrivals, unlike those earlier, coming from eastern and southern Europe (Russia, Poland, Austria-Hungary, and Italy).[127] In October 1906, in an early description of moving-picture shows in Manhattan, for instance, *Views and Films Index* noted that there were already dozens on the Bowery and Park Row, drawing their clientele from the nearby Jewish and Italian immigrant working-class settlements.[128] The following spring, the Chicago newspapers were alarmed at how popular the nickelodeons along Milwaukee and South Halstead (which transected the Jewish Ghetto) were among the "foreigners" of this "slum population."[129] That summer both Currier's survey of New York nickelodeons and a *Chicago Daily News* letter from a "practical man" with long experience in the business singled out "the popularity of these cheap amusement-places with . . . the newly arrived immigrant."[130] That November, in a well-known article, the *Saturday Evening Post* reported that "in cosmopolitan city districts the foreigners attend in larger proportion than the English speakers."[131] Several months later, a Philadelphia journalist wrote that in "cities where a new foreign population swells the census rolls an astonishingly large percentage of the audience in the nickelodeon is drawn from the Latin races who cannot speak English."[132] Although precise evidence is still scant, the nickelodeons catering to an immigrant and usually working-class clientele, whether in the New York districts of the Lower East Side, Jewish Harlem, and Uptown Little Italy, or in Chicago's Jewish, Polish, and Slavic neighborhoods, seem to have been an important market for Pathé films.[133]

The other group to attract attention consisted of women and children, who, according to reports, often made up the greater portion of nickelodeon audiences across the country.[134] As early as May 1907, *Views and Films Index* attributed the nickelodeon boom over the course of the previous year principally to "the patronage [of] women and children."[135] At the same time, the *Chicago Daily Tribune* reported that the early evening audiences on Chicago's lower State Street "were composed largely of girls from the big department stores," while an extensive survey of working-class women in Pittsburgh found them, one Saturday evening, "packed thick at the entrance of every picture show."[136] *Moving Picture World* observed, by contrast, that nickelodeons everywhere were "great places for the foot-sore shopper" and that "mothers . . . take the children and spend many restful hours there at very small expense."[137] That summer, nickelodeons from Boston to Des Moines catered to both women and children: when the Lyric opened in Des Moines, for instance, one of its promises was to be a "ladies and children's resort in earnest."[138] And the Chicago manager for Eugene Cline confirmed that strategy by explaining that "better business in the long run" only came to theaters patronized by "ladies and children."[139] In September, *Views and Films Index* concluded that of the "people who will go to a picture show every day and night if the programme is changed accordingly," most were "women and children."[140] On an average day in New York City, according to a four-month survey taken during the winter of 1907–1908, between 20 and 30 percent of the moviegoers were children.[141] A year or two later, women (both single and married) and children still made up a large percentage of the cinema audience—and reformers like Jane Addams in Chicago and Michael Davis in New York now were writing of their concern for the "thousands of young people in every industrial city" for whom "going to the show" weekly or even daily had become habitual.[142]

This concern about what effect "going to the show" was having on such groups of people was framed in terms of moral uplift, class mobility, and gender hierarchy, especially given what recent historians have documented as an anxiety over the increasing independence of single working-class women.[143] But all of these were caught up in heated questions about the construction of an "American" identity. How would that identity be differentiated from others in an era of heightened nationalism, and how would those without full citizenship—specifically immigrants, women, and children—best be trained to take up that identity and become proper social subjects within an "American" culture? These questions were especially pertinent as the surge of new immigrants into the United States (from southern and eastern rather than northern Europe) rose from three hundred thousand in 1900 to a peak of nearly one million in 1907. This immigration intensified the debate over whether or not the so-called process of assimilation so crucial to "Americanization" was in jeopardy.[144] During the course of several months in 1906 and 1907, for instance, *Munsey's Magazine* ran a thirteen-part series entitled "The Americans in America," which celebrated "the leading races that have contributed" to the development of a still "unfinished" American character.[145] Six months later, in *Century Illustrated*, Brander Matthews insisted on the continuing success of this "melting pot" theory, noting that "we Americans have imposed our ideals on the Irish and on the Germans, as we are now imposing them on the Italians and on the Russian Jews."[146] For "no immigrant culture . . . had the power to resist" assimilation, with American market capitalism undergirding its discursive formulations.[147] Josiah Strong put the matter most bluntly: "Unless we Americanize the immigrants, they will foreignize our cities, and in so doing foreignize our civilization."[148]

For such writers, the vital component in this Americanization process was education, and "every conceivable mode of education," Michael Kammen argues, "was viewed as a potential contribution."[149] By 1908 and 1909, on the evidence of such moral reformers as Simon Patten, Jane Addams, John Collier, and others, education included the cinema, especially the popular nickelodeons, which, according to the *New York Times,* now weekly attracted perhaps half the population of the United States.[150] Those who participated in the National Board of Censorship, for instance, were concerned not only that films offer appropriate or inappropriate models of behavior for immigrants but also that women and children not be exposed to dubious, even deviant, values and attitudes, whether they went to the cinema separately or together. Underlying this concern was a widespread assumption that the function of fiction within mass culture was to generate positive models of imitation.[151] Perhaps the best example was provided by the dime novels of Horatio Alger, which, Michael Denning argues, had their "largest readership between 1900 and 1915" (after the writer's death) and were soon transformed into an "archetypal narrative" of American capitalism in their "individualistic ethic of hard work and self-improvement."[152] What American readers wanted, according to a popular novelist of the time, F. Marion Crawford, was "to see before them characters whom they might really like to resemble, acting in scenes in which they themselves would like to take part."[153] That fictional worlds consisted of fantasy trajectories for individuals to imitate in their own lives seemed as relevant for cinema spectators as it was for readers of magazines, dime novels, and bestsellers.[154]

During these years, I would argue, Pathé's "foreign" films provided one of the principal "others" against which to construct an "American" difference. That difference began to surface in the trade press not long after the articles in *Munsey's* and *Century Illustrated*—and not only in *Variety* reviews. In the summer of 1907, for instance, *Show World* quoted several Chicago film men on "the crying need" for "American capital [to] furnish what now is being supplied by foreign filmmakers," namely Pathé.[155] That fall, the same trade weekly printed an article by the dramatic editor of the *Cleveland News* which bitterly contrasted the Americans, who "relished a Parisian flavor to [their] entertainment," with the French, who wanted "nothing American, except the money." Noted the editor, "It is not a fair exchange."[156] O. T. Crawford was one of the first to try to exploit this difference, when he tried to break into production in November, by advertising his subjects explicitly as "American films."[157] In January 1908, *Views and Films Index* felt compelled to address the question of why "foreign films [were] so eminently successful."[158] Its article not only offered answers but also sought to stimulate American producers at least to equal their foreign competitors. From its initial issues, *Moving Picture World* had polemicized for "clean, wholesome" films, attributing its own "moral reformist" desire for them to "public opinion."[159] By the summer of 1908, that desire was so bound up with the debate over "Americanization" that James Law would turn that desire into a demand for "good, clean, wholesome, national, patriotic, educational films," which was not unrelated to his castigation of "the foremost French maker" for failing to conform to the standards of "American taste," specifically in its handling of marital infidelity and physical comedy.[160] At the same time, the *New York Dramatic Mirror* began to join in this castigation, pointing to the "snap and go" of a new Essanay film, for instance, compared to a "slow and uninteresting" older Pathé title.[161]

The desirability of such films on the American market was widely debated in the trade press throughout 1909. Carl Laemmle (by then an independent distributor) put the case perhaps most strongly as he began to move into production: "I will make American subjects my specialty. . . . I want strong virile American subjects."[162] More than likely, Laemmle's model was the western films that Selig, trading on the public fascination for Buffalo Bill Cody and his Wild West Show as well as the popularity of western stage plays,[163] had done so much to popularize during the previous two years—from *The Girl From Montana* (1907) to *The Cattle Rustlers* (1908).[164] For it was the western, *Moving Picture World* argued, that would serve as the "foundation" of an "American school of motion picture drama."[165] This one-sided debate culminated in the trade weekly's own series on "the urgent necessity of American subjects made by American labor . . . for American moving picture audiences."[166] Even *Films Index* began to lend its support to this "necessity," admitting that there was "a limit to the amount of foreign subjects for which American audiences will stand" and that even some Pathé subjects were "unsuited to American demands."[167] Just as restrictions had begun to stem the tide of immigration into the United States in 1907, so too within the American cinema market were restrictions needed on "foreign subjects," even those bearing the popular "red rooster" trademark.

Besides cooperating with the FSA and the MPPC, Pathé made at least two further moves to meet the demands of "assimilation" and still remain competitive within the American cinema industry. One was to produce and distribute films of "higher quality," specifically adaptations of literary classics, which could both "educate" the masses and attract and hold the "better classes."[168] This strategy originated in France in 1908 with Pathé's investment in two new production companies, Film d'Art and SCAGL: In addition to financing the construction and equipment of their studios, the company contracted to print and distribute their films. And it was coupled with one of the company's unique features, its automated stencil-color process, which allowed it to release at least one "beautifully tinted *film d'art*" each week.[169] These "quality" films also coincided, however, with another shift that was emerging in exhibition. Large vaudeville houses (the first in Chicago was the Orpheum; in New York, the Unique, the Manhattan, Keith's 23rd Street, and Keith's Union Square)[170] began to be converted into movie theaters and to compete successfully with the nickelodeons.[171] As these conversions spread to other cities from Springfield, Massachusetts, to Saint Louis and New Orleans, newly constructed "picture palaces" began to appear—like the Olympic, in Lynn, Massachusetts, and Swanson's Theatre, in Chicago.[172] *Views and Films Index,* of course, promoted the French company's leadership in this move to "quality" films, but both the *New York Dramatic Mirror* and *Moving Picture World* also praised the first SCAGL productions—asserting, for instance, that *L'arlésienne,* which was adapted from an Alphonse Daudet novella, set "a new standard of excellence" and could serve as "a moral object lesson for every American manufacturer."[173]

Despite this deliberate attempt to counter all those earlier charges of "illegitimacy," the mounting complaints against Pathé films were now directed at its "quality" films as well. In November 1908, at the same time *L'Arlésienne* was being praised so highly, *Variety* was describing SCAGL's *Mary Stuart* (drawn from a Victor Hugo novel) as incomprehensible to anyone unfamiliar with the story, although it was playing at the Unique, then "the handsomest popular priced vaudeville theatre" in New York.[174] So vehement was the reviewer's condemnation of such "floppers," with their "intended-to-be-gruesome finales" (in which Mary Stuart lost her head),[175] that he accused the "whole crowd" at Pathé of having the "dope" habit. A month later, *Variety* was citing another SCAGL film, which starred "the well-known Belgian actor Henry Krauss," as an example of the "blood-curdler" that might be suitable for the Cirque d'Hiver in Paris but hardly for the "family ciné-hall" in New York.[176] In February 1909, *Moving Picture World* concluded that the effect produced by *The Assassination of the Duke de Guise* (the famous Film d'Art production based on playwright Henri Lavedan's "original" scenario) was "not so good," partly because "the Duke de Guise is unknown to the great bulk of the audience who gather in an American theater."[177] Despite calling that film "one of the few master-pieces of motion picture production," *New York Dramatic Mirror* acknowledged that its "gruesome" subject was difficult to ignore.[178] Later that year, the *Mirror's* Frank Wood used another Pathé *film d'art, The Wild Ass's Skin* (drawn from a Balzac novel), to set limits to the production of such "high brow" films because they often were "too elevated for popular understanding."[179] The cultural capital of France, even for the new "movie houses" attracting the "better classes," the company discovered, barely had enough exchange value to warrant its export.[180]

In response to such criticism, Pathé began issuing explanatory booklets for its *films d'art,* based on a format developed earlier for its popular *Passion Play.*[181] The company also turned to more familiar subjects like *Cleopatra* (March 1910), which was coupled with a special advertising campaign using the Sunday newspapers in Chicago, Boston, Baltimore, and Detroit.[182] But such moves were hardly enough to meet the overwhelming demand for "American subjects," especially when, according to *Moving Picture World,* those subjects meant "simple life stories . . . represented by clean, good looking actors."[183] For Pathé, the only possible way left to satisfy that demand was to establish its own facilities for producing American subjects with American actors. After testing a similar strategy with its affiliates in Russia and Italy, Pathé finally went ahead with plans to produce and distribute "American" films in the spring of 1910 and finished constructing a studio for that purpose in Jersey City that fall.[184] And what kinds of films did the American affiliate decide to make? None other than "Indian and Western subjects," which the French company had dabbled in successfully for several years but which American companies such as Selig, Kalem, Essanay, and Bison had turned into the most consistently popular genre on the American market.[185] The decision proved profitable, at least in the short run, for throughout 1910, from its very first title, *The Girl from Arizona* (April), through *Cheyenne Brave* (August) and *A Gambler's End* (November), Pathé garnered laudatory reviews in the trade press.[186]

The problem, however, was that Pathé, as a steady supplier of western subjects, was coming rather late to the genre: Whereas once the French company had led the way in producing certain kinds of films for the American market, now it was forced to play "catch up." By 1910, according to Robert Anderson's statistics, "one out of every five pictures produced by American companies . . . was a western," and Pathé could supply only a fraction of those.[187] Moreover, because its "American" films tended to focus on Indians as often as on cowboys and on women as often as on men, the company soon found itself marginalized once again, especially given the increasing emphasis at the time, perhaps best expressed by Owen Wister and exemplified by Selig's *Up San Juan Hill* (1909), on the primacy of the Anglo-Saxon and the masculine in fictional constructions of an American identity.[188] In conjunction with this production strategy, and perhaps as a means of demonstrating the "Americanization" of its weekly programs, the company also took the added step, in the summer of 1910, of cutting back its releases of French and other "foreign" films to just three thousand feet, or three reels, per week.[189] Unfortunately, both strategies would lead to further difficulties within another year or so, when the vogue for westerns began to fade and Pathé sought to import its earliest French feature-length films, for now it was stymied by the MPPC's distribution arm, the General Film Company, which was determined to maintain the production format of single-reel films, leaving the development of the feature film to rival "Independent" companies such as Universal, Famous Players, and Jesse Lasky, as well as other foreign producers in France, Denmark, and Italy.[190] By 1913, with the MPPC fast losing its dominance to the "Independents" (from which would arise the major Hollywood studios), Pathé had to confront the ultimate consequence of its alignment with the MPPC five years before: The company's French films had been almost completely excluded from the American market.[191]

Invoking Horatio Alger, Michael Denning has argued that the history of the dime novel underwent a remarkable rewriting around the turn of the century.[192] Symptomatic of that rewriting was a nostalgic article in the *Atlantic Monthly* in July 1907, which answered such questions as "what did the dime novel stand for . . . and what forces did it represent in the evolution of American society?" with platitudes like this: "The aim of the original dime novel was to give, in cheap and wholesome form, a picture of American wild life. . . . In reading them the American boy's soul soared and sang."[193] Erased in this rewriting, Denning says, was any sense that the usual dime novel reader was "a factory girl" or that the reading focused on "the other, the 'lower classes' and the 'foreigners.' "[194] Something similar happened, I would suggest, to the Pathé films that flooded the American market between 1905 and 1909 and to the role they played, however contradictory, at a crucial stage of the development of an American cinema. In this instance, however, the erasure of a "foreign element" has, perhaps, been even more complete. Once a crucial player in the American cinema's expansion and legitimation, the French company's moves were repeatedly blocked or deflected, stigmatized or appropriated. Once king of the market, the Pathé red rooster had to be suited up so as to appease the new masters just to keep from being run out of town. In the United States, where the cinema's industrialization constituted one of the defining moments of modernity—one which transformed the social space of the nickelodeon into the public sphere of an increasingly homogeneous consumer culture—the "Americanization" process acted as a significant framing, even determining discourse. And, in the context of the debate over that process, Pathé came to serve as a crucial marker of the margin, ensuring that the American cinema would be truly "American."

NOTES

1. Initial drafts of this essay were presented at the Society for Cinema Studies Conference, New Orleans, 11 February 1993, and at the University of Utrecht, 6 April 1994. During the process of revising and expanding those drafts, I have had the support of a John Simon Guggenheim Memorial Fellowship. I also have had helpful suggestions from Leo Charney, Paolo Cherchi Usai, Tom Gunning, Barbara Hodgdon, Roberta Pearson, Lauren Rabinovitz, Vanessa Schwartz, Ben Singer, Judith Thissen, and William Uricchio.

2. Homi Bhabha, "Introduction: Narrating the Nation," in *Nation and Narration*, ed. Homi Bhabha (New York: Routledge, 1900), p. 4.

3. Eric Hobsbawm, *The Age of Empire, 1875–1914* (New York: Pantheon, 1987), pp. 34–83. See also Jean-Marie Mayeur and Madeleine Rebérioux, *The Third Republic from Its Origins to the Great War, 1871–1914*, trans. J. R. Foster (Cambridge: Cambridge University Press, 1984), pp. 94–100, 271–278. For a discussion of early

French cinema within the context of these discourses of imperialism and nationalism, see Richard Abel, "Booming the Film Business: The Historical Specificity of Early French Cinema," *French Cultural Studies* 1 (1990): 79–94.

4. Hobsbawm, op. cit., pp. 142–164.

5. Bhabha, op cit., pp. 1–2.

6. The initial Pathé distribution agencies, other than those in the United States, included Moscow (February 1904), Brussels (October 1904), Berlin (March 1905), Vienna (July 1905), Saint Petersburg (December 1905), Amsterdam (January 1906), Barcelona (February 1906), Milan (May 1906), London (July 1906), and Odessa (July 1906). For further information on Pathé-Frères, especially in France, where its rapid growth into a relatively large corporation was quite unusual, see Richard Abel, "In the Belly of the Beast: The Early Years of Pathé-Frères," *Film History* 5, no. 4 (December 1993): 363–385; idem, *The Ciné Goes to Town: French Cinema, 1896–1914* (Berkeley, Los Angeles, London: University of California Press, 1994), pp. 20–22, 29–35.

7. *Billboard* provided the earliest extensive list of nickelodeons, including each one's seating capacity and number of shows given—see "Electric Theatres and Nickelodeons," *Billboard*, 15 December 1906, pp. 32–33. For concise, thorough histories of the nickelodeon, see Charles Musser, *History of the American Cinema*, vol. 1, *The Emergence of Cinema to 1907* (New York: Scribners, 1991), pp. 417–448; Eileen Bowser, *History of the American Cinema*, vol. 2, *The Transformation of Cinema, 1908–1915* (New York: Scribners, 1991), pp. 1–20; and Douglas Gomery, *Shared Pleasures: A History of Movie Presentation in the United States* (Madison: University of Wisconsin Press, 1992), pp. 18–33. For earlier studies, see Russell Merrit, "Nickelodeon Theaters, 1905–1914: Building an Audience for the Movies," in *The American Film Industry*, ed. Tino Balio (Madison: University of Wisconsin Press, 1976), pp. 59–82; Robert C. Allen, "Motion Picture Exhibition in Manhattan: Beyond the Nickelodeon," *Cinema Journal* 18 (spring 1979): 2–15; and Robert Sklar, "Oh! Althusser! Historiography and the Rise of Cinema Studies," in *Resisting Images: Essays on Cinema and History*, ed. Robert Sklar and Charles Musser (Philadelphia: Temple University Press, 1990), pp. 12–35.

8. One of the classic studies of immigration into the United States at the turn of the last century is John Higham, *Strangers in the Land: Patterns of American Nativism* (New Brunswick: Rutgers University Press, 1955), pp. 106–193. The most important early work on immigrant audiences, particularly those composed of women, comes in Judith Mayne, "Immigrants and Spectators," *Wide Angle* 5, no. 2 (1982): 32–40; Elizabeth Ewen, *Immigrant Women in the Land of Dollars* (New York: Monthly Review Press, 1985), pp. 14–15, 212–217; and Kathy Peiss, *Cheap Amusements: Working Women and Leisure in Turn-of-the-Century New York* (Philadelphia: Temple University Press, 1986), pp. 139–162.

9. Miriam Hansen provides an astute, useful conceptualization of the public sphere, drawing on Oscar Negt and Alexander Kluge's critique of Jürgen Habermas, as well as an excellent summary of the controversy over the social composition of nickelodeon audiences, in *Babel & Babylon: Spectatorship in American Silent Cinema* (Cambridge: Harvard University Press, 1991), pp. 7–15, 61–68, 90–125. Roy Rosenzweig offers a model case study of how working-class audiences in Worcester, Massachusetts, constituted an "alternative" public sphere, in *Eight Hours for What*

We Will: Workers and Leisure in an Industrial City, 1870–1920 (Cambridge: Cambridge University Press, 1983), pp. 191–221.

10. For other, quite insightful essays reconsidering early cinema in terms of "the experience of modernity," see Tom Gunning, "Heard Over the Phone: *The Lonely Villa* and the de Lorde Tradition of the Terrors of Technology," *Screen* 32 (summer 1991): 184–196; idem, "Now You See It, Now You Don't: The Temporality of the Cinema of Attractions," *The Velvet Light Trap* 32 (fall 1993): 3–12; and Gunning's essay in the present collection.

11. The first film historian to draw attention to Pathé's importance as a "foreign" presence in the early American cinema industry was Kristin Thompson in her chapter, "Regaining the American Market, 1907–1913," in Thompson, *Exporting Entertainment: America in the World Film Market, 1907–1934* (London: British Film Institute, 1985), pp. 1–27.

12. Ernest Renan, "What Is a Nation?" (orig. pub. 1882), trans. Martin Thom, in Bhabha, op. cit., p. 20.

13. "Notes from Manufacturers: Pathé," *Moving Picture World*, 16 July 1910, p. 165. Along with Edison, Vitagraph was the only American company, by 1907, to have a distribution agency abroad in London; Vitagraph, however, also had an even larger office, along with a laboratory for printing positive film stock in Paris (Thompson, *Exporting Entertainment*, p. 3).

14. "Editorial: What Does It Mean?" *Moving Picture World*, 26 October 1907, p. 536.

15. For an excellent study of the Edison company, see Charles Musser, *Before the Nickelodeon: Edwin S. Porter and the Edison Manufacturing Company* (Berkeley, Los Angeles, London: University of California Press, 1991).

16. Frank Dyer, Direct Examination, "United States vs. Motion Picture Patents Company and Others, Case No. 889, Eastern Pennsylvania District Court, September 1912–April 1914" (Washington, D.C.: U.S. Government Printing Office), 3:1,573.

17. Dyer, op cit., p. 1,504.

18. For a more extensive analysis of how Pathé achieved such preeminence by 1908, see Richard Abel, "Pathé Goes to Town: French Films Create a Market for the Nickelodeon," forthcoming in *Cinema Journal.*

19. "Growth of the Film Business," *Billboard*, 15 September 1906, p. 16.

20. "To Our Readers," *Views and Films Index*, 30 June 1906, p. 3; and "Atlantic City," *Billboard*, 21 July 1906, p. 7.

21. See, for instance, "News," *Views and Films Index*, 30 June 1906, p. 6; Bob Watt, "Philadelphia," *Billboard*, 29 September 1906, p. 11; "An Unexplored Field and Its Possibilities," *Views and Films Index*, 6 October 1906, pp. 3–4; "Trade Notes," *Views and Films Index*, 10 November 1906, p. 6; and "Trade Notes," *Views and Films Index*, 1 December 1906, p. 6.

22. The best account of the Pittsburgh Nickelodeon's opening in June 1905, and its early success, can be found in Musser, *Emergence of Cinema*, pp. 418–420. See also the profiles on Harry Davis in C. G. Bochert, "Live News Notes from Iron City," *Show World*, 31 August 1907, p. 11; "Surprising Growth of Motion View Industry," *Show World*, 23 November 1907, p. 19; and "The First Nickelodeon in the States," *Moving Picture World*, 30 November 1907, p. 629.

23. "Miscellaneous," *Billboard*, 6 May 1906, p. 30; "Special Correspondence from Important Points," "Kansas City," and "The Moving Picture Shows," *Billboard*, 12 May 1906, pp. 8, 9, and 37; "Davis a Ten-Center," *Variety*, 31 May 1906, p. 13; and "Moving Picture Shows," *Billboard*, 29 December 1906, p. 41.

24. The managers' reports on the weekly programs presented in a half-dozen "high-class" vaudeville houses operated by the Keith circuit, from Boston and Washington in the East to Detroit and Cleveland in the Midwest, make up a large part of the Keith-Albee Collection, University of Iowa Library, Iowa City, Iowa.

25. See, for instance, the Bijou ads in the *Des Moines Register and Leader*, 10 and 31 December 1905.

26. "The Pictures From the Standpoint of One Who Shows Them," *Views and Films Index*, 19 May 1906, p. 6.

27. The Theatre Comique was one of the few nickelodeons (or even vaudeville houses) to report its weekly film programs that year in the trade press. See, especially, the weeks of 13 October, 18 November, and 15 December through 9 February. One of the first Pathé titles shown at the Comique was *Dog Smugglers*, a big hit on the Keith circuit the previous summer.

28. By 1905 Pathé had a studio with two stages at Vincennes, another with two stages at Joinville-le-pont, and a third (with a large pool) at Montreuil. Both Edison and Vitagraph started construction on new studios in late 1905, but neither would be ready until the following summer or fall.

29. See, for instance, "Last Films Out," *Views and Films Index*, 26 May 1906, p. 4, 2 June 1906, p. 4, and 9 June 1906, p. 6; and the Pathé ads in *Views and Films Index*, 16 June 1906, p. 12, and 4 August 1906, p. 11.

30. See, for instance, "Latest Films," *Billboard*, 25 August–22 September 1906, p. 5; and the Pathé ads in *Views and Films Index*, 27 October 1906, p. 11, and in *New York Clipper*, 24 November 1906, p. 1,070. By then, Pathé also had a maze of laboratories in Joinville-le-pont (for perforating, developing, printing, and splicing film stock), Vincennes (for creating stencil-color prints), and Belleville (for manufacturing and servicing apparatuses).

31. "Moving Pictures," *Billboard*, 13 October 1906, p. 21. This figure is for initial orders delivered from Paris, not for additional orders that may have been requested later for the more popular titles. If certain Edison films seem to have sold even more prints (the 1906 *Train Wreckers*, for instance, sold 157), that is because its figures were cumulative, covering one or more years—see Musser, op. cit., p. 317.

32. See, for instance, the Pathé ads in *New York Clipper*, 27 August 1904, p. 613, and in *Billboard*, 9 September 1905, p. 47.

33. See, for instance, the Miles Brothers ads in *New York Clipper*, 15 July 1905, p. 540, and in *Billboard*, 5 August 1905, p. 48; "Motion Picture Films" and "The Passion Play," *Complete Kleine Optical Company Catalog*, November 1905, pp. 206–207, 272–273; and "Pathé Films," *Eugene Cline Catalog* (1906), pp. 19–20. See also "Kleine Optical Company Accounts [1904–1907]," in Musser, *Before the Nickelodeon*, pp. 482–483.

34. See, for instance, the Swanson ad in *Billboard*, 8 September 1906, p. 56; the Laemmle Film Service ads in *Billboard*, 6 October 1906, p. 22, 13 April 1907,

p. 33, and 20 April 1907, p. 37; and the Pathé ad in *Views and Films Index*, 13 July 1907, p. 2. Warren Patrick first called Chicago "the leading film market in the world" in "Pat-Chats," *Billboard*, 1 July 1905, p. 3.

35. See "Trade Notes," *Views and Films Index*, 19 January 1907, p. 6; and "War on Nickel Theatres," *New York Dramatic Mirror*, 23 March 1907, p. 18. The three hundred nickelodeons that *Billboard* had compiled in December 1906 obviously was incomplete; for instance, it had none at all in New York City.

36. By 1907 Georges Méliès was no more than a minor film supplier in the United States, and Gaumont and Eclipse had just begun to distribute films on a regular basis (the latter mostly *actualités*) through Kleine Optical. Also by 1907, Pathé films consistently were deploying most of the basic components of the system of narrative continuity that cinema historians still often attribute to slightly later Vitagraph or Biograph films (or those of D. W. Griffith)—see Abel, *The Ciné Goes to Town*, pp. 121–156.

37. See "The Five Cent Theatres," *Chicago Tribune*, 8 April 1907; "Nickel Theaters Crime Breeders," *Chicago Tribune*, 13 April 1907; "Film Shows Busy, Panic Stops One," *Chicago Tribune*, 15 April 1907; the Laemmle Film Service ad in *Billboard*, 27 April 1907, p. 34; "Editorial: Public Opinion as a Moral Center," *Moving Picture World*, 11 May 1907, p. 147; and "Trade Notes," *Moving Picture World*, 11 May 1907, pp. 152–153.

38. See George Kleine's 10 April letter to the *Chicago Tribune*, reprinted in *Moving Picture World*, 20 April 1907, pp. 101–102.

39. See the Pathé ads in *Views and Films Index*, 1 June 1907, p. 2, and 13 July 1907, p. 2.

40. That spring, Pathé also upped its output to "one novelty for each day of the week"—see its ad in *Views and Films Index*, 20 April 1907, p. 2.

41. See the Radium Theater ad, *Des Moines Register and Leader*, 29 May 1907; the Lyric Theatre ad, ibid., 23 July 1907; "Today's Amusements," ibid., 30 July 1907; "Correspondents," *Show World*, 10 August 1907, p. 12ii; and the Dreamland ads in the *Des Moines Register and Leader*, 30 July and 1, 8, and 15 August 1907. *Two Sisters* was a particularly good example of the relatively sophisticated system of representation and narration which Pathé's filmmakers had developed by 1907; moreover, the film seemed specifically addressed to women.

42. Barton W. Currie, "The Nickel Madness," *Harpers Weekly*, 24 August 1907, reprinted in *The Movies in Our Midst: Documents in the Cultural History of Film in America*, ed. Gerald Mast (Chicago: University of Chicago Press, 1982), pp. 50–51.

43. See "The Rapper," *Views and Films Index*, 17 August 1907, p. 8. Pathé issued a special "booklet of forty-four pages, describing their new Passion Play film," in preparation for the fall season, and later offered a large poster to exhibitors ("Trade Notes," *Views and Films Index*, 17 August 1907, p. 4, and 5 October 1907, p. 4). The film's American release was first announced in *Views and Films Index*, 2 March 1907, p. 11. This was Pathé's third version of *The Life and Passion of Christ*; the other two dated from 1900 and 1902–1903.

44. See the Lyric ad in the *Des Moines Register and Leader*, 29 September 1907, and "Moving Picture News from Everywhere," *Views and Films Index*, 9 November 1907, p. 6.

45. See "Moving Picture News from Everywhere," *Views and Films Index,* 7 December 1907, p. 6; and "Trade Notes," *Moving Picture World,* 14 December 1907, p. 667. Pathé's *Passion Play* also was cited as "a huge success" in George E. Walsh, "Moving Picture Drama for the Multitude," *The Independent,* 6 February 1908, p. 308.

46. See "The Public and the Filmmaker," *Views and Films Index,* 25 January 1908, p. 3; and the front cover of *Views and Films Index,* 29 February 1908. For information on the increasing American film production, see Musser, *Emergence of Cinema,* pp. 466–487.

47. See the Laemmle Film Service ads in *Show World,* 15 February 1908, p. 15, and 22 February 1908, p. 17; the Swanson ad in *Show World,* 7 March 1908, p. 13; and William Fox, Direct Examination, "USA vs. MPPC and Others," vol. 2, p. 676. See also the tribute to Fox in "William Fox," *Views and Films Index,* 8 August 1908, p. 3.

48. See the Lyric ad in *Des Moines Register and Leader,* 22 December 1907.

49. Of those 515 film titles, 458 were from "licensed" manufacturers (grouped in the Film Service Association), with most of the remaining 57 titles coming from Biograph and "independent" distributors of foreign imports. Of those 458 "licensed" films, 14 came from Méliès, 26 from Selig, 32 from Kalem, 40 from Lubin, 42 from Essanay, 45 from Edison, 82 from Vitagraph, and 177 from Pathé. McCoy's survey is reprinted in Musser, *Before the Nickelodeon,* p. 417.

50. "Earmarks of Makers," *New York Dramatic Mirror,* 14 November 1908, pp. 10–11. That summer, the *Mirror* also had singled out Pathé's *Dreyfus Affair* and *Dieppe Circuit* for special praise in its new film review column—see *New York Dramatic Mirror,* 11 July 1908, p. 7, and 22 August 1908, p. 9.

51. Edward Wagenknecht, *The Movies in the Age of Innocence* (Norman: University of Oklahoma Press, 1962), p. 12.

52. These figures come from "Pathé in New Quarters," *Variety,* 1 February 1908, p. 11; "Film Production Increasing," *New York Dramatic Mirror,* 27 June 1908, p. 7; and "Kinematography in the United States," *Moving Picture World,* 11 July 1914, p. 176.

53. Eastman's letter is reprinted in Georges Sadoul, *Histoire générale du cinéma,* vol. 2, *Les Pionniers du cinéma, 1897–1909* (Paris: Denoël, 1948), pp. 465–466. Although undated, it refers to his recent negotiations with Edison and Pathé representatives in the summer of 1907. Sadoul's account of the FSA and MPPC's formation in that volume, on pages 461–478, is still one of the best available.

54. "Compagnie générale de phonographes, cinématographes et appareils de précision," *Les Assemblés générales* (25 June 1906), pp. 656, 658, Carton 1, Pathé Télévision Archive (PTA), Saint-Ouen.

55. "Trade Notes," *Views and Films Index,* 16 March 1907, p. 6. For a more detailed analysis of the negotiations between Edison and Pathé, see Thompson, op. cit., pp. 4–10. See also Martin Sopocy, "The Edison-Biograph Patent Litigation of 1901–1907," *Film History* 3 (1989): 19–22.

56. See G. Croydon-Marks to W. E. Gilmore, 15 March 1907; Gilmore to Croydon-Marks, 10 April 1907; and Dyer to Gilmore, 13 April 1907, 1907 motion picture folder, Pathé file, Edison National Historical Site (ENHS), West Orange, New Jersey.

57. See Marks to Pathé, 21 May 1907, and Gilmore to William Pelzer and Gilmore to Thomas Edison himself, 28 May 1907, 1907 motion picture folder, Pathé file, ENHS.

58. See the translation of the 22 May 1907 letter from Pathé to Marks, 1907 motion picture folder, Pathé file, ENHS.

59. "Trade Notes," *Views and Films Index,* 8 June 1907, p. 4; and "Trade Notes," *Moving Picture World,* 22 June 1907, p. 249. The "incorporators" of the new company were William H. Corbin, Collins & Corbin, Ernest A. Ivatts, and Charles Pathé.

60. "'Duping' of Fine Film Pictures Condemned," *Show World,* 9 November 1907, p. 16.

61. See, for instance, "What Will Pathé Do?" *Show World,* 19 October 1907, p. 18; and "Editorial: What Does It Mean?" *Moving Picture World,* 26 October 1907, pp. 535–536. See also Abel, *The Ciné Goes to Town,* pp. 33–34.

62. "A New Move: The Pathé Contract," *Views and Films Index,* 26 October 1907, p. 3; "Editorial: What Does It Mean?" *Moving Picture World,* 26 October 1907, pp. 535–536.

63. See "American Moving Picture Captains Meet in Pittsburgh," *Show World,* 23 November 1907, p. 21; Warren Patrick, "Chicago Welcomes Captains of Moving Picture Industry," ibid., 30 November 1907, p. 18; "The United Film Service Protective Association," *Moving Picture World,* 30 November 1907, p. 627; "Film Men's Association Needed, Says Swanson," *Show World,* 7 December 1907, p. 14; "Moving Picture Men Organize," ibid., 21 December 1907, p. 88; "The U.F.S.P.A.," *Moving Picture World,* 21 December 1907, p. 682; "United Film Service Protective Association Meets," *Billboard,* 21 December 1907, p. 20; and "Film Convention and Moving Picture News," *Billboard,* 28 December 1907, p. 9. *Views and Films Index* was unusually reticent about these meetings, having only one story devoted to them—see "United Film Service Protective Ass'n," *Views and Films Index,* 21 December 1907, pp. 4–5.

64. Musser, *Before the Nickelodeon,* p. 375.

65. J. A. Berst, Direct Examination, "USA vs. MPPC and Others," vol. 3, pp. 1,768–1,770. See also Musser, *Before the Nickelodeon,* p. 377.

66. The initial listing of the UFSPA included rental exchanges only ("The U.F.S.P.A.," *Moving Picture World,* 21 December 1907, p. 682). By February the FSA was contractually bound to the following licensed manufacturers: Edison, Essanay, Kalem, Lubin, Méliès, Pathé, Selig, and Vitagraph ("Statement by the Licensed Manufacturers," *Views and Films Index,* 29 February 1908, pp. 3–4). For the details of Kleine's ill-rewarded diplomacy in the UFSPA's formation, see Bowser, op. cit., pp. 26–27.

67. "Interview with FSA Members and Others," *Moving Picture World,* 28 March 1908, p. 260. Among those foreign companies excluded from the FSA agreement were Gaumont, Urban-Eclipse, Cinès, and Nordisk, all of which had begun to carve out a niche in the American market.

68. See, for instance, J. A. Berst to George Eastman, 11 February 1908, MPPC box no. 5, ENHS. Pathé also was allowed to hold an "inventory sale" of its "large stock of films on hand"—see the Pathé ad in *Views and Films Index,* 25 January 1908, p. 2.

69. Martin Norden, "The Pathé-Frères Company During the Trust Era,"

Journal of the University Film Association 33 (Summer 1981): 16–17. The Bound Brook factory was producing thirteen thousand meters of positive film stock per day by the summer of 1908, with expectations of twenty thousand meters by the end of the year. See the "Rapport du Conseil d'Administration," Assemblée Générale Ordinaire, Pathé-Frères (2 June 1908), carton 2, PTA.

70. The Biograph licensing group was announced in an ad in *Moving Picture World*, 22 February 1908, p. 130; and then in similar ads in *Show World*, 29 February 1908, p. 28, and in *New York Clipper*, 29 February 1908, p. 52. Kleine had to sell the stocks he controlled in Kalem in order to avoid a conflict of interest.

71. "Moving Picture Men Indorse Independent Movement in Chicago," *Show World*, 14 March 1908, p. 8. See also Musser, *Before the Nickelodeon*, p. 380.

72. See, for instance, "The Position of the American Mutoscope and Biograph Company," *Moving Picture World*, 15 February 1908, p. 112; "Trade Notes: The Film War," ibid., 29 February 1908, pp. 160–161; and "Moving Picture Men Indorse Independent Movement in Chicago," *Show World*, 14 March 1908, p. 8.

73. Sadoul, op. cit., p. 467.

74. "Pathé's Position," *Views and Films Index*, 13 June 1908, p. 4.

75. See "Rumors Regarding Pathé-Frères," *New York Dramatic Mirror*, 12 September 1908, p. 9; "Pathé Will Not Invade Rental Field," *Moving Picture World*, 12 September 1908, p. 192; "Pathé Frères Not to Rent," *Views and Films Index*, 19 September 1908, p. 4; and Bowser, op. cit., pp. 28–29.

76. "Rapport du Conseil d'Administration," Pathé-Frères (2 June 1908), PTA.

77. J. A. Berst, Direct Examination, "USA vs. MPPC and Others," vol. 3, p. 1,778.

78. "Rapport du Conseil d'Administration," Pathé-Frères (2 June 1908), PTA.

79. By November 1905, Pathé was so entrenched on the American market that, along with Kleine Optical, Vitagraph, Biograph, and Méliès (but, significantly, not Edison), it had participated in the first attempt to organize "the leading manufacturers of films," the Moving Picture Protective League of America; see "Moving Picture Makers Organize," *New York Clipper*, 23 December 1905, p. 1,118. *Views and Films Index* often had encouraged the formation of some kind of protective association for the new industry, beginning in the late summer of 1906; see, for instance, "Editorial: Association for Protection Against Dishonest Customers in the Moving Picture Trade," *Views and Films Index*, 18 August 1906, p. 3; "Problems of the Trade and Their Solution," *Views and Films Index*, 25 August 1906, p. 3; and "The Plan to Organize the Protective Association," *Views and Films Index*, 27 October 1906, pp. 3–4.

80. "Increasing American Output," *New York Dramatic Mirror*, 26 September 1908, p. 9.

81. See, for instance, "Release Dates," *Views and Films Index*, 11 April 1908, p. 3; "Now Is the Time," ibid., 30 May 1908, p. 3; and "Association Renters Discuss Schedule," ibid., 6 June 1908, p. 4.

82. Musser, *Before the Nickelodeon*, p. 378; and Bowser, op. cit., p. 28.

83. See, for instance, the front covers of *Views and Films Index*, 22 February and 25 April 1908; and "The Moving Picture Field," *New York Dramatic Mirror*, 30 May 1908, p. 7.

84. See, for instance, "Words From the Knocker and Howler," *Moving Picture*

World, 1 February 1908, p. 72; "The Film Service Association and Ourselves," ibid., 22 February 1908, p. 131; and "About Ourselves," ibid., 21 March 1908, p. 227.

85. Musser, *Before the Nickelodeon*, pp. 380–381.

86. It was Frank Dyer, for Edison, and Harry Marvin and Jeremiah J. Kennedy, for Biograph, who headed these negotiations. For further information on the MPPC's formation, see Thompson, op. cit., p. 10–19; Musser, *Before the Nickelodeon*, pp. 433–438; and Bowser, op. cit., pp. 27–33.

87. The MPPC was even incorporated that September in New Jersey (Musser, *Before the Nickelodeon*, pp. 435–437). For further information on the delay caused by Eastman and Pathé, see Bowser, op. cit., p. 31. Another reason that Pathé briefly considered opening its own rental exchange was to amortize the unsold film prints which were accumulating because of the FSA regulations, but it was able to sell off many of those between September and December, when the MPPC officially replaced the FSA.

88. See the testimony of H. N. Marvin and Frank Dyer, *USA vs. MPPC* (1914), pp. 26 and 1,519.

89. Lucy France Pierce, "The Nickelodeon," *World Today*, October 1908; reprinted in Mast, *Movies in Our Midst*, p. 56.

90. These reviews are reprinted in *Variety Film Reviews, 1907–1920* (New York: Garland, 1983). *The Female Spy* ended with a young Cossack woman being killed and then dragged by a horse, while *A Christmas Eve Tragedy* climaxed with a Breton fisherman throwing his wife's lover, along with the man's horse and cart, over a cliff. This discourse of moral approbation contrasted, however, with the grudging respect that John Collier used to describe New York nickelodeon films in April 1908 (Collier, "Cheap Amusements," *Charities and the Commons*, 11 April 1908, p. 74).

91. See W. E. Gilmore to T. Edison, 28 May 1907, 1907 motion picture folder, EHNS.

92. "Chas. Pathé Makes a Statement," *Views and Films Index*, 16 May 1908, p. 4.

93. T. B., "News from America," *Bioscope*, 24 June 1909, p. 25. See, also, the letter from a Boston nickelodeon manager who argued that only one American company, Biograph, "had attained the standard of quality set by Pathé films" ("Correspondence," *Moving Picture World*, 29 May 1909, p. 716).

94. The phrase "a new social force" was first used by John Collier in "Cheap Amusements." Contrast this with Robert Sklar's statement that Pathé's success in the American market had notably little effect (*Movie-Made America: A Cultural History of American Movies* [New York: Random House, 1975], p. 29).

95. Roberta Pearson and William Uricchio examine a similar contradiction in the appeals made to Italian culture in American discourse on early cinema—see "English, Italian, and American Shakespearean Cinema in the United States: Differences in Signifying Practices and Reception," in *Images Across Borders*, ed. Roland Cosandey (forthcoming from Editions Payot, 1995).

96. Perhaps the earliest evidence of this appeal comes in the Pathé ad in the *New York Clipper*, 28 October 1905, p. 930. Between 1903 and 1905, Lumière's technical advances frequently were highlighted in the prestigious American monthly, *Photo-Era Magazine*. In 1903 France exported 51 million francs worth of automobiles and parts, in 1906, 140 million (Eugen Weber, *France, Fin-de-Siècle* [Cambridge:

Harvard University Press, 1986], p. 207). See also Roger Magraw, *France, 1815–1914: The Bourgeois Century* (London: Fontana, 1983), pp. 232–233; and Paul Greenhalgh, *Ephemeral Vistas: The Expositions Universelles, Great Exhibitions, and World's Fairs, 1851–1939* (Manchester: Manchester University Press, 1988), pp. 154–155.

97. See, for instance, "Trade Notes," *Moving Picture World*, 11 May 1907, pp. 152–153.

98. See, for instance, the full-page ad for the new Pathé projector in *Moving Picture World*, 3 April 1909, p. 390; "French Machine Hits Iowa City," *Views and Films Index*, 5 June 1909, p. 4; "Pathé Professional Outfit," *New York Dramatic Mirror*, 31 July 1909, p. 15; "Pleased with Pathé Machines," ibid., 30 October 1909, p. 17; "Quantitative Competition," *Moving Picture World*, 5 February 1910, p. 158; "N.I.M.P.A. Meeting," ibid., 12 February 1910, p. 214; and "Pathé Machines on United States Warships," ibid., 28 May 1910, p. 885.

99. Sarah Bernhardt made one of the earliest and most influential of such tours in 1880, then returned for another in 1900; Gabrielle Réjane made her first in 1895 and then a second in 1904; see, for instance, Hamilton Mason, *French Theatre in New York* (New York: AMS Press, 1940), pp. 6, 28–29, 31.

100. See, for instance, Arthur Gold and Robert Fizdale, *The Divine Sarah: A Life of Sarah Bernhardt* (New York: Knopf, 1991), pp. 294–298.

101. William Leach, *Land of Desire: Merchants, Power, and the Rise of a New American Culture* (New York: Pantheon, 1993), pp. 99–102. A similar point is made by Kathy Peiss in "Making Faces: The Cosmetics Industry and the Cultural Construction of Gender, 1890–1930," *Genders* 7 (Spring 1990): 157–158.

102. For a good introduction to French grand guignol, see Mel Gordon, *The Grand Guignol: Theatre of Fear and Terror* (New York: Amok Press, 1988). For a more encompassing, more theoretical analysis of turn-of-the-century sensational melodrama, see Ben Singer's essay in the present collection.

103. Vitagraph also briefly stressed the "sensationalism" of its films during this period; see its ad for *The Automobile Thieves* in *Views and Films Index*, 10 November 1906, p. 11.

104. "Vaudeville's Higher Aim," *Des Moines Register and Leader*, 24 March 1907.

105. See the Colonial Theatre ad in ibid., 30 April 1907, p. 5.

106. See the Nickeldom ad in ibid., 13 May 1907, p. 5; and "This Week's Bills," ibid., 26 May 1907.

107. F. C. McCarahan, "Chicago's Great Film Industry," *Billboard*, 24 August 1907, p. 6.

108. See, for instance, "The Melodrama," *New York Dramatic Mirror*, 1 June 1907, p. 14; and "Public Taste in Pictures as Viewed by M. E. Fleckles," *Show World*, 7 September 1907, p. 9. For a further analysis of differences in French and American tastes, particularly in terms of the French penchant for grand guignol melodrama versus the American preference for "bright, happy denouements," see Richard Abel, "A Crisis in Crossing Borders, or How to Account for French 'Bad Taste'," in op. cit.

109. John Wanamaker's advertising editorial in *North American*, 5 April 1906, as cited in Leach, *Land of Desire*, p. 3.

110. "Moving Picture Industry Great," *Show World*, 29 June 1907, p. 29.

111. "The Nickel Madness," *Harper's Weekly*, 24 August 1907, reprinted in Mast, *Movies in Our Midst*, pp. 49–50.

112. See the 2 October 1909 review of *The Servant's Good Joke* reprinted in *Variety Film Reviews, 1907–1920* (New York: Garland, 1983).

113. In 1907 George Kleine had defended French films (especially Pathé's) against press attacks on Chicago's nickelodeons; one year later, allied with the "Independents" against the FSA, he was maligning French films as "racy, risqué, and sensational" ("Interview with George Kleine," *New York Dramatic Mirror*, 27 June 1908, p. 7).

114. See, for instance, "Moving Picture Industry Shows Marked Improvement, Activity and Development," *Show World*, 19 October 1907, p. 22; "Editorial," *Views and Films Index*, 11 April 1908, p. 4; W. Stephen Bush, "Who Goes to the Moving Pictures," *Moving Picture World*, 3 October 1908, p. 378; "Editorial," *Views and Films Index*, 7 November 1908, p. 3; "The Real Problem to be Solved," ibid., 29 May 1909, p. 3; and Lewis E. Palmer, "The World in Motion," *Survey*, 5 June 1909, p. 357. For an analysis of Simon Patten's influential books *The New Basis of Civilization* (1907) and *Product and Climax* (1909), see Daniel Horowitz, *The Morality of Spending: Attitudes toward the Consumer Society in America, 1875–1940* (Baltimore: Johns Hopkins University Press, 1985), pp. 31–37.

115. The descriptive phrase is from Hansen, *Babel and Babylon*, p. 69, but the outlines of this redefinition of the nickelodeon period already were in place in H. F. Hoffman, "What People Want: Some Observations," *Moving Picture World*, 9 July 1910, p. 77.

116. See, especially, Nancy Rosenbloom, "Progressive Reform, Censorship, and the Motion Picture Industry, 1909–1917," in *Popular Culture and Political Change in Modern America*, ed. Ronald Edsforth and Larry Bennett (Buffalo: SUNY Press, 1991), pp. 41–59. It should be noted that in April 1909 the board took unusual measures to approve a large number of Pathé's films, but this changed shortly thereafter—see Bowser, op. cit., p. 50; and Palmer, "The World in Motion," p. 363.

117. See John Collier to Frank Dyer, 10 May 1909, motion picture folder, censorship file no. 1, ENHS. Ironically, Collier had detected not "one immoral or indecent picture" in his investigation of New York nickelodeons just one year earlier (Collier, "Cheap Amusements," p. 74).

118. See Collier to Dyer, 18 June 1909, motion picture folder, censorship file no. 1, ENHS.

119. See Collier to Dyer, 1 February and 9 February 1910, motion picture folder, censorship file no. 1, ENHS.

120. Charles V. Trevis, "Censoring the Five-Cent Drama," *World Today*, October 1910; reprinted in Mast, *Movies in Our Midst*, p. 69. Michael Davis also praises the work of the board in substantially decreasing the number of "morally objectionable" films; see *The Exploitation of Pleasure: A Study of Commercial Recreation in New York City* (New York: Russell Sage Foundation, 1911), p. 34.

121. H. N. Marvin, Direct Examination, "USA vs. MPPC and Others" vol. 3, p. 1,282. See also the 15 January 1910 letter from Charles Sprague Smith, the

board's first director, to Frank Dyer, arguing that Pathé should not be allowed to advertise its films as approved by the Board for fear that that would "tend to discredit the censorship," moving picture folder, censorship file, ENHS.

122. "Regulation of the Cheap Theaters," *Chicago Record-Herald*, 2 May 1907, p. 8.

123. See George Kleine's 10 April 1907 letter to the *Chicago Tribune*, printed in *Moving Picture World*, 20 April 1907, p. 102.

124. See J. Austin Fynes, "Motion Pictures," *Views and Films Index*, 11 January 1908, p. 4; and Collier, "Cheap Amusements," p. 74. The former manager of Keith's Union Square Theater and Proctor's Theater, Fynes operated a number of nickelodeons in the New York area, in association with Miles Brothers.

125. See, for instance, Josiah Strong, *The Challenge of the City* (New York: Eaton & Mains, 1907), pp. 116–118; Sherman C. Kingsley, "The Penny Arcade and the Cheap Theatre," *Charities and Commons*, 8 June 1907, p. 295; William Bullock, "How Moving Pictures Are Made and Shown," *Moving Picture World*, 10 August 1907, pp. 359–360; "Film Shows Win the Press," *Views and Films Index*, 23 May 1908, p. 5; and Collier, "Cheap Amusements," p. 75.

126. See, for instance, the "New York morning paper" that reported, in the spring of 1906, that fifty-two thousand immigrants had entered the city within a period of just four days (cited in Brander Matthews, "The American of the Future," *Century Illustrated*, July 1907, p. 474).

127. Between 1891 and 1900, according to the United States census, 52.8 percent of the new immigrants came from eastern and southern Europe; between 1900 and 1909, the figure rose to 71.7 percent—Frank V. Thompson, *Schooling the Immigrant* (New York: Harper & Brothers, 1920), pp. 29–30. That most of those from Russia, and probably Poland and Austria-Hungary as well, were Jewish has been established by Erich Rosenthal, "The Equivalence of United States Census Data for Persons of Russian Stock or Descent with American Jews: An Evaluation," *Demography* 12 (May 1975): 275–290.

128. "An Unexplored Field and Its Possibilities," *Views and Films Index*, 6 October 1906, pp. 3–4.

129. "Censors Inspect Nickel Theaters," *Chicago Tribune*, 1 May 1907; and "Cheap Shows Lure: Police Aim a Blow," *Chicago Record-Herald*, 1 May 1907.

130. "Correspondence," *Moving Picture World*, 1 June 1907, p. 202; Currie, op. cit., p. 49.

131. Joseph Medill Patterson, "The Nickelodeons, The Poor Man's Elementary Course in Drama," *The Saturday Evening Post*, 21 November 1907, reprinted in George Pratt, *Spellbound in Darkness: A History of the Silent Film* (Greenwich: New York Graphic Society, 1973), p. 48. See also "Low Priced Theatres," *Moving Picture World*, 1 June 1907, p. 202; and Collier, "Cheap Amusements," p. 75.

132. Frederic Haskin, "Nickelodeon History," *Views and Films Index*, 1 February 1908, p. 5.

133. See, for instance, Currie, op. cit. pp. 50–51; "The Nickel Craze in New York," *Views and Films Index*, 5 October 1907, p. 3; "Moving Picture News from Everywhere," ibid., 28 March 1908, p. 6; and H. F. Hoffman, "What People Want: Some Observations," *Moving Picture World*, 9 July 1910, p. 77. One possible source

for determining what films were shown in the New York nickelodeons would be the documents of the Motion Picture Exhibitors Association, formed in June 1907 and led by William Fox—see, for instance, Daniel Czitrom, "The Politics of Performance: From Theater Licensing to Movie Censorship in Turn-of-the-Century New York," *American Quarterly* 44 (December 1992): 533–536.

134. One can argue that nickelodeon exhibitors followed the model already set by vaudeville managers during the 1880s and 1890s, when the latter transformed their theaters into centers of "family" entertainment. See Robert C. Allen, *Vaudeville and Film, 1895–1915: A Study in Media Interaction* (New York: Arno, 1980).

135. See "The Propriety of Some Film Subjects," *Views and Films Index*, 11 May 1907, p. 3.

136. "Nickel Theatres Crime Breeders," *Chicago Daily Tribune*, 13 April 1907; and Elizabeth Beardsley Butler, *Women and the Trades: Pittsburgh, 1907–1908* (New York: Russell Sage Foundation, 1908), pp. 333–334. See also Peiss's ground-breaking study in *Cheap Amusements*, pp. 139–162.

137. "The Nickelodeon," Mast, *Movies in Our Midst*, pp. 44–45.

138. See "Trade Notes," *Views and Films Index*, 15 June 1907, p. 4; "Business in Massachusetts," ibid., 22 June 1907, p. 3; the Radium ad, *Des Moines Register and Leader*, 29 May 1907; and the Lyric ad, ibid., 23 July 1907.

139. McCarahan, "Chicago's Great Film Industry," p. 4. See also F. C. Aiken, "Moving Pictures a National Industry," *Show World*, 14 December 1907, p. 24.

140. "Editorial," *Views and Films Index*, 21 September 1907, p. 4.

141. Collier, "Cheap Amusements," p. 74.

142. Jane Addams, *The House of Dreams* (New York: Macmillan, 1909), reprinted in Mast, *Movies in Our Midst*, p. 72; and Davis, op. cit., pp. 29–30, 34–35.

143. See, for instance, Mayne, op. cit., pp. 32–40; Hansen, *Babel and Babylon*, pp. 90–125; Ben Singer, "Female Power in the Serial-Queen Melodrama: The Etiology of an Anomaly," *Camera Obscura* 22 (1990): 91–129; and Lauren Rabinovitz, "Temptations of Pleasure: Nickelodeons, Amusement Parks, and the Sights of Female Sexuality," *Camera Obscura* 23 (1990): 91–106.

144. Matthews, op. cit., p. 477. See also Michael Kammen, "Millions of Newcomers Alien to Our Traditions," in Kammen, *Mystic Chords of Memory: The Transformation of Tradition in American Culture* (New York: Knopf, 1991), pp. 228–253.

145. See Herbert N. Casson, "The Americans in America," *Munsey's Magazine* 36 (January 1907): 436.

146. Matthews, op. cit., p. 476. Interestingly, Matthews also drew attention to the contribution (out of all proportion to their numbers) of early French Protestant immigrants to the American concept of citizenship; but he also deliberately excludes both African-Americans and Asian-Americans.

147. Leach, *Land of Desire*, p. 5.

148. Strong, op. cit., p. 153.

149. Kammen, op. cit., p. 244. See also "Low Priced Theatres," p. 202.

150. See "Nation-Wide Wave of Motion Pictures," *New York Times*, 3 January 1909.

151. See also the turn-of-the-century French sociologist, Gabriel Tarde, whose influential theory of imitation included the notion that imitative behavior took

place in a semiconscious state. For an analysis of Tarde's social theories, see Susanna Barrows, *Distorting Mirrors: Visions of the Crowd in Late Nineteenth-Century France* (New Haven: Yale University Press, 1981), pp. 137–161; and Rosalind H. Williams, *Dream Worlds: Mass Consumption in Late Nineteenth-Century France* (Berkeley, Los Angeles, London: University of California Press, 1982), pp. 342–384.

152. Michael Denning, *Mechanic Accents: Dime Novels and Working-Class Culture in America* (London: Verso, 1987), pp. 172, 202–203.

153. F. Marion Crawford, *The Novel: What Is It* (New York, 1893), p. 23, quoted in Tom Lutz, *American Nervousness, 1903* (Ithaca: Cornell University Press, 1991), p. 29.

154. For two excellent studies of the construction of an "American" subject in turn-of-the-century magazines, advertisements, and best-sellers, see Amy Kaplan, "Romancing the Empire: The Embodiment of American Masculinity in the Popular Historical Novel of the 1890s," *American Literary History* 2 (winter 1990): 659–690; and Richard Ohmann, "History and Literary History: The Case of Mass Culture," in *Modernity and Mass Culture,* ed. James Naremore and Patrick Brantlinger (Bloomington: Indiana University Press, 1991), pp. 24–41.

155. See the interviews with Robert Bachman of 20th Century Optiscope and an unidentified "Chicago film man," in "The Popularity of Films Grows," *Show World,* 13 July 1907, p. 10.

156. Archie Bell, "American Actors Fail in France," ibid., 28 September 1907, p. 3. Although Bell is speaking about stage performance, his attitude was shared by many of the Chicago renters interviewed in *Show World.*

157. See, for instance, the O. T. Crawford ad, ibid., 2 November 1907, p. 36. Crawford was a very successful renter and exhibitor, headquartered in Saint Louis.

158. W. Livingston Larned, "The Public and the Filmmaker," *Views and Films Index,* 25 January 1908, p. 3. Larned may have been a pseudonym for a young man whom J. Austin Fynes described, in his brief introduction, as a freelance writer "of 'scenarios' for play-pictures."

159. See, for instance, "Editorial: Public Opinion as a Moral Center," *Moving Picture World,* 11 May 1907, pp. 147–148.

160. James D. Law, "Better Scenarios Demanded," ibid., 29 August 1908, pp. 153–154. Lary May refers to another critic asking for "American subjects" in June 1908 but does not provide a specific citation (May, *Screening Out the Past: The Birth of Mass Culture and the Motion Picture Industry* [Chicago: University of Chicago Press, 1980], p. 64).

161. "The Moving Picture Field," *New York Dramatic Mirror,* 6 June 1908, p. 6.

162. "Interview with Carl Laemmle," *Moving Picture World,* 5 June 1909, p. 740.

163. See, for instance, "Western Plays Hold the Stage," *Chicago Tribune,* 4 November 1906; and James C. Dahlman, "The Cowboy in Drama," *Show World,* 21 December 1907, p. 24. In May 1907, Buffalo Bill's Wild West Show returned to the United States after a five-year tour of Europe and received a tumultuous welcome over the course of three annual farewell tours.

164. *The Cattle Rustlers,* which survives at the National Film Archive in London, nicely exemplifies the so-called superiority in plotting which the trade press was beginning to single out in American films vis-à-vis "foreign films"; see, for instance,

"Earmarks of Makers," *New York Dramatic Mirror,* 14 November 1908, p. 10. For an analysis of Selig's development of the western genre between 1907 and 1909, see Robert Anderson, "The Role of the Western Film Genre in Industry Competition, 1907–1911," *Journal of the University Film Association* 31 (spring 1979): 22–24. See also Denning, op. cit., p. 203.

165. "An American School of Motion Picture Drama," *Moving Picture World,* 20 November 1909, p. 712.

166. "What Is an American Subject?" ibid., 22 January 1910, p. 82.

167. "American vs. Foreign Films," *Film Index,* 10 April 1909, p. 7. *Views and Films Index* changed its name to *Film Index* in October 1908.

168. Vitagraph became involved in a similar strategy of producing "quality" films at this time; see Roberta Pearson and William Uricchio, *Reframing Culture: The Case of Vitagraph Quality Films* (Princeton: Princeton University Press, 1993).

169. See David Hulfish, "Colored Films of Today," *Nickelodeon,* January 1909, p. 15; and Palmer, "The World in Motion," p. 356.

170. The Orpheum (with seven hundred seats) became a moving picture theater in November 1907; see Charles Morris, "The Chicago Orpheum Theater," *Nickelodeon,* January 1909, pp. 3–5. The Alhambra became the Unique; both Keith theaters became Bijou Dreams; see "New Name for Twenty-Third Street," *New York Dramatic Mirror,* 4 January 1908, p. 14; "Unique Theatre," *Variety,* 15 February 1908, p. 11; "Manhattan a Money Maker," ibid., 22 February 1908, p. 10; "Pictures at Union Square," *New York Dramatic Mirror,* 22 February 1908, p. 13; and Palmer, "The World in Motion," pp. 357, 359. Most of these new cinemas offered longer programs (of approximately one hour), small orchestras, and uniformed attendants.

171. For a list of New York vaudeville houses turned into moving picture theaters, see "The Moving Picture Field," *New York Dramatic Mirror,* 6 June 1908, p. 6. In New York, in the summer and fall of 1908, William Fox and Marcus Loew were two leaders in this conversion; both used these large "movie houses" to establish major cinema chains. See also Allen, op. cit., pp. 9–13; Czitrom, op. cit., pp. 536–537; Bowser, op. cit., pp. 121–129; and Gomery, op. cit., pp. 29–37.

172. See the photograph of the Olympic Theatre and accompanying caption (it seated 1,475) in *Views and Films Index,* 9 May 1908, p. 6. The Swanson Theatre, on 39th Street and Cottage Grove, seated seven hundred; see "William Swanson's New Theater," *Show World,* 27 June 1908, p. 26c.

173. See, for instance, "Future Pathé Films," *Views and Films Index,* 11 April 1908, p. 3; "Stories of the Films," *Moving Picture World,* 28 November 1908, p. 433; "Reviews of New Films," *New York Dramatic Mirror,* 9 December 1908, p. 8; "First in Pantomime Art: Pathé Frères' Films D'Art Lead the World in Finished Film Production," ibid., 1 May 1909, p. 38; and "Looking Forward," *Film Index,* 7 August 1909, p. 2.

174. "Moving Picture Reviews," *Variety,* 28 November 1908, p. 10.

175. The ending of the initial scenario for this film, which was cut in the revised version, had the executioner hold up Mary Stuart's severed head for the audience's pleasure; see the Pathé-Frères Scenario Collection, Département des Arts et Spectacles, Bibliothèque Nationale, Paris.

176. "A French Sample," *Variety,* 2 January 1909, p. 10.

177. "Comments on Film Subjects," *Moving Picture World,* 27 February 1909, p. 236. See also "Correspondence," ibid., 6 March 1909, p. 277.

178. "Reviews of New Films," *New York Dramatic Mirror,* 27 February 1909, p. 13. Before the film was shown in New York, it was being treated much like a new French stage production; see, for instance, "'Film d'Art' Plays," *New York Daily Tribune,* 3 December 1908.

179. "Spectator's Comments," *New York Dramatic Mirror,* 11 September 1909, p. 15.

180. One question demanding further research is whether certain kinds of films (produced by certain companies) tended to be shown in nickelodeons and others tended to be shown in the vaudeville houses or new "movie houses," especially during the transition period of 1908 to 1910.

181. See "Pathé Notes," *Film Index,* 20 November 1909, p. 2.

182. The Pathé ads in the *Chicago Tribune,* for instance, ran from 10 February to 27 March and singled out the genres of comedy, tragedy, travel pictures, educational films, juvenile films, and historical pictures. See also "Pathé Pointers," *Film Index,* 26 March 1910, p. 6, and "Novel Advertising Campaign," *New York Dramatic Mirror,* 26 March 1910, p. 20.

183. W. C. S., "What Is an American Subject," *Moving Picture World,* 12 February 1910, p. 206. A change in attitude toward the acting style in Pathé films seems to have occurred in parallel with this demand for American subjects: Even Frank Wood, who generally praised Pathé's actors, began to assert the values of American acting versus European acting; see his "Spectator's Comments," *New York Dramatic Mirror,* 20 November 1909, p. 15, and 11 December 1909, p. 15. For more on the issue of acting style during this period, see Hansen, *Babel and Babylon,* pp. 78–79; and Roberta Pearson, *Eloquent Gestures: The Transformation of Performance Style in Griffith Biograph Films* (Berkeley, Los Angeles, London: University of California Press, 1992), pp. 10–12.

184. Although announced during the spring, this studio was not completed until December ("Pathé American Studio Announced by Mr. Berst," *Film Index,* 9 April 1910, pp. 1, 3; "New Pathé Studio," *New York Dramatic Mirror,* 9 April 1910, p. 21; "New Pathé Studio," *Film Index,* 6 August 1910, p. 3; and "Berst Returns," ibid., 8 October 1910, p. 2. For further information on Pathé's strategy in Russia, see Richard Abel, "Pathé's Stake in Early Russian Cinema," *Griffithiana* 38/39 [October 1990]: 242–247).

185. Pathé westerns ranged from *Indians and Cowboys* (1904) to *Indian Justice* (1907) and *The Hostage* (1908), the latter of which *Variety* singled out as a "perfect example of Pathé craft and popularity" ("Moving Picture News and Reviews," *Variety,* 25 January 1908, p. 11). According to a New York Child Welfare survey in late 1910, young boys who were frequent filmgoers preferred "Indian and Cowboy" pictures above all others; see "Pictures that Children Like," *Film Index,* 21 January 1911, p. 3. See also Davis, op. cit., pp. 29–30, 34–35.

186. *Pathé Weekly Bulletin,* 16 May 1910. The company's success with its westerns can be gathered from "News from America," *Bioscope,* 9 June 1910, p. 29; "Topics of the Week: The Popularity of Western Films," ibid., 18 August 1910, pp. 4–5; and "Editorial," *Moving Picture World,* 15 October 1910, p. 867.

187. Anderson, op. cit., p. 25, n65.

188. See, for instance, Owen Wister, "The Evolution of the Cow-Puncher," *Harper's Monthly,* September 1895, pp. 602–617. For arguments about the Anglo-Saxon, masculine turn in American mass culture in the early twentieth century, see Denning, op. cit., pp. 204–206; Kaplan, op. cit., pp. 659–690; and Jane Tompkins, *West of Everything: The Inner Life of Westerns* (New York: Oxford University Press, 1992).

189. See "Pathé Film Selection," *New York Dramatic Mirror,* 23 April 1910, p. 20; and "Notes from the Manufacturers: Pathé," *Moving Picture World,* 16 July 1910, p. 165.

190. By late 1911, Pathé had set up its own distribution office, CGPC, in order to release imported French features and used General Film to distribute its American product, including the popular newsreel, *Pathé-Weekly.* After a year of less than stellar results, CGPC was reorganized as the Eclectic Film Company, whose principal success would turn out to be not French films but the famous *Perils of Pauline* serial (1914), starring Pearl White. For further information on the development of feature-length films, see David Bordwell, Janet Staiger, and Kristin Thompson, *The Classical Hollywood Cinema: Film Style and Mode of Production to 1960* (New York: Columbia University Press, 1985), pp. 128–134; Bowser, op. cit., pp. 191–215; and Abel, *The Ciné Goes to Town,* pp. 298–388.

191. Charles Pathé finally acknowledged this exclusion from the American market in the company's 1920 stockholders meeting; see "Pathé-Cinéma," *Information financière, économique, et politique,* 26 September 1920, p. 3.

192. Denning, op. cit., pp. 201–213.

193. Charles M. Harvey, "The Dime Novel in American Life," *Atlantic Monthly,* July 1907, pp. 37–45.

194. Denning, op. cit., p. 202.

PART THREE

Ephemerality and the Moment

EIGHT

Panoramic Literature and the Invention of Everyday Genres

Margaret Cohen

"The anarchy of the halflight of the everyday."
MICHEL DE CERTEAU, QUOTING GEORG LUKÁCS

From the first shorts of Thomas Edison and the Lumière brothers, cinema has been fascinated with representing the everyday. The following essay argues that such fascination marks one of cinema's important roots in the nineteenth century. My argument takes as starting point a materialist lineage of cultural theory which proposes the everyday as a historically specific form of daily life emerging along with the problematic this lineage characterizes as "modernity."[1] For thinkers like Walter Benjamin, Henri Lefebvre, and Michel de Certeau, the everyday designates the way individuals' daily gestures of production and reproduction are shaped by the conjunction of the capitalist logic of surplus value, industrialization, urbanization, and the increasing atomization and abstraction of the bourgeois-dominated social formation.[2]

Much important work has been done on cinema's prehistory in nineteenth-century technologies of the spectacle. But if modernity is also characterized by a historically specific phenomenology, a full account of cinema's genesis requires a genealogy of intelligibility: cinema's prehistory in nineteenth-century ways of making sense of the world.[3] As Benjamin's work on Baudelaire suggests, one cultural site where this historically specific phenomenology takes concrete shape is in the nineteenth century's invention of new representational strategies and genres. What, I ask here, does the cinematic representation of the everyday share with nineteenth-century everyday genres?[4]

The greater part of my essay will be spent describing important features of a characteristic nineteenth-century genre for representing the everyday. My attention will be to what we might call an everyday genre for representing the everyday: a genre that is part of everyday experience with minimal

227

transcendent aesthetic claims. The essay closes by indicating points of comparison between nineteenth-century everyday genres and the first cinematic shorts. I choose this point of cinematic reference because the early shorts are closest in time to nineteenth-century everyday genres. I also choose them in adherence to the materialist precept that, as Richard Terdiman puts it, "in the period of its early institutionalization a sociocultural form leaves traces of its operation which later, as it solidifies its domination, become considerably harder to detect."[5] In addition, early cinema has the advantage of clearly being an everyday genre, a popular form of spectacle. The status of cinema's relation to the everyday becomes more complex as its aesthetic ambitions increase.

JULY MONARCHY PANORAMA

In France, the social transformations at issue in the problematic of modernity emerged across the middle decades of the nineteenth century. The July Monarchy (1830–1848) was the beginning of that emergence, the time when the bourgeoisie came to cultural, political, and economic dominance.[6] The genesis of modernity is characterized by the creation of the everyday as practice. It is also characterized by the conceptual emergence of the everyday, the recognition of everyday life as a valid object of scientific inquiry.

The conceptual attention given the everyday during the July Monarchy has played an important role in intellectual developments with what used to be called "world historical" impact. Henri Lefebvre writes that "in the nineteenth century the axis of thought was redirected from speculation towards empirical practical realism, with the works of Karl Marx and the budding social sciences forming landmarks on the line of displacement."[7] Numerous watershed events emblematize July Monarchy France's contributions to the redirection. This was the period when Auguste Comte invented sociology and when Adolphe Quetelet devised the statistical concept of the average man.[8] "Engels told me how in 1848 in Paris in the Café de la Régence, one of the first centers of the Revolution of 1789, Marx for the first time put forth to him the economic determinism of his theory of a materialist conception of history."[9] With these words, Paul Lafargue dramatized Marx's first exposition of a theory grounding the movement of world history in the daily gestures of production and reproduction.

Along with the recognition of everyday life as a valid object of scientific inquiry, the July Monarchy saw the emergence of the everyday as a valid object of representational attention. Such attention resulted in a number of new representational genres. I focus here on one of these genres, collections of descriptive sketches of contemporary Parisian life and habits inaugurated by *Paris, ou le livre des cent-et-uns* (1831). "The plan of this book is very simple," wrote the publisher Ladvocat in his introduction. "Modern Paris will parade by; we will show it as it is, undecided, capricious, angry, impatient, poor, bored, still thirsting for art and emotions but moved only with difficulty, often absurd, sometimes sublime."[10] Contributions to *Le Livre des cent-et-uns* were provided by leading members of the literary establishment of the time. A selection of titles from its first volume indicate the variegated nature of the reality it put on display: "The Palais-Royal," "The Parisian Bourgeois," "The Jardin des Plantes," "Artist Soirées," "Public Libraries," "To M. de Chateaubriand," "Political Ingratitude," "Opening Night," "The Morgue." The collection's format, Ladvocat claimed in his preface, was absolutely modern. This was "a new book if ever there was one; new in its content, new in its form, new in its procedure of composition which makes it a kind of encyclopedia of contemporary ideas, the monument of a young and brilliant period."[11]

With his multivolume collection, Ladvocat inaugurated an ephemeral July Monarchy genre that Walter Benjamin has termed panoramic literature.[12] Other titles include *Paris au XIXe siècle* (1841); *Recueil de scènes de la ville de Paris* (1838); *Le Museum parisien* (1841); *Le Prisme, encyclopédie morale du XIXe siècle* (1841–1850); *Les Français peints par eux-mêmes* (1840–1842); *Scènes de la vie privée et publique des animaux* (1842); *La Grande ville, nouveau tableau de Paris, comique, critique, et philosophique* (1842–1843); *Le Diable à Paris, Paris et les parisiens* (1845–1846).[13] Like the panoramas to which Benjamin compared it, the panoramic genre aimed to give a masterful and entertaining overview of the present.

Benjamin compared panoramic literature to a visual medium not only to emphasize the scope of its project but also to emphasize the important role these texts accorded visual illustration. The panoramic texts pursued their ambitions to represent the present by juxtaposing descriptions of daily Parisian life and lithographs illustrating these descriptions. This format grounds the panoramic genre in the same technological innovations that enabled the consolidation of the mass press. As Richard Sieburth comments, panoramic books were "byproducts of the recent technological advances in printing and paper manufacturing which had made illustrated books more commercially feasible."[14] If the panoramic texts were closely related to the inexpensive *physiologies*—mass-produced pamphlets providing description and commentary on contemporary social types, institutions, and mores—these more expensive books were consumed in a different social space.[15] Sieburth notes that "whereas such deluxe albums as Curmer's *Les Français peints par eux-mêmes* were designed to take their place within the cozy confines of the bourgeois *intérieur*, . . . the physiologies were aimed instead at the buyer off the street."[16]

The details of everyday life were central to the panoramic texts' descriptions of contemporary social practice. From the grocer and the grisette

opening *Les Français peints par eux-mêmes* to the description of the daily
press in *La Grande ville,* from vignettes on how Parisians greet each other
in *Le Diable à Paris* to commentary on a most humble object of daily urban
survival, the umbrella, in the chapter of *Le Livre des cent-et-uns* entitled "The
Parisian Bourgeois," these volumes are replete with material belonging
to the uneven fabric of daily Parisian experience. "Count then how few
moralists have deigned to enter into these simple details of daily life," wrote
the eminent literary critic Jules Janin in his introduction to *Les Français
peints par eux-mêmes,* giving epistemological dignity to a zone that aristocratic society had dismissed as trivial and banal.[17] Janin continued:

> Yes, let us consider this, a day will come when our grandchildren would like
> to know who we were and what we were doing *in those days;* how we were
> dressed, what dresses our women wore; what our houses were like, what were
> our habits, our pleasures; what we understood by beauty, this fragile word
> which is eternally undergoing transformations? They will want to know ev-
> erything about us: how we rode our horses, how we dined, what were our fa-
> vorite wines? What type of poetry did we prefer, did we powder our hair or
> wear boots with cuffs? To say nothing of a thousand other questions that we
> dare not foresee, which would make us die of shame, and which our neph-
> ews will pose to us out loud as the most natural questions.[18]

Panoramic literature is but one short-lived genre of the everyday produced during the July Monarchy. If its limited production suits it to the fi-
nite field of the essay, I use it to encapsulate the July Monarchy contribution to a number of representational genres whose importance continues
into the present. The realist novel is at the high end of the spectrum; this
most celebrated nineteenth-century genre for representing the everyday
emerged in France during the July Monarchy.[19] Balzac described his novels as providing readers with "the history that so many historians forget,
that of *moeurs.*"[20] His attention was to the *moeurs* of postrevolutionary society. "This drama is neither a fiction nor a novel," he wrote at the opening
to *Le Père Goriot. "All is true* [English in the original], it is so true that everyone can recognize its elements at home, in the heart perhaps."[21] The mass
press is at the everyday end of the spectrum of everyday genres. This genre,
too, was consolidated during the first decade of the July Monarchy. "July 1
1836, Emile de Girardin succeeds in putting into practice the simultaneously social and technical idea that has haunted him for five or six years:
that of a cheaper daily paper [*quotidien*] that will have, as a result, more
readers and which will thus attract advertising."[22] As Terdiman has observed, the homonym of the newspaper and the category of the everyday
studied by cultural theory is more than fortuitous.[23] A celebrated genre of
modernity's everyday, the mass daily plays a vital role in the processes of
consumption and exchange constituting this form of daily life.

PARISIAN ZOO

The panoramic texts announce an epistemological project allying them with the nascent social sciences. Janin's introduction makes clear that the panoramic text's stated aim is to give an objective overview of the phenomena constituting contemporary everyday experience. We might term this aim the project of panoptic representation, invoking Foucault's visual figure for the epistemological and institutional practices framing such an ambition.[24] The phenomena to come under the panoramic text's panoptic gaze range from typical people and places to customs and habit, likes, dislikes, quirks, and memories.

Various features of the panoramic genre clearly serve its stated project of panoptic representation. The panoramic text approaches the phenomena of daily life with the characteristic panoptic gestures of description and classification. The close attention to external, above all visible, material details (objects, clothes, physical appearance, food, gestures, weather, speech) gives the reader vivid access to the sensuous materiality of contemporary Parisian reality. The panoramic text simultaneously treats this materiality as the key to the less visible social relations structuring the present. Thus, to return to the humble umbrella in "The Parisian Bourgeois," the narrator dwells with loving care on who uses the object, concerned to get its social semiology just right:

> Ignorant painters always weigh him [the bourgeois] down with an umbrella; this is one of the crudest prejudices that ill-will and partisan politics [*l'esprit de parti*] have ever spread. The umbrella belongs to people living off unearned income, to employees, that is to say to the invalids and eunuchs of industrial society. The Paris bourgeois has a cane to give himself presence, to chase away dogs and to threaten rascals. But he is not afraid of bad weather; if it starts to rain, he takes a cab, as he tells you with a satisfied air.[25]

In addition to providing objective information on the contours of everyday life, the panoramic text's attention to detail functions as a rhetorical performance related to Barthes's "effect of the real." Giving texture to the tiniest corners of daily life, it conveys a sense of the density of everyday experience, of its lived complexity.

The panoramic genre's treatment of place functions similarly to its treatment of objects and daily details. Panoramic texts map the contours of contemporary Paris with great precision. This precision gives "real" information on daily Parisian life. In addition, it constitutes a rhetoric emphasizing these texts' exact grounding in a referentially verifiable space. The fact that all panoramic texts represent a single geographical location also adds to their reality effect; Paris recurs as a stable object across textual variation.[26] The existence of this object is, moreover, one that the reader can verify. Paris is a celebrated place for visits and is frequently represented in other genres with claims to referential accuracy.

Panoramic texts evince a characteristic narrational mode: They are composed of micronarratives with no direct continuity from plot to plot. Their narratives' temporal concentration is accompanied by a concentration of subject matter. Panoramic texts focus on a knowledge that the structuralists might have called a "Parisianeme," a distinctive minimal unit of Parisian life. This minimal unit is presented from the viewpoint of a single narrator. The micronarrative is a textual index of the panoramic text's scientific ambitions. Brevity is a principle of encyclopedic narrative, as the encyclopedic article "concentrates *the maximum* of knowledge in *the minimum* of time."[27] In his introduction to *Le Livre des cent-et-un*, Ladvocat calls his text "a kind of encyclopedia of contemporary ideas."[28]

The variety of contributing authors is another essential feature of the panoramic genre. From the first *Livre des cent-et-uns*, the panoramic text stresses that its diverse authorship constitutes a substantial divergence from previous descriptive texts about Paris. That these authors write in a variety of genres is also an important characteristic of panoramic texts. The generic spectrum of *Les Français peints par eux-mêmes* runs from a detailed physical and moral description of the grocer by an "objective" narrator to a fictionalized novella about a lady of fashion who implicitly exemplifies the type named by the text's title. The spectrum also includes an encounter with that paragon of respectable, chic, and seductive Parisian womanhood, "la femme comme il faut," from the mobile subjective viewpoint of an individual strolling through everyday reality (*flâneur*), a satirical description of the art apprentice (*rapin*), and a poem glorifying the young girl.

In other examples of panoramic literature, what I will call this genre's constitutive *heterogenericity* is yet more varied. To describe contemporary Paris, for example, *Le Diable à Paris* opens with a factually accurate "history of Paris." It passes to a satirical-fantastic prologue representing Hell, then moves on to a letter that a devil sends from Paris to his master, a description of Parisian class stratification addressed to this devil by George Sand, an ethnographic description of "how Parisians greet each other," and a generically hybrid "album" meditating on "what constitutes a Parisian woman," with maxims, opinions, fragments of dialogues, an extract from one such creature's own "album," an example of her memoirs, and a fairy tale.

The editors of the panoramic texts relate the panoramic genre's multiple authors and heterogenericity to its panoptic aims. The introduction by the editor of *Le Livre des cent-et-un* states that postrevolutionary social reality has grown too complex to be encompassed by a single individual.

> What writer could suffice for this multiplied and tricolored Paris? Who would suffice for these small graces, these sharp angers, these stormy passions? Pas-

sions of old people, passions of young men, passions of women, passions of heroes. Paris trembles, Paris threatens, Paris cries to arms, Paris wants to go to war, Paris wants to remain calm, Paris bursts out laughing, Paris cries and sobs, centrist Paris, extreme Right Paris, extreme Left Paris; what writer would want to take this monster in hand!

Well then! Give up unity for a manifold painting, call all contemporary imaginations to your aid.[29]

When Janin rewrites this topos in his introduction to *Les Français peints par eux-mêmes,* he shifts the focus from individual authors to the discourses they employ. He makes the point that the panoramic text's diversity is not just a diversity of individuals but a reflection of social heteroglossia.[30] Janin explains this heteroglossia as a consequence of the revolution.

The more French society found itself divided, the more the study of *moeurs* became difficult. This great republic was cut up in so many small republics, each one of which has its laws, its customs [*usages*], its jargons, its heroes, its political opinions in the absence of religious beliefs, its ambitions, its short-comings and its loves. . . . Now, how could the same moralist, the same writer of *moeurs* penetrate in all these far-away regions when he knows neither the roads, nor the language, nor the customs? How could the same man understand all these strange dialects, all these languages that are so diverse?[31]

De Certeau asserts that with the inception of modern science, the novel became "the zoo of the practices of everyday life."[32] During the July Monarchy, de Certeau's statement is even truer of the panoramic genre, if we understand representational genres themselves to figure among a society's daily practices. For while the realist novel (the form that de Certeau designates as the nineteenth-century novel *tout court*) unifies its representations of daily life within the framework of a single genre, open-ended as it may be, the panoramic text uses clearly differentiated genres to represent differing social species. The young girl is painted with poetry, the woman of fashion with a sentimental novella, the grocer with a detailed portrait similar to those found in realist narratives.

This point is literalized in a panoramic text that took a trip to the Parisian zoo as its organizing conceit. *Scènes de la vie privée et publique des animaux* (1842) starts off as a revolution in the Jardin des Plantes. "Here," the introduction tells us, "the Animal worries about Man and judges him in judging himself." *Scènes de la vie privée et publique des animaux* systematizes the panoramic text's use of differing genres to represent different aspects of social reality. Each animal species is distinguished by a characteristic species of narration. Balzac's "Peines de coeur d'une chatte anglaise" studies contemporary *moeurs* among the fine flower of cat aristocracy with conventions familiar from his *Scènes de la vie privée*; Sand's proletarian sparrow in search of a better world employs the genre of political allegory to talk about the differing political and economic organizations of animal kingdoms and republics; Madame Menessier Nodier's "Lettres d'une hirondelle à une sérine élevée au couvent des oiseaux" uses an epistolary exchange marked by the generic conventions of the sentimental novel to describe the vicissitudes of feminine life.[33]

TWILIGHT AT THE ZOO

These features of the panoramic text do not all further its stated panoptic project. The fact that the text is the product of multiple authors works against—as well as bolsters—its claims to social authority. Each author may well represent a distinctive face or jargon of Parisian reality. No overarching subjectivity, however, steps forward to guarantee the referential veracity of the panoramic whole.

The panoramic genre's heterogenericity only accentuates the hermeneutic complexities introduced by its lack of authorizing point of view. The panoramic text mixes up genres that position themselves in relation to contemporary reality in widely differing fashions. *Les Français peints par eux-mêmes* is the panoramic text where the mix-up is the most muted. The physico-moral portrait of a type offers social reality through objective transcription; the novella constitutes "reality plus," holding up the more faithful mirror in its resort to make-believe; the satirical description exaggerates social reality; the poem glorifies it; the texts of flânerie alloy social reality with another subject's fantasy, speculations, and offhand "spontaneous" thoughts. *Le Diable à Paris* is the panoramic text where the relation of representation to Parisian referent varies most. To understand Paris and the Parisians (*Le Diable à Paris*'s subtitle), the reader negotiates a spectrum ranging from straightforward history and impressionistic ethnography to frankly fantastic scenarios, descents into hell, a Paris where supernatural creatures intermingle with the common spectacles of everyday life.

As a result of such mix-up, panoramic texts generate little referential stability through their narrative practices. The reader must decide for him- or herself how to sort through representational anarchy, how to negotiate texts whose representational codes and referential claims differ widely, how to read through these codes to the reality they represent.[34] This anarchy induces a form of reader response which is a characteristic feature of panoramic texts, as well as of everyday genres more generally. Rather than offering the secure position of objective mastery proposed in its opening panoptic claims, the panoramic text pushes the reader towards what Lukács has called "the anarchy of the half-light of the everyday."[35] It throws the reader into an epistemological twilight, a state where objective knowledge, externally verifiable experience, socially sanctioned fictions, and individual phantasmatic projection interact in unstable and unruly fashion. Henri Lefebvre makes the point that this interaction encourages the intrusions of the reader's own fantasy life into the seemingly stable, referentially verifiable details of external social reality when he characterizes the reader response solicited by everyday genres of his own present. He writes of the generically uneven woman's magazine (the woman's magazine assumed its modern form in July Monarchy France):[36]

> A single issue may include practical information on the way to cut out and sew up a dress or precise information such as where and at what price to buy another, alongside a form of rhetoric that invests clothes and other objects with an aura of unreality: all possible and impossible dresses, every kind of dish from the simplest to those whose realization requires the skill of a professional, garden chairs and occasional tables, furniture worthy of a castle or a palace.[37]

He writes of the more homogeneric genre of the horoscope:

> What, indeed, do people expect from horoscopes, why do they consult them, how do they interpret the signs and how are they influenced by the interpretations? A zone of *ambiguity* is established half way between belief and make-believe, yet directed towards action by justifying individual tactics so that those concerned believe and do not believe what they say, and behave as if they believed, while following their own inclinations, feelings, or interests—their vaticinations.[38]

ANOTHER POINT OF VIEW

Heterogenericity is only one example of the fondness of panoramic texts for categorical transgression. This transgression can occur in the relation of micronarrative to micronarrative, or within one narrative frame (the panoramic text's interest in the *album* form). It can occur through the juxtaposition of texts holding out differing opinions on the same subject, sometimes by the same author: Arsène Houssaye's "Why One Leaves Paris," "written with a view of Berg-op-Zoom," immediately followed by "Another Point of View" from Harlem in *Le Diable à Paris.* It occurs as thematic heterogeneity: Panoramic texts are peopled by figures who incorporate categorical transgression into their social being. In *Les Français peints par eux-mêmes,* Janin's grisette is a "strange assemblage of beauty and wretchedness, of ignorance and art, of intelligence and apathy."[39] Grandville's animals in *Scènes de la vie privée et publique des animaux* constitute the imagistic equivalent of such strange assemblages in their odd and inconsistent mixtures of social and animal species. "One evening my mistress asked one of the young Misses to sing," states the English cat, Beauty, and Grandville illustrates the sentence with a "young Miss" who is part dog and part human, and who is clad in human dress (fig. 8.1). To what social species does the creature belong?

Un soir, ma maitresse pria l'une des jeunes Miss de chanter.

Fig. 8.1. "One evening my mistress asked one of the young Misses to sing."
Illustration by J.-J. Grandville. In *Scènes de la vie privée et publique des animaux*.
Paris: Hetzel and Paulin, 1842.

The panoramic genre also transgresses categories in the way it brings together visual and verbal representations. In "Une Mère de famille" from *Le Diable à Paris,* Gavarni juxtaposes this commonplace phrase from bourgeois ideology with an image of a disheveled woman wearing the longshoreman costume then fashionable at masked balls. On her head, she wears a kerchief tied in a shape reminiscent of the revolutionary Phrygian cap.

Such categorical transgression can help introduce readers into the twilight zone, throwing them into "the anarchy of the half-light of the everyday." When de Certeau details the consequences of this mix-up, he makes the point that the epistemological twilight zone is not simply the suspect realm where knowledge is diluted by phantasmatic deviation. For de Certeau, the juxtaposition of "*qualitatively heterogeneous dimensions*" provides one potentially creative opening in the repetition and habit of the everyday.[40] This repetition tends to reproduce the dominant social formation. De Certeau finds that the juxtaposition of qualitatively different elements, in contrast, produces an experience with the potential to reconfigure it in new and illuminating ways. He terms the experience "the occasion."

> The occasion always escapes definitions because it cannot be isolated from a conjuncture or an operation. It is not a fact that can be separated from the 'trick' [*tour*] that produces it. Inscribed in a sequence of elements, it twists their relations. It expresses itself there as *torsions* produced in a situation by bringing together *qualitatively heterogeneous dimensions* that are no longer only oppositions of contraries or of contradiction.[41]

The occasion produces knowledge illuminating the situation in a minimal moment of encyclopedic brevity. De Certeau terms this knowledge a knowledge of praxis, irreducible to theory, inseparable from the moment in which it occurs. "Reduced to its most minimal format, in an act transforming the situation, this concrete encyclopedia partakes of the philosopher's stone."[42] De Certeau finds the representational analogue to this moment of the occasion in what he calls "*the minimal unit.*"[43] "It can have a comic form with the memory which, at the right moment, turns a situation around—of the sort: 'But . . . [*sic*] you are my father!' 'Good God, my daughter.' . . . There is a form found in thrillers, where the past, in returning, overthrows the givens of a hierarchical order: 'He is then the murderer!'"[44] A similar dramatic use of the minimal unit is common to all manner of panoramic categorical transgression, exemplified, for example, by the clichéd phrases which Gavarni provides as punch lines to his images.

For de Certeau, the occasion is a moment producing a knowledge disrupting established hierarchies and orders. If we return to the transgressions of the panoramic genre, we see them work a similar overthrow. Thus, Janin's grisette and Grandville's "young Miss" indicate the limits of

the nineteenth-century project to classify social difference with categories
from eighteenth-century natural science. In the case of Gavarni's "Mère
de famille," the juxtaposition of image and text complicates the important
bourgeois ideologeme of the "mother," opening it towards frivolity, towards sexuality, towards politics, towards the carnival of the established
social order. At the same time, we remember that during the July Monarchy, the carnival is a constitutive part of that order. Misogynistic representations of seemingly proper women engaged in all manner of socially
transgressive behavior are common in a cynical, materialist discourse of the
bourgeoisie. It would thus be a mistake to align the transgression of categories in everyday genres with a uniform politics of resistance. Such resistance may or may not be at issue; each instance of transgression needs to
be understood and evaluated on its own.

THE PHANTOM REFERENTIALITY OF THE EVERYDAY

Following theorists of the everyday, we may understand the distinctive
features of the panoramic genre as bringing to representation distinctive
features of modern daily life. The panoramic text's use of discontinuity
captures the discontinuities in sense perception characterizing the urban
metropolis and processes of industrial production, what Benjamin has
famously termed the shocks of the modern life. Its brevity brings to representation the way the logic of capital penetrates the interstices of the
everyday. If the production of surplus value is the fundamental motor of
capitalism, capitalist economic processes are characterized by a construction of temporality as transformation—specifically, as expansion and innovation. In the domain of everyday life, these processes take the form
of practices of the ephemeral, where the new is valorized for a brief moment and then discarded: advertising, fashion, the newspaper.

The discontinuities of the everyday genre can also be seen as seizing
aspects of the phenomenology of the commodity form. The commodity
works through mobilizing the subject's desire. As Lefebvre points out, in
daily life this mobilization is necessarily discontinuous, intermittent. In the
realm of the everyday, we conflate our use of objects to assuage a material
need with the psychical satisfaction of desire: "We might say that everyday
life is the place of desire, so long as we specify that it is also—indeed primarily—the nonplace of desire, the place where desire dies of satisfaction
and re-emerges from its ashes . . . the power of material objects is part
of everyday life . . . everyday life tends to merge with material objects,
whereas desire does not—which is the secret of its power."[45]

The everyday genre's zone of ambiguity registers one more feature of the commodity's phenomenology. As Marx suggested with his famous notion of commodity fetishism, in capitalist society, commodities are simultaneously material objects and representations of material processes which they both abstract and screen. These processes are the human labor that produced them.[46] As a result, commodities occupy an epistemological twilight that Benjamin found emblematized in the halflight filtering through the arcades (one of their privileged July Monarchy sites of display). They have a curious "melting" presence that Benjamin as well as Marx termed "phantasmagorical."[47]

The domain of rhetoric provides a useful way to clarify the commodity's phantasmagorical displacement from itself. If, as Marx suggested, the commodity's material objecthood derives its power from the fact that it is an abstraction of the material processes of human labor, this operation can be expressed with a rhetorical analogy. The commodity's literal existence is always already figurative, an expression of the processes of production and circulation which lend commodities their appeal. The commodity thus has a referential presence akin to the rhetorical figure of catachresis; it is fundamentally "improper."[48] A catachresis is a literal signifier that is always already a figure: We have no "proper" term for the "leg" of a table, the "arm" of a chair.

Panoramic texts may be responding to this aspect of the commodity form in their own fascination with the "improper." This fascination is visible, for example, in their treatment of social space. The panoramic text's grounding in referentially verifiable space in part reinforces its panoptic project, as does its interest in classifying and ordering the activities of city life. At the same time, however, the panoramic text is not content to classify the city from on high. Rather, it descends to experience unsystematically the interstices of the city. The experience of wandering in the city figures prominently in its descent. According to de Certeau, the experience of urban wandering takes place in an epistemological twilight. For de Certeau, wandering both seeks the "proper" and displaces it precisely in an arena where the "proper" would seem most immovable: space.

> To walk is to lack a place. It is the indefinite process of being absent and seeking a proper. Wandering, which multiplies and brings together the city, makes of it an immense social experience of the loss of place—an experience, it is true, eroded in countless and minute deportations (displacements and promenades), compensated for by the relations and crossings of these exoduses, which constitute intertwinings creating an urban fabric, and placed under the sign of what should ultimately be place but which is only a name, the City.[49]

Circulation is the term for the displacement of the "proper," both in the discourse of the commodity and the discourse of flânerie.

THE IMAGE STANDARD

When Terdiman characterizes the July Monarchy newspaper's use of the image, he suggests it as an example of disjunctive heterogenericity that works to destabilizing effect. "In the image, distinction itself receives an authentically differential signifier."[50] This occurs in part because

> images were *new*. As a form immediately distinguishable from the dense flux of printed text, *as image*, visual representation in the satirical daily could serve distinctively as a representation of the Other: as an alternative to the dominant real, to its discourse, to its characteristic system of expression. . . . Lithography thus remained for some time under the sign of its difference, as the medium of *specifically oppositional, counter-discursive illustration.* The medium itself was, in this early period, a distinctive *sign* of protest and critique.[51]

Panoramic literature, too, depends on the lithographic image crucial to the newspaper, and the same caricaturists contributed to newspapers and to the panoramic genre. But in panoramic literature, the image functions somewhat differently. The panoramic image, as I now want to show, is a vehicle of homogenization rather than of disjunction, exhibiting the diversity of neither genre nor artist characteristic of panoramic literature's written texts. As a result, the image here does not function in counterdiscursive fashion. Rather, it works to facilitate the reader's introduction into the twilight zone of everyday genres.

If the contrast between the panoramic genre's imagistic and textual practice is evident from the first work in the genre, it is most visible in *Les Français peints par eux-mêmes*. This collection includes textual genres that gesture to referential experience in oscillating fashion. On the level of the image, in contrast, an *identical* series of portrayals punctuates every micronarrative. The narrative is introduced by an image the table of contents identifies as the "type," a full-page, full-body representation of the character under discussion, dressed in typical costume and striking a distinctive pose. External social setting is almost always effaced, and the character is shadowed as if placed under the scrutiny of a light (fig. 8.2). The narrative is uniformly punctuated by two smaller forms of images: the "page heading" (*tête de page*) providing a view of the species's environment, and the "letter" (*lettre*), a bust of the character where the first letter appears, more or less ingeniously worked in (figs. 8.3, 8.4). Many of the narratives conclude with a smaller third image as well: a "tail-piece" (*cul de lampe*) providing a typical scene from the character's life, often connected with his or her characteristic pleasures.[52]

The mutation of scale, perspective, and scope of visual field differentiating these imagistic forms might best be described in photographic terms as the lithographic equivalent to different kinds of shots. To call them

Fig. 8.2. The "type" for "L'Epicier." Drawn by Gavarni. In *Les Français peints par eux-mêmes*. Paris: L. Curmer, 1840.

L'ÉPICIER.

Fig. 8.3. The "tête de page" for "L'Epicier." Drawn by Gavarni. In *Les Français peints par eux-mêmes*.

genres would be overstating the case, for despite differences in imagistic form, all the images position the reader in similar fashion in relation to the reality they represent. (The whimsical improvisations with the letter are the only deviation from this similarity.) They offer slightly pointed, but not particularly satirical, exaggerations of the salient features of the character under discussion. That the images unfold in regular sequence and predictable pattern reinforces their stabilizing effect.

The image in the panoramic text also creates an effect of stability through the way it displays the presence of the illustrating hand. Stylistic differences among images are minimal for one of two opposing reasons, both of which work to similar effects. Either one or a select few artists do all or most of the images and set the style for the rest, or the images are by anonymous artists who mute their stylistic differences. As index of this treatment of images, we may look at the way panoramic texts credit their illustrators. Either the panoramic text completely effaces the identity of the artists producing its images, or it links all images to a minimal number of master artists. Thus, while the introduction to *Le Livre des cent-et-un* credits at least 101 writers, it credits no artists for its largely (but not entirely) decorative figures. Grandville does all the illustrations in *Scènes de la vie privée et publique des animaux*, although the volume collects texts by multiple authors. The dedicatory page of the first volume of *Les Français peints par eux-mêmes* lists all of its authors but only the two principal July Monarchy caricaturists, Gavarni and Monnier, who provide and sign all its types. In fact, a number of illustrators assisted Gavarni and Monnier in the pro-

Fig. 8.4. The "lettre" for "L'Epicier." Drawn by Gavarni. In *Les Français peints par eux-mêmes*.

duction of the secondary images. They are, however, absent from the title page and do not identify themselves in their drawings. The secondary illustrators receive credit only in the concluding tables of contents.

This contrast in the panoramic genre's textual and imagistic diversity works to specific readerly effect: Images intervene in the textual economy in which they appear. Providing a stable form of symbolic representation across authorial difference and heterogeneric textual codes, images help unify multiplied and tricolored texts into one panoramic whole. The deployment of the image as leveler among authorial diversity, social heteroglossia, and textual heterogenericity is a characteristic feature of the panoramic genre.

The contrast between the mutating text and the homogenizing image is not identical in every panoramic work. A heterogeneric use of illustration characterizes *Le Diable à Paris*. The images in this text range from panoramas of old and new Paris, satirical sketches of hell, and whimsical drawings of animated objects of daily life to sketches where, similar to the "types" and "têtes de page" of *Les Français peints par eux-mêmes*, typical Parisian figures and scenes are slightly schematized but not in particularly satirical fashion. Nonetheless, even here, I would argue, imagistic diversity is restrained when compared to textual diversity. The ratio of artists to authors credited can serve as index of this restraint. In the one-volume edition of *Le Diable à Paris*, the 1845 *Le Tiroir du Diable*, five illustrators supply images for twenty-three authors.

In any case, *Le Diable à Paris* does not negate the homogenizing tendency of the image in other examples of the panoramic genre. Nor does it negate the homogenizing tendency of the image in modernity more generally. Visual theorists have analyzed this tendency, working from the starting-point of photography, a medium that carries on the anonymization of the image already initiated by lithography. Jonathan Crary writes that "photography is an element of a new and homogeneous terrain of consumption and circulation. . . . As Marx said of money, photography is also a great leveler, a democratizer, a 'mere symbol,' a fiction sanctioned by the so-called universal consent of mankind."[53] What Crary calls the "photography effect" is better named the "image effect," for, as Crary himself observes, photography is but one medium in which this deployment of the image can occur. We might also call it the image *standard*.

> Since the *image* does not disclose what has been transformed into it, everything, *representation* or not, is convertible into *image*. . . . Not even are the bones of saints, and still less are more delicate *res sacrosanctae extra commercium hominum* [sacrosanct things outside the commerce of men] able to withstand this alchemy. Just as every qualitative difference between *representations* is extinguished in the *image*, so the *image*, on its side, like the radical leveler that it is, does away with all distinctions.[54]

In this paragraph, I have rewritten a passage from *Capital*'s "Money or the Circulation of Commodities" by changing "gold" to "image" and "commodity" to "representation." I can do so because while Marx here diagrams the structure of economic value in capitalist society (the form of value which capitalist society equates with value *per se*), his diagram applies to the structure of value in capitalist society more generally, including the structure of symbolic value. The image is the gold of modernity's symbolic field.

The image standard, too, belongs to the twilight zone of everyday genres, furthering at least two conflicting readerly effects. On the one hand, it supports the panoptic project, offering the promise of an authoritative metalanguage in a situation of discursive instability. This use of the image will find its fulfillment in the documentary use of photography, a medium inaugurated during the July Monarchy, and in the documentary use of film. At the same time, however, the panoramic image derives its power from another aspect of the image in modernity: its important role in the subject's social access to his or her desires. We privilege the image because of the importance of the visual in the complex phenomenology of the commodity form. To cite Guy Debord:

> This is the principle of commodity fetishism, the domination of society by 'intangible as well as tangible things,' which reaches its absolute fulfillment in the spectacle, where the tangible world is replaced by a selection of images which exist above it, and which simultaneously impose themselves as the tangible *par excellence*.[55]

My rewriting of Marx on the gold standard is thus doubly motivated: because Marxian notions of value hold true across modernity's different practices of value *and* because the visual occupies a privileged place in Marx's analysis of how value is *experienced* in modernity. Seen from this angle, the image standard has a phantasmatic as well as panoptic dimension, furthering the ebb and flow of the reader's fantasy with the text.

Discussions of the power of the image in modernity have overwhelmingly been preoccupied with its link to the phenomenology of the commodity. Introducing the notion of the image standard, I want to stress that the image's appeal cannot be explained by reference to the economic practices of modernity alone. It must be understood, too, by resituating the image among the complicated discursive and semiotic practices framing it. The image standard, I have argued, results from the image's power to intervene *inter-semiotically*, to provide a common currency unifying the discursive chaos that characterizes the abstract and complex social formations of modernity.

JUMP CUT

In this essay, I have used panoramic literature to exemplify salient features of nineteenth-century everyday genres. To conclude, I want to gesture to the continuity between nineteenth-century everyday genres and early cinema. The nature of this continuity is, it should be stressed, the subject of another essay that would discuss the variegated relations constituting historical causality. There certainly is a direct lineage leading from nineteenth-century everyday genres to the first cinematic projections, as the fact that Méliès got his start staging popular visual spectacles suggests. At the same time, nineteenth-century everyday genres and cinema are effects of the practices structuring the modern everyday.

Like nineteenth-century everyday genres, early cinematic shorts are fascinated with everyday life. "Yes, let us consider this, a day will come when our grandson would like to know who we were and what we were doing *in those days*," as Janin wrote. Among these daily activities, Janin included "how we were dressed" (Lumière, *Baby's Quarrel*); "what dresses our women wore" (Biograph, *Those Awful Hats*); "what our houses were like" (Lumière, *The Demolition of a Wall*); "what were our habits" (Lumière, *Cockfight*); "our pleasures" (Edison, *The Kiss*); "how we understood beauty" (Gaumont, *A Fine Woman*); "how we rode our horses" (Lumière, *Train Entering the Station*); "how we dined" (Lumière, *Baby's Lunch*); "what were our favorite wines" (Edison, *The Eating Contest*); "what type of poetry did we prefer" (Edison, *Annabelle Serpentine Dance*); and "did we powder our hair or wear boots with cuffs" (Edison, *Sandow Flexing His Muscles*).

I have also suggested that everyday genres are characterized by the juxtaposition of minimal distinctive units. Early cinema makes use of the minimal distinctive unit; indeed, Tom Gunning has suggested this use as one of early cinema's defining features. Gunning finds that it characterizes what he describes as the cinema of attractions. He notes that "the cinema of attractions directly solicits spectator attention, inciting visual curiosity and supplying pleasure through an exciting spectacle—a unique event, whether fictional or documentary, that is of interest in itself."[56]

The minimal distinctive units at issue in the early cinematic shorts cover a range of everyday subject matter similar to that covered in the panoramic text. In many panoramic entries, the minimal unit is a distinctive social type (Edison, *Old Maid in a Drawing Room* [the old maid was played by the female impersonator Gilbert Saroni]). But the unit can also be a geographical site (Lumière, *The Tuileries Basin*); a historical event from the distant past or the more recent present (Lumière, *The Landing of the Congress Participants* [Congress of Photographers] *at Neuville-sur-Saône*); a distinctive custom, institution, or happening (Lumière, *Cardgame*), or even a distinctive Parisian discourse, sometimes one associated with a distinctive contemporary social type, as in a chapter from *Le Diable à Paris* entitled "Leaves from the Album of a Young Art Apprentice" (Gaumont, *The Neo-Impressionist Painter*). In cinema, as in panoramic texts, the subject matter at issue in these distinctive units can range well beyond common experiences in the modern, urban everyday. The equivalent of *Le Diable à Paris*'s range of subject matter is promised by "THE MARVELOUS ELECTRIC PHANTOSCOPE":

> By means of this wonderful invention, you see a perfect reproduction, full life-size, of the living originals, every act and motion absolutely perfect even to the wink of an eye. Repertoire includes two acts from Trilby; one act from 1492; Carmencita, Sousa's Band; dances, fist fights, Annabelle in the Sun and Serpentine dances; a cock fight, and numerous other interesting subjects.[57]

Gunning suggests the notion of the cinema of attractions to include the two pioneers of cinema who have been used to exemplify the two opposing poles of cinematic illusion. "Whatever differences one might find between Lumière and Méliès, . . . one can unite them in a conception that sees cinema less as a way of telling stories than as a way of presenting a series of views to an audience. . . . The cinema of attractions . . . is a cinema that bases itself on . . . its ability to *show* something."[58] My characterization of everyday genres allows us a further insight into a feature unifying Lumière's and Méliès's practice. I have suggested that everyday genres introduce the reader into an epistemological twilight zone. The films of both Lumière and Méliès, I think, do just that, unmooring the separation of reality from representation, albeit in rather different ways. (If the distinction between Lumière and Meliès has been drawn with such emphasis, it is perhaps because this unmooring is a disconcerting feature of everyday genres.)

Dai Vaughan glosses "a story so frequently repeated as to have assumed the status of folklore [which] tells how members of . . . [Lumière's] first audiences dodged aside as a train steamed towards them into a station. We cannot seriously imagine that these educated people in Paris and London expected the train to emerge from the screen and run them down."[59] Vaughan explains: "It must have been a reaction similar to that which prevents us from stepping with unconcern on to a static escalator, no matter how firmly we may assure ourselves that all it requires is a simple stride on to an immobile flat surface. What this legend means is that the particular combination of visual signals present in that film had had no previous existence *other* than as signifying a real train pulling into a real station."[60] Perhaps. But could not these spectators rather have been theatrically registering their pleasure at being transported into the epistemological twilight of everyday genres? Such reactions have by no means disappeared with the maturing of cinema and its audiences. We still use our bodies to stage our participation in its halflight, a participation facilitated by our lack of self-consciousness in the darkened space where cinematic projection occurs. I bite my nails, avert my eyes, smile, feel tears welling up at moments drawing me into cinema's zone of ambiguity with compelling force.

A similar epistemological twilight is generated in the work of Méliès. I have suggested that panoramic literature juxtaposes texts, positioning the reader in unstable relation to the reality they represent without providing a single authority to guide the reader through their variation. We can, I think, see a related instability in the way Méliès's films refuse to take responsibility for locating the "reality" of their representation. There is no stable alignment of filmic technique with the film's "reality" or "fantasy"; the viewer lacks a guide on the level of the code. Thus, to take the example of the sequences making up the *Dream of a Rarebit Fiend*: the fantasy of the fiend's illusion is sometimes depicted with obviously trick photography, sometimes with neutral photography that derives its fantastic quality from its place in the narrative sequence in which it is inserted, sometimes with obviously painted scenery, and sometimes with characters dressed up in fantastic fashion or objects manipulated illusionistically. This instability concerning the constitution of the illusion is exhibited in the final sequence, where the rarebit fiend crashes through the ceiling back from his dream into ordinary reality and his bed. The final frame does not show whether the ceiling was demolished "in reality" or only in the fiend's imagination: What is the referential status of the depicted event?

In cinema, the photographic image replaces the dialogue between textual diversity and lithographic stability. The panoramic genre's constitutive heterogenericity, however, is not lost. It can become, as we have seen, an effect of narrative: generic difference among micronarratives (the different kinds of films collected in one program), or, as with Méliès's film, a referential instability produced by shifting codes of representation within the scope of one narrative flow. It can also penetrate the image standard itself. In early cinema, this penetration occurs when the seemingly stable photographic image is unmoored from its referential function, its "proper" place (the dancing lamppost in the *Dream of a Rarebit Fiend*). It also occurs when text or drawn images are inserted into photographic uniformity. In Gaumont's *Merry Bacteria,* the animated bacteria mutate from pseudo-medical drawings into social caricatures of the patient who had started out claiming that he has never felt better in his life. He feels increasingly unwell, however, as he contemplates these mutations. As if to literalize the cause for his destabilization, the film concludes with the doctor smashing the image that has become the measure of all things: he breaks a framed picture over his patient's head.

Finally, it should be remarked that cinema carries through on some distinctive features of everyday genres which were not completely realized in the panoramic text. In large measure, it is able to do so as a consequence of its new technology.[61] Thus, I have detailed the panoramic text's attack on the author's power to guarantee the reality of social relations he or she represents.[62] The panoramic text performed this attack by multiplying authors but did not do away with the guaranteeing subjectivity of individual authorial presence. The reality of a cinematic sequence, in contrast, appears an effect of the operation itself. This is particularly true of early cinema, which does not yet restore the effaced author as it will when it lays claim to the realm of Art.

Benjamin writes, "Lithography enabled graphic art to illustrate everyday life, and it began to keep pace with printing. But only a few decades after its invention, lithography was surpassed by photography."[63] Photography not only kept pace with everyday life but also proved better able to accommodate a feature of the image standard only imperfectly served by the image practice of the panoramic text. While lithography provides a stabilizing note in discursive diversity, the medium inscribes the trace of the illustrating hand. With photography, this trace gives way to the pencil of light.[64] The image's link to an individual producer is, however, still implicit in the photograph's single point of view. Moving pictures erase the mark of the individual on viewpoint. With the invention of cinema, the image standard finds a medium adequate to its illusion.

NOTES

1. The term generalizes a wide variety of social practices in uneven and not always homologous relation to one another. I designate modernity as a problematic to make the point that the term is a site of critical debate rather than a firmly established thing.

2. For a critique and contextualization of Lefebvre's work, see Alice Kaplan and Kristen Ross, eds., *Everyday Life*, Yale French Studies no. 73 (New Haven, 1987). The editors comment, "When it is successful, everyday life analysis offers a new alternative to a subject/object opposition so basic to postwar continental thinking as to correspond to its major intellectual movements: phenomenology and structuralism. By this we mean that everyday life is situated somewhere in the rift opened up between the subjective, phenomenological, sensory apparatus of the individual and reified institutions" (p. 3).

3. Stanley Cavell makes a related point using the notion of medium: "The invention of the photographic picture is not the same thing as the creation of photography as a medium for making sense" (Cavell, *The World Viewed* [Cambridge: Harvard University Press, 1979], p. 38).

4. In this essay, I use the notion of genre to designate a set of representational codes shared by a set of texts. My assumption is that these codes extend to the way a text positions the reader or viewer towards the reality it represents, a positioning deriving from the relation a text constructs among implied author, subject matter, and implied reader or viewer. I thus fuse what Fredric Jameson suggests as the two traditional poles of genre theory: the apprehension of genre as a mode (the phenomenological approach) and as a model (the structuralist approach) (see Jameson, "Magical Narratives: Romance as Genre," *New Literary History* 7, no. 1 [autumn 1975]: 137).

5. Richard Terdiman, *Discourse/Counter-Discourse* (Ithaca, N.Y.: Cornell University Press, 1985), p. 120.

6. On the residue of aristocratic dominance in the July Monarchy social formation, see François Furet's chapter on the July Monarchy in Furet, *Terminer la Révolution* (Paris: Hachette, 1988), pp. 121–209.

7. Henri Lefebvre, *Everyday Life in the Modern World*, trans. Sacha Rabinovitch (London: Penguin, 1971), p. 12.

8. Quetelet set forth the notion in *Sur l'homme et le développement de ses facultés, ou essai de physique sociale* (1835). A Belgian scientist, Quetelet published this

important book in Paris where he had received his statistical training in the 1820s. On Quetelet's connections with Paris, see Stephen Stigler, *The History of Statistics* (Cambridge: Harvard University Press, 1986), p. 162.

9. Cited from Walter Benjamin, *Das Passagen-Werk*, in *Gesammelte Schriften* (Frankfurt: Suhrkamp, 1983), vol. 5, pt. 1, p. 164. Unless otherwise noted, all translations from German and French are my own.

10. "Au public, le libraire-editeur," in *Paris, ou le livre des cent-et-un* (Paris: Ladvocat, 1831), vol. 1, p. vi.

11. Ibid., vol. 1, p. ix.

12. The panoramic genre is a subgenre of a more durable Parisian everyday genre, the *tableaux de Paris,* although a discussion of the relation between later *tableaux de Paris* and panoramic literature is beyond the scope of the article.

13. Translations of these titles are: Paris or the Book of the Hundred and One; Paris in the Nineteenth Century; Collection of Scenes from the City of Paris; The Parisian Museum; The Prism, Moral Encyclopedia of the Nineteenth Century; The French, Painted by Themselves (less literal but more elegant would be French Self-Portraits), Scenes from the Private and Public Life of Animals; The Great City; New Comical, Critical, and Philosophical Picture of Paris; The Devil in Paris; Paris and the Parisians.

14. Richard Sieburth, "Same Difference: The French *Physiologies*, 1840–1842," in Sieburth, *Notebooks in Cultural Analysis* (Durham: Duke University Press, 1984), p. 166.

15. On the *physiologies*, see also Judith Wechsler, *A Human Comedy* (Chicago: University of Chicago Press, 1982).

16. Sieburth, op. cit., p. 166.

17. Jules Janin, *Les Français peints par eux-mêmes* (Paris: L. Curmer, 1840), vol. 1, p. iv.

18. Ibid., vol. 1, p. v. Emphasis in original.

19. On the realist novel and the everyday, as well as on the novel and the everyday more generally, see Mikhail Bakhtin, *The Dialogic Imagination,* trans. Caryl Emerson and Michael Holquist (Austin: University of Texas Press, 1981).

20. Honoré de Balzac, "Avant-propos à la *Comédie Humaine*," in *Oeuvres complètes* (Paris: Gallimard, 1976), 1:11.

21. Honoré de Balzac, *Le Père Goriot*, in *Oeuvres complètes* 3:50.

22. Claude Bellanger et al., *Histoire générale de la presse française* (Paris: Presses Universitaires de France, 1969), 2:114.

23. Terdiman notes that "the daily paper itself takes a privileged place as figure for the constant, recurring practices by which daily life is produced and reproduced" (Terdiman, op. cit., pp. 119–120).

24. On the value and limits of the notion of the panopticon for characterizing nineteenth-century panoramic representations of Paris more generally, see Christopher Prendergast, *Paris and the Nineteenth Century* (Cambridge: Blackwell, 1993), p. 47.

25. *Le Livre des cent-et-un,* vol. 1, pp. 42–43.

26. Even *Les Français peints par eux-mêmes,* which claims to represent the spectrum of contemporary French society, offers in practice an inventory of the inhab-

itants of a central urban metropolis, a great many of whom participate in specifically Parisian institutions of social life.

27. Michel de Certeau, *L'Invention du quotidien* (Paris: Union Général d'Editions, 1980), p. 157.

28. *Le Livre des cent-et-un,* vol. 1, p. ix.

29. Ibid., vol. 1, pp. vi–vii.

30. The term "heteroglossia" is used by Mikhail Bakhtin to designate "the internal stratification of any single national language into social dialects, characteristic group behavior, professional jargons, generic languages, languages of generations and age groups, tendentious languages, languages of the authorities, of various circles and of passing fashions, languages that serve the specific sociopolitical purposes of the day, even of the hour" (see Bakhtin, op. cit., pp. 262–263).

31. *Les Français peints par eux-mêmes,* vol. 1, p. ix. It is important to recognize the limits of the social spectrum represented in the panoramic texts. As Sieburth suggests, these texts represent a fundamentally bourgeois universe. Left-wing, working-class, and criminal figures and discourses appear only in occasional and picturesque fashion.

32. De Certeau, op. cit., p. 151.

33. English translations of these titles are Sorrows of an English Cat, Scenes of Private Life, and Letters from a Swallow to a Canary Raised in the Convent of the Birds.

34. In Sieburth's view, the *physiologies* offer an extreme example of this panoramic emphasis on codes. In them, the referent has simply dropped away: "If they imitate anything, then, it is not contemporary social life, but rather the immense fund of the *déjà-écrit* and *déjà-lu* which Barthes identifies with *la doxa*" (Sieburth, op. cit., p. 173).

35. I take the citation from Michel de Certeau's *L'Invention du quotidien,* p. 333.

36. Anne Higonnet writes: "The women's magazine became a real cultural force only toward the middle of the nineteenth century. More than one hundred fashion periodicals were created between 1830 and 1848" (*Berthe Morisot's Images of Women* [Cambridge: Harvard University Press, 1993], p. 90).

37. Lefebvre, op. cit., p. 86.

38. Ibid., p. 83.

39. *Les Français,* vol. 1, p. 15.

40. De Certeau, op. cit., pp. 158–159.

41. Ibid.

42. Ibid., p. 157.

43. Ibid., p. 161.

44. Ibid.

45. Lefebvre, op. cit., p. 118.

46. Lefebvre writes that "every object and product acquires a dual existence, perceptible and make-believe" (Lefebvre, op. cit., p. 108).

47. I discuss Benjamin's and Marx's understanding of this term at length in *Profane Illumination* (Berkeley, Los Angeles, London: University of California Press, 1993).

48. Derrida develops the relation between the catachresis and Marxian notions

of the commodity in "La Mythologie blanche," in *Marges de la philosophie* (Paris: Editions de Minuit, 1975).

49. De Certeau, op. cit., p. 188.

50. Terdiman, op. cit., p. 150.

51. Ibid., pp. 151–152. Emphasis in original.

52. Occasionally the texts are punctuated by several secondary, smaller format types as well.

53. Jonathan Crary, *Techniques of the Observer* (Cambridge: MIT Press, 1991), p. 13. See also John Tagg, "The Currency of the Photograph," in *Thinking Photography*, ed. Victor Burgin (London: Macmillan, 1982).

54. In this quote, I change "gold" to "image" and "commodity" to "representation." Karl Marx, *Capital*, trans. Samuel Moore and Edward Aveling (New York: Modern Library, 1906), p. 148. Emphasis mine.

55. Guy Debord, *Society of the Spectacle* (Detroit: Black and Red, 1983), chap. 36.

56. Tom Gunning, "The Cinema of Attractions," in *Early Cinema: Space, Frame, Narrative*, ed. Thomas Elsaesser (London: BFI, 1990), p. 58.

57. Ad quoted in Charles Musser, *The Emergence of Cinema: The American Screen to 1907* (New York: Charles Scribner's Sons, 1990), p. 104.

58. Gunning, op. cit., p. 57.

59. Dai Vaughan, "Let There Be Lumière," in Elsaesser, op. cit., p. 63.

60. Ibid.

61. As other essays in this volume illustrate, however, it results also from transformations in the representational practices of everyday genres in the time between the panoramic texts and the invention of cinema.

62. Comparing the magician to the painter and the surgeon to the cameraman, Benjamin writes, "In contrast to the magician—who is still hidden in the medical practitioner—the surgeon at the decisive moment abstains from facing the patient man to man; rather, it is through the operation that he penetrates into him" (Benjamin, "The Work of Art in the Age of Mechanical Reproduction," in *Illuminations*, trans. Harry Zohn [New York: Schocken, 1969], p. 233).

63. Ibid., p. 219.

64. As Martin Jay observes, "So powerful has the assumption of photography's fidelity to the truth of visual experience been that no less an observer than the great film critic André Bazin could claim that 'for the first time an image of the world is formed automatically, without the creative intervention of man.' . . . And even Roland Barthes could argue in his early essay on 'The Photographic Message,' . . . 'Thus can be seen the special status of the photographic image: *it is a message without a code*'" (Jay, *Downcast Eyes* [Berkeley, Los Angeles, London: University of California Press, 1993], p. 126).

NINE

Moving Pictures: Photography, Narrative, and the Paris Commune of 1871

Jeannene M. Przyblyski

Photography is a kind of primitive theater, a kind of tableau vivant, *a figuration of the motionless and made-up face beneath which we see the dead.*
ROLAND BARTHES[1]

Let me begin with this photograph, taken on the barricades hastily erected across the rue Saint-Sebastien on 18 March 1871 (fig. 9.1). Although there are particular things about it that interest me—the frame-filling press of volunteers; the enthusiastic brandishing of guns, drums, and trumpets; the domesticizing presence of women and children—for all that, it is a typical enough image. Dozens like it were made in the popular quarters throughout the city on the day that opened the way for the declaration of the Commune. Bits of play-acting for the camera, they were meant to prove the willingness of Parisians to defend their neighborhoods against hostile invasion. To be sure, resolute citizens such as these had done so when the Prussians had surrounded the city during the long winter months of the siege of 1870–1871, and they now proposed to do the same against a national government scheming to bring the unruly city under its thumb. But on 18 March, this new enemy quickly folded, and the barricades were dismantled, at least temporarily. For the next ten weeks, while the Commune occupied the Hôtel de Ville, business went back to something like usual on the neighborhood streets.

This is an image of urban revolution and one that fairly bristles with the uneasy tensions of modernizing Paris, that much is certain. But as the photographic image, it is nothing if not a strange hybrid. At once a cityscape, a group portrait, a sort of street theater, and a slice of life, it offers us an unstable mix of photographic cues—topographic, physiognomic, and narratological. The mapping of perspectival space interrupted by the span of the barricade, the wealth of specific detail documenting costume and physical appearance woven into the representation of a collective body, the variety of self-conscious poses converging into the spectacle of a *tableau vivant*—all these are bound together, inseparably, on the photograph's

Fig. 9.1. Anonymous, *Barricades on the rue Saint-Sebastien,* 18 March 1871.
(Courtesy of the Bibliothèque Historique de la Ville de Paris.)

frozen surface. Such photographic cues and representational codes were
still in formation in 1871, and just as the photograph disperses any notion
of authorship into the space between cameraman and collective subject, it
is not quite clear just what was expected of its blend of formal gravity and
plein air casualness, of the semiofficial and the improvised, the evidentiary
and the anecdotally eloquent. But these concerns also seem slightly beside
the point. However ambiguously the photograph positions itself within the
emerging discourses of photography, what seems most important is the
conviction with which these men, women, and children faced the camera,
for it speaks to their determined belief not only that they should be photographed at such a moment but also that such a moment—out of the studio and into the streets—should be photographable at all. Standing before the camera's eye, the photograph seems to suggest, might be a way to
occupy history itself, by making it visible and rendering it into an artifact.
Of course, this will toward making visible had much to do with a broad
cultural belief not only in photography's aptitude for topographic and
physiognomic description but also in the facility through which, on the

Fig. 9.2. Alphonse Liébert, *Hôtel de Ville in ruins*, 1871. (Courtesy of the Bibliothèque Nationale de France, Paris.)

basis of its dumbly mechanistic propensity for "truth-telling," photography negotiated more complex claims of possession and presence. These claims were part and parcel of the invention of the medium. It also had something to do with a just-forming notion of another sort of telling—one that connected the surface vividness of the photograph to the storytelling of a specific event.

Side by side with this image of Paris blockaded, let us place another image of the city, equally vivid in its descriptive power, and equally contrary in its mixing of photographic cues (fig. 9.2). Alphonse Liébert's photograph shows the Hôtel de Ville in ruins, burnt down during the *semaine sanglante*, the bloody week of street fighting which ended the Commune in May 1871. Despite the evidence of monumental disaster—the gaping windows and heaps of rubble, the blank absence of the building's gabled, fairy-tale roof—once again, it is not a singular image. Such photographs of "ruined Paris" circulated widely after the Commune fell. Meant in part to support the government's claim that the Communards were little more than common criminals—vandals, arsonists, and murderers—they also lent the city's significant architectural landmarks a satisfyingly antiqued look, perversely attractive to a sophisticated viewer well schooled in the aesthetics of French neoclassicism, who might be expected to make a connection between the fall of Rome and the situation of post-Napoleonic Paris.[2] Topographic document; conservative propaganda; an arty, touristic view of modern Paris (a Paris made strange to the returning bourgeoisie, who had largely fled the city for the duration of the Commune), Liébert's photograph also has another interest. For against an image of the city made visible as property—as both national patrimony and damaged goods—it also records the partial erasure of the city's inhabitants, who are in motion, unmindful that the photograph was being made and so rendered next to invisible.

Taken together, these two images locate us at an important moment in the late nineteenth-century uses of photography and the demands being made upon it. They offer compelling evidence as to what photography recorded then, and what it did not. Against its voracious appetite for immobile, or immobilized, surface detail—the look of a face, the angle of a gesture, the particularities of dress, the lay of the land, the leavings of an architectural facade—we might place photography's occupation of a continual present and the slow fixity of its stare. This was both a strength of photography and, increasingly, a perceived limitation. For in one sense, photography's inability to record movement operated as a given in 1871: People held still in order to be seen by the camera (indeed, as evidenced by the barricade photograph, they played at stillness *for* the camera), or people were not the issue. The displacement of concrete human presence by what we might call effects of "instantaneity"—the residual blurs and snapshot-like imperfections that attest to a photograph's having been made on the spot and under less than ideal conditions—was not expected to be seen in such a photograph as Liébert's, which was *not* meant to be a dynamic image of a city in motion. Instead, these effects constituted the sort of meaningless "afterimages" that were tolerated as inevitable aberrations of a machine's-eye view. In this case, they might even be excused by some viewers, for photography's technical limitations seemed to work to official advantage in Liébert's image by dramatizing that the destruction of property was foremost at issue in the aftermath of the Commune, precisely because it could be made visible (photographically speaking), rather than the loss of life resulting from the Commune's suppression (the summary execution of between twenty and thirty thousand Communard soldiers and civilians which went largely unseen by the camera's eye).

So the camera's limitations could work both ways. And despite—or, perhaps, because of—them, these images suggest that photography was increasingly looked upon as a tool to record not only faces and places but also episodes in "real" time. In general, these photographs speak to the growing tendency throughout the 1860s and 1870s to turn the camera upon contemporary events, as well as to the popular desire that the camera, cumbersome and slow as it was, be there as significant happenings were occurring.[3] Yet this desire, produced out of both the recognition of photography's accomplishments and the envisioning of its future, also helps us to understand how the task of photographing movement (a physiological process that posed a technical problem for photography, one rooted in the speed and acuity of photographic materials and apparatus), while raising one set of questions, seems related to but also different from the task of photographing historical narrative (which suggests not simply a need for mechanical refinement, but, more importantly, the necessity to constitute representational codes through both appropriation and invention). The questions of how to piece together a photographic account of the events of the Commune and what demands would be made upon such an account were predicated not simply upon the ability or inability to excerpt such events from continuous time but likewise upon engineering the intersection between such established narrative cues as the photographic "pose" (that which was eloquent and legibly intended, rooted in existing conventions of both theater and painting) and the photographic "document" as a product of a certain phenomenological attachment—something both uncanny and commanding, conjured out of the aura of "that has been" that clings to the photograph-as-indexical-sign.[4]

To survey the photographic artifacts produced in and around the Paris Commune is to come time and again upon their desire for narrative eloquence; it is to appreciate both their naiveté and their imagining of the modern conventions of photographic reportage, and to note both their strategic economies and their significant absences. Most consistently absent are scenes of action, whether of the fighting on the barricades or the fires of the *semaine sanglante*. Photographers worked around this in several ways. One otherwise little-known cameraman named Leautté juxtaposed "before" and "after" shots of the barricades on the Avenue Victoria in his album *Photographs from Life Under the Commune of Paris*, published late in 1871.[5] In a similar vein, Bruno Braquehais, one of the most significant photographers at work during this period, produced something very close to the modern notion of a photo-essay when he turned his camera upon one of the central events of that spring, the Commune-sanctioned toppling of the Vendôme Column on May 16. Through a series of images, Braquehais focused methodically on the preparation of the column for demolition, the activities of the crowd (who took a special delight in playfully posing before the ill-fated monument), and the spectacle of the column destroyed, its broken image of Napoleon scattered upon the ground. Such photographs were often captioned with references to time—asserting, for example, that a particular image was made just five minutes before the column fell—and we might group these images as examples of narrative "unfolding" accumulating around the idea of a photograph *instantanée*, bound to the imperceptible lapse and sudden capture of time, but also predicated upon the comparative ease of photographic image-making and the ability to proliferate an event across several exposures.

Yet it should be quickly noted that the term *instantanée* is both helpful and unhelpful here. Helpfully, the term points toward the connection increasingly being made between the *actualité*, or practice of journalistic reportage (with its double sense of the "real" and the "topical" and its links to the commodification of news as entertainment), and the instantaneous image made "on the spot." But it is misleading in the way that it invokes our modern notion of instantaneity, a notion binding photography's ability to witness unfolding events to its mechanical propensity for arresting time in such a way as to call attention to itself as a slice of life. The look of such a modern photograph tends to be the now-familiar look of the snapshot (the look that probably passed unnoticed in Liébert's photograph), with its crops and blurs, impromptu angles, false attachments, and abrupt shifts of scale—that is, the set of photographic conventions that made their way from the spaces of the turn-of-the-century family album to the frame of modernist photography, whether the dynamic New Vision of the 1920s and 1930s or the gritty street aesthetic of the 1950s and 1960s. But the snapshot did not come into being until the invention of the handheld box camera in 1888, and the appearance of instantaneity to a viewer of photographs around 1871 is much more troublesome to define.[6]

To be sure, *vues instantanées* were produced during the 1850s and 1860s, and the notion of instantaneity was often attached to a notion of "motion transfixed" or arrested.[7] Yet the look of such instantaneous views is not particularly the look of the Commune photographs. In these earlier examples, the up-close and immediate scrutiny that marks the most compelling of the images made during 1871 was habitually deferred in favor of a panoramic view, one that obviated the problem of figures illegibly blurred by motion by hewing to a higher ground and a greater distance. Moreover, discussions of the potential interest of the *vue instantanée* were habitually tempered by allowances for photography's difficulty in achieving it in practice. In 1855 Ernest Lacan, critic and editor of the photographic journal *La Lumière*, offered an account of one such "instantaneous view" that conveys both great enthusiasm and a probably unintended irony. Speaking of a Crimean battle scene by the Romanian photographer Carol Popp de Szathmari, Lacan wrote:

> In the foreground, the Danube flows tranquilly, as if all were only joy, sunshine, and life on its devastated banks. To the right, the great pontoon bridge below Silistria sketches its somber form against the silvery waters of the river. Further in the distance, on the hilltops over which the wind chases and scat-

ters the whitened clouds, can be seen some intersecting black lines that break off and then reunite in indistinct masses: These are the fighting armies. This is the battle.[8]

The rendering of action into *masses indécises*, the material bleakness of battle vaporized into contrapuntal play with the clouds above: Clearly, the *vue instantanée* was something of a trade-off. On the one hand, it offered a sense of exact location and the vicarious thrill of "being there." On the other hand, it threatened to disperse this hard-won immediacy into mere photographic effect, an effect more pictorially decorative than descriptively vivid, and one whose generalized terms stood in marked contrast to Lacan's responses to other images by Szathmari of the military encampments in the Crimean theater, the troops, and their leaders, in which he lingered equally lovingly upon photography's aptitude for recording costuming, placement, expression, and gesture—a Turkish general's ingenious mélange of oriental and European uniform styles, the gravity of the Russian leaders meeting in conference, the ethnically distinct bearing of a Cossack or Bedouin foot soldier, the picturesque embellishment provided by an improvised camp of a nomadic family following the troops.[9]

Two things interest me about Lacan's reading of Szathmari's photograph *instantanée*. One is the way in which physiognomic and topographic richness, the emotionally moving acuity of detail long associated with photography, could stand in for the experience of a more narrowly defined temporal instantaneity. Indeed, this richness consistently holds its own in comparison with a delight in any marginal success in capturing the effects of physiological movement. The other turns upon the way textual narrative could also make up the difference between the greater sense of immediacy offered by an instantaneous photography and the trade-off loss of the telling detail. For Lacan's writings on photography in general are remarkable for the vigor with which he grafted onto the new technology a model of art criticism bent upon bringing images to life and more broadly rooted in the mid-nineteenth-century discovery of Denis Diderot's lively, but theretofore privately circulated, essays on the Salons of the 1760s.[10] It is as if text and photograph must always supplement one another, each propped upon and borrowing a vividness that the other lacked. And this compensatory double play for photographic stillness and muteness leads me to the second set of narrative conventions which might be said to characterize photography during the Paris Commune. For this set of conventions was based not so much on "narrative unfolding" as on what might be best characterized as "narrative compression" (that is, the impetus to define a "significant moment," to establish a photographic shorthand by which an instance stands in for the entire event). Produced out of the tensions of balancing the as yet unmeetable demand for a photography *instantanée* against the particular sort of vividness that photography *could* provide—a vividness rooted in the legibility of descriptive detail—the impetus toward narrative compression locates us at a particular moment of instability, when photography's smooth functioning within one language of reality-effects intersects the hesitant and provisional search for another.

Well after May 1871, Guglielmo Marconi produced a number of photographs of soldiers fallen in battle, heaped in awkward, tangled masses under the camera's painstaking scrutiny. The series also included a compelling study of two well-dressed bourgeois children, a boy and a girl, sprawled as if in sleep-heavy abandon. Only upon closer scrutiny is one to understand that they have fallen dead under enemy bombardment. Marconi, a studio photographer by trade, regularly produced photographic *académies* for the Ecole des Beaux-Arts, and these new images were intended to be no less so: staged tableaux destined to serve as documentary studies for artists working on large-scale battle scenes or contemporary history paintings related not only to the Commune but also, and this was more likely the case, to the Franco-Prussian War. The photographs were clearly labeled as such when they were placed on deposit in the Bibliothèque Nationale and yet they migrated from this initial frame to that of the *actualité*, appearing as photographs *instantanées*, tendered as having been lifted straight from the scene of confrontation, not only in late-nineteenth-century compilations of photographic artifacts related to the Commune but also in more recent historical accounts.[11]

Clearly, it might be argued that Marconi's theatrical re-creations fall off the mark in their ability to forge a connection between the immediately real and the topical, for whatever look of instantaneity they accrue depends on their misrepresentation as historical artifacts rather than as artist's "documents" and on their misrecognition as images made on the spot. Yet it does not seem so easy to discount a more ambitious and notorious series of photographic inventions, the composite scenes of the capital events of the Commune produced by Eugène Appert and published as *Crimes de la Commune*. These appeared in a number of formats—portfolios, postcards, and *cartes-de-visite*—and were disseminated widely until the official tolerance for images related to the Commune came to an end in December 1871.[12] Cutout portraits, location shots, and complex restagings, often involving many hired extras, were more or less skillfully sutured into single images. Each was envisioned on a grand scale, and one re-creation of the execution of sixty-two hostages on the rue Haxo during the height of the *semaine sanglante* brought together such a crush of "victims" and "villains" that it reportedly necessitated a call for actors "from all the theaters of Paris."[13]

Combinations of the fake and the real, the prop-like and the relic-like, the layered accumulation of fairy-tale illusion and the tissue-thin veneer of documentary truth, like the barricade photographs, Appert's composites were also hybridized objects, complex in their assembling of photographic cues and contrary in the way they complicated the legibility of a photographic point of view. Moreover, like the photographs of ruined Paris, these images did service as conservative propaganda, emphasizing the most sensational "atrocities" committed under the Commune and targeting a middle-class audience eager to justify to itself the Commune's brutal suppression. Yet, like Marconi's images, they quickly became such staples of illustrated accounts of the Commune, whether pro- or anti-Communard, that eventually the line between reality and artificial simulation hardly seemed to matter.

Contemporary historians of photography have tendered this partial fictionalizing of the documentary authority of the photographic sign as an indictment of sorts. Frequently fingered as the "bad guy" in accounts of photography and the Commune, Appert's fakes have been understood to offer a small but pointed homily on the dangers of too gullible a faith in the photographically real and have been condemned as typical of photography's use as a potential vehicle for disinformation.[14] That's right to a certain extent, and yet it seems to me falsely reassuring and falsely flattening in terms of the complex discursive field inhabited by these images. For in one sense it is as if Appert's images might thus be bracketed off from the larger field of photographic discourse, as if the exposure of a rupture in the photographic surface might be sufficient in itself to discount the influence of the photographic message, as if documentary authority were no less constructed in so-called unmanipulated, or straight, photography. In another way, it assumes that the persuasiveness of these images depended upon their being unquestioningly consumed as seamlessly real in 1871. While their illusory effects of reality were no doubt relished by their intended audience—indeed, such effects were precisely the point—I wonder whether this enjoyment precluded understanding them as fakes, or (perhaps better, in terms of contemporary photographic practices) if fakery-as-such would have been as much an issue to a viewer in the 1870s as it is to his counterpart in the late twentieth century, a counterpart whose anxiety about photographic authenticity has been increased (only, perhaps, to be rendered finally pointless) by such virtual-reality techniques as "image-morphing" and matting.[15]

The remainder of this essay grapples with the implications of Appert's contrary mixing of reality and artifice. Its concerns circle around the demands and frames of reference that a contemporary viewer might be expected to bring to these images, as well as the slippages between established viewing habits and potential new ones these images seem to anticipate. The relationship between photography and entrepreneurial practices within the mass media is central to understanding the encounter

between Appert's images and their audience(s), particularly as this encounter engages notions of the photographic "document" and the demands of making history popularly visible as an image. This line of investigation will necessitate looking into not only the practice of composite
photography as it stood in 1871 but also the contingent frames of reference conjoining Appert's work with other practices of visual reportage.
For now, let me suggest across the range of photographs examined thus
far that what was apparently asked of photographic *actualités* in 1871 was
not so much that they capture reality in motion (most spectators would
have granted that this could not be done), but that they exhibit bits of the
"real," that they operate fragmentary and reliclike, with a metonymical
claim to authenticity. In their almost mummified condition midway between
historical artifact and simulated re-creation, there is something about Appert's composite images that seems to me particularly modern and particularly central to understanding the terms by which both photography and
other contemporary modes of mass-imaging were bound up in defining
the conditions by which reality, precisely in terms of the *actualité*, or contemporary event, was to be produced as novelty entertainment.

The first thing that should be said is that composite photography was
nothing new in 1871. Debates about its uses and abuses had preoccupied
amateurs of the new photographic "art" throughout the 1850s and 1860s,
while pieced-together pantheons of the great or merely famous, and con-
cocted glimpses of the Empress Eugénie without her clothes, for example,
were objects of popular fascination and scandal.[16] *The Two Ways of Life,* a
complex and ambitious allegory printed from more than thirty combined
negatives by the English photographer O. G. Rejlander in 1857, was widely
discussed on both sides of the Channel, and Henry Peach Robinson's *Pictorial Effect in Photography: Being Hints on Composition and Chiaroscuro for Photographer,* published in 1869 and soon thereafter translated into French,
concluded with a chapter on using combination printing to achieve natu-
ralistic effects. The eminently successful Parisian photographer and entrepreneur A. A. E. Disdéri tended to dismiss these artful efforts as little
more than "ridiculous simulacras" running a poor second to painting in
the attempt to represent a "reality" both emotionally moving and actively
in motion.[17] Yet his own "mosaic" photographs—most notably those featuring the shapely legs of female dancers—represented another sort of
manipulated image, nonnarrative but still rooted in the techniques of the
composite.[18]

For Appert as well, the manipulated image amounted to nothing more
than more of the same. A composite photograph of Napoleon III and his
generals lined up in stiff little rows outside the emperor's tent at Châlons
on the eve of the Franco-Prussian War suggests that Appert's attempts
to broaden the offerings of his portrait and *carte-de-visite* business by recy-

cling existing images of notables and dignitaries into new, topical products dated from before the Commune.[19] Like Disdéri's photomosaics, works like this belong at the intersection between the artful and entrepreneurial uses of the still-new photographic technology. And dismissing them out of hand as fakes because they do not respect the integrity of the photographic surface does not adequately register the fluid situation of photography at that time, a situation in which such techniques as combination printing and photomontage were among many that a photographer might use in producing a more convincing and true-to-life image.[20]

Moreover, Appert's were not the only composite images associated with the Commune. Charles Soulier, a Parisian photographer who specialized in stereoscopic views and reproductions of artworks, compiled an album of images by several different cameramen, including Appert, Disdéri, and Liébert. The album opens with an image of Paris in flames that is a pastiche of photographic, engraved, and hand-drawn, hand-colored elements, and it later features another composite photograph of the Hôtel de Ville on fire (fig. 9.3). A closer look reveals this last image to be Liébert's photograph of the city hall in ruins, doctored by an unknown hand to include shooting flames, a smoke-filled sky, and little firemen busily wetting down the building with spurting hoses. To be sure, the *photomonteur* did not do a very good job of it here—the flames are clearly hand-drawn, the firemen are out of scale, and the sharpness cut by their active figures is at odds with the blurry bodies of the casual spectators milling about nearby. As one quickly appreciates, Appert's photographs, despite their occasional lapses, are much more accomplished—small wonder that they soon cornered the market in such photographic relics. Still, Soulier's efforts point to a broader demand for images that married the vividness of photography's "reality-effects" to the action-packed events that the camera had not been there to witness, and they militate against understanding Appert's composites as singularly suspicious historical curiosities.

If there were those, like Disdéri, who understood photography to be competing with painting in its quest for a language of visual narrative, then photography's equally recognized and ongoing competition with engraving in terms of reproductive facility, exactitude, and vividness was just as relevant to the reception of Appert's images. Indeed, the two processes of mechanical reproduction were intimately linked from the very invention of photography.[21] During and after the Commune, the histories of photography and engraving intersected within the spaces of popular journalism, most particularly those of such illustrated weeklies as *L'Illustration* and *Le Monde illustré.*[22] Although these publications included poems, fashionable sketches, literary reviews, and puzzles, their main business was in *actualités,* offering the reader a glance across contemporary events in such a way that gave images, often half- and full-page spreads, pride of place.

Fig. 9.3. Charles Soulier, *Hôtel de Ville in ruins*, 1871. (Courtesy of the Bibliothèque Historique de la Ville de Paris.)

These images were, of course, drawings engraved onto wood plates, for the technology did not yet exist to embed photographs in mechanically printed text.[23] Yet photography was by no means invisible or uninvoked within the pages of the illustrated journals. It might even be said that, in 1871, the two processes—photography and engraving—were involved in a series of compensatory exchanges by which the terms of modern visual reportage were to be imagined.

In June of that year, a series of images of the ruined buildings left in the aftermath of the *semaine sanglante* appeared in *L'Illustration*.[24] These images were based upon photographs by Franck Gobinet de Villecholle, and this was the way photography was most typically annexed into spaces of the illustrated journals. The connection to a photographic prototype is credited in the captions, and it also seems important to the particular sort of images these are: topographic views of Paris scarred by revolution, and of a type, as we have seen, common to many photographers working at this time. The ruins are pictured through multiple frames of archways and apertures—the rubble-strewn streets of the modern city seen through timeworn, crumbled forms reminiscent of Roman viaducts. Such engravings are careful in their marshaling of the cues of perspective and comparative scale to channel the viewer into the image and offer a means by which to measure the magnitude of destruction. These are also the visual cues by which engraving claimed a common bond with photography through their mutual connection to such mechanical devices for viewing and drawing as the camera obscura. They are also painstaking in their richness of detail, less like sketches than like tracings of the spidery networks of cracked mortar, the jagged edges of broken lumber and shattered stone. It is as if *L'Illustration* were trying to appropriate the topographic authority of the photographic document, hoping that some of its vivid luster would rub off onto the journal's flimsy, matte pages, even as it was attempting to capitalize on the popularity of photographs of ruined Paris by supplying its own version of the product. And in order to conjure its own effect of the index (of the trace rather than the sketch), *L'Illustration* had to negotiate its depiction of the real at one remove, claiming to see it through photography rather than witnessing it on the spot.[25]

Photography also made its way into the mass press in other, equally telling ways, for the making and merchandising of photographs related to the Commune quickly became integral parts of the Commune's story. On 24 June the *London Illustrated News* featured a sketch on its cover of a cameraman so eager to set up his apparatus amidst the smoldering wreckage of the *semaine sanglante* that he was in danger of crowding out the firemen still battling the flames. Obviously, the image exaggerates the speed with which photographers had rushed to the scene (its joke is as much a matter of wishful invention as the montage in Soulier's album). Yet it was no less an indication that an awareness of photography had thoroughly infiltrated the journalistic coverage of these events. The widespread demand for photographs quickly became a part of the hyped-up haze of notoriety and fascination through which mass journalism participated in the process of mythologizing and commodifying the Commune. In July, Jules Moinaux reported in *Le Charivari* that an English businessman had purchased fifty thousand images of the toppled Vendôme column for sale abroad. These pictures apparently made such a hit that, a few weeks later, Adrien Hunt related an anecdote about an English tourist who had reputedly sent a telegram to the government asking that clean-up of the debris along the rue de Rivoli be delayed until he and his wife had had a chance to "contemplate the disasters."[26] Such commercial opportunities did not go unnoticed by Parisian photographers; that month, Disdéri took out a paid advertisement in the same publication for his *Ruins of Paris and the Surrounding Areas*, billed as complete with an itinerary to aid the diligent tourist in visiting each site.[27]

Appert's series of Communard portraits and composite photographs first began to appear in September, on a market already crowded by photographers eager to cash in on the Commune, and they also demonstrated their relation to the conventions of the illustrated journal. Not only were their subjects—the assassination of Gustave Chaudey, the massacre on the rue Haxo, the execution of the Dominicans of Arcueil—crisply topical in nature, responding to the set of reportorial conventions by which the unfolding of events in real time would be compressed as a series of discrete and climactic "incidents," but they also stayed close to the same repertory of incidents previously packaged and made familiar by the illustrated press. Indeed, it is not suggesting too much to say that Appert's task was not so much the production of meaning through an original act of narrative compression as the entrepreneurial annexation of this device of journalistic reportage into the contiguous and equally commercial discursive spaces of photographic souvenirs and memorabilia. Nowhere is this act of annexation more dramatically evidenced than in the close congruence demonstrated on more than one occasion between the composition and components of Appert's photographic representations and those graphic images that had appeared several months earlier in the pages of *L'Illustration*.[28]

The deaths by firing squad of Generals Clément Thomas and Claude-Martin Lecomte on the rue des Rosiers on 18 March 1871 was one of the most pivotal in a day full of pivotal events, including the confrontation between the army and neighborhood residents over the cannons of Montmartre, the occupation of the Hôtel de Ville, and the flight of the national government to Versailles. An image of the execution was quickly produced for the 25 March issue of *L'Illustration* (fig. 9.4). It shows the two generals: the one, in plainclothes, a popularly despised leader of the suppression of the Blanquist revolution in 1848; the other, in uniform, a recently promoted veteran of the Franco-Prussian War. They resolutely face their executioners in the garden behind the house where they had been provisionally detained. In the accompanying notes, Henri Vigne assured *L'Illustration*'s readers that its representatives had fanned out across the city from morning to night of that fateful day, claiming that "the sketches of our drawings were made on the spot, and our readers can consider the account that we are going to render here to be exact."[29] The draftsman had visited the garden, noting its configuration of flowerbeds, espaliered fruit trees, and crowd-trampled ground. Relying on eyewitness testimony, his drawing faithfully locates each man on the exact patch of earth where he was slain. Yet despite these claims to maplike accuracy, Vigne's written narrative of the event does nothing if not contradict the image of the execution that it accompanied. For, as the text proceeds to relate, the generals

Fig. 9.4. Engraving of *Execution of Generals Clément-Thomas and Lecomte*, *L'Illustra-tion*, 25 March 1871, p. 164.

were not executed together, but one after the other, and not by a single volley of gunfire, but military-style, with each rifleman taking a shot in turn. According to Vigne, the white-bearded Thomas took fourteen rounds and remained standing ("with each bullet, the body of the victim shook with a convulsive start, but remained firmly in place, like a statue") before a shot taken above his right eye felled him.[30] Pale and uttering words of protest, the young Lecomte was led out to meet a similar, though more summary, fate.

To bring the two accounts, one visual and one textual, into contact with each other is to confront the contradictions between the stiffly posed conventions of formal execution images and the breathless sensationalism, complete with the *frissons* of italics and multiple exclamation points, of contemporary journalistic narrative. It is to place us back again in the territory of Lacan's voluble quickening of the "instantaneous" yet indistinct photographs of the Crimean War. Yet it is also to begin to understand the way in which Appert's image of the same event sharpened and heightened certain component parts of the popular representation of this event while fictionalizing it to no greater extent (fig. 9.5). Indeed, the photograph offered up the same configuration of buildings, courtyard and trees, and

Fig. 9.5. Eugène Appert, *Execution of Generals Clément-Thomas and Lecomte*, 1871. (Courtesy of the Bibliothèque Nationale de France, Paris.)

executioners and victims. Its main innovation was to step back slightly from the scene in order to permit the inclusion of an irregular little line of onlookers.

No less than in the images of ruins, we might understand the engraving of the generals' execution as an attempt to claim for itself the topographic and physiognomic authority of the photograph; this desire stands behind Vigne's representation of the image as made "on the spot." In turn, no greater sense of narrative action (nor luridness, for that matter) was conjured up by Appert; the topographic and physiognomic potentials of the photographic document were, rather, directly exploited, patiently laid over the armature of the engraved tableau in such a way as to negate the need for Vigne's written assurances while even supplying an image whose own authority as a visual "witness" rested to some extent on familiarity with an engraved representation already in circulation. It does not seem quite right to say that Appert animated the engraving per se, but he did attempt to enliven it with a greater sheen of the real, derived in part from using such montage elements as preexisting photographic portraits of Generals Thomas and Lecomte. Such an attempt also seems the proper frame for understanding the significance of the onlookers' presence. For they do nothing if not heighten the sense of spectatorship attached to Appert's image, providing a mirror image of the curious, souvenir-hunting gaze that would in turn be directed at the photograph itself. It is as if the narrative value of the moving picture were to be deferred in favor of the exhibition value of the photographic trophy, as if the unfolding of an event in time could be displaced by the operation of putting reality, selectively, on display.

Thus, in one sense, it seems most accurate to say that Appert's composite photograph is as much "of" *L'Illustration's* engraving as "of" the actual event, even as it is equally and partially "of" the site where that event took place. Yet in another way, this nearly seamless overlapping of photographic subjects points to the complex condition of transparency by which the world at large and its construction into "current events" were coming to be regarded as interchangeable.[31] This condition was increasingly shared across the discursive spaces of the mass press and topical photography, and it begins to suggest how *actualité* might be said to inhabit the same discursive framework as such urban consumerist mechanisms as the *grands boulevards,* the new department stores, and the wealth of novelty attractions mapped across modern Paris, a framework within which distinctions between the real and the commodified were blurred according to the logic of commercial enticement.[32] Within such a framework, it seems only appropriate that the contemporary life span of Appert's images can be mapped from their beginnings in the strategies of the illustrated press, through their insertion into a specialty market for photographically enhanced souvenirs of the Commune, to their use as promotional giveaways tucked inside boxes of tapioca pudding to encourage discriminating Parisian shoppers to purchase one brand over another.[33]

Moreover, those operations bent on pleasurably blurring the consumer's perception of the distinction between the real and the commodified are precisely the point insofar as they traverse those ideological contingencies breaking around the Commune in general, and around Appert's images in particular. Objectivity—the claim of photography and journalism to an authoritative point of view that is persuasive because it masquerades as no point of view at all—was not only one ideological guise by which popular opinion might be swayed but it was also, and more accurately in terms of the evolution of the commercial press in the nineteenth century, the device by which the news was increasingly sold. In this sense, it has been argued that such perceived objectivity was the necessary precondition for a mass press, whose products—both its journalistic nuggets of information and entertainment and the paid advertisements that framed them—had to appeal to the widest possible range of potential consumers.

It points to the functional leveling of the relationship between the "news item" and the commodity item by which the popular press became economically viable.[34] *L'Illustration,* in particular, had long been recognized for its "consummate prudence" in straddling the political fence; though firmly located in the mainstream, it was even noted for its occasional moments of opposition.[35] Certainly, it was not banned after the Commune fell and its sympathies with the national government's call to order were quickly made apparent, most tellingly in the semantic shifts through which, by June, the *fédérés* engaged in civil war had been reframed as insurgents and *pétroleuses* implicated in a mass riot. Significantly, however, and as opposed to several other mainstream journals, neither was it banned during the Commune.[36]

Further, when one considers the eventual appearance of Appert's photographs in such manifestly pro-Communard publications as *Paris Under the Commune by a Faithful Witness: Photography* (1895) and Dayot's *Invasion, Siege, and Commune, 1870–1871* (1901), one finds that the argument for their interest was presented much in the same way that Vigne's comments position *L'Illustration's* engravings.[37] The publisher of *Paris Under the Commune* introduced the collection of photographic artifacts by arguing for the camera's objectivity:

> Numerous volumes have been written on the Commune, some to defend it, others to attack it. We want to present, simply and without commentary, photographic reproductions of the men and matters of the Commune, which are the only incontestable documents. We have gathered together from all sides and from every source, the materials most likely to clarify opinion. Their authenticity is unquestionable and they are, perhaps, the only living witness of the events that followed the Franco-Prussian war.[38]

Not only was a faith in photographic objectivity shared across commercial ventures floated by pro- and anti-Communard entrepreneurs, but Appert's images occupied a place in both. Of course, this was possible in part because such topical representations seldom stood alone. Despite the publisher's assurances to the contrary, *Paris Under the Commune* is nothing if not a subjective account, the captions for each image displacing Vigne's sensationalist narrative with a passionate and equally sensationalized endorsement of the Communard point of view. Further, to present Appert's composites in such a context did not necessarily assume a blindness to their fictional devices. Dayot reproduced Appert's *Execution of Generals Clément Thomas and Lecomte* with the caveat that the photograph was largely a product of invention, but he allowed that it was still valuable for its accurate picturing of the site of the execution and the positioning of the two generals.[39] Such an assertion of the visual interest of Appert's image reiterates and doubles back upon the terms of Vigne's initial presentation of the engraved representation of the event.

By aligning the pages of *L'Illustration* with Appert's composite photographs and their appearance in late-nineteenth-century publications related to the Commune, I mean to point to several things. One concerns, as I have suggested, displacing a focus upon image-authoring and its "subjective" point of view with an alternative attention to the entrepreneurial strategy of commodifying objectivity, of packaging up contemporary events as the "real," which characterizes photography's appeal in all three contexts. Appert's images would appear well matched to such a project of displacement, precisely because the technique of the composite fairly does away with a fixed point of view, vacating the monocular authority of photographic vision for a potentially contradictory montage of fragments and cuts that disperses points of view across the surface of the photograph. Moreover, these contradictions also begin to displace our contemporary notion of the documentary photograph (with its implicit equation of mastery and truthfulness, within which framework Appert's image can only be see as a "lie") with a more historically determined definition of the photographic document. For the term "document" as it pertained to French photography in the nineteenth century was nothing if not an unstable category, referring not so much to something "fixed" as to something contingent—to the photograph as a sort of "raw material" defined less by what was contained within the frame than by the uses to which its various elements might be put, as much by the particular demands of a particular task of image-making as by the photograph's "aura" of indexical authenticity.[40]

In both *L'Illustration*'s full-page spread and Appert's composite photograph, the intention to display reality movingly was related to but also held in tension with a narrative, either textual or popularly recited, with its own conventions and lapses, one that was just as widely known and had accrued its own sheen of notoriety. Yet, the effect of the photograph when considered as a component of a historical narrative, that is to say, as a product of ordering "what actually happened" into a tellable and telling story, is to dislodge the appearance of visual reality from a registration of sentient corporeality (that which Vigne's text attempts to provide and both images refuse to reveal). Instead, "reality," as it is referenced by the photograph, is reattached to a web of spectral forms, both more and less real, which shift easily from frame to frame, register to register, which migrate unresistingly across the spaces from photographic document to that of the *actualité* as a form of commodity enterprise. This series of exchanges might be put this way: Appert's image claims to represent the execution of the two generals as it actually occurred, but it clearly does not, and those familiar with the events of 18 March might have been expected to know that. At the same time, it claims to reproduce a standard account of the execution contained within the mass press, and yet it does more, and its audience would have appreciated that. For, finally, there is a way in which Appert's photograph not only images but foretells the future of those it pictures, exacerbating the distinction between lived experience and image-making by conceiving of the photographic process as enacting the repetitive return of the living to a state of stillness, the obsessive re-presentation of its subject in death. This is to bring us back to the status of the photograph as indexical sign, back to its funereal property of record-ing that which has been but is no longer. But it is also to suggest that such an indexical status, insofar as it is central to not only the truth value but also the market value and the propaganda value of Appert's image, is not "simply" the property of photography as such, but a potentially localizable effect within the photograph as a (composite) whole.

One thing has always fascinated me about Appert's work: To seek out the face of General Lecomte or General Thomas, or to look into the faces of any of the "victims" or "perpetrators" re-presented in his images of the Commune, is to experience a sensation of detachment provoked by the realization that these people give no indication that they know what is happening to them. They face their fate with total sangfroid in the midst of disaster. A monk looks out blandly from the massacre of the Domin-icans of Arcueil, one hand stanching the bleeding from a gaping wound on his chest, while the numerous corpses scattered at his feet have appar-ently met their fate with the same stoic composure they had assumed in the portrait studio. In the same vein, the lineup of victims to be executed on the rue Haxo look as if they are queuing for the autobus, and their ex-ecutioners appear equally disengaged. Appert's images place on display not so much the simulation of an event as the spectacle of unknowing bodies that the spectator knows will become corpses. It is in this way, as much by their engagement of the viewer in an intricate give-and-take between artifice (the fictive witnessing of the real) and reality-effect (the effect of immanence exhibited by these particular bodies), as by any com-pensations for the inability of contemporary photography to capture phys-iological movement, that the particular strategies of Appert's composite photographs might be characterized as striving toward a new language— as envisioning, hesitantly and imperfectly, the compelling displays of real-ity presented by the first moving pictures.

This last assertion is a bald one, but also to my mind a much needed one, for by it, I mean to locate Appert's images within the complex condi-tions under which reality was increasingly consumed as artifice in the spaces of urban Paris, and to conjoin them to larger issues of precinematic spectatorship in the late-nineteenth-century city. This positioning chal-lenges the terms of our habitual understanding of these photographs, which has lodged their propaganda value against the assumption of a viewer consuming artifice as if it were real, and refuses to pair them with the "image of the naive spectator" which Tom Gunning has rightly criticized as haunting accounts of early cinematic *actualités* and their spectators.[41] Insofar as Appert's images participate in such constructions of spectatorship (and I think they do), their family resemblance to the conventions of documentary photography would seem less relevant than their proximity to such precinematic spectacles as the diorama, panorama, and wax museum, spaces bound to topicality (particularly in their insistent pairing of celebrity and disaster) and yet equally invested in the simultaneous pleasures of deception and recognition through which one experienced a never-before-seen reality as a clever simulacrum.[42] Acknowledging a nineteenth-century viewer's familiarity with such illusionistic entertainments might suggest an alternative and more historically located contemporary consumer for Appert's images, a consumer who would be able to differentiate well enough between the vividly realistic aspects of the *Execution of Generals Clément-Thomas and Lecomte* and its narrative conveniences and shorthands and who would relish it precisely because the ability to do so was the real evidence of "having been there," the true mark of a Parisian insider.[43]

In the end, I might be accused of trying to have it both ways—of bringing Appert back into the mainstream fold and normalizing the obvious strangenesses of his images, even as I question the sorts of ideological readings that these images have habitually attracted. Yet, by emphasizing what might be called the entertainment value of Appert's photographs, I do not mean to recuperate or "explain away" their partisan content, as if to say, somehow, that Appert didn't really mean it when he pictured a female Communard taking deadly aim against a lineup of gendarmes (in *Massacre on the Rue Haxo*), or the benign submission of the clergy to mob rule (in the various representations of Archbishop Darboy and the *Execution of the Dominicans of Arcueil*). Don't mistake me: his images remain a nasty bit of business. They were deeply implicated in the public relations game by which the national government sought to construct its own version of the events of spring 1871, and Appert was well rewarded with official titles and support for his diligent services to the government.[44]

But I do mean to shift the discussion of ideology as it engages these photographs away from partisanship per se, away from the temptation neatly to niche particular photographic productions into anti- or pro-Communard, Right-leaning or Left-leaning camps. (To do so successfully would entail not only explaining away the sort of contextual analysis I have mapped out here but also accounting for the unbuttoned familiarity with which not only the men and women of the Commune but also the Versailles troops confronted the camera of Bruno Braquehais, perennially celebrated as the pro-Communard photographer par excellence.) No, this account is not meant to be ideologically indifferent. Rather it proposes to understand ideology differently, less as a fixed sum of political beliefs into which Appert's images might be pigeonholed, and more as a "system of representations" within which these photographs must be positioned in contact with other institutions and practices insuring the stability of the dominant culture.[45] Within such an understanding of ideology, it is imperative that we be more self-conscious about the moments when we attach partisan readings to the "big lie" of photographic misrepresentations of an authentic reality and to the presumption of a gullible, "reality-seduced" public.

For Appert's gambit reminds us that photography's other is not "reality" at all, but a matrix of representational structures, already existing and only dreamt of, which photography appropriates, compresses, displaces, and occludes.[46] This seems to me the most eloquent context for Appert's entrepreneurial, reportorial, and yet undeniably propagandistic images. For they are most precious not for unmasking the untruth of the composite photograph but for reminding us that all photographs demand this unmasking and that it is only by this unmasking that we might begin to apprehend not so much the "meaning" of the photograph—and all that entails about quixotic pursuits of the positivist and essentialist—but instead what orders of meaning, as photography intersects the social formation, are at stake.

NOTES

In addition to the editors of this volume, I would like to thank Carol Armstrong and Marcus Verhagen for their helpful suggestions during the writing of this essay, and Charlotte Eyerman for extraordinary efforts in Paris.

1. Roland Barthes, *Camera Lucida* (New York: Hill and Wang, 1981), p. 32.

2. Liébert's photographs were published in two volumes and three versions as *Les Ruines de Paris et de ses environs* (Paris: Photographie américaine, 1871–1872). The accompanying text by Alfred d'Aunay, explicitly anti-Communard in tone, lovingly lingered on the destruction wrought upon the architectural heritage of France.

3. For example, see Roger Fenton's photographs of the Crimean War in 1854–1855, Gustave Le Gray's photographs of the barricades erected in Palermo during Garibaldi's campaign for Italian unification in 1860, and Mathew Brady & Co.'s images of the American Civil War in 1861–1865.

4. On "that has been," see Barthes, op. cit., p. 77. On photography and the index, see Rosalind Krauss, "Notes on the Index: Part 1," in Krauss, *The Originality of the Avant-Garde and Other Modernist Myths* (Cambridge and London: MIT Press, 1985), p. 203.

5. A. Leautté, *Photographies d'après nature sous la Commune de Paris, du 18 mars au 21 mai 1871* (Paris, 1871).

6. Kirk Varnedoe rigorously separates the modern vision exemplified by advanced (i.e., Impressionist) painting of the 1860s and 1870s from the more con-

servative practices of contemporary photography. See "The Artifice of Candor: Impressionism and Photography Reconsidered," *Art in America,* January 1980, pp. 66–78. On the anachronistic use of the term "snapshot" to describe photographic vision in the 1850s and 1860s, see especially p. 78, n.18.

7. Aaron Scharf cites an English critic writing in the *Photographic News* (London) of 1861 as well as a portfolio of Parisian *Vues instantanées* published by Hippolyte Jouvin in 1861 (Scharf, *Art and Photography* [New York: Viking Penguin, 1986], p. 182).

8. "Au premier plan, le Danube coule tranquillement, comme si tout n'était que joie, soleil et vie sur ses bords dévastés. A droite, le grand pont de bateaux sous Silistrie dessine sa forme sombre sur les eaux argentées du fleuve. Puis au loin, sur les collines, on aperçoit des lignes noires qui se croisent, s'isolent ou se réunissent en masses indécises, sous des nuages blanchâtres que le vent chasse et disperse: ce sont les armées aux prises, c'est la bataille" (Ernest Lacan, *Esquisses photographiques à propos de l'exposition universelle et de la guerre d'orient* [Paris: Grassart, 1856], p. 160).

9. Ibid., pp. 160–166.

10. Michael Fried provides an elegant and intensive reading of Diderot's art criticism in *Absorption and Theatricality: Painting and Beholder in the Age of Diderot* (Chicago and London: University of Chicago Press, 1980). On the nineteenth-century interest in Diderot's essays on art, see Louis Asseline, *Diderot et le dix-neuvième siècle* (Paris: Conférences de la rue de la Paix, 1866).

11. Marconi's "Prisoners" is reproduced in *Paris sous la Commune par un témoin fidéle: La Photographie* (Paris and Sceaux: Charaire et cie., 1895) and Henri Lefebvre's *La Proclamation de la Commune* (Paris: Gallimard, 1965), as well as in Alistair Horne's illustrated survey, *The Terrible Year: The Paris Commune, 1871* (New York and London: Macmillan, 1971), pp. 83, 129. Even Donald English's otherwise meticulous account of photography under the Commune reproduces this image without comment as to its origins (English, *The Political Uses of Photography in the Third French Republic, 1871–1914* [Ann Arbor, Michigan: UMI Research Press, 1984], pp. 57–59).

12. English's essay, "Photography and the Paris Commune: Symbol, Myth, Censorship, and Identification," in English, *The Political Uses of Photography,* provides the most thorough publication history of Appert's photographs, and I am deeply indebted to his research.

13. Georges Bourgin, *La Guerre de 1870–71 et la Commune* (Paris: Flammarion, 1971), p. 373.

14. This tactic has generally taken the form of pointing out the propaganda value of these images and then immediately pointing to inaccuracies and inconsistencies in their production, as if the distastefulness and dishonesty of the message were somehow affirmed by the ineptitude of its execution. Claude Nori thus identifies Appert as among the first to exploit the propagandistic potentials of the medium, his "ignoble" example contrasted to that of the photographer most often named as a sort of hero of the Commune, Bruno Braquehais. See *French Photography from its Origins to the Present* (New York: Pantheon, 1979), p. 21. Jean-Claude Gautrand does the same, adding that it supposedly took years to discern the falseness of certain images. See "Les Photographes et la Commune," *Photo-ciné revue*

(February 1972): 57–59. Gen Doy is at pains to point out the static, obviously posed quality of these photographs and their impossible lack of blurriness, speculating that even these defects would not deter a public predisposed to accept these images as "factual." See "The Camera Against the Paris Commune," in *Photography/ Politics: One*, ed. Terry Dennett and Jo Spence (London: Comedia Publishing Group, 1979), pp. 19–21. More recently, Susan Buck-Morss dismisses Appert's images as "falsified documents" bent upon obliterating all traces of artifice. See *The Dialectics of Seeing: Walter Banjamin and the Arcades Project* (Cambridge and London: MIT Press, 1989), p. 67.

15. Christine Lapostolle raises a similar concern, arguing that the gap between the abilities of the photographic apparatus and the taste for photographic "reality" necessitates a more subtle reading of the relationship between Commune photography and ideology than is habitually the case. See "Plus vrai que le vrai: Stratégie photographique et Commune de Paris," *Actes de la recherche en sciences sociales* 73 (1988): 67. This article and her essay "La Commune de Paris: De la barricade à la ruine," *Recherche photographique* 6 (1989): 20–28, are among the best recently published on photography and the Commune, and Lapostolle's work has been a constant spur to my own.

16. Such an image of the empress was rumored to have been for sale at the 1867 Universal Exposition. See Robert A. Sobieszek, "Composite Imagery and the Origins of Photomontage, Part I: The Naturalist Strain," *Artforum* (September 1978): 62. On Parisian debates about the artistic use of composite photography, see James Borcoman's very informative "Notes on the Early Use of Combination Printing," in *One Hundred Years of Photographic History: Essays in Honor of Beaumont Newhall*, ed. Van Deren Coke (Albuquerque: University of New Mexico Press, 1975), pp. 16–18. Interestingly, Borcoman suggests that Rejlander's *Two Ways of Life* may have been an attempt to provide an English product that could compete with continental advancements in this area of photographic practice.

17. "A la place del la réalité émouvante qu'il veut montrer, il n'obtiendrait que de ridicules simulacres." A. A. E. Disdéri, "Des scènes animées, sujets de genre— sujets historiques," in *L'Art de la Photographie* (Paris: J. Claye, 1862), p. 301.

18. Disdéri's mosaic photographs are widely reproduced. For the legs, see, for example, Robert A. Sobieszek, "Composite Imagery and the Origins of Photomontage, Part II: The Formalist Strain," *Artforum* (October 1978): 42.

19. For a reproduction, see Bourgin, op. cit., p. 59.

20. Sobieszek, op. cit., p. 62.

21. See, for example, Lacan's account of Nicéphore Niépce's contribution to the invention of photography, framed in terms of the inventor's interest in techniques of lithographic reproduction (op. cit., p. 5ff). In his opening remarks on photography at the Salon of 1859, Louis Figuier notes that "si nous n'avons pas eu dans notre siècle la *querelle des anciens et des modernes*, nous avons eu la *querelle des graveurs et des photographistes*" (Figuier, *La Photographie au Salon de 1859* [Paris: Hachette, 1860], p. 1). Emphasis in original.

22. Most especially, the *Illustrated London News* gave widespread coverage to the events of the Paris Commune.

23. Photographic illustrations, produced by transferring photographic images directly onto wood engraving plates, first appeared in the pages of *L'Illustration* in

1891. Prior to that, woodcut engraving was the sole means of mechanical reproduction used by the journal. For a discussion of the old and new technologies of reproduction used by *L'Illustration*, see the excellent article by Anne-Claude Ambroise-Rendu, "Du dessin de presse à la photographie, 1878–1914: Histoire d'une mutation technique et culturelle," *Revue d'histoire moderne et contemporaine* 39 (January–March 1992): 6–28.

24. *L'Illustration*, 17 June 1871, pp. 340–341.

25. During the June days of the 1848 revolution, a daguerreotypist named Thibault made several "before and after" images of the barricades erected on the rue Saint-Maur, comprising bird's-eye views of the street deserted and tightly battened down before the battle and repopulated and opened up in the battle's aftermath. These daguerreotypes served as models for a pair of woodcut engravings that appeared in *L'Illustration* in July 1848, thus establishing the pattern of "borrowings" between photography and the illustrated press that I am pointing to. For reproductions of these images, see Musée Carnavalet, *Paris et le daguerreotype* (Paris: Paris-Musées, 1989), pp. 170–171, 256–257.

26. Jules Moineux, "Revue comique des tribunaux," *Le Charivari*, 3 July 1871, pp. 2–3. Adrien Hunt, "Chronique du jour," ibid., 21 July 1871, p. 4. See also English, op. cit., p. 24.

27. *Les Ruines de Paris et ses environs* advertised for sale in *Le Charivari*, 9 July 1871.

28. Among recent writers on Commune photography, only Lapostolle has commented on this connection. See "Plus vrai que le vrai," pp. 75–76.

29. "Pendant la journée du 18, nous avons, le matin et le soir, parcouru tous les quartiers des hauteurs de Montmartre. Les croquis de nos dessins ont été pris sur place, et nos lecteurs peuvent considerer comme exacts les renseignements que nous allons consigner ici" ("Nos gravures," *L'Illustration*, 25 March 1871, p. 170).

30. "A chaque balle reçue, le corps de la victime était agité d'un tressaillement convulsif, mais restait ferme en place come une statue" (ibid.).

31. Richard Terdiman, *Discourse/Counter-Discourse: The Theory and Practice of Symbolic Resistance in Nineteenth-Century France* (Ithaca and London: Cornell University Press, 1985), p. 118.

32. On the connection between the mass press and department stores, see Terdiman, op. cit., pp. 135–146.

33. On the tapioca pudding incident, see English, op. cit., p. 68.

34. Terdiman, op. cit., p. 122.

35. Claude Bellanger et al., *Histoire générale de la presse française* (Paris: Presses Universitaires de France, 1969), 2:300–301.

36. For an interesting discussion of the semantic distinctions entailed in describing the Commune in official publications, see Michel Barat, "Le Vocabulaire des ennemis de la Commune," *La Pensée: Revue du rationalisme moderne* 156 (April 1971): 52–67.

37. *Paris sous la Commune par un témoin fidéle: La Photographie* and A. Dayot, *L'Invasion, le siège, la Commune, 1870–1871* (Paris: Flammarion, 1901).

38. "Nombre de volumes ont été écrits sur la Commune: les uns pour le défendre, les autres pour l'attaquer. Nous avons voulu apporter simplement et sans

commentaires la reproduction photographique des hommes et des choses de la Commune, seul document incontestable. Nous avons recueilli de tous côtés, à toutes les sources, les matériaux susceptibles d'éclairer l'opinion; leur authenticité n'est pas discutable et c'est peut-être le seul témoignage vivant des événements qui suivrent la guerre franco-allemande" (*Paris sous la Commune,* unpaginated preface).

39. Dayot, op. cit., p. 237.

40. For a discussion of the inflections of the concept of the photographic document as it applied specifically to French usage, see Molly Nesbit, *Atget's Seven Albums* (New Haven and London: Yale University Press, 1992), pp. 14–19.

41. "An Aesthetic of Astonishment: Early Film and the (In)credulous Spectator," *Art & Text* 34 (spring 1989): 33.

42. On the wax museum, diorama, and panorama as precinematic spectacles, see Vanessa R. Schwartz, "The Public Taste for Reality: Early Mass Culture in Fin-de-Siècle Paris" (Ph.D. diss., University of California, Berkeley, 1993).

43. Nicholas Green's account of the diorama seems particularly apt here: "The diorama twinned illusionism and artifice . . . [and] projected nature both as the 'real' and as the material for cunning transformations, scintillating surprises. Switching easily between registers was, of course, a sign of the urban initiate" (*The Spectacle of Nature* [Manchester and New York: Manchester University Press, 1990], pp. 97–98).

44. Appert's business cards included such honorifics as "Peintre-photographe de S. M. la Reine d'Espagne, du Grand Duc Constantin, expert auprès du Tribunal de la Seine" and "photographe de la Magistrature de l'Armée, du Sénat et de la Chambre des Députés," suggesting an ongoing, mutually profitable relationship with the government.

45. For a cogent discussion of the distinction between "ideology" as individual politics and a more Althusserian account of "ideology" as the complexly related social mechanisms through which the individual "subjects" himself to social formation, see James H. Kavanagh, "Ideology," in *Critical Terms for Literary Study,* ed. Frank Lentricchia and Thomas McLaughlin (Chicago and London: University of Chicago Press, 1990), pp. 306–320.

46. On this point, see John Tagg, "The Currency of the Photograph: New Deal Reformism and Documentary Rhetoric," in Tagg, *The Burden of Representation: Essays on Photographies and Histories* (Amherst: University of Massachusetts Press, 1988), pp. 154–156.

TEN

In a Moment: Film and the Philosophy of Modernity

Leo Charney

Practically we perceive only the past, the pure present being the invisible progress of the past gnawing into the future.
HENRI BERGSON[1]

The post-1870 transformations of modernity generated a perceptual climate of overstimulation, distraction, and sensation, characterized by Georg Simmel in 1903 as "the rapid crowding of changing images, the sharp discontinuity in the grasp of a single glance, and the unexpectedness of onrushing impressions."[2] In the midst of this environment of fleeting sensations and ephemeral distractions, critics and philosophers sought to identify the possibility of experiencing a moment. Experiencing a moment in these contexts meant feeling the presence of the moment, fully inhabiting it. The moment exists to the extent that the individual experiences immediate, tangible sensation. This feeling is so intense, so strongly felt, that it tapers off as soon as it is first felt. The experience of strong sensation articulates the possibility of a moment both through an intensity of feeling which communicates immediate presence and through the waning of intensity by which the moment contrasts with the less intense moment that follows it.

Through the category of the moment, such writers as Walter Pater, Walter Benjamin, Martin Heidegger, and Jean Epstein sought to rescue the possibility of sensual experience in the face of modernity's ephemerality. The concept of the moment provided a means to fix an instant of feeling, yet this effort at stability had to confront the inescapable fact that no moment could stay still. This dilemma led these writers towards the two interlocking concepts that defined their investigation of the modern as momentary: the evacuation of stable presence by movement and the resulting split between sensation, which feels the moment in the moment, and cognition, which recognizes the moment only after the moment. These two aspects of the modern moment came together to create a new form of experience in cinema.

The category of the moment as the discrete marker of sensual response was first put forward by the aesthetician Walter Pater in the Preface and Conclusion to the book first published as *Studies in the History of the Renaissance* in 1873, then republished in 1877, with the Conclusion excised, under the title *The Renaissance: Studies in Art and Poetry,* the title it retained in the third edition, with a revised Conclusion, in 1888. As this checkered history suggests, Pater's Conclusion was in its time a polarizing and controversial document that, in the delicate words of Pater's latter-day editor Harold Bloom, "cost Pater considerable preferment at Oxford."[3] In his Introduction to Pater's work, Bloom gleefully quotes a scornful paraphrase of Pater's aesthetic by "this very minor Wordsworth"—William's grandnephew John, who, after the first edition, summed up Pater's position as, in part, a belief that "the only thing worth living for is momentary enjoyment." Pater's dry response to this charge indicated that it was not really wrong: "I wish they would not call me a hedonist. It gives such a wrong impression to those who do not know Greek."

Although such statements oversimplify his stance, Pater basically did believe that "the only thing worth living for is momentary enjoyment." "Art comes to you," he wrote in the Conclusion's last sentence, "professing frankly to give nothing but the highest quality to your moments as they pass, and simply for those moments' sake" (p. 62). Sensual response isolated the moment, marked it off experientially as one moment distinct from the moments that preceded and succeeded it. The moment in turn described sensual response, whose intensity was also recognized from its contrast with the more ordinary moments that surrounded it. Defining "pleasurable sensations" as "each of a more or less peculiar and unique kind" (p. 18), Pater detached sublime experience from continuity and emphasized that it could reside only inside unique moments of sensual immersion. Artworks "are valuable . . . as we say, in speaking of an herb, a wine, a gem; for the property each has of affecting one with a special, a unique, impression of pleasure" (p. 18). The concept of the "impression" reinforced Pater's emphasis on the momentary instant of sensation, and Pater further underlined this momentariness by adding the adjectives "special" and "unique."

By isolating sublime feeling in the moment, Pater cannily gave sensual response the status of a discrete entity, a "fact" as observable as the "primary data" of the natural world. In so doing, Pater turned on their heads the Positivist ideas that held sway during the period in which he wrote. Positivism stressed the centrality of individual observation; Pater twisted this emphasis to suggest that the individual's subjective response therefore constituted a "fact" of the natural world as inarguably as numbers or light. "In aesthetic criticism," he wrote in the Preface,

> the first step towards seeing one's object as it really is, is to know one's own impression as it really is, to discriminate it, to realise it distinctly. . . . What is this song or picture . . . to *me*? What effect does it really produce on me? Does it give me pleasure? and if so, what sort or degree of pleasure? The answers to these questions are the original facts with which the aesthetic critic has to do; and, as in the study of light, of morals, of number, one must realise such primary data for oneself, or not at all. (pp. 17–18)

This emphasis on momentary sensation begun in Pater's aesthetic criticism was more fully developed by the two emblematic critics of modernity, Walter Benjamin and Martin Heidegger, both of whom allied the momentary to the experience of vision. " 'In the moment of vision' nothing can occur," Heidegger wrote in *Being and Time*,[4] putting "in the moment of vision" in quotes to underline the impossibility of inhabiting, being "in," a moment of vision. "Nothing can occur" inside a moment of vision because it always "leaps away," in Heidegger's phrase, before we can acknowledge it. We can acknowledge the moment's occurrence only after the moment in which it seemed to occur. The cognition of the moment and the sensation of the moment can never inhabit the same moment.

As Heidegger persuasively identified, this evacuation of the present had far-reaching consequences for the experience of time in modernity. For if sensation and cognition cannot inhabit the same moment, then the present is always lost. To the extent that "presence" names a category of consciousness, it exists only through the ability to recognize it. Yet that recognition cannot happen in the same moment that the presence happens; it can arrive only after the present of the presence. The present, really, cannot occur, since the mind can recognize the present only after it is no longer present; the present can be acknowledged only once it has become past. We can never be present in a present.

This "falling into lostness," as Heidegger called it, inscribed a fundamental alienation into the structure of daily life. With modernity came the awareness that people were always already alienated from the time in which they were living. Yet the present's lostness could be partly redeemed by valorizing the sensual, bodily, prerational responses that retain the prerogative to occupy a present moment. To say we cannot recognize the present inside the moment of presence is not to say that the present cannot exist. It is merely to say that it exists as felt, as experienced, not in the realm of the rational catalog but in the realm of the bodily sensation. This possibility of a sensual present as antidote to the alienation of modernity was the path taken in modernity from Pater's promotion of the sublime moment to Walter Benjamin's notion of shock to Jean Epstein's concept of *photogénie* to Heidegger's own speculation that the "moment of vision" allowed an ecstatic break in the otherwise elusive passage of lost time.

Heidegger proposed that in the moment of vision we experience a direct sensation that we can grasp in the immediacy of a present presence: "The moment of vision," he continued, "permits us to encounter for the first time what can be 'in a time' as ready-to-hand or present-at-hand." In the moment of vision, we "encounter" sensation in the practical realm that Heidegger called the "ready-to-hand or present-at-hand." We experience the moment of vision in a nonrational way, and this experience fills us with the sensation of being present inside the present. This sensation, Heidegger went on to specify, marks the place of ecstasy, bliss, rapture: The moment of vision "must be understood in the active sense as an ecstasis. It means the resolute rapture with which [the subject] is carried away to whatever possibilities and circumstances are encountered in the Situation."[5] As in traditional theories of the sublime, Heidegger depicted the individual as "carried away" in the transporting moment. This rapture, Heidegger implied, relocates the individual to a moment so full of feeling that it can contain no other sensations.

Walter Benjamin, the poet laureate of the modern as the momentary, similarly allied momentary sensation to vision through what he called in his Arcades Project the "Now of recognizability."[6] Writing in Thirties Berlin, Benjamin sought to understand the urban modernity that had emerged in the Teens and Twenties by way of the culture of late-nineteenth-century Paris which gave rise to that modern environment. "For the materialist historian," as he observed in the Arcades Project, "every epoch with which he occupies himself is only a fore-history of the one that really concerns him" (p. 65). This three-way series of Chinese boxes allowed Benjamin, from his retrospective position in the Thirties, to synthesize most of the conceptual and experiential elements that had defined modern experience into the Twenties.

Looking back at the emergence of the modern environment, Benjamin found in late-nineteenth-century Paris the blueprint for the developing conditions of modern experience. If modern life, as Benjamin wrote in his essay on Charles Baudelaire, initiated "a change in the structure of . . . experience,"[7] this change lay in the direction of the momentary and fragmentary, qualities that for Benjamin transformed the nature and experience of time, art, and history. Benjamin developed this theme throughout this work but brought it to fullest fruition in the so-called Arcades Project, which was left unfinished at his death in 1940. This work, as described by translator Richard Sieburth was

> composed of hundreds of 22 × 28 centimeter sheets of yellowish paper that
> have been folded in half to create 14 × 22 folios, the first and third sides of

which contain Benjamin's minuscule notes in blue or black ink. Each group of these folios is in turn gathered into a *Konvolut* or sheaf according to its central paradigm or theme. The manuscript is divided into 36 such sheafs, their titles keyed to the letters of the alphabet.[8]

As this description implies, the very form of the Arcades Project was fragmented and fragmentary. It proceeded not as a linear argument but as a series of discrete ideas, observations, and quotations, presented without the transitions and intervening commentaries that generally characterize essayistic argument. As Sieburth indicates, "it may be a misnomer to speak of it as a *work* at all. . . . Benjamin, by contrast, describes his Arcade not as a work but as an ongoing event, a peripatetic meditation or *flânerie* in which everything chanced upon en route becomes a potential direction his thoughts might take."[9]

Benjamin associated this conceptual collage with the montage of cinema. "This project . . . is intimately linked to that of montage" (p. 45), he explicitly stated, and a few sections later elaborated: "Method of this project: literary montage. I need say nothing. Only exhibit" (p. 47). More important, the project aimed "to carry the montage principle over into history" (p. 48). Benjamin strove not just to propose the momentary as a defining trope of the modern but to illustrate it through his own sensibility and style. In this effort, he relied above all on the refusal to distinguish between quotations and commentary, using quotations not as illustrative but as the project's core. As Sieburth reports, "Of the quarter of a million words that comprise Tiedemann's edition, at least 75 percent are direct transcriptions of texts Benjamin collected over thirteen years."[10]

This panoply of voices and disjunction of ideas would reflect stylistically Benjamin's sense of the experience of modernity as filled with anarchic juxtapositions, random encounters, multiple sensations, and uncontrollable meanings. The experience of wandering through the Arcades Project would resemble as closely as possible the lost experience of wandering through the arcades. The arcades would be not just exhumed but re-evoked, reexperienced. Benjamin's endeavor to derive a fragmentary style reflected his insistence that the nature of perception in modernity was intrinsically fragmentary, and that a critical record of those perceptions could, therefore, not imbue them with a false and inappropriate continuity.

Benjamin's work suggests, in other words, the interdependence between the moment and the fragment. As a way to express the prevalence of the moment in modern experience, Benjamin took recourse in a fragmentary method. He associated this method with "montage," a term that for Benjamin contained the vital allusion to cinema. The history and criticism of the fleeting, fragmentary shocks of modernity will itself be fleeting, fragmentary, and shocking. And Benjamin, of course, was not just prescribing that history but writing it himself.

This approach to writing history stemmed from Benjamin's broader reconceptualization of the experience of time in modernity and therefore of time-as-history and history-as-time. These concerns placed Benjamin in the mainstream of the rethinking of presence which emerged from modernity. For Benjamin, the reiteration of the past could occur only as a fleeting moment. "The past," he famously wrote, "can be seized only as an image which flashes up at the instant when it can be recognized and is never seen again."[11] In the Arcades Project, this sense of the present moment as a "flash of lightning" became Benjamin's governing view of both time and history. "It isn't," he wrote,

> that the past casts its light on what is present or that what is present casts its light on what is past; rather, an image is that in which the Then and the Now come together into a constellation like a flash of lightning. In other words: an image is dialectics at a standstill. For while the relation of the present to the past is a purely temporal, continuous one, the relation of the Then to the Now is dialectical: not of a temporal, but of an imagistic nature. (p. 50)

In this highly compressed formulation of the momentary present, Benjamin, like Heidegger, linked the possibility of presence to vision, to what he called throughout the Arcades Project the "Now of recognizability." The possibility of a "Now" could occur only through its tangible—that is, visual—"recognizability." As Benjamin elaborated, "The dialectical image is a lightning flash. The Then must be held fast as it flashes its lightning image in the Now of recognizability. The rescue that is thus—and only thus—effected, can only take place for that which, in the next moment, is already irretrievably lost" (p. 64).

These three sentences crystallize Benjamin's conception of the momentary. The moment of presence, the Now, takes place as a hiatus in the otherwise ceaseless cycle of the dialectic, which circles between future and past. Benjamin clarified this idea: "Thinking involves both thoughts in motion and thoughts at rest. When thinking reaches a standstill in a constellation saturated with tensions, the dialectical image appears. This image is the caesura in the movement of thought" (p. 67). The possibility of a moment occurred in the form of an image because the perception of an image represented for Benjamin the best option for immediate perception. This image was what Benjamin called the "Now of recognizability": The Now could occur only in recognizability and recognizability in turn inscribed the possibility of an instantaneous Now "blasted out of the continuum of the historical process" (p. 67).

Yet this tentative and unstable present represents a futile "rescue," since the image it freezes "in the next moment, is already irretrievably lost." The dialectical image cannot halt the inevitability of the moment's erasure by the next moment, the unstoppability of serial moments. For Benjamin, the upheaval of modernity arose in this movement away from experience conceived as a continuous cumulation towards an experience of momentary shocks that bombarded and shattered subjective experience like hand grenades. Benjamin came increasingly to define modern experience as this ephemeral experience he called "shock." Baudelaire, he emblematically suggested, "placed the shock experience at the very center of his artistic work" and as a result "indicated the price for which the sensation of the modern age may be had: the disintegration of the aura in the experience of shock."[12]

Benjamin's concept of "shock" delineated a category, which Benjamin elsewhere allied to the "constant sudden change" of film and modern life,[13] of sharp ephemeral sensations that hit the modern subject with great intensity. The more intense the sensation, the more abruptly the modern subject would feel the waning of its initial strength. The combination of immediate intensity and just as immediate tapering off was felt as shock. To experience shock was to experience a moment. Shock could occur only in a flashing, fleeting moment; more exactly, shock framed and defined a moment as a moment. The intensity of feeling that marked shock as shock placed brackets around the heightened moment in which the shock was felt. The moment of shock returned to sensation, and then to consciousness, the immediacy of the present moment, even as it slipped away. Shock jolted the modern subject into tangible reawareness of the presence of the present. Inside the immediate presence of the moment, what we can do—the only thing we can do—is feel it. The present presence of the moment can occur only in and as sensation.

Yet that present is, at the same time, always already moving away. In this symbiosis between the possibility of a sensual moment and the equally potent evanescence of the moment, film became the defining art form of the temporal experience of modernity. The writer who captured this link between the emerging aesthetic of film and the philosophical upheavals of modernity was Jean Epstein, the French filmmaker and film theorist, who in the Twenties argued that film's essence arose from the form of the sensual moment that he called *photogénie*—fleeting fragments of experience that provide pleasure in ways that the viewer cannot describe verbally or rationalize cognitively. Epstein conceived film as a chain of moments, a collage of fragments that elicited not an even flow of attention but sudden, unpredictable peaks and valleys. Inside those bumps of attention the viewer scavenges moments of pure immersion in image. For Epstein, this indefinable *photogénie* marked the specificity of cinema as a unique art form of modern experience. "With the notion of *photogénie*," he said in a 1924 lecture, "the idea of cinema-art is born. For how better to define the indefinable *photogénie* than to say: *Photogénie* is for cinema what color is for painting, volume for sculpture—the specific element of that art."[14]

What, then, was this great discovery, the element that defined "the essence of cinema"? Herein lies the paradox. Epstein's conceptual leap was to ally film to irrationality, indefinability, instability—to those qualities that a film theorist cannot specify, quantify, or describe. Epstein set out to define cinema, but the definition was indefinable. Cinema's essence relied on its elusiveness, its always-moving-away. For Epstein, the essence of cinema dwelt not in its narrative capacities but in the evanescent moments of powerful feeling that certain images provide. *Photogénie* marks the place of these uncanny effects. "One racks one's brains in wanting to define it," he wrote of *photogénie*. "Face of beauty, it's a taste of things. I recognize it like a musical phrase" (p. 91). Moreover, *photogénie* is momentary and ephemeral: "*Photogénie* is a value on the order of the second. If it is long, I don't find continuous pleasure in it. . . . Until now I have never seen pure *photogénie* lasting an entire minute" (p. 94).

Photogénie thus exists inside, and defines the possibility of, a moment. For Epstein, however, the wider significance of the moment emerged from the displacement of space and time characteristic of modernity and embodied in cinema. "We therefore return again and always to the question," he said in a 1923 interview, "'What are the aspects of things, beings, and souls that are photogenic, aspects to which the cinematic art has the duty to limit itself?'" (p. 120) Epstein answered this question in three terse sentences: "The photogenic aspect is a component of space-time variables. This is an important formula. If you want a more concrete translation, here it is: an aspect is photogenic if it displaces itself and varies simultaneously in space and time" (p. 120).

Epstein here suggests that rapid movement through space and time creates an environment of flux, ephemerality, and dis-placement that found its home in the cinema. More pointedly, Epstein embodied in his own expression this conceptual emphasis on elusivity and ungraspability. His "concrete" position was anything but concrete, as it embodied the generative paradox of his idea of *photogénie*, which defined the essence of cinema as indefinable. Pressed in this interview for "concrete" specification, Epstein first employed bluster, bafflement, and irony, until he found his best revenge in a grudging "definition" that was only about movement and change. Epstein's definition of *photogénie* deconstructed itself: Claiming concreteness, it reconfirmed *photogénie*'s elusiveness.

Photogénie, Epstein insisted through this definition, was defined as change and variation. Its essence lay in its inability to be pinned down to the graspability of a concrete definition. It is dis-placed. Epstein expressed his distaste for the concreteness even of language in a characteristic passage from a 1924 lecture: "Around what one wants to say words skid like wet bars of soap," he said, destabilizing the very form of the lecture in which he expressed these thoughts. "This evening," he continued, a friend who wanted to explain everything to me too exactly suddenly raised his arms twice and said no more. . . . And when the scholar labors to use words with precision, I no longer believe. . . . There are twelve good words for each thing, and at least twelve things for each word. . . . On the line of communication the static of unexpected feelings interrupts us. Everything remains to be said, and we give it up, exhausted. (p. 146)

The disruption of a linear message by "the static of unexpected feelings" precisely describes *photogénie*'s relation to narrative cinema.

In Epstein's writings, the cinema became emblematically modern in yoking together space and time; film's essence arose from its ability to move and change across space and time. "The lamentable poverty of scenarios," he suggested, "arises in the first place from the failure to appreciate this primordial rule: There are no inactive feelings, that is, not displacing themselves in space; there are no invariable feelings, that is, not displacing themselves in time" (p. 121). This was why, with his typically careful wording, he emphasized that "only the mobile . . . aspects of things, beings, and souls can be photogenic" (p. 140). Here we return to the definition of *photogénie* as an element that "varies simultaneously in space and time." Cinema is above all about movement: "*Photogénie* . . . does not let in stasis" (p. 94). And movement crosses both space and time.

Epstein went on to link this cinematic conception of space and time to the evacuation of the present in modernity. "There is no real present," he wrote in one of his most philosophically serious passages:

Today is a yesterday, perhaps old, that brings in the back door a tomorrow, perhaps far-away. The present is an uneasy convention. In the midst of time, it is an exception to time. It escapes the chronometer. You look at your watch; the present strictly speaking is already no longer there, and strictly speaking it is there again, it will always be there from one midnight to the next. I think, therefore I was. The I future bursts into I past; the present is only this instantaneous and incessant molt. The present is only a meeting. Cinema is the only art that can represent this present as it is. (pp. 179–180)

Like Heidegger, Epstein presented the present as something that could exist only as the site where past and future collide. Cinema, for Epstein, marked the emergence of an art form that could reflect this temporal reality.

At the same time, Epstein's writings suggested that the sublime moment was also the epiphanic moment, the moment of defamiliarization. To the extent that the moment stands out from the ordinary life that contains it, it becomes vehicle and exemplar of defamiliarization. The moment defamiliarizes and defamiliarization occurs in a moment; defamiliarization describes the comparison between an intense moment and the less intense moments that surround it.

For Epstein, the defamiliarizing moment occurs at the intersection of mechanical reproduction and the external world. By becoming part of the photogenic, the object on screen differs from what it was before; the new context makes it a new object, even if it can be traced referentially to the concrete object that existed in front of the camera. *Photogénie* embodies repetition, yet the repetition is ineffably different. In mechanical reproduction's reproduction of the physical universe, something new emerges. "Our eye, without very long practice, cannot discover it directly. A lens centers it, drains it, and distills *photogénie* between its focal planes" (p. 91). In the mechanically reproduced image, we resee something familiar and this reproduction elicits qualities that our habituated perceptions cannot discover. "On screen," Epstein writes, "we resee what the cinema has already seen once" (p. 91).

Photogénie conceived in this way marked both the moment of hedonistic bliss and the moment of defamiliarizing ephiphany. The juncture of these aspects represents the crucial move in the effort to rescue sensation through the moment, and it was echoed in Victor's Shklovsky's 1917 manifesto for defamiliarization, "Art as Technique," in which Shklovsky mournfully noted, "If the whole complex lives of many people go on unconsciously, then such lives are as if they had never been."[15] To remedy this anonymity and mundanity of modern life, Shklovsky proposed the category of the sensual moment he called defamiliarization: "Habitualization devours works, clothes, furniture, one's wife, and the fear of war. . . . And art exists that one may recover the sensation of life; it exists to make one feel things, to make the stone stony. The purpose of art is to impart the sensation of things as they are perceived and not as they are known."[16] Through aesthetic perception, defamiliarization would return the subject's awareness of sensation. "Art is in this context," as Fredric Jameson has put it, "a way of restoring conscious experience, of breaking through deadening and mechanical habits of conduct . . . and allowing us to be reborn to the world in its existential freshness and horror."[17]

The most overt form of film's defamiliarizing moment appeared in what Tom Gunning has called the "cinema of attractions" of the period before 1908.[18] At a time when early film technology did not allow full-length storytelling, the cinema of attractions presented viewers with brief images that would shock, thrill, or incite curiosity—for instance, the 1895 Lumière short of a train arriving at a station; or the 1903 Edison short in which an elephant is electrocuted, falls over, and dies. Rather than contrive an elaborate story, the cinema of attractions accosted the viewer with cinema; attractions solicited the viewer's attention not as the narratively absorbed voyeur of later cinema but as the gaping, amazed observer also engaged by the circus or amusement park. The attraction linked the emerging form of cinema to the culture of the moment from which it arose: "The attraction," Gunning has noted, "seems limited to a sudden burst of presence . . . to the pure present tense of its appearance."[19]

These attractions were often shown as part of a longer program of skits or short films; their momentary nature was subsumed into their place in a continuous entertainment.[20] This interaction between the momentary and the continuous set the terms for the development of cinema, as the incorporation of moments of attraction into the continuity of full-length cinema mirrored the inculcation of momentary experience into the general continuity of movement and experience. The disruption of a film's putative continuity by moments of attraction was first identified in 1923 by Sergei Eisenstein, who wrote that what he called attraction in theater

> is every aggressive moment in it, i.e. every element of it that brings to light in the spectator those senses or that psychology that influence his experience—every element that can be verified and mathematically calculated to produce certain emotional shocks in a proper order within the totality.[21]

As Jacques Aumont has written, Eisenstein derived this concept of the attraction from the kinetic spectacles of modernity: "The attraction," Aumont indicates, "is originally the music hall number or sketch, a peak moment in the show, relatively autonomous, and calling upon techniques of representation which are not those of dramatic illusion, drawing upon more aggressive forms of the performing arts (the circus, music hall, the sideshow)."[22] Marked off from what surrounds it, the attraction represents a momentary apex of attention or stimulation; it offers a mode of experience different from the dramatic storytelling that enmeshes it.

Eisenstein identified the attraction as a peak moment in a film's program which must find its "proper order" within the totality." This interaction between the fixity of the moment and the mobility of time—the imputation of continuous movement across a chain of discrete moments—becomes clear from the precinematic motion studies of Eadweard Muybridge and Etienne-Jules Marey in the 1870s and 1880s. In striving to capture the continuity of movement, both Marey and Muybridge successfully indicated its impossibility—they captured the nature of movement as a series of moments and fragments, as an illusory discontinuity.

Marey innovated a "chronophotographic gun" whose trigger, when pulled, registered successive moments of movement, up to twelve each second, which Marey then printed on the same glass plate. Marey transformed serial moments into a form of collage, each moment superimposed on the next, which re-created the movement yet was riddled with gaps undermining that movement's apparent continuity. Muybridge's work overtly rendered these gaps, as it segregated each moment of movement into its own box, sternly separated by a black frame. In his ruminative theoretical meditation on Marey, François Dagognet suggests that

Marey's aim was not to render the surface of the world, as in Positivism, but to show us the hidden, secret, and invisible: "No one as well as he succeeded in making visible what resides in shadow. . . . The forces of life are hidden: he transposed them and exposed them to the light of day."[23] For Dagognet, "Marey really tackled only one question: tracking down and registering what escapes our view. . . . He exteriorized, exposed . . . what hides itself or, because of its smallness, escapes us."[24]

From this perspective, Marey's gaps become not an accidental or incidental by-product undermining a positivist effort at complete controlled representation but the very point of the enterprise: to show not just movement, which we can all see for ourselves, but the hidden spaces between movement, the spaces that reveal that movement is really movements, that the motion of humans and other animals occurs only through the same series of progressive fragments ultimately allied to cinema.

In her recent book on Marey, Marta Braun asserts that "Marey's studies of human and animal movements are everything that Muybridge's are not: disinterested, accurate, analytic, and systematic."[25] When Braun inexplicably writes that "Muybridge's concern, then, is with narration, not with movement,"[26] she misses the very point exemplified by both Marey and Muybridge, whose visual narratives were defined in the crossing of time and space by movement. Marey and Muybridge signaled a new form of narrative which was defined as structured movement through time and space. Their work linked the self-conscious elaboration of a beginning, middle, and end to the effort to imagine a continuity that could vanquish the isolation of fragmentary moments and the hollowness of empty presence. As Marey's representations of a bird's flight indicate, the narrative structure of beginning, middle, and end was even more germane to Marey's carefully composed paths of movement than to Muybridge's haltingly fragmentary serials. Dagognet ably articulates this aspect of Marey's project: "The universe knows only surges and drops, fragments that we reassemble and that we thereby diminish. We ourselves fabricate a smoothed-out, rounded spectacle. Mareyism must shatter this lie, which philosophy (Bergson) reinforced."[27]

Muybridge and Marey thus anticipated the soon-to-emerge aesthetic of cinema in a simple and schematic manner: Both men used new technologies to re-present continuous motion as a chain of fragmentary moments. Whether through Marey's collage form or Muybridge's more explicit recognition of separation, both efforts made clear that in the constitution and reconstitution of movement, it is never possible to recapture the whole movement. The fissures between the separate moments remind us that we are seeing something that simply replicates a continuous movement but can never be one. We have, that is, entered the zone of representation, which with the bond to the real introduced by photography became representation. The difference of the re-presentation is inscribed in the representation of motion by the gaps that render it discontinuous and fragmentary, whereas the original motion—the present motion—was seemingly continuous.

In film, this union of fragmentation and representation, or fragmentation as representation, posed a double problem. Like other early technologies of movement, film re-presented images in apparently continuous movement. Yoked to photography, cinema then re-presented both the appearance of movement and the appearance of the real. As Christian Metz noted, film's inculcation of movement provides its closest bond to the real, since the people on screen are actually moving. "The objects and the characters we see in a film are apparently only effigies," Metz writes, "but their motion is not the effigy of motion—it seems real."[28] Yet Metz's phenomenological perspective privileges the original movement over the represented movement, as if the first movement were more self-evidently present than its reiteration. "Because movement is never material but always visual," in Metz's words, "to reproduce its appearance is to duplicate its reality. In truth, one cannot even 'reproduce' a movement; one can only re-produce it in a second production belonging to the same order of reality, for the spectator, as the first."[29]

This view of representation does not acknowledge that the original movement was never self-present to begin with. The hollowing-out of movement reiterates and forms part of the general hollowing-out of presence. What we perceive as our movement has in fact already happened; our cognition of the physical fact of movement lags behind the movement itself, so that movement is always displaced. What we call "movement" is really, like presence in general, two parallel tracks: what the body does and what the mind construes. Both progressions carve a forward path through time and space but because presence is always lost, what seems like continuous movement is really a construction of fragments.

Film, Marey and Muybridge remind us, is composed of two things: moving pictures and the spaces between those moving pictures. The pictures do not really move: they just follow each other. Editing thus creates a collage of fragments that cannot help render the viewer's experience discontinuous. Editing's discontinuity opens up gaps and spaces throughout the action, nagging echoes of discontinuity which haunt the film's premise of continuity.[30] As Dziga Vertov wrote in 1929, filmmaking in modernity "calls for construction of the film-object upon 'intervals,' that is, upon the movement between shots, upon the visual correlation of shots with one another, upon transitions from one visual stimulus to another."[31] Because of editing, because of the fissures created by editing, a film can never be fully present as continuous movement; a film's gaps make it always a chain of moments, as segregated as the frames of Muybridge's motion studies.

This fragmentation marks the heart of film as re-presentation: because it is always fragmentary, always a string of moments, it is never complete and present. Re-presentation, in its very form, played into the evacuation of presence that characterized the modern. If there was no present, then re-presentation did not simply reiterate a previous presence. There was no present to re-present. Representation in this sense confirmed the artificiality and evacuation of presence in general.

However, the emerging form of cinema, as such Soviet filmmakers as Vertov and Eisenstein keenly perceived, allowed modernity's potential drawbacks to become aesthetic advantages: Shock, speed, and dislocation became editing, and the evacuation of presence, in the technique of cinema, became the means by which the viewer could find a place in the film's ceaseless forward movement. As Joel Weinsheimer has articulated this concept in a different context, "That it never is (self-present) means that it is always to be interpreted, is always open to interpretation and to a future."[32]

In this way, cinema transformed the hollow present into a new form of experience, as the vacated present opened space for the viewer's activity. Experience arose in—was defined by and in—the space vacated by the present's movement away from itself. The present's self-evacuation opened up niches, breathing room inside the possibility of presence, what Ross Chambers has called "room for maneuver."[33] Modernity's empty, invisible present expanded into a new art composed of a series of empty, invisible presents. These moments were stitched into continuity by the viewer's activity, itself interior and invisible inside the viewer's body. "The animation and the confluence of these forms," as Epstein wrote,

> produce themselves neither on the film strip nor in the lens but only in the individual himself. Discontinuity becomes continuity only after penetrating the spectator. It is a purely interior phenomenon. Outside the subject who looks, there is no movement, no flux, no life in the always fixed mosaics of light and shadow that the screen presents. Within, there is an impression that, like all the others given by the senses, is an interpretation of the object—in other words, an illusion, a phantom. (p. 261)

Yet Epstein predicates film's fragmentation on the unity and coherence of "the individual himself," much as Metz hinges film's fragmentary movement on an imaginary self-presence of "real" movement. If the present disappears, and thereby hollows out presence, this shift also hollows out the subject who constructs that presence. The modern subject is always already alienated, since consciousness of the body can never coincide with the lived body. The modern self can never be present, in a present, to or as its self: "Before itself, behind itself: never itself," as Jean-Paul Sartre put it.[34]

It was above all this form of moving experience which tied the experience of film to the experience of daily life in modernity. The experience of cinema mirrored the wider epistemological experience of modernity. Modern subjects (re)discovered their place as buffers between past and future by (re)experiencing this condition as film-viewers. Past and future clashed not in a hypothetical zone but on the terrain of the body. This alienation both grounded and arose out of the modern aspiration to seize fleeting moments of sensation as a hedge against their inexorable evisceration. The quest to locate a fixed moment of sensual feeling inside the body could never succeed.

NOTES

1. Henri Bergson, *Matter and Memory*, trans. Nancy Margaret Paul and W. Scott Palmer (New York: Zone Books, 1988), p. 150. I am grateful to Annette Kuhn for bringing this quote to my attention.

2. Georg Simmel, "The Metropolis and Mental Life," in *The Sociology of Georg Simmel*, ed. Kurt Wolff, trans. H. H. Gerth (1903; reprint, New York: Free Press, 1950), p. 410.

3. *Selected Writings of Walter Pater*, ed. Harold Bloom (New York: Columbia University Press, 1974), p. xxi. Subsequent references will appear in the text.

4. Martin Heidegger, *Being and Time*, trans. John Macquarrie and Edward Robinson (New York: Harper and Row, 1962), p. 388.

5. Ibid., p. 387.

6. My citations from the Arcades Project will be to the partial translation by Leigh Hafrey and Richard Sieburth in *Benjamin: Philosophy, Aesthetics, History*, ed. Gary Smith (Chicago: University of Chicago Press, 1989). Subsequent references will appear in the text. Also see Susan Buck-Morss, *The Dialectics of Seeing: Walter Benjamin and the Arcades Project* (Cambridge: MIT Press, 1989). My discussion of the "Now of recognizability" is indebted to Margaret Cohen, *Profane Illumination: Walter Benjamin and the Paris of Surrealist Revolution* (Berkeley, Los Angeles, London: University of California Press, 1993).

7. "On Some Motifs in Baudelaire," in *Illuminations*, ed. Hannah Arendt, trans. Harry Zohn (New York: Schocken, 1969), p. 156.

8. Smith, op. cit., p. 38.

9. Richard Sieburth, "Benjamin the Scrivener," in Smith, op. cit., pp. 26–27.

10. Ibid., p. 28.

11. "Theses on the Philosophy of History," in *Illuminations*, p. 255.

12. "Some Motifs in Baudelaire," in *Illuminations*, pp. 163, 194.

13. "The Work of Art in the Age of Mechanical Reproduction," in *Illuminations*, p. 238.

14. Jean Epstein, *Ecrits sur le cinéma, 1921–1953;* tome 1, *1921–1947* (Paris: Seghers, 1974), 145, my translation. All subsequent citations of Epstein will be from this volume and will be my translations; references will appear in the text. Selections from some of Epstein's most important articles and lectures appear in English translation in *Afterimage* 10, *October* 3, and *The Avant-Garde Film: A Reader of Theory and Criticism*, ed. P. Adams Sitney (New York: New York University Press, 1978).

15. *Russian Formalist Criticism: Four Essays*, trans. Lee T. Lemon and Marion J.

Reis (Lincoln: University of Nebraska Press, 1965), p. 12. On Russian Formalism see Victor Erlich, *Russian Formalism: History - Doctrine,* 3d ed. (New Haven: Yale University Press, 1981).

16. In Lennon and Reis, op. cit., p. 12.

17. Fredric Jameson, *The Prison-House of Language* (Princeton: Princeton University Press, 1972), p. 51.

18. Tom Gunning, "The Cinema of Attraction: Early Film, Its Spectator, and the Avant-Garde," *Wide Angle* 8 nos. 3–4 (1986); and idem, "An Aesthetic of Astonishment: Early Film and the (In)Credulous Spectator," *Art and Text* 34 (spring 1989).

19. Idem, "'Now You See It, Now You Don't': The Temporality of the Cinema of Attractions," *Velvet Light Trap* 32 (fall 1993): 6–7.

20. Charles Musser has made this point in *The Emergence of Cinema* (New York: Scribner's, 1990), pp. 179–181 and 258–261, as well as in "Rethinking Film History: Early Cinema/Primitive Cinema/Cinema of Attractions," paper delivered at "The Movies Begin: A Conference Commemorating the 100th Anniversary of Motion Pictures," Yale University, May 1993.

21. Sergei Eisenstein, "Montage of Attractions," *The Film Sense,* trans. and ed. Jay Leyda (New York: Harcourt Brace, 1942), pp. 230–231.

22. Jacques Aumont, *Montage Eisenstein,* trans. Lee Hildreth, Constance Penley, and Andrew Ross (Bloomington: Indiana University Press and the British Film Institute, 1987), p. 42.

23. François Dagognet, *Etienne-Jules Marey: La passion de la trace* (Paris: Hazan, 1987), p. 15, my translation. This book has received a notably poor and stilted translation, *Etienne-Jules Marey: A Passion for the Trace,* trans. Robert Galeta with Jeanine Herman (New York: Zone Books, 1992).

24. Dagognet, op. cit., pp. 137–138.

25. Marta Braun, *Picturing Time: The Work of Etienne-Jules Marey, 1830–1904* (Chicago: University of Chicago Press, 1992), p. 254.

26. Ibid., p. 249.

27. Dagognet, op. cit., p. 13.

28. Christian Metz, "On the Impression of Reality in the Cinema," in Metz, *Film Language,* trans. Michael Taylor (New York: Oxford University Press, 1974), p. 8.

29. Ibid., p. 9.

30. Scott Higgins has examined how this fragmentation dominated the films of the so-called transitional period between 1907 and 1917. "Motivation and Spatial Fragmentation in the Cinema of Narrative Integration," paper delivered at the Society for Cinema Studies Conference, Syracuse, N.Y., March 1994.

31. *Kino-Eye: The Writings of Dziga Vertov,* ed. Annette Michelson, trans. Kevin O'Brien (Berkeley, Los Angeles, London: University of California Press, 1984), p. 90.

32. Joel Weinsheimer, *Gadamer's Hermeneutics* (New Haven: Yale University Press, 1985), p. 163.

33. Ross Chambers, *Room for Maneuver: Reading (the) Oppositional (in) Narrative* (Chicago: University of Chicago Press, 1991).

34. Jean-Paul Sartre, *Being and Nothingness,* trans. Hazel Barnes (New York: Washington Square Press, 1966), p. 201.

PART FOUR

Spectacles and Spectators

Cinematic Spectatorship before the Apparatus: The Public Taste for Reality in *Fin-de-Siècle* Paris

Vanessa R. Schwartz

"No people in the world are so fond of amusements—or *distractions* as they term them—as Parisians. Morning, noon and night, summer and winter, there is always something to be seen and a large portion of the population seems absorbed in the pursuit of pleasure."[1] Cassell's 1884 Paris guidebook confirmed that many visitors to France's capital expected to find a good time. Paris, by the last third of the nineteenth century, had become the European center of the burgeoning entertainment industry. But more important than pleasure, perhaps, the guidebook promised that "there is always something to be seen." Life in Paris, I would like to suggest, became powerfully identified with spectacle. Yet real life was experienced as a show at the same time that shows became increasingly lifelike.

By examining a field of novel cultural forms and practices in late-nineteenth-century Paris, I hope to situate early cinema as a part of the public taste for reality. Rather than understand cinematic spectatorship through a universal and timeless theory of psychic spectatorship constructed in direct relation to the cinematic apparatus, or as an idealized vision produced through discourses about perception and embodied in technological innovations, I frame spectatorship within a particular cultural moment. As Giuliana Bruno has suggested, spectatorship is most aptly conceived of as an embodied and "kinetic affair."[2] It must also be taken as a practice whose history can be understood by examining, on the one hand, the relation between technologies and contents represented, which thus produces possibilities for observation; and, on the other hand, the discourse produced by the experiences of those technologies in a specific context.

I begin, then, with the premise that cinema's spectators brought to the cinematic experience modes of viewing which were cultivated in a variety of cultural activities and practices. By looking at practices that were coterminous with cinema in its initial moments, I suggest that cinema ended up as more than just one in a series of novel gadgets because it incorporated many elements that already could be found in diverse aspects of so-called modern life.

In three sites of popular pleasure in late nineteenth-century France—the Paris Morgue, wax museums, and panoramas—I situate flânerie, which has begun to be used as a shorthand for describing the new, mobilized gaze of the precinematic spectator, in its proper context as a cultural activity for those who participated in Parisian life and claim that the late nineteenth century offered a sort of flânerie for the masses.[3] But I also connect this flânerie to the new mass press which served as a printed digest of the flâneur's roving eye. Spectacle and narrative were integrally linked in Paris's burgeoning mass culture: The realism of spectacle was in fact often contingent on the familiarity of supposedly real-life newspaper narratives.

THE PARIS MORGUE

"There are few people having visited Paris who do not know the Morgue," wrote Parisian social commentator Hughes Leroux in 1888.[4] Listed in practically every guidebook to the city, a fixture of Thomas Cook's tours to Paris, and a "part of every conscientious provincial's first visit to the capital,"[5] the Morgue attracted both regular visitors and large crowds of as many as forty thousand on its big days, when the story of a crime circulated through the popular press and curious visitors lined the sidewalk waiting to file through the *salle d'exposition* to see the victim.

A large and socially diverse audience went to the Morgue. The crowd was composed of "men, women and children," of workers, *petits rentiers*, flâneurs, women workers, and ladies.[6] In fact, the location was so well frequented that vendors lined the sidewalk outside, hawking oranges, cookies, and coconut slices.[7]

The morgue in question was built in 1864 in the center of Paris, behind the cathedral of Nôtre Dame on the quai de l'Archevêché (where the Mémorial à la déportation stands today) and was open to the public seven days a week from dawn to dusk. The institution began in the eighteenth century as the *basse-geôle* of the Châtelet prison in a dark and dank room where "visitors could only present themselves one after another, . . . forced to press their faces against a narrow opening"[8] in order to identify corpses that had been found in the public domain. By the late nineteenth century, the Morgue, whose name comes from an archaic verb meaning "to stare," featured a *salle d'exposition*, wherein two rows of corpses, each on its own marble slab, were displayed behind a large glass window that had green curtains hanging at each side. In contrast to the *basse-geôle*, large crowds could gather and gaze at this almost theatrical display. Of the three large doors at the front, the middle one remained shut, and visitors would file through, entering at the left and exiting at the right, prompting the Morgue's registrar to comment that the Morgue was nothing more than an *entresort*—a carnival attraction in which one purchased entry, then walked through a barrack to gape at the sight within.[9]

The *salle d'exposition* was comparable to other displays that dotted the Parisian landscape in the second half of the nineteenth century. Ernest Cherbuliez, in an article in *La Revue des deux mondes*, highlighted this quality by recounting an anecdote in which a man walked down the boulevard Sébastopol, stopped in front of a store window, and asked the window dressers for work. They suggested he ask at the Morgue.[10]

Most often, however, the Morgue was celebrated as public theater. Emile Zola remarked in *Thérèse Raquin* that it was a "show that was affordable to all. . . . The door is open, enter those who will."[11] A poem in a popular edition called *Les Chansons de la Morgue* described the scene in the *salle d'exposition*: "The crowd, gay and without remorse, comes to the theater to take its place."[12] Upon the closing of the Morgue to the general public in March 1907, one journalist protested:

> The Morgue has been the first among theaters this year to announce its closing. . . . As for the spectators, they have no right to say anything because they didn't pay. There were no subscribers, only regulars, because the show was always free. It was the first free theater for the people. And they tell us it's being canceled. People, the hour of social justice has not yet arrived.[13]

In a time of increasingly private and commercial entertainment, the Morgue was open and free, and the display of dead bodies existed for the public to come and see. As a municipal institution, however, the Morgue's principal goal was to serve as a depository for the anonymous dead, whose identity, administrators hoped, might be established by their being publicly displayed. Yet the Paris Morgue was like no other municipal institution. Despite its location in the shadows of Nôtre-Dame, its deliberately undramatic facade, and its seemingly somber subject matter, the Morgue was "one of the most popular sights in Paris."[14] The identification of dead bodies was turned into a show.

Why did this show attract so many visitors? The historical record does not offer many direct answers. Looking at descriptions of the Morgue in the popular press and in administrative literature, however, offers a means through which one may attempt to reconstruct the Morgue's allure. The vast majority of visitors probably did not go to the Morgue thinking they actually might recognize a corpse. Under the pretense of acting out of civic duty, they went to look at real dead bodies. This was public voyeurism—flânerie in the service of the state.

Many commentators suggested that the Morgue satisfied and reinforced the desire to look which permeated much of Parisian culture in the late nineteenth century. Clovis Pierre, the Morgue's registrar and a sometime poet, wrote that visitors came "to exercise their retinas at the window."[15] Why, however, go to the Morgue when there was so much to see in the city most often associated with the "spectacle of modern life?"[16]

The Morgue served as a visual auxiliary to the newspaper, staging the recently dead who had been sensationally detailed by the printed word. The late nineteenth century in France has been called the "golden age of the press,"[17] and it is critical to understand the central role it played in the development of Parisian spectacle. Current events became the daily fare of the popular Parisian dailies, whose overall circulation increased 250 percent between 1880 and 1914.[18] Newspapers replaced opinion with so-called truth as the world "entered the age of information."[19] In the Parisian press, political life took a backseat to theater openings, horse races, and charity events, but it was the *fait divers*—reports of horrible accidents and sensational crimes—which filled the columns and the coffers.

The *fait divers* was a popular newspaper rubric that reproduced in extraordinary detail, both written and visual, representations of a sensational reality. In addition to the sensationalism of the *fait divers*, newspapers offered serial novels. Clearly demarcated from the rest of the newspaper by a bar across the bottom of the page, these popular narratives were often based on actual newspaper stories, especially the *faits divers*.

Because of its featured role in so many *faits divers*, material about the Morgue appeared regularly in the newspaper. As Alphonse Devergie, medical inspector of the Morgue, explained, "Once the newspapers announce a crime, one sees a great number of the curious arrive at the Morgue."[20] And, of course, when a large crowd gathered at the Morgue, *it* then became the subject of further news reports, which in turn kept the corpse, the unsolved crime, and the Morgue in the public eye and guaranteed a steady stream of spectators on the quai de l'Archevêché.

Press coverage heightened public awareness and interest. Guillot argued that the newspaper constituted a source that stimulated public interest for what "in newspaper jargon is called the *plat du jour*."[21] He believed that all the reporting turned the Morgue into a "glass house," and that if the Morgue could be considered a theater of crime, then the newspaper was its program.[22] One of the Morgue's registrars argued that reading the newspaper prompted women workers to visit the Morgue because their spirits had been haunted by the newspapers' serial novels.[23] Other comments suggest that the Morgue was a version of the newspaper's *feuilleton*. *L'Éclair*, for example, described the Morgue as "this living illustration of a serial-novel mystery."[24]

Some people believed that the popularity of public visits to the Morgue, like interest in newspapers themselves, stemmed from the public interest in so-called reality. "What if, rather than your stories, your most frightening paintings, they prefer reality, and what a reality," suggested Firmin Maillard, one of the Morgue's earliest historians.[25] An article in *Le Paris* boasted that the Morgue was worth a visit because what one saw "are not imitations, not trompe l'oeil."[26] Yet, while the newspapers may have encouraged many visits, a look at one of the many causes célèbres of the Morgue reveals that the spectacular show in the window was far more than just an ordinary placement of corpses on slabs.

In August 1886, the cover of *Le Journal illustré* featured a doyenne of the Morgue, the "Enfant de la rue du Vert-Bois"—a four-year-old girl found on 29 July 1886 in a stairwell at 47, rue du Vert-Bois, near the Conservatoire des Arts et Métiers. The corpse, which was transferred to the Morgue, showed no apparent signs of injury except a slight bruise on the right hand. The newspapers reported that the display attracted "a considerable crowd," which by 3 August was estimated at about fifty thousand.[27] The body, clothed in a dress, was mounted in the *salle d'exposition,* "on a chair covered in a red cloth that brought out the paleness of the little dead one even more" (fig. 11.1).[28] *Le Matin* reported that despite the "service d'ordre" that had been established, the size of the crowd forced traffic to a halt, and vendors hawked coconut, gingerbread, and toys, turning the quai de l'Archevêché into "a genuine fairgrounds."[29] On 5 August, the papers reported severe disorder: "The mob rushes the doors with savage cries; fallen hats are tromped on, parasols and umbrellas are broken, and yesterday, women fell sick, having been half suffocated."[30]

By then, *Le Matin* estimated that 150,000 people had filed past the body (in groups of no more than 50 at a time, in rows of 5, who were forbidden to tarry in front of the glass). Each night, the corpse was put in a refrigerated case to preserve it. In order to avoid altering it in any way, attendants simply strapped the corpse to the red velvet chair and deposited the complete display in the refrigerator.

Because of the state of decomposition, Morgue doctors decided to perform an autopsy on 6 August.[31] *Le Petit journal* reported the sentiments of the crowds that had gathered that day, only to "have had the disappointment not to have caught sight of the child displayed on its little chair."[32] After the autopsy, doctors concluded that the child had died a natural death, having suffocated by choking on an earthworm.

Images of both the child and the crowd at the Morgue appeared in the popular press throughout the period of display. *Le Journal illustré* featured an illustrated narration—a sort of illustrated serial novel—a genre that often accompanied a cause célèbre at the Morgue (fig. 11.2). The scene opens with the building on the rue du Vert-Bois. Next, two men discover the corpse in the stairwell in the building. The crowd outside the Morgue

Fig. 11.1. Display of corpse of the "Child of Vert-Bois Street," *Le Monde illustré*,
15 August 1886.

occupies the center of the page, and the scene in the *salle d'exposition*
covers the bottom. When these illustrations appeared on 15 August, part
of the case had already been resolved, but the child's civil status and the
reasons she had been abandoned remained a mystery. She was buried on
17 August, and, although her photograph remained on display at the entrance, the child went unidentified.[33]

The Morgue's visitors came neither to identify corpses nor simply to see
them laid out on slabs. No doubt the Morgue was a morbid attraction.[34]
More significantly, however, it was "part of the cataloged curiosities, of
things to see, under the same heading as the Eiffel Tower, Yvette Guilbert,
and the catacombs."[35] In other words, this public service was experienced
as a Parisian attraction. Newspapers featured stories about the crowds at

Fig. 11.2. "The Mystery of Vert-Bois Street," *Le Journal illustré*, 15 August 1886.

the Morgue, and, like newspapers, the Morgue re-presented a spectacularized Parisian life. The *salle d'exposition,* its curtain, the lines outside,
corpses dressed and seated on chairs, and newspaper illustrations guaranteed that the Morgue's reality was re-presented, mediated, orchestrated,
and spectacularized.

In part a visual digest of the printed word, the Morgue transformed real
life into spectacle. It is worth noting that the Morgue was finally closed
to the public in 1907—a year often considered a watershed among cinema historians which in France was marked, in particular, by a proliferation of institutions devoted exclusively to cinema.[36] The audience, it
seems, had moved from the *salle d'exposition* to the *salle du cinéma.*

In trying to explain the Morgue's popularity, its administrative director
remarked, "The Morgue is considered in Paris like a museum that is much
more fascinating than even a wax museum because the people displayed
are real flesh and blood."[37] He was not alone, however, in drawing a connection between these two institutions of Parisian spectacle.

THE MUSÉE GRÉVIN

When the Musée Grévin opened in 1882 on the boulevard Montmartre,
in the heart of "modern" Paris, a newspaper cartoon linked the wax museum to the already popular Morgue. In it two working-class men gape at a
wax figure laid out on a slab. One says, "Geez, you'd think it was a real
stiff." His friend replies, "This is almost as much fun as the real Morgue."[38]
An immediate success, the museum attracted half a million visitors yearly
and remains open to this day. An emblem of the burgeoning entertainment industry, it had a fundamental tie to the public. "It is not from the
Institute that Grévin will seek approval," noted one reviewer; "it's from the
public."[39] Why did a wax museum capture the public imagination in *fin-de-
siècle* Paris?

The Musée Grévin was modeled, in part, after London's very popular
Madame Tussaud's, itself a direct descendant of the well-known wax cabinet of Philippe Curtius, popular in Paris during the revolutionary era. Unlike Madame Tussaud's, the Musée Grévin was founded by a well-known
boulevard journalist, Arthur Meyer, and the newspaper caricaturist Alfred
Grévin. Both men envisaged the museum as an improvement upon newspapers, as a more realistic way to satisfy the public interest in current
events. The museum's founders promised that their display would "represent the principal current events with scrupulous fidelity and striking precision," serving as "a living newspaper."[40]

The two men believed that written reporting did not entirely satisfy the
public. As the preface to the museum's first catalog, written by *Le Figaro*'s
Albert Wolff, explained,

By adding an image to the text, illustrated newspapers . . . have made a decisive advance in modern communication. The museum's founders correctly figured that one could go even further and create a *journal plastique,* where the public would find those people who occupied their attention reproduced with a scrupulous respect for nature.[41]

Critics constantly remarked on the museum's verisimilitude, calling it a chronicle in action and an animated newspaper, despite the fact that the tableaux did not move.

The realism of the displays relied on many devices other than the lifelike quality of the wax figures themselves. Accessories, ornaments, and the framing device of the tableaux worked together to effect the real. For example, the museum used authentic accessories. The figure of Victor Hugo held one of the writer's actual pens; a tableau of the death of Jean-Paul Marat featured the actual tub in which he had been murdered (and for which the museum had paid a hefty five thousand francs), a genuine soldier's pike from the revolutionary era, and a 1791 edition of *L'Ami du peuple,* the newspaper edited by the murdered revolutionary. The figure of Emile Zola wore a suit donated by the author.

A tableau's realism might also be derived from its status as an authentic copy. For example, the president's library was a replica of the library at the Elysée palace, and a tableau of a scene from the new opera *Françoise de Rimini* was the "exact and absolute facsimile of the National Academy of Music," from the costumes to the furniture and the sets.[42]

The tableaux created recognizable, taxonomical, and appropriate settings for the figures—mini-narratives in the form of peepholes into Parisian life. As the museum catalog explained, "it was necessary to make the museum interesting not only by the exact likeness of the characters but also by the composition of groups, by showing individuals in their milieu."[43]

Left unsaid, however, was the necessity of the tableaux for public recognition of the figures. Visitors, for the most part, had probably never seen, either in a newspaper or in person, most of the subjects represented at the museum, since the only mass-produced visual images available were color engravings. Photographs would not be easily reproduced for newspapers until the twentieth century. The tableaux and their abundant details—whether genuine objects or copies—were essential in effecting verisimilitude simply because of the crowd's inability actually to assess the likeness of the various personalities represented.

Aside from the vivacity of the wax sculpture and taxonomic groupings of the dioramas, the museum formed a pantheon that relied on the public's recognition of and familiarity with its characters; its success dwelled ultimately in the eye of the beholder. Rather than the definitive collection decided on from above found at most museums, the Musée Grévin held a rapidly changing collection whose content was contingent on the public's interest and visual recognition. Whereas traditional pantheons may be characterized by their selectivity, the Musée Grévin boasted of its range and inclusiveness. The novelist Paul Bourget celebrated the museum, noting, "In three or four rooms is it not the abridged version of the modern city?"[44]

As a wide-ranging pantheon, the museum mimicked the newspaper's form: Tableaux most often stood side by side in no particular relation to one another, as did newspaper columns filled with seemingly unconnected stories.[45] The juxtaposition of political leaders, actors, and artists attested to a modern social order dominated by celebrity and based on popularity. With what seemed like "intrepid whimsy," celebrities filled this "Parisian Pantheon."[46] That the café-concert singer Yvette Guilbert and the president of the republic might stand side by side suggested that the wax museum also echoed the basis of political legitimacy in Third Republic France, in which politicians—like performers and artists—rose and fell seemingly by virtue of the crowd's fancy. The wax museum materialized that new social order based on the whims of the crowd.

While representing a social order created in and by the public eye, the museum also offered its visitors visual privilege by providing an apparent proximity to celebrities. One newspaper review explained, "The likenesses of our great men, of our famous artists or society people pleases us . . . and it is to see them up close that the public crowds to the Musée Grévin."[47]

Beyond representing celebrities, the tableaux also afforded museumgoers something special: an up-close-and-personal view of dignitaries who might otherwise be seen only in official functions, if seen at all. For example, a tableau featuring Napoleon seeking shelter from the snow during his retreat from Russia represented the emperor huddling in the cold. The catalog explained, "Napoleon's look is poignantly filled with anxiety: You can already see foreshadowed there the Empire's destiny."[48] One found the country's fate in its leader's emotional physiognomy rather than on the battlefields. Visitors also saw the famous explorer Savorgnan de Brazza relaxing in his tent and Bismarck meeting with Field Marshal Von Moltke in a "private visit" at Varzin, where the prince "often rested from the fatigues of politics."[49] These tableaux personalized politics, transforming the scale of history and contemporary politics into something with which visitors might identify.

But privilege did not stop at the relation between the viewer and the subjects represented. The three-dimensional tableaux created a particular perspective between the spectator and the display, which functioned as one of the museum's lasting attractions. At the Musée Grévin, visitors could inhabit multiple perspectives—panoramic views—at the same time that the displays often offered privileged access, serving as peepholes into Paris.[50]

Fig. 11.3. Workers looking at dignitaries on the Eiffel Tower, Musée Grévin, 1889. (Musée Grévin Archives, Paris.)

In 1889 the museum opened a tableau of the Eiffel Tower. Rather than reconstruct the sight that could be seen on the Champ de Mars, the museum offered a view, in mid-construction, of a visit by Eiffel and three officials, Lockroy, Alphand, and Berger (fig. 11.3). The scene included workers who had been interrupted by the visit and who were represented as watching the visiting dignitaries (fig. 11.4). The museum visitor, therefore, saw what most people had never seen: the tower under construction—a sort of dress rehearsal. At the same time, the scene depicted a panoramic view of Paris as it would have been seen from the second level of the Eiffel Tower. The catalog boasted that "everything is rendered with a fidelity that can be appreciated by only the rare privileged who have already made this marvelous ascent."[51] The display represented a privileged view of a privileged view of Paris. Visitors enjoyed not only a panoramic view of the city but also the peephole view of workers being interrupted by a visit of dignitaries. Not one but three sights confronted the museum visitor: the panoramic view of Paris, the view of the visiting dignitaries, and the view of the workers watching the visit.

Fig. 11.4. View from the Eiffel Tower, Musée Grévin, 1889. (Musée Grévin Archives, Paris.)

Over the years, the Musée Grévin's tableaux featured several scenes from the *coulisses* (backstage)—representations of a perspective not usually accessible to most spectators and the domain most often reserved for allegedly privileged flâneurs. Here *their* voyeurism was extended to every visitor who could pay the museum's small admission price. The museum spectator's privilege resided in the tableau's offer of more than one view at a time: that of both a spectator of the show and a spectator of other spectators.[52] In 1885, for example, the museum represented a dancer's loge at intermission. The scene showed a dancer being visited in the dressing room by an elegant man. In 1890 that tableau was replaced by "*Les Coulisses de l'Opéra: Le Foyer de la danse.*" Here, the visitor simultaneously saw both onstage and off. The catalog underscored the tableau's privileged perspective: "All works to give the spectator the illusion of a visit to so curious a corner of the grand Parisian stage, a visit only permitted an elect few."[53] While the themes may not have been unfamiliar, at least to those visitors who had attended various Impressionist salons, the display's three-dimensionality and verisimilitude were touted as effecting the illusion of

Fig. 11.5. A Rehearsal at the Comédie Française, Musée Grévin, 1887. (Musée Grévin Archives, Paris.)

presence, or reality, in a way that paintings simply could not. An 1887 diorama further reveals what the wax museum offered that paintings did not. "A Rehearsal at the Comédie-Française" represented the director's loge during a dress rehearsal (fig. 11.5). There the museum's visitors observed Juliette Adam, editor of *La Nouvelle revue*; Ambroise Thomas, director of

the Opéra; Jules Claretie, director of the Comédie-Française; and Edouard
Pailleron, author of *La Souris,* watching a scene from that play. The tableau
was structured around its three-dimensionality and the visitor's mobility. It
was assumed that the spectator would approach the tableau from the left,
where the figures in the box appeared to be watching something. As the
spectators walked to the right, they could then see the inset of the dress
rehearsal being watched, which was represented as seen through the eyes
of those seated in the box, and which, because of its angle, could not really
be seen by museum visitors until they aligned themselves with the visual
perspective of the wax figures. The tableau's designers intended for people to walk through and thus offered them movement through sequential
points of view. This not only vested spectators with the power of making
the scene happen through their own motion but also offered a primitive
way of introducing motion into the display—an effect that the museum actively pursued in another way. In 1892 the Musée Grévin became the first
institution to offer projected moving images in the form of Emile Rey-
naud's "*Pantomimes lumineuses.*"[54]

If spectators' movement might have been incorporated into the museum's display, narrativity also built motion into the displays. The response
to "L'histoire d'un crime"—the museum's serial novel—clarifies the imbrication of serial narrative to motion at the Musée Grévin. A series of seven
tableaux, the display portrayed the vicissitudes of a crime from start to finish: the murder, the arrest, the confrontation of the murderer and his victim at the morgue, the trial, the cell of the condemned, the preparation
for execution, and the execution. An early review noted that its "thrilling
realism made it the display that most interested the crowd; it was difficult
even to approach, the crowd was so enormous."[55] One reviewer explained
that "it is a *fait divers* in seven tableaux, of an extraordinarily realistic execution that creates an intensity of effect that is stunning."[56] Another simply called it a "living *fait divers.*"[57]

The enhanced realism of the series of tableaux was embedded in its familiar narrativity, while its seriality presented a series of freeze-frames set
into motion by the spectator's walk through the display. "*L'Histoire d'un
crime*" also offered a familiar form of narrative in its conceptualization
as a serial novel—a standard feature of almost all newspapers by the late
nineteenth century. "*L'Histoire d'un crime*" announced itself as a serial
novel, yet it was reviewed as though it were a *fait divers.* Not only does this
echo the blurring between reality and fiction that characterized each
genre but it also suggests that what was so strikingly real about "*L'Histoire
d'un crime*" was neither its props nor its wax figures but rather its serial narrativity. The seven wax tableaux seemed more realistic than even a serial
novel. The spectator's motion infused the display with its seemingly lifelike quality; such serial motion linked "*L'Histoire d'un crime*" to real life. It

should come as no surprise that Ferdinand Zecca, an early filmmaker at Pathé, established his fame with a 1901 film entitled *L'Histoire d'un crime,* based on the Musée Grévin display.[58]

The content of the tableaux and the way they situated spectators helped turn museum visitors into flâneurs. It offered the public, at the very least, views of the places and perspectives which seemed to belong only to the hounds of modern life. But visitors to the Musée Grévin also entered a plastic newspaper—a world dominated by events (the making of the sight-bite, so to speak) and a pantheon of the present—where the will of the crowd might determine the content of the collection and the powerful were rendered familiar and personable. The technology of the tableaux offered museum visitors a world of visual mastery and access to privilege, giving them both panoptic and peephole visual fields. The Musée Grévin's dedication to the public taste for reality, its use of wax sculpture to reproduce that so-called reality, its focus on current events and rapid change, its link between both spectacle and narrative, and the scopic organization of its tableaux are all elements associated with early cinema and yet found at the Musée Grévin well before the alleged invention of film.

PANORAMAS

While crowds gathered at the Musée Grévin, Parisians and tourists sought out other realist entertainments. Cassell's 1884 *Guide to Paris* remarked, "With the last few years there has been a perfect eruption of panoramas in every quarter of Paris."[59] "We are entering Panoramania," declared an article in *Le Voltaire,* in response to the opening of the third panorama in a year's time.[60] Indeed, this late eighteenth-century entertainment, which had virtually disappeared by midcentury, witnessed a renaissance in the 1880s and 1890s.

Panoramas and dioramas have often been discussed as technological inventions of the early nineteenth century that can be understood as antecedents to film. In particular, scholars have drawn attention to the way panoramas and dioramas marshaled vision to transport spectators in time and place through the illusion of realistic representation.[61] Rather than simply limit a discussion of panoramas and similar entertainments to the moment of their invention in the early nineteenth century, I want to show how, like wax museums, panoramas flourished in the 1880s and 1890s because they attempted to capture and re-present an already familiar version of reality—a reality in which life was captured through motion. The panorama's realism hinged on the notion that, to capture life, a display had to reproduce it as bodily, and not merely as visual, experience.

The 1880s and 1890s witnessed a proliferation of realistic details in the panoramas. Photography helped. Some panorama painters painted from photographs; others projected enlarged slides onto the canvas and then traced the projected images. Even before photography, panoramas mixed three-dimensional objects with the painted canvas to improve the display's realism. Langlois incorporated a real set in the 1830s in his "Battle of Navarino," in which spectators found themselves on an actual battleship. In his 1881 panorama "*Les Cuirassiers de Reichshoffen*," which depicted a defeat by French troops in the Franco-Prussian War, Poilpot used tinsel for the weapons and for the buttons on the military costumes on his canvas. The catalog of "*Les Cuirassiers de Reichshoffen*" acknowledged sculptor Jules Talrich for providing the wax figures that "represent the bodies strewn out on the natural setting in such an astonishing and true manner."[62]

The caricaturist Robida mocked the increasing verisimilitude of panoramas in a cartoon featuring a panorama of the Battle of Champigny during the siege of Paris. One of the captions explained that in order for visitors to understand what the siege was really like, they would be forced to stay for three days and be given only one smoked herring to eat. Another caption noted that the attraction was freezing and visitors could be drenched by a simulated rainstorm. With the cartoon depicting exploding shells and military music in the background, Robida concluded that "one deserved a military medal upon exiting." Although no panorama actually went as far as Robida's parody, his point was clear: People delighted in the realistic re-creation of this terrible event.

Whereas panoramas of the early nineteenth century may have provided news in a world prior to the mass press, in the 1880s panoramas served as visual corollaries of the popular press in much the same way that the wax museum did.[63] Panoramas began to represent daily events reported in newspapers, such as the Tsar's coronation or the visit of the French president to the Russian fleet. A definition of panoramas and dioramas from the 1890s described their realism as generated by the subjects they represented rather than as a product of their technologies:

> Scenes of current events have the knack of attracting the crowd, which is still struck with emotion about a recent event, a catastrophe, an execution or a famous assassination. They reexamine the accident or the crime in a tableau that creates the illusion of reality.

Late-nineteenth-century panoramas broke with traditional, landscape-oriented panoramic representations despite the fact that illustrating individuals was not as effective as depicting landscape in the creation of the realistic panorama effect. Realism was no longer simply an effect of visual representation. For example, the success of Charles Castellani's panorama "*Le Tout Paris*" resided in cultural fascination with representations of celebrities in the familiar sights of modern Paris. The tableau grouped Paris's celebrities around the Opéra, one of the symbols of modern Paris. Spectators were positioned as though standing in front of the Opéra; around them were the boulevard des Capucines, the Grand Hôtel, the rue du Quatre Septembre, the Café de la Paix, and, at the end of the long avenue de l'Opéra, the Louvre. A review celebrated the choice of the place de l'Opéra: "No better place could have been chosen in this shining and noisy Paris to represent Parisian life in all its ardor, vigor and feverishness."[65] "*Le Tout Paris*" was intended to satisfy a public interest and curiosity that was clearly tied to press culture. One review explained that the panorama would attract many of the people who "always wanted to know and see the poets, writers, painters, sculptors, actors and politicians whose names they read in the newspaper every day."[66] The gallery served as a *summa* of the popular press.

This panorama contained none of the foreground objects that had been added to other attractions at the 1889 Exposition, but only by virtue of circumstance. Located within the actual exposition grounds on the esplanade des Invalides, it was nonetheless situated in what was considered a dead area of the exposition.[67] This poor location worried the panorama's financiers who insisted on keeping expenses down. As a result, as Catellani complained about the attraction, "We had neither accessories, nor false terrains, nor any of the things that are absolutely indispensable for producing what the public likes: trompe l'oeil and illusion."[68] The reviews suggested, however, that the illusion of life might be otherwise generated.

Popular despite its poor location, the panorama remained open for the entire exposition, during which time more than three hundred thousand people visited.[69] Aside from celebrating the range and sheer number of celebrities represented, reviews noted the panorama's lifelike qualities. A simple circular painting, without props and sets, one would imagine that it could not compete with other panoramas in terms of its verisimilitude. Yet critics celebrated "the astonishing expression of activity and life that animates the entire composition."[70] It was as if its subject matter somehow animated the composition itself. Another review described the panorama as if it were a freeze-frame, an instant

> seized while passing by in a carriage, on horseback, in groups, with even more truth than an instant photograph can give the idea of. What's more, isn't there the charm of color, the representation of gestures and looks, the entire Parisian spirit spread among the brilliant, animated crowd that is so lively that we have the perfect illusion of its movement and its reality?[71]

Although the painting did not portray an actual moment, it depicted an idealized and possible moment in Parisian life which most readers of the daily press could have imagined, based on their familiarity with the location and the people populating it. In other words, the painting seemed lifelike because it visually materialized a world that formed a familiar popular narrative: the real world that one found represented in the Parisian press. Like the wax museum, the panorama's success was in the eye and the mind of the beholder; realism was not merely a technological evocation.

Of course, public interest in reality also drove many other panoramas toward ever-increasing realism in the form of simulation. The panoramas of the late nineteenth century relied less on an imagined transport and more on simulations of voyages and literally moving landscapes.

The first moving panorama was the "Panorama of the Fleet of the Compagnie Générale Transatlantique," where visitors boarded a re-creation of the company's newest steamer, *La Touraine*.[72] Opened in May 1889, on the quai d'Orsay, within the exposition grounds, the attraction received more than 1.3 million visitors.[73] The painter Poilpot served as the artistic director of the display, which incorporated a view of the entire port of Le Havre, including a view of the company's eighty other ships harbored. The attraction also featured eleven other canvases and a coastal landscape that moved as the ship "went by." Passengers climbed aboard this life-size reproduction of the ship through an elegant vestibule and walked up a set of stairs and then out onto the captain's deck in the "open air." Wax figures of crew members in lookout positions and of the captain describing the port to a female passenger mingled with live sailors and officers dressed in the uniforms of the Transatlantic Company. One reviewer noted that Poilpot had "succeeded in reconstituting scenes from life on board in its most minor details with surprising fidelity. . . . The artist has completely achieved his goal; he has mixed reality and fiction in such a way that we are practically fooled."[74]

With as many visitors as the attraction had, all paying the small sum of one franc, it should come as no surprise that reviewers remarked on the diversity of the crowd, which included peasants, workers (who had never seen the sea, the reviewer noted), bourgeois men and women, shopkeepers, and diplomats.[75] Visitors of different classes must have had divergent experiences on *La Touraine*. Those bourgeois visitors who had actually taken a cruise could judge the quality of the simulation. For others, it might be the only time that they set foot on a ship, and one imagines that the Compagnie Transatlantique hoped that it would not be their last time.

Poilpot continued in his attempts to achieve a more realistic effect by simulating motion. His 1892 panorama, which represented the 1794 sinking of the French ship *Le Vengeur* during the war against the British, provided a technological watershed. Spectators stood on the deck of the battleship *Le Hussard*, surrounded by enemy ships and across from the sinking *Vengeur*. The deck of *Le Hussard* pitched back and forth, giving spectators the feeling that they were on a ship.[76] Reviewers celebrated what they considered an advance toward greater illusion in this panorama which opened on 25 May 1892. In July, Poilpot added the feature of sound to his spectacle in the form of cannons firing, a chorus singing the Marseillaise and two actors reciting a lyric poem about the accomplishments of the sinking ship. Despite its critical acclaim, "Le Vengeur" did not stay open for more than a year; its enormous costs simply did not allow the two-franc panorama to make a sufficient profit.[77]

Between 1892 and the next exposition in 1900, many attractions successfully simulated motion. For example, starting in October 1892, Parisians could see the *"Pantomimes lumineuses"* at the Musée Grévin. In 1894 they could see moving photographs in Edison's kinetoscope; and, as of December 1895, the Lumière brothers' films could be seen at the Grand Café.

Entrepreneurs sought to incorporate the new moving pictures into already existing amusements. Moving pictures were initially considered simply a novel technique for representing motion, and it was not clear that they might suffice as an entertainment in their own right. Moving pictures did, however, blend well with the cultural agenda of the panoramas. So, for example, in 1898, Louis Régnault opened "Maerorama" on the boulevard across from the porte Saint-Martin. A simulated boat ride, it incorporated the moving platform used in "Le Vengeur," adding compressed air to make wind and waves. The exhibitor, dressed in a captain's uniform, warned "that those susceptible to falling seasick should abstain."[78] The lights then dimmed, and instead of a painted canvas rolling by, visitors watched "movies" of coastal views photographed from boats: the Corsican coast, Africa, the Italian lakes, and, finally, a view of Marseille, where, after two toots of the ship's horn, passengers were asked to descend and allow other tourists "eager to experience the wonders of 'Maerorama'" to be given their chance.[79] Régnault presented a similar attraction at the 1900 Exposition; there, passengers were seated in a funicular instead of on a boat. The advent of film did not replace mechanical panoramas: Film was not, at least in its early years, perceived as the answer to the public's taste for reality.

Panoramas and similar entertainments reproduced reality in a variety of ways: by relying on spectator-generated optical illusions, by echoing other realist genres such as the press, and by simulating reality. One can find no technological telos toward ever more perfectly realistic reproduction culminating in the invention of cinema. Rather, as this focus on panoramas during the 1880s and 1890s has tried to suggest, these spectacles technologically generated "reality" and its concomitant animation in a variety of ways during the same period. Further, the various representations of "real-life" experiences offered sensationalized versions of reality—a sensationalism that ranged from narrative suspense to physical simulations.

To many *fin-de-siècle* observers, Parisians demonstrated a new and marked

taste for reality. By stretching beyond the bounds of realism and illusionism, I have tried to argue that their taste for the real was posited on the
blurring of life and art—on the way that reality was spectacularized (as at
the Morgue) at the same time that spectacles were obsessively realistic.
Reality, however, was complexly constituted and defined. Looking at contemporaneous observations suggests that, as in any technological apparatus, the reality-effect also resided in spectators' abilities to make connections between the spectacles they saw and the familiar press narratives they
already knew.

To understand cinematic spectatorship as a historical practice, it is essential to locate cinema in the field of cultural forms and practices associated with the burgeoning mass culture of the late nineteenth century. It is
not mere coincidence that apart from people's interest in reality, the activities described here transpired among large groups of people in whose
mobility some of the spectacles' realistic effects resided. Those practices
suggest that flânerie was not simply the privilege of the bourgeois male but
a cultural activity for all who participated in Parisian life. Thus, rather
than identify the seeds of cinematic spectatorship, this sort of flânerie for
the masses points to the birth of the audience, for it is necessarily in a
crowd that one finds the cinematic spectator.

NOTES

1. *Guide to Paris* (London: Cassell's, 1884), p. 111.

2. Giuliana Bruno, *Streetwalking on a Ruined Map* (Princeton: Princeton University Press, 1993), p. 38.

3. See Anne Friedberg, *Window Shopping* (Berkeley, Los Angeles, London: University of California Press, 1993) on the relationship between flânerie and modern
spectatorship.

4. Hughes Leroux, *L'Enfer parisien* (Paris: 1888), p. 353. Unless otherwise
noted, all translations from the French in this essay are my own.

5. *Le Temps*, 25 September 1882.

6. Ernest Cherbuliez, "La Morgue," in *La Revue des deux mondes*, January 1891,
p. 368; Emile Zola, *Thérèse Raquin* (Paris: Flammarion, 1970), p. 131; and Adolphe
Guillot, *Paris qui souffre: Le Basse-geôle du Grand-Châtelet et les morgues modernes*, 2d ed.
(Paris: Chez Rouquette, 1888), p. 177.

7. Leroux, op. cit., p. 353, and Guillot, op cit., p. 177.

8. Guillot, op cit., p. 43.

9. Clovis Pierre, *Les Gaietés de la morgue* (Paris: Gallimard, 1895).

10. Cherbuliez, op. cit., p. 360.

11. Zola, op. cit., p. 131.

12. Angelin Ruelle, *Les Chansons de la morgue* (Paris: Léon Varnier, 1890).

13. Pierre Véron, "La Morgue," in *Le Magasin pittoresque*, March 1907, pp. 171–
172.

14. E. A. Reynolds-Ball, *Paris in Its Splendours* (London, 1901), 2:312.

15. Pierre, op. cit.

16. Georg Simmel, cited in Walter Benjamin, "Some Motifs in Baudelaire," in Benjamin, *Charles Baudelaire*, tr. Quintin Hoare (London: New Left, 1973), p. 151.

17. Jacques Wolgensinger, *L'Histoire à la une: La Grande aventure de la presse* (Paris: Decouvertes Gallimard, 1989).

18. Anne-Marie Thiesse, *Le Roman du quotidien* (Paris: Le Chemin Vert, 1984), p. 17.

19. Emile Zola, cited in Wolgensinger, op. cit., p. 67.

20. Alphonse Devergie, *Notions générales sur la Morgue de Paris* (Paris: Félix Malteste, 1877), p. 11.

21. Guillot, op. cit., p. 182.

22. Ibid., pp. 199, 258.

23. *La Presse,* 22 March 1907.

24. *L'Éclair,* 21 March 1907.

25. Firmin Maillard, *Recherches historiques et critiques sur la Morgue* (Paris: Delahays, 1860), pp. 94–95.

26. *Le Paris,* 31 August 1892.

27. *Le Petit journal,* 3 August 1886.

28. *Le Matin,* 2 August 1886.

29. Ibid., 4 August 1886.

30. *La Liberté,* 5 August 1886.

31. Archives of the Police Prefect of Paris, morgue registers, 1886.

32. *Le Petit journal,* 6 August 1886.

33. Archives of the Police Prefect of Paris, morgue registers, 1886.

34. See Anne Margaret and Patrice Higonnet, "Façades: Walter Benjamin's Paris," *Critical Inquiry* 10 (March 1984): 391–419, in which the Morgue is discussed as part of the nineteenth-century bourgeois obsession with death.

35. *Le Voltaire,* 22 July 1892. Yvette Guilbert was a well-known singer in the café concerts.

36. For more on the closing of the Morgue, see my dissertation, "The Public Taste for Reality: Early Mass Culture in *Fin-de-Siècle* Paris" (University of California, Berkeley, 1993).

37. *La Presse,* 22 March 1907.

38. Cartoon from the Musée Grévin Archives, hereafter cited as MGA.

39. *Le Monde illustré,* 22 May 1882.

40. Stock prospectus, Bibliothèque Historique de la Ville de Paris, Actualités Anciennes, series 102. Hereafter cited as BHVP.

41. *Catalogue-Almanach du Musée Grévin,* 1882, MGA.

42. Ibid.

43. Ibid.

44. *Le Parlement,* 8 June 1882.

45. See Richard Terdiman, *Discourse/Counter-Discourse* (Ithaca, N.Y.: Cornell University Press, 1985), p. 122, for a discussion of newspapers.

46. Jules Lemaître, *Impressions de théâtre* (orig. pub. 1887), 2d ser., 8th ed. (Paris: Société Française de l'Imprimerie, 1897), p. 325.

47. *L'Indépendance belge,* 12 June 1882.

48. *Catalogue du Musée Grévin,* 54th ed., MGA.

49. *Catalogue-Almanach du Musée Grévin,* 32d ed., MGA.

50. For an important discussion of spectator position at wax museums, see Mark Sandberg, "Missing Persons: Spectacle and Narrative in Late Nineteenth Century Scandinavia" (Ph.D. diss., University of California, Berkeley, 1991).

51. *Catalogue du Musée Grévin,* 57th ed., MGA.

52. As Robert Herbert has noted, this theme could be found represented in many Impressionist paintings and in other more popular images as well (Herbert, *Impressionism* [New Haven: Yale University Press, 1988], p. 104).

53. *Catalogue-Alamanch du Musée Grévin,* 82d ed., MGA.

54. For more on the cinema at the Musée Grévin, see my article, coauthored with Jean-Jacques Meusy, "Le Musée Grévin et le Cinématographe: L'Histoire d'une rencontre," *1895* 11 (December 1991): 19–48.

55. *Le Temps,* 7 June 1882.

56. *L'Express,* 7 June 1882.

57. *Le Parlement,* 6 June 1882.

58. This 140-meter film, lasting between five and six minutes, was based on the tableaux that could still be found at the Musée Grévin, with one exception: Whereas the wax scene of the convict in his cell shows him playing cards, the film version shows him in an activity that would later become the primary metaphor of the filmic experience. He is dreaming.

59. Cassell's *Guide to Paris* (Paris, 1884), p. 117.

60. *Le Voltaire,* 3 January 1881, as cited in François Robichon, "Les panoramas en France au XIX siècle" (Doctoral diss., University of Paris, Nanterre, 1982), p. 216.

61. Friedberg, op. cit., pp. 20–22. Jonathan Crary has made a distinction between the two; in the panorama, one is compelled to turn one's head and look around, while the diorama actually turns its spectators, transforming the observer, he argues, into a component of the machine (Crary, *Techniques of the Observer* [Cambridge: MIT Press, 1990], p. 113).

62. *Les Cuirassiers de Reichshoffen* (Paris: Société des Grands Panoramas, 1881), BHVP, Actualités Anciennes, series 103.

63. See Richard Altick, *The Shows of London* (Cambridge: Harvard University Press, 1978). Altick argues that panoramas provided news for those who could not get it. The problem here is that the audience for panoramas and newspapers was one and the same: Only the bourgeoisie read newspapers or could afford panoramas.

64. *Encyclopédie enfantine recommandé pour les écoles,* BHVP, Actualités Anciennes, series 103.

65. *Le Figaro,* 23 February 1889.

66. *Le Petit moniteur,* 16 May 1889.

67. See Charles Castellani, *Confidences d'un panoramiste* (Paris: Maurice Dreyfous, n.d.), p. 281.

68. Castellani, op. cit., p. 281.

69. Charles Rearick, *Pleasures of the Belle Epoque* (New Haven: Yale University Press, 1985), p. 173.

70. *Le Rappel,* 12 March 1889.

71. *Le Courier des expositions,* March 1889.

72. Readers will note that many of the attractions were sponsored by companies that actually offered the real trips on their modes of transport. That fact should serve as an important corrective for those who associate such corporate entertainment with twentieth-century America in general and, say, the Disney theme parks in particular.

73. Robichon, op. cit., p. 504.

74. P. Bluysen, *Paris en 1889* (Paris: P. Arnould, 1890), p. 19.

75. *La Nature,* 15 June 1889, p. 34, cited in Robichon, op. cit., p. 507.

76. A two-horsepower, gas-generated machine activated the pistons of a hydraulic press that moved the platform. See Robichon, op. cit., p. 520.

77. Ibid., p. 516.

78. R. M. Arlaud, *Cinéma-bouffe* (Paris: Jacques Melot, n.d.), p. 66. I thank Jean-Jacques Meusy for this reference.

79. Ibid., p. 67. It should be clear that this well predates Hale's Tours. See Raymond Fielding, "Hale's Tours: Ultra-Realism in the Pre-1910 Motion Picture" in *Film before Griffith,* ed. John Fell (Berkeley, Los Angeles, London: University of California Press, 1983).

TWELVE

Effigy and Narrative: Looking into the Nineteenth-Century Folk Museum

Mark B. Sandberg

The visual objects of a museum resemble the scattered bones on the battlefield of Ezekiel's vision. Pour a living, coherent idea into these soulless, often anonymous objects; sort them, order them, group them around their centers; . . . in this way let the meaningless receive its meaning, let the apparently worthless find an ingenious use, and the scattered bones will arrange themselves into figures; ethnographic objects in their unsurveyable mass will gather themselves into types, and the visitor will leave the collection with a total impression of a people now living and breathing in the provinces, in the fatherland, in the Scandinavian North.
ZACHRIS TOPELIUS, "Hauszeichen," in
Das Nordische Museum in Stockholm: Stimmen aus der Fremde, 1888

Out of the great international exhibitions of the nineteenth century arose a new sort of museum dedicated to the display and continued visibility of folk culture. This institution, generally referred to as the "folk museum," originated in Scandinavia between 1870 and 1905. As ethnographic collections of folk costumes, furniture, and tools from rural districts, the Scandinavian folk museums were founded in order to preserve a concentrated, frozen, tableaulike image of traditional culture at the very moment that culture seemed most threatened by the changing conditions called modernity. As the museums developed, the displaced objects appeared in increasingly elaborate, contextualized displays, complete with mannequins, scenery, and accompanying narratives. These framed images of folk culture combined to form a larger cultural story, with the scenes of folk life standing in for what was perceived as a lost "original" cultural experience. The public responded enthusiastically to these contextualization efforts, and the popularity of the earliest folk museums (housed in buildings in Stockholm and Copenhagen) led to the development of "open-air museums" at the turn of the century throughout Scandinavia and beyond.[1] These predecessors of living-history museums around the world further contextualized the material traces of folk culture in an outdoor, naturalized milieu of relocated rural buildings, flora, and fauna.

As popular turn-of-the-century institutions, the folk museums form a useful point of comparison with other forms of spectating during the time of cinema's birth and early growth.[2] At first glance, they appear to be situated at the opposite end of the cultural spectrum from the spectacles and visual attractions associated with modernity. One would not, that is, immediately think of looking at folk museums to trace the genealogy of the modern gaze. The function of these national-ethnographic collections in the urban landscape seems on the contrary primarily nostalgic, prompted by a longing for simpler, more coherent cultural forms in a time of rapid urbanization, industrialization, and commodification. Indeed, in Scandinavian cultural histories the folk museums are most often seen as a tidy corollary to the dominant literary trends in the 1890s, usually labeled "neoromantic" due to the increased interest in historical novels and the premodern Scandinavian heritage.[3] A good deal of neoromantic reaction to modernity did in fact contribute to the founding of the folk museums, but a closer examination of the ways early folk museum visitors articulated the impressions of their visits suggests that the received experience of spectating sometimes exceeded the founding paradigm in important ways.[4] Many spectators who patronized the folk museums left behind written accounts that make one thing clear: they brought with them composite viewing habits from a variety of late-nineteenth-century attractions, habits usually identified with modernity (a taste for distraction, mobile subjectivity, panoptic perspectives, and voyeuristic viewing). The disjunction between the institution's ostensible purpose and the variety of its uses by spectators highlights the fact that a museum's founding definition and its eventual social function are not necessarily identical.

The turn to spectatorship as the paradigm of investigation helps to coax this perspective out of the historical material, because one quickly realizes that viewing habits were not institutionally specific. For example, it is easy for a theoretical placeholder term like "cinema spectator" to mask, if just for a moment, the fact that late-nineteenth-century spectators pursued a variety of other visual entertainments; the very formulation of the term as a separate category encourages conceptualization of early film viewers as somehow distinct from other "kinds" of spectators. As scholars in cinema studies have argued with increasing frequency, however, the audience in the cinema seats did not constitute a discrete group. Instead, in varying combinations, cinema spectators patronized other visual attractions as well. This is particularly true of the late nineteenth century, a period that witnessed the development of recording technologies, increased circulation of mass-produced images, invention of a bewildering number of new optical devices, and new institutionalized forms of viewing pitched at the middle classes. All of these factors created new possibilities for a roving patronage of visual culture. Crossover spectating potentially linked each institution of the visible to its neighbors on the boulevard (such as the wax museum, the freak show, the magic-lantern show, the cinema), not just in formal aspects of presentation and display, but in the modes of watching they encouraged in spectators.[5] In Copenhagen, where Bernhard Olsen, former director of the Tivoli amusement park, founded both the Danish wax museum and folk museum in the same year (1885) and in the same building (right across from Tivoli and next to the train station), the implicit relationships of the public sphere were made literal in a shared physical space. Many institutions of the visible in the late nineteenth century, though, shared audiences in less explicit ways. Media-specific theories of spectatorship fail to account for the cumulative effect of composite viewing habits, instead attributing most aspects of spectating to the visual technologies imposed by the particular mode of display. Lost in an institutionally specific approach is a sense of how a variety of viewing experiences could together school spectators' viewing habits, and how spectators carried with them expectations about viewing from experiences at competing visual attractions.

Treatment of the folk museum as one of several institutions of the visible also helps emphasize the historical aspect of vision, but without depending solely on a technology-driven shift in the "historical eye." Attempts to redirect the teleological emphasis of cinematic history often remain too closely tied to the mechanical metaphor of the apparatus to successfully shift the argument from technology to discursive circulation.[6] By replacing the apparatus metaphor with a notion of institution as discursive formation, one can include in a constellation of visual attractions forms of viewing that lack an obvious connection to optical machines and devices, attractions linked instead by available spectator positions and similar narrative contextualizations of visual experience. Especially in the late nineteenth century, one of the most distinctive features of visual culture was a burgeoning discourse of programs, guidebooks, souvenir biographies, and promotional material, all made possible by the proliferation of mass media printing and graphic techniques. This printed matter, the most constant companion of late-nineteenth-century spectators, linked institutions of the visible by steering interpretations of visual attractions in directions acceptable to middle-class viewers. If in fact vision is best seen as the social construction of particular historical moments, the best place to look for the historical variability is perhaps not in the eye or the device, but in the printed narrative that interprets and places the representational practice in a social and discursive context. Cinema itself is still worth explaining, to be sure, but one way to do that is to see it as one of the many turn-of-the-century entertainments that settle down and begin to cultivate habitual viewing in a regular audience by attaching themselves to a permanent building; by developing consistent promotional publicity, guidebooks, and programs; and by eliciting regular journalistic reviews. In this light, cinema becomes a parallel rather than a cumulating case study. That is, the institutionalization and narrativization of "sights" in the late nineteenth century is a historical tendency worth attention in its own right, one that requires devoting more attention to extra-cinematic kinds of spectatorship in the late-nineteenth-century public sphere. The present study offers one such juxtaposition by examining the visual logic and spectator appeal of the folk museum, especially as it relates to the issues of corporeality and narrativity. The hope is that this kind of inquiry will not only elicit new perspectives on early cinema spectatorship but will also help demonstrate how the cinema, the folk museum, and other visual attractions participated in a more general discursive circulation at the turn of the century.

NARRATIVE AS CULTURE:
EFFIGY AND THE FUNCTIONALIST DISPLAY

The important work that has been done in recent years on the narrativization of early cinema traces a general trajectory from spectacle-oriented entertainment to the narrative form of feature films. In this line of inquiry, it has not always been easy to answer questions of why narrativity appealed to film audiences. If, on the one hand, the need for narrative is seen as a transhistorical given, then the narrativization of cinema (or other nineteenth-century institutions of the visible) appears as an inevitable outcome accompanying the institution's maturation process. Given enough time and the right economic conditions, the argument would go, any spectacle entertainment will tend to develop into a "fuller" narrative form. If, on the other hand, there is something historically variable about this narrative turn, then the narrativization of cinema might be better understood in terms of a larger push toward a consolidation and institutionalization of visual culture at a compelling historical moment.

The idea of narrativity is particularly important to the display of rural culture in Scandinavia because of the problems posed by the museum object and the folk body, both of which were charged with the tensions of changing social experience. A late but sudden industrialization in the northern countries made the relation of bodies and objects more highly fraught, as the growing commodity culture both introduced new objects of mass production and increased the circulation of objects and bodies in new social and commercial networks. Transformations in modes of agricultural labor not only displaced rural workers but also made many traditional work procedures obsolete. The tools, costumes, and buildings of traditional folk life began to lose their use value or, to put it another way, their obvious and seemingly necessary connection to a body. Especially in the 1870s, improved transportation possibilities (longer railroad lines, increased steamship travel, new highways) and communication networks (such as the telegraph and dramatically expanded postal systems) made possible a relatively sudden increase in social mobility between formerly isolated rural districts themselves, between country and city, and between Scandinavia and foreign lands. The increased circulation of people and goods sometimes created possibilities for striking juxtapositions; as one scholar has put it, in remote areas of Sweden the situation was such that "from a train window or the deck of a steamship a traveler could catch a glimpse of a living folk culture with archaic features."[7]

There is reason to see the effects of modernity as particularly potent in Scandinavia. Although there is a range of opinion about the most relevant dates, most scholars place the "industrial revolutions" of these three countries during the 1870s and 1880s significantly later than similar developments in England, Germany, France, or the United States.[8] Since industrialization came later to Scandinavia, other industrial markets and existing technologies were already available for export and import, making possible a more rapid modernization process once things got underway.[9] Encounters with modernity also had a more dramatic impact on Scandinavia because of the relatively small scale and isolated location of the countries. The populations of the Scandinavian cities, for example, still quite modest in the mid-nineteenth century, had grown dramatically by the end of the 1890s, due in large part to the influx of surplus rural labor.[10] This growth occurred in spite of significant emigration to the United States (especially from Sweden and Norway). By 1915 about 750,000 Norwegians had emigrated to America, and between the years 1820–1930, about one and a quarter million Swedes did the same.[11] All of these forms of social movement left indelible marks on what previously were relatively stable rural societies.

For many Scandinavians, the rapid arrival of modernity and industrialization led to a sense of cultural dispersal and dilution. By the time the Danish Folk Museum opened in 1885, that process was perceived as well underway. Looking back on the collecting efforts for the Danish Industrial Exhibition six years earlier, one journalist wrote: "The country had already been plowed through for many years, mostly by foreign collectors and buyers, and much that would have been desirable to preserve was already long gone."[12] At the opening of the Norwegian Folk Museum in 1902, Moltke Moe (son of the famous Norwegian fairy-tale collector) echoed those sentiments: "Every railroad and every new highway that flattens out the path into our closed valleys, in fact just about every tourist who visits our country, carries out with them one piece after the other of our disappearing culture."[13] All of this resulted in an extraordinary investment in the folk body as a desirable, nostalgic object—the vanishing, former owner of now-displaced artifacts. As actual folk bodies from the rural population increasingly crossed the line from country to city, becoming urban spectators of their former culture themselves, the absent folk body, collectively imagined, acquired great representational currency, as did that body's props: the artifacts, tools, clothing, and buildings that had once been in contact with it. The more irretrievable that body seemed to be, the more evocative—and potentially frustrating—its metonymic traces became. Zachris Topelius, whose impressions of Artur Hazelius's Nordic Museum were published in a 1888 German guidebook, stages the desire to get beyond the signifying artifacts when he states, "But where are the people [*das Volk*]? I hear their voices, I recognize their breath, I feel their hearts beat, but I don't see them: they stand behind their achievements; raise the veil, let the curtain fall, give me the living people!"[14] Traces of the "folk" were not enough for this viewer, even though tools, clothing, and artifacts could point evocatively to the abstract concept they represented; for him they acted as both a tease and a barrier, preventing a more intense experience of the folk body itself.

The problem the folk museum faced, then, was how to collect and display the displaced objects of traditional culture in such a way as to deny the representational status of the display. If they could manage that, they could avoid duplicating in the museum's activities of collection and display the rootlessness many perceived in modernity. As the Norwegian Anders Sandvig (founder of Maihaugen, Lillehammer's folk museum) put it, "It was the arranged, museumlike effect I wanted to avoid; I really wanted the visitor to forget that it was a collection he had in front of him, but rather to get the impression that it was a real home he was visiting."[15] In older museums, classification, seriality, and historical rubrics were seen as sufficient contextualizations for the discrete objects of a collection. For the Scandinavian folk museum founders, such principles of display seemed to concede too readily the distance between the museum objects and the visitor, a distance that paralleled the growing social detachment from traditional culture that the folk museums were intended to counteract. The traditional scientific museum model was too much a monument to loss; late-nineteenth-century museums needed a new kind of display aesthetic, a compensatory narrativizing technique that could perform damage control by re-situating objects in an "unbroken" context, allowing spectators both accessibility and the illusion of an experiential connection with the objects of their vision.

The solution developed in the folk museums was the "functionalist" display, which restored contexts to objects by placing them in relation to a body, a scene, and a narrative anecdote or description. The mimetic project of the folk museums, which eventually reached truly hyperbolic proportions, began by situating folk artifacts such as traditional costumes in relation to wax or plaster mannequins and then expanded to take on more elaborate groupings of figures in anecdotal, theatrical tableaux. The display of folk culture culminated in the heroic project of moving actual buildings and samples of their former milieux to the open-air museums. Set in relation to a human form and a context perceived as authentic, the museum artifact eventually was turned into a purposeful theatrical prop instead of a "stranded object," to use Eric Santner's term.[16] The curator in turn became a *metteur-en-scène*. Narrative coherence could substitute for cultural coherence, in a compensatory way to be sure, but if the story-telling were accomplished in a skillful manner, perhaps visitors would be satisfied with the substitution—or even prefer it. Claës Lundin, who visited Hazelius's folk museum in Stockholm, was enthusiastic enough to claim: "The thing that distinguished this [museum] and gave it the advantage over the majority of ethnographic collections in other countries was that it in every respect sought to provide completely watchable pictures [*'åskåd-liga bilder'*] of reality itself."[17] The phrase "watchable pictures of reality" is in one sense a logical contradiction, but it is also a constitutive feature of vision in modernity, which seeks the advantages of the image's absence and circulation in new visual media ("watchability") while enjoying the security of an imagined presence delivered up by hyper-mimetic production values. Even though "reality itself" is not inherently watchable, the folk museum's pictures of reality promised to spectators both surveyability and seemingly direct experience.

The functionalist display drew heated criticism from more established voices in the Scandinavian museum community. One of the most conservative voices, that of Sophus Müller,[18] saw all narrative compensation as unscientific, the stuff of marketplace entertainment rather than of a museum proper. Müller wanted to reserve the latter term for more disciplined, serious work, as did an opponent of state funding for the Norwegian Folk Museum, who called the proposed folk museum a "more refined variety show/wax museum sort of institution."[19] Reactionary though these voices may have been in their defense of traditional notions of the scientific, scholarly museum, their protests are valuable because they highlight the logical contradictions of the functionalist display. One principal objection was that in order to be consistent, the functionalist technique would demand an additional figure and room for every duplicate object the museum owned. Notes Müller, "Altogether only a pitiful amount of material can be placed in original use-contexts and surroundings. . . . Say one had several hundred clay pots; in order to display them in interiors one would need a good many pottery workshops, even if each of these were plentifully equipped. Several hundred bronze swords would require raising a small army."[20] The thoroughgoing functionalist museum would simply require too many buildings and too many bodies, which in their "folk" varieties seemed increasingly to be in short supply at the turn of the century.

In practice, the early folk museums in Stockholm and Copenhagen could not in fact mount consistently functionalist displays. The perpetually scarce financial resources of the early folk museums (before state and community funding became more predictable, the founders were initially dependent on their own limited resources and voluntary donations from the public) placed inescapable limits on recontextualization; to resuscitate folk culture completely in story form would have required an enormous fortune, and even then the absurdity of the enterprise would soon have become evident.[21] The mannequin figures that Hazelius insisted upon in his museum's early days in order to make the folk costumes "watchable," as he put it, were expensive enough that it would be impossible to populate an entire museum with effigies for the objects.[22] Moreover, the number of objects in the collections was continually growing; Hazelius and several of the other folk museum directors were notorious victims of collecting mania, due in part to their particular personality traits and in part to the perceived urgency of their task (when one sets out to "rescue" a culture, how many objects are enough?).[23] The vast numbers of duplicate objects they eventually collected, undisplayable in the relatively small number of re-created interior scenes, spilled over either into more traditional serial displays or the museum's crowded storage rooms. In practice, then, the functionalist display created two competing collections—one purposeful, complete, and self-sufficient, and the other (consisting of the leftovers) inescapably miscellaneous.

In the early days of the folk museums, one could see both kinds of collection on the display floor. Artur Hazelius's Scandinavian-Ethnographic Collection, for example, included both mannequin tableaux—"life itself," in niches on the left—and more traditional displays of objects grouped in series on the walls or in glass cases, shown here on the right and in the rear of the room (fig. 12.1). These objects were those without specific prop value for the particular scenes presented by the mannequins and were accordingly relegated to other spaces, where Hazelius packed the walls and even the ceiling with the rest of the objects he had rescued from oblivion. For example, one part of the museum, called the "Iron Room," had as its organizing principle the simple fact that all of its objects were made out of iron (fig. 12.2). A similar situation existed at the Dansk Folkemuseum in the center of Copenhagen, where in addition to the main attraction of functionalist interior rooms, one could find in larger halls "great collections and series of individual objects illuminating the different aspects of life and customs in the past."[24] The inclusion of overflow rooms, juxtaposed with the functionalist tableaux displays, meant that the early folk museums displayed their contradictions up front. Objects presented

Fig. 12.1. Interior of Artur Hazelius's Scandinavian-Ethnographic Collection. (Illustration by R. Haglund, n.d., photograph in Nordiska Museet Archives, Stockholm.)

themselves in some parts of the museum as discrete units worthy of individual attention and in other sections as less conspicuous props in a dramatic context.

The mannequin effigy helped mediate these tensions between miscellany and diegesis,[25] as can be seen in a later photograph from the Stockholm museum in which both modes compete for attention in the same picture (fig. 12.3). Along the back wall of this scene are objects from the wall of Hazelius's "Iron Room," in this case locks and keys displayed in cumulative, serial fashion ("here is one, and here is another one"). The inclusion of a single mannequin facing the viewer would not change that effect significantly, but with two mannequins grouped in interactive poses as they are here, turned at a ninety-degree angle from the viewer, a scene is created and the sense of diegetic space greatly strengthened. The parallels to the development of early cinema are instructive; Tom Gunning has argued in that context that the overt solicitation of the spectating gaze in the early "cinema of attractions" turns in on itself and "goes underground" when it introduces more consistent forms of storytelling.[26] The most literal manifestation of this turn toward narrative absorption in cin-

Fig. 12.2. The "Iron Room" at the Scandinavian-Ethnographic Collection around the turn of the century. The change of the museum's name to "Nordiska Museet" had likely taken place by the time of this photograph. (Photographer and date unknown, in Nordiska Museet Archives, Stockholm.)

ema practice is the eventually adopted convention that actors not look directly at the camera, but a variety of other techniques make possible the impression in cinema that one has stumbled onto a story in progress. Similarly, in Hazelius's "Iron Room" the mannequins are placed so that they interact directly with each other, not with the spectator. Even more significantly, this particular arrangement endows them with the ability to see and, by extension, with consciousness. The purposeful, interactive sight lines (the man showing the object while looking at the woman, the woman reacting by looking at the object) let the scene proceed unmindful of the museum visitor's own spectating activity. The visual information of this mannequin scene remains sketchy—one has no idea why he is showing her the object, or even what exactly it is. The artifact in the mannequin's hand, however, has acquired a fundamentally different display status from

Fig. 12.3. Mannequins in the Iron Room of Nordiska Museet. (Photograph by
Anton Blomberg, 1902, in Nordiska Museet Archives, Stockholm.)

the objects on the wall. It is perhaps even more difficult to notice in this contextualized display that the folk costumes worn by the mannequins are also collected objects, which themselves could also have been displayed in serial fashion along the wall. The clothing's proximity to the displayed bodies make it even less noticeable as collected material. To different degrees, then, the mannequin bodies help efface the "object-ness" of both artifact and dress, giving them a context that approximates an original connection to a body.

This representation, though, is fundamentally circular. If the folk museum object is invested with a heightened realism and "life" by virtue of its proximity to a human effigy, one must also recognize that the body on display in turn achieves its lifelike appearance by being surrounded by the same objects, seemingly set out for its use. Without the props to activate the viewer's imagination, the mannequin remains a dummy; with them, the figure simulates agency and consciousness. The circularity of the representation necessitated a shoring up of the visual anecdotal force of the early folk-museum groupings. That is, in order to ensure a satisfactory narrative compensation for vanishing cultural forms, the "story" implied by each tableau scene needed additional help from accompanying prose descriptions. The museum guidebook served such a function and proved to be an indispensable guarantee that the carefully orchestrated parts of the display would remain securely in their story and not remind the viewer of their status as miscellaneously collected objects. In Hazelius's museum, the guidebooks were particularly elaborate, with extensive information and rich illustrations.[27] Although much catalog space was still devoted to historical information and the traditional museological information about provenance, the written tour through Hazelius's museum never failed to improvise a more elaborate story each time it turned its attention to the mannequin tableaux. At the end of each descriptive section in the commemorative guidebooks from 1892 and 1902, for example, the printed text referring to the interior scenes shifts register and enters storytelling mode. Using a narrative present tense, these concluding sections would tell the visual anecdote of the display in more detail, identifying relationships between characters, attributing feelings to each figure involved in the action, and speculating on the continued course of the story in time and space beyond the depicted scene. Typical is the description of the Bålastuga display depicting an interior scene at Christmastime, with the mannequins representing an older, rural couple:

> The following illustration reproduces an interior room at the start of a holiday. Tapestries and wall-hangings have been hung up; the shelves are gleaming with freshly shined dishes and bowls; no objects reminiscent of everyday life have been left inside. The two old people have dressed themselves in their festive apparel, although for the sake of comfort the old man has kept

his wooden shoes on. It is almost as if they are waiting for some dear relative. In the meantime, the old woman reads aloud from a devotional book, and the old man is occupied with his tobacco kit. Even so, he isn't an inattentive listener, because now and then he stops his tobacco cutting to ponder what is being read.[28]

This account alludes to past and impending action, attributes agency to the mannequins (making them "characters" in the story), implies continuity of the story beyond the moment ("now and then he stops"), and speculates on the meaning of the depicted moment. (In a similar fashion, the wax museum guide, the souvenir freak biography, or the later cinema program would supplement the narrative tendencies of the visual display itself by filling in holes and elaborating the story beyond the actual representation.) The guidebook thus reassured the viewer that the figures would indeed continue to be "alive" even after the spectator stopped looking, by showing that the story went beyond the immediately visible. The catalog eventually became a crucial component of the folk-museum experience, prompting one visitor to Anders Sandvig's collection in Lillehammer in 1901 to state explicitly: "If the collections get their own catalog, completely carried out in the spirit of this remarkable collector, they will become a whole, whose equal will surely not easily be found in the North."[29] Without that catalog, the implication seems to be, they will remain a collection of parts; with it, the "body" of the museum—the narrative effigy—is complete.

When studying the reception history of hypermimetic modes of representation, one becomes skeptical when spectators or promotional materials effuse about having reached the ultimate in realistic effect. So too here—and, in fact, the "amazingly lifelike" representations in the Stockholm folk museum in the 1870s and '80s were soon superseded by the reality-effect experienced by visitors to the open-air museums in the next decade. There, the attempts to re-create entire milieux of relocated buildings surrounded spectators with a cultural "story" that filled the entire museum space, and spectators could thus to an even greater degree act as if the open-air museum was not at all representational—here, at last, they could encounter the real thing. Claës Lundin, in a retrospective article on the creation of Skansen in 1898, expressed a common reaction: "He [Hazelius] had already shown the interiors from the homes of Swedish peasantry in the two pavilions on Drottninggatan, but these interiors are merely *reproductions* [*afbildningar*]. It was through *real* homes that he wanted to acquaint the public with the old customs and practices of the Swedish rural population, both the festive and the everyday—real, vernacular houses in a natural milieu, which perfectly resembles the one they came from."[30] On another occasion, the same writer claimed, "What stands in front of us now is not some more or less faithful imitation, but rather *reality itself*," and one of his companions apparently enthused on the same occasion, "This is altogether different than going around peeking into boxes and cabinets, like at the usual exhibitions."[31] Gone were the conspicuous displays of leftover objects in overflow rooms; in order to represent a thoroughly organic milieu at the open-air museum, none of the space could appear to be museum space, but instead had to seem as if it were the genuine "folk space" of actual homes.

Even so, the folk museum, like all realist representation, necessarily failed in the impossible substitution of representation for reality. Even real homes that had been inhabited by real bodies had been collected and recontextualized at the open-air museums—for all their reality-effect, they were still on display. In spite of the inordinate energy museum directors and staff expended on the recontextualization of folk life, the museum did not and could not, of course, deliver up the "real" folk or "real" cultural-historical experience, if in fact such a thing existed. If the appeal of the institution were simply due to an irresistible nostalgia for "a vanished time without steam and electricity, when people were still people and not cogs in a huge, thundering machine,"[32] the inadequacy of mimetic representation would ultimately frustrate the spectator-patriots seeking in the representation of folk life the presence of traditional culture. But some folk-museum visitors seem in fact to have been more like spectators at the cinema or other institutions of the visible—they were complicit in the illusion-making and found pleasure in both the attempt and the failure of the representation. As I will argue in the following sections, spectators were more often intrigued by the in-betweenness of the folk museums, by the ways in which they both managed the losses of modernity—the weakened connections between body and culture—and celebrated the powers it endowed on spectators—powers of mobility, invisibility, and panopticism. The availability of "watchable pictures" of folk culture, taken together with the sense that one could encounter "reality itself," was an appealing combination for modern, urban spectators, one which eventually led spectators to prefer the representational project to the "real thing."

THROUGH THE FOURTH WALL:
VOYEUR SPECTATORS AND THE TABLEAU

The functionalist technique at work in the folk museum's display space allowed spectators to pursue a complex imaginative relationship to the bodies on display therein. In much the same way that the narrativization of cinema created stories on screen that seemed not to need the spectator's presence in order to proceed and yet depended for their effect on the viewer's powers of imagination and identification, the construction of a coherent diegetic space in the folk tableaux likewise allowed spectators to assume invisible positions of observation that freed them to pursue imaginary relationships with the displayed scene. A look at early spectator accounts of visits to the folk museums reveals, in other words, that the cinema had no exclusive rights to voyeurism; self-conscious references to that model of spectating are strewn throughout the written sources from the early days of the folk museums, but with an important difference. The transition of the folk-museum display from indoor, framed tableau to the surround-style open-air milieu provides a context in which the voyeur metaphor and its contradictions are played out more fully than in the cinema. In that medium, the spatial limitations of the two-dimensional screened image prevented anything more than an imaginary immersion in the visual field. If the spectators of the early folk-museum tableaux experienced these same limitations, approaching the displays as voyeurs peeking into interior cottage scenes (but separated from the display spaces by cords and ropes, as in fig. 12.1), visitors to the vacant rooms of the later open-air museums did not. At these later folk museums, which surrounded spectators with an entire milieu of folk culture, visitors could act out an extension of the voyeuristic fantasy by actually inserting themselves into the domestic space while the supposed inhabitants had "momentarily stepped out."

Such early films as Edwin Porter's *Uncle Josh at the Moving Picture Show* (Edison, 1902) make the tension between voyeuristic distance and immersion in the visual field the subject of comedy. In that film a naive cinema spectator is shown interacting inappropriately with a series of cinematic images because he cannot understand their representational status (after a series of reactions he eventually rips down the screen in anger). Although the early folk-museum tableaux maintained the same strict spatial division between display and spectator, the later open-air museum did not. There, the insertion of the spectator into the visual field of display was not an extreme test case of the medium's boundaries but an essential part of that museum's logic. A primary appeal of the open-air format was in fact that it allowed spectator-trespassers to inspect at close hand the interior display space that had previously been off-limits in the earlier folk tableaux. *Uncle Josh* is not just about dimensionality, however; it is also about training spectators to perceive in conventional ways, with the comic Uncle Josh serving as a ridiculous example for real cinema audiences of how *not* to behave at the cinema, of how to occupy a more sophisticated position with respect to the visual field. When examining some of the clumsier moments of transition at the folk museums, one gets the same impression of spectator pedagogy, of curators teaching visitors how to react to different levels of representation and illusion. As in the cinema, the goal of the institution was not to keep fooling an audience of perpetually naive spectators, but to create spectators who could manage with ease the representational status of the world provided there.

As a starting point, early spectator reactions to the mannequin display deserve a closer look. Wax or plaster figures of folk characters first appeared in the tableau displays of national material culture at the international expositions of the second half of the nineteenth century, and their first spectators were thus the great crowds visiting those fairs.[33] At the Parisian exposition of 1867, the Swedish display featured mannequins with heads and hands carefully sculpted by C. A. Söderman, a Swedish sculptor who would go on to create figures for later exhibitions and Hazelius's Scandinavian-Ethnographic Museum. Söderman's technique was apparently excellent, with many viewers expressing astonishment at the figures' lifelike appearance. Jonas Berg quotes a Danish journalist who visited this exhibit: "The accomplishment is so illusory that many visitors mistook the figures for living persons; not only are the costumes exquisitely beautiful, but they are also worn by actual folk characters, whose grouping, faces, and hands make the whole display a collection of genre sculptures rather than costumed mannequins."[34] This realistic display technique, which at this 1867 exhibit involved presenting the mannequins in niches behind glass, usually grouped in twos, was further developed at international exhibitions in Vienna (1873) and Philadelphia (1876) to include furniture, larger groups, and much stronger anecdotal content in the grouping. The Philadelphia exhibits improved on the previous arrangements by adding scenery and titles reminiscent of rural genre paintings; about half of the exhibits there used the visual compositions of well-known genre paintings as a guide.[35] The story of these popular paintings, often quite familiar to viewers, gave the tableaux the recognizable content of stereotypic scenes from folk life.

The general tendency toward more illusionistic narrative in the tableaux culminated at the 1878 International Exposition in Paris, where Hazelius was put in charge of arranging the mannequins for Sweden's display in the Trocadero Palace. This time the Swedish figures and their highly anecdotal naturalized settings were one of the exposition's most popular attractions. One journalist wrote that at the exhibit, one could hear "a guard confirm that every day between midday and six in the evening, at least 10,000, maybe even as many as 15,000 people crowd in like us in order to see the Swedish groups."[36] The sentimental tableaux reportedly had an extraordinarily gripping effect on the exhibition visitors. One French journalist wrote:

> Even I stood transfixed there, strongly interested, soon quite touched, especially when in passing by the scene I had in front of my eyes, my thought penetrated into the customs of this life of bygone days; because, alas, it

appears that the vertiginous evolution of modern progress is making itself felt even up to those frigid regions where the good old days seemed intent on lasting forever, demolishing in hurried strokes the ancient edifice of costumes and practices, as well as ideas.[37]

This account, tinged by a sense of the impending disaster of modernity, shows why the freezing of a moment of folk life could seem so evocative. Surrounded by the context of the international exhibition's panegyric to modernity, the folk tableau represented a counterpoint of secure, composed images of traditional life, the very life that to some seemed threatened by what was going on elsewhere in the exhibition.

One scene in particular, entitled "The Little Girl's Last Bed," elicited powerful reactions at the 1878 Exposition (as it did earlier in Philadelphia and would later at Chicago's Columbian Exposition in 1893). The composition of the figures, taken directly from a well-known Swedish genre painting of the same title by Amalia Lindgren (1853), depicts a group of mourning figures gathered around an infant's deathbed (fig. 12.4). The theme of the premature loss of an infant, a theme repeated in other Scandinavian genre paintings,[38] apparently gripped the audience more than any other scene in the exhibit. A French journalist reported: "Never have figures of wax or wood nor theatrical settings achieved an equivalent artistic and emotional effect. All of the mothers weep in front of these seven figures from Rättvik parish, posed around 'The Little Girl's Last Bed.' "[39] The journalist was surely exaggerating the scope of the reaction, but from today's perspective, it is difficult to imagine even one viewer moved to tears by a group of mannequins, so familiar are they to the display spaces we encounter. Perhaps for these weeping spectators the depiction of the dead infant served some cathartic effect for the exhibition-going experience as a whole. Perhaps nagging anxieties about the costs of modernization accompanied visitors as they viewed the wonders of industrial progress, so that when they came upon these scenes from folk life, the tiny corpse in this display concretized those apprehensions about a traditional culture threatened with premature extinction.

Also contributing to the intensity of that reaction, though, was the mannequins' ontological status between life and death. As noted, enthusiasm about the mannequins' lifelike qualities depended to a large degree on the elaborate staging in the tableaux and the supporting printed materials; stripped of the narrative trappings and ontological hierarchies of the functionalist display,[40] the mannequins had the potential to appear more absent than present, more dead than alive. But the barely recognized absence that haunted the mannequin display was part of its attraction too, since it could facilitate the imaginary substitution of spectators for mannequins by having the figures "stand aside" when the viewers "stepped

Fig. 12.4. Nordiska Museet's display of one of the most popular of the mannequin tableaux, "The Little Girl's Last Bed," which was also exhibited at expositions in Philadelphia in 1876, Paris in 1878, and Chicago in 1893. (Photograph by Axel Lindahl, n.d., in Nordiska Museet Archives, Stockholm.)

into" the story. I use the word "imaginary" as a deliberate echo of the term Christian Metz has used to characterize the process of cinematic signification ("the imaginary signifier"). For Metz, the recorded status of cinema (its essential absence) distinguishes it from modes of display dependent on the simultaneous presence of performer and spectator, like the theater. The filmic signifier is both absent and present, a highly mimetic recorded representation (a filmed image) of a representation (the scene arranged for filming), a status Metz sees as crucial to a complex range of spectator identifications.[41] Metz's argument, an evocative and influential one, to be sure, deserves some historical contextualization nevertheless, and it is in this light that the popularity of mannequin tableaux at the turn of the century suggests that the attraction of the cinematic signifier's "in-between" status may have been more generally available in other modes of display. Mannequin tableaux, although they did not literally constitute a "recorded" medium, approximated that status in both the freezing of action and in the bodies of the wax figures themselves, which like the filmed body had a lifelike presence and yet were strangely absent as well.

The element of absence implicit in recorded representation and mannequin displays held a particular appeal for many spectators at the turn of
the century, namely that of insulation from the visual field of the representation and the potential returned look from the bodies on display. A description of the Swedish display in Paris by a French journalist hints at how
easily the voyeuristic pleasure of the tableau could slide into an uncanny
sense of being watched in return:

> The figures, modeled for the most part from life . . . convey a striking truth-
> fulness. . . . The heads and the hands are made of plaster; the eyes have
> been glazed by one of the foremost eye-makers in Sweden. All of this is
> so real, so alive, so intelligent, that one experiences a feeling of uneasi-
> ness [*malaise*]. Evidently not much is required to make people out of these
> mannequins.[42]

In this account, the presence effect of the mannequins (their lifelike qualities) is too strong, precluding enjoyment of the in-between pleasures of
looking at figures carefully situated between life and death. (One notes especially this viewer's emphasis on the mannequins' realistic eyes.) For most
spectators, the stagelike tableau with the invisible fourth wall removed
guaranteed that the mannequins would not return their "penetrating"
looks. The closer the mannequins came to real life, however, the more they
threatened the hierarchy of the viewing situation.

The tensions implicit in maintaining the voyeuristic hierarchy are most
evident in another account from the 1878 exposition, in which one Swedish visitor to his country's display apparently acted out a literal insertion
into the display. Perhaps because he was a fellow countryman (or perhaps
because he was a journalist), he was given special permission to walk into
the display space for a closer look. This reporter's description of viewing
several mannequins grouped in an outdoor scene, as well as the "Last
Bed" tableau adjacent to it, is worth quoting at length:

> Look at this landscape from the Mora district! Walk in among these good
> men of the valley and their wives, if like me you obtain permission to do so,
> and you will think yourself transported to the "beautiful shores of Siljan."
> Way down there is the magnificent lake—not even the church boats are
> missing. What a view!
>
>   And these groups are "artificial" (yes, really!), and the view can be found—
> just a few steps away from you!
>
>   There, just to the left, is a cottage. If you aren't permitted to "peek in
> through the windowpane," climb down among the crowd, move yourself a
> little to the left, and you will have an unobstructed view of what is happening
> in this humble dwelling. . . . The poor people in there! They take no notice
> of what is outside. The poor mother! With what sentiments do you lie there,
> bent over your little loved one's useless cradle? Yes, it is a heavy burden after
> all your waiting, after all your agony, now to lift your little one and place her

in the black coffin, her last bed. To the degree that the spectators comprehend the significance of this scene they have in front of their eyes, their voices are lowered and they walk silently away.[43]

As this reporter walks into the display, toys with the idea of peeking voyeuristically through the window on the side wall to the adjacent exhibit, and then adopts the more standard position of viewing the "Last Bed" mannequins through the invisible fourth wall along with the rest of the crowd, he acts out many of the various spectatorial positions and fantasies available to viewers of a tableau. Michael Fried claims that in Diderot's tableau aesthetic, the beholder of a painting is both encouraged to think of himself as invisible in front of the painting and simultaneously invited to enter imaginatively into the represented world.[44] A literal insertion into a scene, which as Fried points out is an "absurd" proposition in painting, was on the contrary literally possible (at least with special permission) in a three-dimensional tableau. The appeal of literally invading the display seems to have been considerable; Hazelius apparently won over other journalists by allowing them the same privilege at his Stockholm museum.[45] With three-dimensional mannequin exhibits, the only constraints were social and institutional norms of spectating behavior, not limitations inherent in the medium of representation, as in painting, or eventually (as Uncle Josh would discover) in the cinema.

SHARED QUARTERS: THE LIVING AND THE STUFFED

The interiors, as they continued to be displayed in Hazelius's Nordic Museum, remained organized around the idea of the missing fourth wall. Some museum founders, however—including Hazelius, as his ideas developed—found the detachment of the voyeuristic model too reminiscent of the social distance between folk culture and modernity, insertion fantasies notwithstanding. As the tableau interior moved toward the open-air museum technique, however, contradictions between the new display spaces and the mannequin effigies become apparent. The first significant attempt to break the plane of the invisible fourth wall in Scandinavia was carried out by Bernhard Olsen in Copenhagen. He too visited the Swedish display at the 1878 exhibition and found it to be a stimulating model. He even reported being profoundly affected by the Hazelian tableaux: "The impression was particularly unusual and stood out sharply and clearly from that of the rest of the exposition, with its heaps of industrial-artistic wonders and useless objects, fabricated for the day and worthless when it was over."[46] Even so, when folk culture was at stake, Olsen found the voyeuristic model ultimately too frustrating. He preferred a competing model that he discovered on display at the same exposition, which he himself would pursue both at Danish expositions and at his Danish Folk Museum:

The Dutch had, either through their own invention or instructed by Hazelius's participation in earlier international exhibitions, set up their own little folk museum that contrasted with the Swedish and Finnish ones. Whereas
these depicted interiors in smaller rooms whose fourth wall is open to the
public, in other words as it is done in the wax museums, the Dutch had here
a complete room which one could walk into. Every single thing had been
taken out of old houses and stood in its proper place. In contrast to the
Swedish manner, the effect was stirring, and from the moment I walked into
this old room, which was like another world, far in time and space from the
teeming, modern exposition, it became clear to me that this was the way a
folk museum should be arranged.[47]

The whole-room interior of the Dutch display, in constrast to Hazelius's
half-room tableaux, allowed visitors the opportunity to occupy the space
of the display and to surround themselves with an interior scene from folk
culture, with no special permission necessary. As one of Olsen's friends
put it in a retrospective article: "In Hazelius's farmers' rooms the fourth
wall was open; in other words, one merely peeked into the room; one
wasn't *actually* there. In contrast, at the Dutch display at the international
exposition there was a *closed* farmer's room, and Bernhard Olsen was not
slow to distinguish between the good effect of the one and the far stronger
effect of the other."[48]

Olsen applied this principle a year later in 1879, when he was made
responsible for the displays of folk culture at the industrial exhibition in
Copenhagen. He created the rooms by paneling the walls and ceilings
of existing interior spaces and furnishing them with appropriate period
pieces. These interiors then formed a suite of rooms, each from a different period or location. Visitors could thus actually walk into a room from
folk life and inspect objects at much closer range than was generally possible with the Hazelian model. At the exhibition, these rooms were still inhabited by mannequins, but the presence of these effigies at close range
created more problematic juxtapositions of the living and the dead than
had been the case with the Hazelian tableaux. These tensions are easy
to imagine when one takes a look at one such whole-room interior from
the exhibition, the Hedebostuen (fig. 12.5).[49] The visitor's intended path
through the room is clear, but the tantalizing proximity of the mannequins now potentially calls attention to their lifelessness, an aspect previously counteracted by the spectator's more distant, gathering perspective
in relation to the framed composition in the tableau. In the whole-room
interior, nothing prevents the visitor from sitting down next to the mannequins at the table and slapping them on the back, except perhaps social
decorum.

Social constraints were apparently not enough to hold back spectators
at Olsen's Danish Folk Museum when it opened in August 1885. Encour-

Fig. 12.5. The exhibit of the "Hedebostuen" with seated mannequins at the Copenhagen "Kunst-og Industriudstilling" of 1879. (Woodcut illustration by I. T. Hansen, 1879, photo courtesy of Nationalmuseet, Brede, Denmark.)

aged by his success at the exhibition six years earlier, Olsen applied the so-called whole-room principle in the more permanent displays of his new folk museum in the Panoptikon building. It opened with eight reconstructed interiors—this time apparently without mannequins.[50] Even though the rural rooms at the 1879 exhibition had introduced a wide spectrum of Copenhagen society to the whole-room interior, visitors were apt to test the conventions of museum-going in the new folk museum, where the lack of overtly demarcated space allowed visitors to feel a bit too much at home. One journalist complained on opening day: "If there is anything we miss in this excellent museum, it is signs placed here and there forbidding people to touch the displayed objects. But that is a lack that will probably be rectified, especially if the visitors continue so unabashedly to finger everything as one could see them do on the first day."[51] That freedom was, however, part of the inherent appeal of the experience—or, as another visitor put it, "to feel, study, and look through all of the past's curiosities, which up until now only dry letters and dead woodcuts have told about."[52] Viewers felt they had been allowed into the privileged space of the display and made themselves at home; now they needed to learn a less obtrusive presence in the display space.

Back in Sweden, where Hazelius was ready to put on display an entire outdoor milieu at Skansen (founded in 1891 in a park area overlooking Stockholm harbor), the transitional moment between interior and exterior space involved yet another intriguing juxtaposition of the living and the stuffed. The popular appeal of the folk mannequins at Hazelius's Nordic Museum led him to move five of them over to Skansen's Morastugan building, two of them to be placed inside and the others to be arranged outside (these were moved inside or outside depending on the weather!). He also brought along several figures from his Lapland tableau and set them up in a re-creation of a Sami (Lapp) camp, where they sat motionless next to a live dog brought down from northern Sweden (Hazelius had originally intended to stuff the dog as well, but grew too fond of him).[53] In the meantime, however, the rest of Skansen was being populated not by mannequins but by living guides in folk costumes. In this photo, and in many like it produced for postcards, one can see two living guides in the foreground, with the two Mora mannequin "natives" grouped behind them (fig. 12.6). Hazelius apparently often duplicated the trick implicit in the photo in real life in order to surprise his guests. One visitor described how a group Hazelius was leading on tour was "set up" to mistake the outdoor mannequin group for real, then was led to "discover" that all the figures were mannequins, only to find in turn that the "young man with intelligent appearance" was actually alive after all—he was a museum worker planted among the figures, who came to life when called by Hazelius.[54] Another account highlights the same amusing juxtaposition:

> Look, there outside are a man and a woman in Mora costumes standing and talking to each other. We are just about to join in on the conversation, but realize to our surprise that we only have effigies [*bilder*] before us. Inside the cottage we look around and find everything to be as if in a farmer's home in Mora—at least the way it was in certain areas a few decades ago. If only those two women sitting on the bench also were living people and not just costumed wax effigies! We could start up a chat with them and hear about this and that from their beautiful hometown. But what's this? Now one of them is moving her eyes. Have they perfected the effigies to such a degree that they have managed in some way to make a movable eye? While we stand there looking at the effigy, it starts to laugh. We had been duped; it was two living women who were sitting in there.[55]

Such lighthearted play was apparently a regular feature at Skansen in the early years, and it reinforced the point made by the folk museum—that folk culture could live on in representational form and that the world of representation could be entertaining—by exploiting the power of the mannequins to elicit mistakes in the viewer's perception and put into question their assumptions about the display space.

In this account it is again the eye that betrays the living guide as "real."

Fig. 12.6. Exterior of the "Morastugan" of Skansen's operation. The two female figures in the foreground are living guides; the male and female figure behind are mannequins out enjoying the nice weather. (Photograph by Axel Lindahl, 1892, in Nordiska Museet Archives, Stockholm.)

As mentioned previously, the more voyeuristic dynamic of the tableau depended on guarantees that the figures would not look back; in this account, the feeling of insulation from the display forfeited in the open-air format is further destroyed by the returned look of the figure in that space. The previously mentioned photograph of the mannequin couple exchanging glances at the Nordic Museum (fig. 12.3) showed that Hazelius was aware of the importance of a sort of eyeline match in overcoming the displacement effects of the collecting process (a technique that would later be used to create "natural" shot transitions in Hollywood film editing, which in itself is a kind of "collecting"). At his outdoor museum, Hazelius seems to have insisted on the same coordinated interaction. That is, since the figures around Morastugan were often moved, they would sometimes not end up correctly posed. In a reminder note to several women of Skansen's staff, dated 10 July of either 1899 or 1900, Hazelius emphasizes: "May I remind especially the morning inspectress to keep a careful eye on the displayed figures outside Morastugan so that they 'correspond' with one another, that their looks are aimed at each other. *That was not the case today!*"[56] The implication, as in the earlier case, is that if the figures' sight lines match up, they are more than simply mannequins.

For spectators schooled in tableau-viewing in other contexts, surround-style displays posed challenges to the previously well-defined spaces of spectating and display. Visitors to museums like Skansen, especially in that museum's transitional moments, tested the boundaries of the display and encountered playful, reciprocal substitutions between the living and the dead. This essentially pedagogical process taught spectators how to negotiate the new kinds of display space. Eventually, however, Skansen shifted to the more consistent technique of using living guides, dressed in folk costumes, as sources of information about the houses. The simultaneous presence and absence of the mannequins, which had served the tableau displays so well, seems to have become an uncomfortable contradiction in the three-dimensional space of the open-air museums.[57] Folk museum spectators had gone on to other pleasures—attractions of a smoother substitution of themselves for the absent folk body.

IMMERSION, TRESPASSING, CLAUSTROPHOBIA

Olsen's Danish Folk Museum in Copenhagen had introduced spectators to the idea of immersion in the display space, and when his rooms were eventually cleared of mannequins, spectators could act out an insertion of their own bodies into the space made vacant by the room's previous inhabitants—the folk bodies whose traces were felt in every detail of the display. The Norwegian folk museums adopted this principle from the start, beginning as open-air museums and never going through substantial phases of tableau-interior displays. At the Norwegian Folk Museum in Oslo (opened to the public in 1902), founder Hans Aall simply could not reconcile himself to entertainment effects like mannequins; his earlier experiments with "false, imitated half-interiors" later became an embarrassment to him. They were his museum's adolescent errors, he wrote later, "mistakes that were common at that time."[58] He sought a more contemplative spectator than those attending the wax museums, one who would be more attracted by the idea of museum as memorial, as a "quiet place of memories."[59] The reigning metaphor for spectating at Aall's museum was that of walking into an old, locked room untouched by time: "Far better to keep the interiors slightly distant from reality, something like locked-off rooms in an old house. They always get our fantasy going, so that we ourselves try to create pictures for ourselves of the real life that has pulsated there before."[60] Aall wanted to attract the spectator with the pleasures of historical melancholy, to preserve the sense that although the inhabitant of the room was missing, it was only temporary; the missing person would soon return to the space they had left. The evocative gap created by the missing folk body could then spur on the spectator fantasy to create personal pictures, which would be much more imaginative than an actual representation and "recovery" of the lost body.

At Anders Sandvig's Maihaugen, another important Norwegian open-air museum (officially established in 1904, but open to the public as early as 1895), illusionism was on the contrary cultivated and carefully orchestrated at lively folk festivals (perhaps more than at any other Scandinavian folk museum). The basic principle of the missing person, however, was still observed, as at the Norwegian Folk Museum. In 1909 the architect Carl Berner visited Maihaugen and commented:

> The people themselves can of course not come back from the dead [*gaa igjen*], even though some folk museums, such as Skansen in Stockholm, try with costumed wax figures to blow life into the dead. But when these homes are correctly displayed, are wax figures necessary? No, our own fantasy can much better than any wax figure conjure up the deceased, old and young.[61]

The awkward experience of entering a room occupied by mannequins was unsatisfactory for both of the Norwegian museum founders, but Sandvig in particular did not want to give up the powerful imaginary presence of the folk body, which animated the museum buildings and made them into a "collection of homes, in which one could walk right into the people who lived in them and learn of their ways of life, their tastes, their work."[62] At Maihaugen, the ubiquitous rhetoric of the museum as home encouraged visitors to exclaim, as one apparently did, "My goodness, it's so cozy—here is a place I'd like to live."[63]

The homey effect depended both on making the room look inhabited and on leaving an appealing vacancy for the visitor to occupy in his or her imagination and enter into the display. The first was accomplished by arranging small objects around the room, traces of the room's previous inhabitants. Sandvig was especially adept at this technique. A Bible would be left open, a bedspread turned back, a costume left draped over a chair, shoes placed "carelessly" by the bed—anything that could have been in direct contact with a human body or hand. The effect was apparently both convincing and appealing for spectators (and is still today the display technique of choice at most open-air museums). By having the visitor do the "conjuring up," the open-air museum hit upon a way of evoking the folk body without incurring the financial cost or risking the representational contradictions of delivering it up literally in the display.

The most evocative details were those that showed how the body of an actual former inhabitant physically imprinted itself on the environment. At the Norwegian Folk Museum, for example, one could still see "traces of the sword blows, which the groom at the wedding had to strike with his sword to show the bride his strength."[64] The chief architect at the Danish Frilandsmuseet in more recent times, Arne Ludvigsen, seems to have been alert to the same effect:

In order to give the building as much life as possible it also helps to preserve
the wear that has occurred through the years, both inside and outside. The
doors show wear where the hand repeatedly has reached, the alcove bed
frames are worn smooth and the paint has vanished, the floors are especially
worn near the doors, and the open hearthstones show clear marks from
pots and kettles, bumps and blows. In the stalls, the livestock have gnawed
and rubbed themselves, and the stones have been worn smooth by their
walking. Many more people than one thinks are especially receptive to these
small effects, which, taken together, give a picture of the genuine and the
convincing.[65]

Each mark, scrape, and worn plank (like the objects, tools, and costumes
laid out for view) bears mute metonymic witness to the absent body that
imprinted itself on its environment, whose former presence assures the
viewer that the room is "genuine."

Imagined folk bodies populate almost all of the journalistic accounts of
visits to the open-air museums. After describing the clothing left out in one
of the rooms, one Maihaugen spectator in 1903 playfully wrote, "Then we
go out again; on the door threshold we turn around: Hush! Can't you
hear the old people snoring over there in the bed?"[66] Sometimes it is even
unclear from the language of an account whether the bodies described
are there in literal effigy or merely in the visitor's imagination, giving the
described figures a rhetorical in-betweenness to match that of the display.
The most striking example of conjuring up folk bodies, however, comes
from a forged postcard depicting the Ramloftstue building at Maihaugen
(fig. 12.7). This card was forged both in the sense that it was not autho-
rized by Sandvig, who owned the photographic rights to his collection,
and in the sense that the costumed bodies were pasted on the card and
were not in the original photograph. As Tonte Hegard points out, the costumes were not even authentic to the building's region, and the location
of the museum is listed incorrectly (it is in Lillehammer, not Skjåk).[67] The
forgery is interesting not only for the way it raises issues of image ownership but also because it asks the question of why it would seem appropriate to superimpose onto the photograph folk bodies that were not there
in the original. One is reminded of Hazelius's comments about mannequins making costumes more "watchable." Here, a picture of a building
with "original" inhabitants was also more visually appealing, and it probably seemed more in line with the spectator's experience of visiting the
museum, in which bodies—in imaginary form—seemed everywhere. The
clumsy postcard approximation of that effect affirms that potential viewers
expected a corporeal experience at the open-air museum.

The visitor's body, however, competed for space with the bodies "conjured up" in the imagination, placing the spectator in the position of a
trespasser who occupies the folk space only momentarily, until the owner's

De Sandvigske Samlinger. Skiaker   Ramloftstuen fra Løhre

Fig. 12.7. The forged postcard of the "Ramloftstuen" at Maihaugen. (Photographer unknown, ca. 1900, photo courtesy of Maihaugen—De Sandvigske Samlinger, Lillehammer, Norway.)

return. As with the voyeuristic peeking into the folk tableau, at the open-air museum the spectating remains slightly illicit. Opening up the display space did not, in other words, completely legitimize the looking. In one sense, the feeling of unauthorized looking was only augmented by the spectator's physical presence in "someone else's" home. In numerous accounts of visiting the early open-air museums, visitors often continued to use the same voyeuristic rhetoric, linking the pleasures of "taking a peek" into a room with a sense of the owner's impending return. At Skansen, a journalist described one building interior in this way: "When one enters, it seems almost as if one has sneaked inside while the house inhabitants have momentarily stepped out."[68] A visitor at the Norwegian Folk Museum used similar imagery: "It is as if the people had just stepped out and forgotten to lock up after themselves."[69] The imagined possibility of being discovered by the original owners as one snooped around their house added an extra *frisson* for the spectator-trespasser, the appeal of breaking and entering the space of a display that had previously been off-limits for viewers except in the imagination.

In its most optimistic, appealing version, the folk museum display allowed for easy movement in and out of representational homes and created an evocative, temporary position for the viewing subject. For the immersion experience to be pleasurable, however, the spectator had to have not only easy access to the display space but an easy exit as well; otherwise, it was just another womb fantasy gone bad. The potential for claustrophobic reactions to the surround-style display hover around the margins of several spectator accounts, but in one hyperbolic anecdote that Sandvig tells about the opening of Maihaugen, the issues are quite explicit. It seems that when the Maihaugen "inhabitants" (historical role-players stationed around the museum for the day) moved in for the opening festivities on a long summer night around Midsummer's Eve, the celebrating went long into the morning. One of the men who was dressed up in uniform at the captain's manor in the museum finally grew tired and fell asleep on a sofa in the re-created interior room. When he awoke in the early morning, he panicked, not recognizing himself or his surroundings. Collecting himself momentarily, the role-player discovered that he was trapped in the representation—he had been left behind and locked in. Finding no other exit, the officer had to wriggle down through the toilet opening at the end of the second-floor gallery.[70]

One would be hard-pressed to insist on the literal truth of the account; even Sandvig conveys a good-natured skepticism of its veracity. But the fact that he finds the story appropriate to tell as a paradigmatic, founding anecdote for his museum is suggestive in several ways, because it stages an extreme version of the representational tensions inherent in this new museum practice of walking into re-created private spaces. The anecdote, that is, expresses the nightmare version of the new display principles. The same antique objects that elicited unanimous enthusiasm in actual spectator accounts are here depicted as threatening "old things" menacing the soldier. Likewise, the experience of immersion in represented historical spaces, which seemed so intoxicating to most Maihaugen visitors, becomes claustrophobic and panic-inducing in the anecdote's reverse image of the museum. Awakened abruptly, the soldier finds himself in the situation of a spectator without narrative material or guided tour, a visitor who does not know he is a visitor. He experiences an entrapment in history, not the smooth insertions in and exits from historically re-created milieux enjoyed by the folk-museum visitors during the opening day's festivities.[71] The baroque imagery of the anecdote makes the joke that the soldier has been swallowed alive, and that the only way out is to be defecated through the house's sewer onto the hillside. As an amusing "nightmare" tale of the visitor who was not able to get himself back out of the representational field, the story congratulates more capable museum visitors on their powers of mobility. The account underscores the fact that the attraction of the folk museum for many visitors was the hope that they would experience not a literal transportation to a real historical milieu but instead a simulation of that experience in a represented home. A viewer's consciousness of the play between presence and absence could greatly enhance the museum-going experience and made it something other than simple nostalgia or romanticism.

FOLK MUSEUMS AND "CINEMATIC" MODERNITY

The mix of identification and distance which allowed the temporary role-play at the folk museum, the momentary suspension of a subjectivity rooted in time and place, created a modern sort of pleasure. For many visitors, the atemporality and displacement effects of the folk museum functioned more as an urban distraction than as a longing for vanishing folk culture. One spectator talked of experiencing a "cultural-historical intoxication," and another put the museum at Maihaugen in sequence with other attractions of modernity: "The railroad rushes by—one hears the noise from the electric power station—sees a motley crowd of tourists and summer visitors—what can strike one more abruptly than the sight of the old Ramloftstue building and its bower?"[72] Despite the shock effect this writer attributes to the sight of a restored, relocated building in the midst of the quintessentially modern visual field of railroad tourism and electricity, the folk museum in one sense belongs precisely to this series of attractions and sights. Take the suggestive account of an enthusiastic visitor to the Danish Folk Museum in 1885, who found the mixed mode of the spectating experience there to be its main attraction. After describing in detail his tour through the museum, he recommended that visitors stop in a room at the end of the tour and take a look out of one particular window, which, although part of the display, apparently faced directly out onto the street of the actual Copenhagen cityscape outside (which included the railway station and Tivoli gardens across the street). Given the anxiety about the deluge of modernity which motivated founders of the folk museums like Hazelius, Olsen, and Sandvig, one might expect this writer as well to be repelled by the urban scene he saw after experiencing the traditional interiors. His account reveals quite the contrary:

> And if during your wandering past all of the old treasures, stopping in front of this or that rare showpiece—a tooled mug, a majestic four-post bed, or a precious, nicely inlaid wardrobe—if you have for a moment been envious of the people who then enjoyed and lived surrounded by such magnificence, then just look out the window in front of you. Over there, under the train station's open hall, a train is about to depart. The bell rings, the locomotive whistles, the steam billows up beneath the ceiling's iron beams and flushes out the pigeons nesting up there. In great arcs they circle around in the sunlight that gilds their wings. But the train is already far away, the last wagon is

now passing the last telegraph pole you can see. Reconsider, and tell me then, if you want to trade. I didn't.[73]

The writer of this account juxtaposes the mechanical grandeur of the locomotive departure with the beautiful handcrafted articles inside the museum, as if to say, "We moderns have our own sort of beauty." In fact, the descriptive stance he adopts with regard to the train's departure creates a competing, equally aestheticized tableau. The visitor should not be filled with longing for past glories, he seems to say; he, at any rate, would not trade for a premodern position. The key point of this account is not simply that the journalist prefers the modern world outside; instead, he seems to enjoy the city because it gives him the potential to be in multiple places and times. Positioned at the window between past and present, he can be part of either world simply by turning one way or the other. For this viewer, the appeal of the museum was the mobility of the modern gaze. At the urban folk museum, the writer seems to say, one can walk into other earlier times and settings on any afternoon and then return to the city, as easily as one enters and leaves a streetcar.

Accounts from the other folk museums corroborate the importance for spectators of having it both ways. Some, of course, felt that museums like Skansen should remain "a coherent whole, a free space for old memories, away from the modern industrialism."[79] This was a minority voice, however, contradicted by many others who saw advantages in the museum space as representation. For example, when it was proposed at the turn of the century that electric cables be installed at Skansen to improve lighting around the restaurant area, the letter writer quoted above protested strongly. A rebuttal to his nostalgic position appeared a week later in the same paper, however, taking the point of view that Skansen's representation of traditional culture was indeed important but did not need to be a "demonstration against the modern age's real accomplishments," such as electricity. Besides, the writer continued, just because one has electric capabilities at Skansen does not mean one always needs to use them: "An electric switch can, all according to whether one feels it called for by the situation, be turned on or off."[75] On days when Hazelius wanted to create a particular "historical" mood, that is, the lights would remain off; however, when comfort and convenience around the restaurant areas or tourist rest stops were desired, the switch could be turned on. Visitors at Skansen, like the visitor positioned at the threshold of the window at the Danish Folk Museum, could enjoy the availability of potential positions in both the traditional and modern.

In the more remote town of Lillehammer, modernity was not felt to the degree it was in the capital cities. Located in an interior valley of Norway, it had only 1,686 inhabitants in 1885 and did not acquire electric power

Fig. 12.8. The "Ramloftstuen" when it was still located in Sandvig's garden in Lillehammer in the late 1890s. (Photographer unknown, photo courtesy of Maihaugen—De Sandvigske Samlinger, Lillehammer, Norway.)

or a railroad connection to the capital until 1894.[76] It was here in his own backyard that Anders Sandvig first displayed his collected buildings and artifacts before they were moved up to the present location of Maihaugen in 1904. Even in this small-town setting, however, visitors sensed the contrast between the modern and the traditional in the folk museum, especially since Sandvig's home was quite close to the new train station. His collections, opened to the public a year after the railroad in 1895, were thus easily accessible to tourists interested in a day trip from Oslo. Alhed Schou suggested, "You can use the waiting time between two trains to take a look at 'Gudbrandsdalens Museum' and the six old buildings."[77] The contrast is easy to imagine: After riding a train (itself one of the most powerful tutors of modern spectators) one briefly entered the apparently stable, coherent world of the folk museum and then returned to the high-speed impressions of train travel and life in the capital. A photograph of one of Sandvig's buildings makes visible this relation between the museum and modernity (fig. 12.8). Behind the Ramloftstuen, pictured here in Sandvig's garden, one can make out a telegraph pole—an evocative juxtaposition of old and new. The point is not one of simple contrast, though; it is rather that the folk museum embodied the modern as much as it marked it off as distinct. It is useful to remind oneself, for example, that the very transportation networks that made the open-air museums seem necessary (due to increased exposure of traditional culture to modernity) also made them possible (since railroads were needed to gather in the artifacts and freight the disassembled buildings to central locations). Despite appearances, Sandvig's building pictured here was not on original ground—it was brought there by the same railroad of which one sees traces in the background of the photo.

When the prominent Norwegian artist Christian Krogh visited Sandvig's collection, he was in fact more impressed by this montage effect than by the museum's narrative seamlessness. His humorous account of the visit begins with a comment about meeting his tour guide: "I turned around and saw a woman from the nineteenth century, who held in her hand a key ring with a key from the seventeenth, one from the sixteenth, and three from the fifteenth century."[78] His admiration for the various time periods represented at the museum grows throughout his report, but he experienced the strongest effect when he entered Sandvig's own modern villa at the end of the visit:

> It was remarkable, this sudden transition, this leap through three or four centuries, from the simple and the solid to the soft and the varnished, which one went through by entering in here. . . . I felt almost a stranger in the milieu of my own age, so much had I thrown myself into and felt at ease in the one I have just left. I had the feeling of the man in the fairy tale, who had been taken into the mountain for ten minutes, but when coming out discovered that one hundred years had passed. Everything I saw here seemed new and unknown. But this violent opposition between the impressions of different times has its own great interest, and because of that I changed my opinion, which was the general one that holds that bringing these old remnants into the middle of the city is mistaken. . . . If I had any say in the matter, I would vote against it [that general opinion], precisely because the comparison with the new is so interesting and the juxtaposition so striking.[79]

Even in tiny Lillehammer, Krogh could appreciate in Sandvig's garden the free space created by the atemporality and estrangement effects of the open-air museum, to the point that he preferred that one retain hints of both worlds in the experience in order to strengthen the effect.

The advantages of this openly representational relation to folk culture eventually led visitors to prefer the idea of collection to that of "original" culture (which is where the matter stands today). As Maihaugen became more established, for example, towns still more remote than Lillehammer began to discuss the creation of even more local folk museums. The town of Vågå, from which the parsonage building at Maihaugen had been moved, was encouraged by the success of the folk museum in Lillehammer to start its own local museum in 1908.[80] The problem, however, was that now Maihaugen had one of their best buildings. When the town council requested that it be returned, the response in the Lillehammer newspapers was vociferous:

> Say that we went and tore something away, say we moved the parsonage back to Vaage [sic]. That would be to destroy the effect of totality, one would no longer retain the surveyability that distinguishes these collections. It would seem as if a wall were missing in the living room. The coherence would be broken and destroyed, a great thought would be killed. . . . It would be a kind of desecration to move the parsonage.[81]

The collection had by this point replaced the original in people's minds, the protests of "desecration" echoing precisely the earlier objections of people like Sophus Müller to moving buildings to museums in the first place. Ironically, the buildings at Maihaugen had by this point already been moved twice, once to Sandvig's garden in the 1890s and again up the hill to their present location at Maihaugen in 1904. The narrative powers of the museum, which had given the buildings the aura of originality by virtue of the new milieu's "coherence," had helped to create the impression that the Lillehammer residents were defending traditional life instead of modernity. Just beneath the surface in this debate, however, lay the idea that there were no more originals, only collections—or, as this same writer concluded, "You don't want to start one town's collection by ruining another."[82]

By the 1910s, the narrative and mimetic powers of the folk museums seem to have enabled spectators to enjoy the various displacements and atemporalities inherent in the process of collecting without experiencing its costs. The representation of folk life in the museums eventually replaced the need for the real because the spectator's relationship to the representation was seen as more advantageous. It allowed mobility, detachment, and a panoptic point of view, all the while delivering up a contained yet potent dose of cultural experience and the necessary assurances that the representation came as close as possible to the "real" itself. The development of the Scandinavian folk museum, in summary, suggests that the compensatory social functions of narrative helped make modernity attractive, turning a sense of "displacement" into "mobility" and a feeling of "rootlessness" into "liberation." The concentrated, seamless display spaces offered by the folk museums in this way allowed their visitors, sometimes the very people displaced by the processes of modernity, to continue a representational relationship with vanishing ways of life while pursuing spectating activities more typical of surrounding visual attractions in other institutions of the visible. Not every folk-museum visitor had this sensibility, of course; for every amused account like Christian Krogh's, there are others with more naive, hyperbolic exclamations of admiration for the reality effect of the museums. Many spectators did, however, express pleasure about the "in-betweenness" of the experience, about the peculiar mix of presence and absence which made a visit to the folk museum as appealing as a number of other visual attractions of the turn of the century, including the cinema.

The parallels with the general narrativization process in early cinema suggest that the storytelling power of the contextualized folk museum display may be part of a larger trend toward narrative in turn-of-the-century visual culture. Just as the transition from spectacle-oriented cinema to longer, storytelling films created more complex, oblique spectating positions, the development of a functionalist display at the folk museums allowed spectators to participate in more complex negotiations of subject and object boundaries than was the case with the more direct address to the viewers in more traditional museum displays. The narrative turn in many other institutions of the visible at the turn of the century could profitably be examined for this same dynamic. It may well be that narrative was more important to spectating at the turn of the century than has often been assumed, serving as the unobtrusive safety net that made the unmooring of the eye in modernity possible and pleasurable. Perhaps a neglected component, even a buried precondition of modern vision may in fact be the narrative controls surrounding the modes of display, which unobtrusively yet efficiently make possible the games of visual pleasure.

The more obvious social stakes of the representational game at the folk museum (where cultural transformation was the subject matter of the display) pose further questions about the compensatory social function of cinematic narrative. For example, did it perform a similar sleight-of-hand substitution of narrative coherence for cultural coherence (and were the cultural stakes as high in other countries)? Did the cinematic body mediate the narrativization process in the early transitional stages of cinema, gathering in and anchoring the disparate modes of display as the mannequin folk body did in the folk museum? Discussions of identification and imaginary involvement in the visual spaces of the cinematic image could benefit from this turn from the psychoanalytic to the social body. Perhaps the "in-betweenness" of both the phantom body on screen and the mannequin effigies at the museums could profitably be seen as indices of new social relations between bodies and objects in the late nineteenth century, a line of inquiry that leads to investigation of the many other institutions of the visible surrounding cinema's founding moment. It may well be, in this light, that the relation between effigy and narrative is a key to unlocking the social context of viewing at the turn of the century.

NOTES

1. Of the earlier type of folk museum, the two that I will discuss at length are Artur Hazelius's Skandinavisk-Etnografiska Samling (Scandinavian-Ethnographic Collection), founded in 1873 in Stockholm and later renamed Nordiska Museet (The Nordic Museum), and the Dansk Folkemuseum (Danish Folk Museum), founded by Bernhard Olsen in Copenhagen in 1885. The open-air versions of the folk museums considered here will be Hazelius's Skansen, which opened in Stockholm in 1891, Olsen's Frilandsmuseet, founded outside of Copenhagen in 1901, Oslo's Norsk Folkemuseum (Norwegian Folk Museum), founded by Hans Aall in 1902, and Maihaugen, which opened in Lillehammer, Norway, in 1904. The latter, which developed out of Anders Sandvig's private collection, was also open to the public as early as 1895 under the name De Sandvigske Samlinger (The Sandvigian Collections).

2. I group the various types of Scandinavian folk museums together in this article as essentially the same cultural form so as to emphasize similar aspects of spectatorship at a specific historical moment. By so doing, I admittedly lose some national and institutional specificity, but existing histories convey those perspectives quite ably. See, for example, Arne Björnstad, ed., *Skansen under hundra år* (Höganäs, Sweden: Wiken, 1991); Tord Buggeland and Jakob Ågotnes, eds., *Maihaugen: De Sandvigske Samlinger 100 år* (Oslo: Cappelens, 1987); Holger Rasmussen, *Bernhard Olsen: Virke og Verker* (Copenhagen: Nationalmuseet, 1979); and Tonte Hegard, *Romantikk og fortidsvern: Historien om de første Friluftsmuseene i Norge* (Oslo: Universitetsforlaget, 1984). In English, see Holger Rasmussen, ed., *Dansk Folkemuseum & Frilandsmuseet: History and Activities* (Copenhagen: Nationalmuseet, 1966); Edward P. Alexander, "Artur Hazelius and Skansen: The Open Air Museum," in *Museum Masters: Their Museums and Their Influence* (Nashville: The American Association for State and Local History, 1983), pp. 239–275; and the proceedings of a conference on Skansen's centennial, Mats Janson, ed., *Report of the Conference, 1991, European Association of Open-Air Museums* (Stockholm: Skansen, 1993). The latter contains numerous articles both about the Scandinavian context and the open-air museum idea.

3. Tonte Hegard's thorough study of the history of the Norwegian folk museums promotes the view that such institutions are primarily nostalgic and "romantic" in ideology; the title of her book translates as "Romanticism and Saving the Past: The History of the First Open-Air Museums in Norway."

4. A wealth of information about spectating at the folk museums can be gleaned from the numerous newspaper accounts of early visits. The populist outlook of the folk-museum founders made them quite eager students of public opinion, and they followed descriptions of their museums in the press quite closely. One of the tangible benefits of this preoccupation for the modern researcher is that the major Scandinavian folk museums have fairly complete collections of journalistic articles describing impressions of visits to their institutions. I am especially grateful for the kind assistance of personnel at the museum archives at Skansen, Maihaugen, and the Danish Nationalmuseet, nyere tid, who have provided such generous access to this and other archive material.

5. The term I use here, "institutions of the visible," is intended to echo Jean-Louis Comolli's oft-quoted phrase "machines of the visible," used in his essay of the same title in Teresa de Lauretis and Stephen Heath, eds., *The Cinematic Apparatus* (New York: St. Martin's Press, 1980), pp. 121–142. The rephrasing in institutional terms is intended to shift the attention from technologies of display to the ways visual culture is consolidated, commodified, and narrativized at the end of the nineteenth century in Europe. My use of the term here claims a certain historical specificity for this process—that the institutionalization of the visual is particularly characteristic of the late nineteenth century—but the phenomenon is of course not exclusive to the historical and cultural contexts of late-nineteenth-century Europe.

6. Comolli, for example, attempts to move the discussion in the direction of discursivity by expanding the idea of the machine or apparatus to include social configurations of economics, politics, and ideology. But when he writes of a "social machine" that "manufactures" representation, the mechanical aspect of the metaphor still tends to subsume the sense of the social he is trying to promote. Retention of the apparatus image never allows Comolli to completely disassociate himself from the technological teleologies he criticizes. See Comolli, op. cit., especially pp. 121–122.

7. Nils-Arvid Bringéus, "Artur Hazelius och Nordiska Museet," *Fataburen: Nordiska Museets och Skansen Årbok* (1972): 7. (This and subsequent translations, unless otherwise noted, are my own.)

8. See Vagn Dybdahl, *De nye Klasser, 1870–1913*, vol. 12 of *Danmarks Historie*, ed. John Dahlstrup and Hal Koch (Copenhagen: Politikens Forlag, 1965), pp. 33–35, and Franklin D. Scott, *Sweden: The Nation's History* (Carbondale: Southern Illinois University Press, 1988), pp. 436–437. The decades identified with industrialization coincide with developments in the literary and cultural production of the Scandinavian countries, which during the 1870s and 1880s was marked by the realistic, socially engaged literature and cultural discussions of Georg Brandes, Henrik Ibsen, August Strindberg, and many others. Interestingly, the standard designation among Scandinavian cultural historians for this important moment is "the modern *breakthrough*," the last term pointing to the perception that an abrupt shift took place not only in terms of social mobility and work practices but also in the cultural arena.

9. Scott, op. cit., p. 437.

10. Total national populations of the Scandinavian countries during the nineteenth century approximately doubled, while the major cities typically quadrupled in size. Norway's capital city Kristiania (now Oslo) grew from a small provincial population of 33,000 in 1845 to 250,000 in 1900. Stockholm grew from 75,000 in the year 1800 to 300,000 in 1900, while Copenhagen during the same period grew from 104,000 to 370,000. Although this left the Scandinavian capitals with significantly smaller populations than Paris, Berlin, New York, or London, which had between two and six million inhabitants at the turn of the century, the Scandinavian cities' relative growth from provincial outposts to significant population centers was still a dramatic social transformation for the northern cultures. See Hans Try, *To Kulturer, En Stat*, vol. 11 of *Norges Historie*, ed. Knut Mykland (Oslo: J. W. Cappelens Forlag, 1979), p. 103, and Scott, op. cit., p. 344.

11. In terms of percentage of the total population, Norway had a more significant emigration than Sweden, and was exceeded only by Ireland. See Try, op. cit., pp. 66–67, and Scott, op. cit., p. 369.

12. Adolf Bauer, "Dansk Folkemuseum," *Dagbladet* (Copenhagen), 8 August 1885.

13. Moltke Moe, quoted in Hans Aall, *Norsk Folkemuseum, 1894–1919: Trekk av dets historie* (The Norwegian Folk Museum, 1894–1919: Aspects of Its History) (Kristiania: Kirstes Boktrykkeri, 1920), p. 4.

14. Zachris Topelius, "Hauszeichen" (Signs of Home), in *Das Nordische Museum in Stockholm: Stimmen aus der Fremde* (Stockholm: P. A. Norstedt & Söner, 1888), p. 92.

15. Anders Sandvig, speech at Maihaugen's opening ceremonies (copy in clipping book 4, page 127), Maihaugen Archives, Lillehammer.

16. Santner uses this evocative term in a different, but not entirely unrelated context—that of objects seen in relation to the lost bodies of the Holocaust. See Eric Santner, *Stranded Objects: Mourning, Memory, and Film in Postwar Germany* (Ithaca, N.Y.: Cornell University Press, 1990).

17. Claës Lundin, "Nordiska Museet," *Ny Illustrerad Tidning*, 22 October 1898, p. 348.

18. Müller (1846–1934) was a Danish archaeologist and scholar of Danish prehistory, the traditional subject matter of museum display before the late-nineteenth-century shifts in museological practice. He was made director of the Danish National Museum's ancient history section in 1892.

19. Quoted in Rune Kjellberg, *Et halvt århundre: Norsk Folkemuseum, 1894–1944* (Oslo: Tanum, 1945), p. 7.

20. Sophus Müller, "Museum og Interiør," *Tilskueren* (1897): 690.

21. A satirical article in a Swedish periodical from the turn of the century took delight in the contradictions of the open-air museum's recontextualization efforts; with witty parody the author imagined a future time in 1950 when Skansen would have expanded to turn the entire city of Stockholm into one giant open-air museum, open to visits by its former residents at the price of half a crown. See Joker [pseud.], "Storskansen" (Greater Skansen), *Söndags-Nisse* (Stockholm), 17 March 1901.

22. Hazelius mentioned to a potential donor that the mannequins could cost four times as much as the folk costumes themselves (he quotes costs of 230 *riksdalar* for a mannequin, and 50 to 100 for a costume)—a discrepancy one must simply "put up with," Hazelius claims, if one wants to reach the public. ("Brefväxling emellan A. Hazelius och O. Dickson") (Correspondence between A. Hazelius and O. Dickson), *Meddelanden från Nordiska Museet 1898* (Stockholm: P. A. Norstedt & Söner, 1900), 320.

23. Hazelius was criticized strongly by some for his inability to rein in the enterprise once it started; one newspaper correspondent called his collecting habits "normal for children, ravens, lunatics, magpies and kleptomaniacs, but ridiculous for a mature, wise, and honorable man." See "En vacker hänförelse, som bör—stäfjas" (A beautiful enthusiasm, which should—be put in check), *Smålandsposten* (Kronoberg), 27 December 1895.

24. Jørgen Olrik, "Dansk Folkemuseums Jubilæum," *Illustreret Tidende*, 7 August 1910, p. 558.

25. I borrow this term from film theory because of its usefulness in describing a consistently constructed, seemingly self-sufficient fictional space. The tableaux scenes are more properly called diegetic than narrative, although some elements of character identity, temporality, and offstage action are introduced by accompanying printed matter as well. The scenes themselves, lacking any discernible sequence in the early folk museums (except perhaps a general geographic organization), are not visually narrative, but when taken with the supporting information of living and written guides, might be considered so in a more general sense.

26. Tom Gunning, "The Cinema of Attractions: Early Film, Its Spectator and the Avant-Garde," in *Early Cinema: Space Frame Narrative,* ed. Thomas Elsaesser (London: BFI Publishing, 1990), pp. 56–62.

27. Hazelius and others realized that the visibility of folk material could be augmented not only by gathering it in a central location but also by reproducing the images and making them available to people who could not visit the museum in person. For the actual visitors as well, the illustrated catalogues could take on a souvenir function, providing a "more secure memory" of their visit, as Hazelius puts it in the introduction. See Artur Hazelius, *Minnen från Nordiska Museet: Afbildningar af föremål i museet jämte åtföljande text* (Memories from the Nordic Museum: Illustrations of artifacts in the museum together with accompanying text), 2 vols. (Stockholm: P. B. Eklunds Förlag, 1892–1902).

28. Ibid.

29. "Sandvigs Samlinger" (Sandvig's Collections), *Intelligenssedlerne,* 14–15 June 1901. The author of this article is likely Alhed Schou; if so, she followed her own recommendation. She wrote the first guidebook for Maihaugen, which was published in 1905.

30. Lundin, "Nordiska Museet," p. 348. Emphasis in the original.

31. Idem, "I svenska allmogehem, bland dalfolk och lappar: Nutidsbild från Stockholms Djurgård" (In the homes of Swedish commoners, among Dalecarlians and Lapps: A modern picture from Stockholm's Djurgård), *Stockholms Dagblad,* 27 September 1891.

32. "Skansens utveckling" (Skansen's Development), *Svenska dagbladet* (Stockholm), 24 August 1899.

33. For a more thorough history of mannequin display in the Swedish folk-museum contexts, see Jonas Berg, "Dräktdockor—Hazelius' och andras" (Costume Mannequins—Hazelius's and Others'), *Fataburen: Nordiska Museets och Skansens Årbok* (1980): 9–28 (pp. 12–15 deal specifically with the mannequin displays at the late-nineteenth-century industrial exhibitions).

34. Quoted in Berg, op. cit., p. 13.

35. Berg., op. cit., pp. 14–15.

36. F. A. Wulff, "Skandinavisk-etnografiska museet på verldsutställningen i Paris 1878," *Aftonbladet* (Stockholm), 12 October 1878.

37. Ernest Allard, "Exposition d'ethnographie scandinave," quoted in J. H. Kramer, *Le Musée D'Ethnographie Scandinave à Stockholm. Fondé et Dirigé par le Dr. Artur Hazelius. Notice Historique et Descriptive,* 2d ed. (Stockholm: Norstedt & Söner, 1879), p. 44.

38. Two more well-known examples are Christen Dalsgaard's "The Town Carpenter Arrives with a Coffin for the Dead Child" (1857) and Albert Edelfelt's "A Child's Funeral Procession" (1879).

39. "A travers les pays Scandinaves" (Across the Scandinavian Countries), *Le Rappel,* 6 August 1878.

40. A prevalent technique in the Scandinavian wax museums involved depiction of wax figures in a variety of states of consciousness, from "dead" or "sleeping" figures to "alert" mannequins engaged in visual activity similar to that of the spectator. The juxtaposition contributed to the sense that some of the mannequins were more alive than others, when in reality of course all shared the same waxen status. A folk museum tableau like "The Little Girl's Last Bed" adopts much the same technique, gathering "live" figures around a "dead" one.

41. See especially the section entitled "Identification, Mirror" in Christian Metz, *The Imaginary Signifier: Psychoanalysis and the Cinema,* trans. Celia Britton et al. (Bloomington: Indiana University Press, 1982), pp. 42–57.

42. M. G. de Molinari, "Visites a l'exposition universelle," *Le Journal des débats,* 13 July 1878.

43. Wulff, op. cit.

44. Michael Fried, *Absorption and Theatricality: Painting and Beholder in the Age of Diderot* (Chicago: University of Chicago Press, 1980), pp. 121–122.

45. A visitor to Hazelius's museum four years earlier in 1874, Johanne Mestorf, also describes being allowed to walk into the display space for a closer look. Although mostly interested in seeing the objects up close, he also seems to have been acting out a fantasy of interacting with the mannequins, which he described in this way: "All ages are represented and the life-size figures are so life-like that one forgets that they are not made of flesh and blood and feels tempted to talk to them" (see *Das Nordische Museum in Stockholm* [Stockholm: P. A. Norstedt & Söner, 1888], pp. 65–66).

46. Bernhard Olsen, "Dansk Folkemuseum." *Illustreret Tidende,* 2 August 1885, p. 573.

47. Ibid.

48. Emil Hannover, "Bernhard Olsen ved hans 70-aarige Fødselsdag den 9. September" (Bernhard Olsen on his 70th birthday, the 9th of September), *Tilskueren* (1906): 706–707. Italics in original.

49. It is not always easy to discern from a photograph whether a represented figure is a mannequin or a costumed "actor"—an ontological dilemma for the visual historian that duplicates the challenge folk-museum spectators themselves faced as they viewed such exhibits in person. In this case, however, multiple pictures from different angles by different photographers and artists show these figures in exactly the same poses, so it is unlikely that they were dressed-up guides.

50. One journalist (Adolf Bauer, op. cit.) mentions that folk costumes would be displayed at the Folk Museum when the financial resources allowed sculpting of the necessary mannequins. Olsen, however, seems to have decided rather soon to phase out the mannequins in favor of either living guides demonstrating craft techniques or empty rooms with only traces of missing bodies, the two techniques that eventually were adopted by most open-air museums, as I will discuss below.

51. L. Lund, "Mere om Dansk Folkemusæum," *Morgenbladet* (Copenhagen), 10 August 1885.

52. Curt [pseud.], "I Folkemuseet," *Illustreret Tidende,* 2 August 1885, p. 576.

53. One account mentions that the live Lapp dog previously had the habit of sitting in the midst of the tableau interior display of Lapland back at the Nordic

Museum before the mannequins were moved, which created similar potential for surprising contrasts there (see *Das Nordische Museum in Stockholm*, p. 65).

54. Lundin, "I svenska allmogehem."

55. *Hemlandsvännen*, 21 October 1892.

56. Quoted in Arne Björnstad, "Artur Hazelius och Skansen, 1891–1901," in *Skansen under hundra år* (Höganäs, Sweden: Wiken, 1991), p. 69. Emphasis in original. My thanks to Mr. Björnstad for personal correspondence providing extra contextual information on the date and situation of this note.

57. In fact, I am told that several years ago at Skansen, when a curator attempted to place mannequins back in one building at the modern museum as a historical retrospective, public response was so negative that the staff decided to remove them again. Mats Jansson, personal conversation with author at Skansen, July, 1992.

58. Aall, op. cit., p. 34.

59. Ibid., p. 10.

60. Ibid., p. 36.

61. Carl, Berner, "De Sandvigske Samlinger paa Lillehammer" (Sandvigs Collections at Lillehammer), *Morgenposten* (Kristiania), 8 March 1909.

62. Anders Sandvig, *De Sandvigske Samlinger i tekst og billeder* (Oslo: J. W. Cappelens Forlag, 1928), p. 11.

63. "Kvinderne paa Maihaugen," *Gudbrandsdølen* (Lillehammer), 18 April 1905.

64. "En Visit til Det Norske Folkemuseum paa Bygdø," *Vestlandstidene,* 11 June 1902.

65. Arne Ludvigsen, "Om Flytning af gamle Bygninger" (On the Moving of Old Buildings), in *Fra Nationalmuseets Arbejdsmark 1940* (Copenhagen: Nationalmuseet, 1940), p. 46.

66. "De Sandvigske samlinger, Lillehammer." Article from an unnamed Gjøvik newspaper, clipping book 4, p. 102, Maihaugen Archives.

67. Hegard, op. cit., p. 94.

68. "På Skansen," *Vårt land* (Stockholm), 5 October 1891.

69. "Gudbrandsdalens Folkemuseum paa Maihaugen. en Seværdighed," *Aftenposten* (Kristiania), 31 May 1903.

70. Anders Sandvig, *I praksis og på samlerferd* (Oslo: Tanum, 1943), pp. 185–186.

71. Several films about wax museums provide an interesting parallel to this nightmare of confinement. An early Danish comedy, *Christian Schrøder i Panoptikon* (1910), depicts an exhausted tourist from the countryside who falls asleep in the wax museum at closing time and is locked in, only to have the wax figures come to life. Likewise, two American wax museum films, *Mystery of the Wax Museum* (1933) and Vincent Price's 3-D remake, *House of Wax* (1953), both play up the idea that after hours the pleasurable entertainment of the wax museum has a more sinister aspect and end with entrapment scenarios in the cellars of the buildings, where actual corpses are being dipped in wax.

72. "Dansk Folkemuseum," *Husvennen* 13 (1885–1886): 326–328; "Ramloftstuen paa Lillehammer," *Verdens Gang,* 26 July 1895.

73. Curt, op. cit., p. 578.

74. "Elektriciteten och Skansen," *Dagens nyheter* (Stockholm), 2 May 1899.

75. "Elektriciteten och Skansen: Ett genmäle till 'En Skansvän'" (Electricity and Skansen: A reply to "A friend of Skansen"), *Dagens nyheter,* 10 May 1899.

76. Ågotnes and Buggeland, op. cit., p. 43.

77. "Sandvigs Samlinger," *Intelligenssedlerne.*

78. Christian Krogh, "Lillehammer," *Verdens gang* (Kristiania), February 1901.

79. Ibid.

80. Buggeland and Ågotnes, op. cit., pp. 90–91.

81. Midttun, Gisle, "Flytning af Prestegaarden," *Dale-Gudbrand* (Lillehammer), 28 February 1908.

82. Ibid.

THIRTEEN

America, Paris, the Alps: Kracauer (and Benjamin) on Cinema and Modernity

Miriam Bratu Hansen

GENEALOGIES OF MODERNITY

On the threshold of the twenty-first century, the cinema may well seem to be an invention "without a future," as Louis Lumière had predicted somewhat prematurely in 1896.[1] But it is surely not an invention without a past, or pasts, at least judging from the proliferation of events, publications, and broadcasts occasioned by the cinema's centennial. What actually constitutes the past, however, and how it figures in history—and helps to figure history—remains very much a matter of debate, if not invention.

For more than a decade now, scholars of early cinema have been shifting the image of that past, from one of a prologue or evolutionary stepping-stone to the cinema that followed (that is, classical Hollywood cinema and its international counterparts) to one of a cinema in its own right, a different *kind* of cinema.[2] This shift has yielded detailed studies of early conventions of representation and address and of paradigmatically distinct modes of production, exhibition, and reception. At the same time, it has opened up the focus of investigation from a more narrowly defined institutional approach to a cross-disciplinary inquiry into modernity, aiming to situate the cinema within a larger set of social, economic, political, and cultural transformations.

In the measure in which historians have uncoupled early cinema from the evolutionist and teleological narratives of classical film history, studies of cinema and modernity have gravitated toward the nineteenth century. More specifically, there is a tendency to situate the cinema in the context of "modern life," prototypically observed by Baudelaire in nineteenth-century Paris. In this context, the cinema figures as part of the violent restructuration of human perception and interaction effected by industrial-capitalist modes of production and exchange; by modern technologies such as trains, photography, electric lighting, telegraph, and telephone; and by the large-scale construction of metropolitan streets populated with anonymous crowds, prostitutes, and not-quite-so anonymous flâneurs. Likewise, the cinema appears as part of an emerging culture of consumption and spectacular display, ranging from world expositions and department stores to the more sinister attractions of melodrama, phantasmagoria, wax museums, and morgues, a culture marked by an accelerated proliferation—and, hence, also by an accelerated ephemerality and obsolescence—of sensations, fashions, and styles.

These contexts give us considerable purchase on understanding the ways in which modernity realized itself in and through the cinema, whether early cinema in particular or the cinematic institution in general. They elucidate, for instance, how the cinema not only epitomized a new stage in the ascendance of the visual as a social and cultural discourse but also responded to an ongoing crisis of vision and visibility.[3] They account for the cinema's enormous appeal in terms of a structural "mobilization of the gaze"—which transmutes the traumatic upheaval of temporal and spatial coordinates not just into visual pleasure but also into a "*flânerie* through an imaginary elsewhere and an imaginary elsewhen."[4] They complicate assumptions about the sexual and gender dynamics of the gaze predicated on the model of classical cinema by tracing detours and ambivalences in the development of female consumption. Moreover, once we locate the cinema within a history of sense perception in modernity, in particular the spiral of shock, stimuli protection, and ever greater sensations ("reality!"), we can recast the debate on spectatorship in more specific historical and political terms.[5]

But I am interested here in what this genealogy of cinema and modernity tends to leave out: the twentieth century—the modernity of mass production, mass consumption, and mass annihilation, of rationalization, standardization, and media publics. I wish in no way to contest the legitimacy and value of anchoring the cinema's modernity in the mid- to late-nineteenth century, but I find something symptomatic in the ease with which so many studies seem to speak from one *fin-de-siècle* to another. What is at issue here is not just the choice of focus on different periods or stages of modernity but the status of competing or alternative versions of modernism, as the cultural discourses co-articulated with modernity and processes of modernization.[6] In this competition, the eclipse of the twentieth century is not limited to cinema studies. Marshall Berman, for instance, explicitly endorses a Baudelairean vision of modernity, which he dubs "modernism in the streets," making it part of a cultural-political program for the present. As Berman proclaims: "It may turn out, then, that . . . remembering the modernisms of the nineteenth century can give us the vision and courage to create the modernisms of the twenty-first."[7]

Despite Berman's polemical stance against postmodernism, this is quite a postmodern gesture, not only because of its patent nostalgia but also because the very notion that there is more than one modernity—and that modernism can, and should, be used in the plural—only emerged with the passing of the modern as, to use Jameson's term, a "cultural dominant."[8] It became possible to think that way with, among other things, the decline of Fordist industrialism and the end of the Cold War; the increased presence of marginalized social groups and cultures in institutions of art, literature, and the academy; and the emergence of a global perspective that highlights modernism and modernity as specifically Western phenomena tied to a history of imperialism and masculinism. In the wake of these multiple, staggered, and interlinked shifts, it has become possible to question the hegemony of modernism in the singular—a modernism that, its own attacks on the Enlightenment legacy notwithstanding, reinscribed the universalist therapies of the latter with the ostensibly unitary and value-free truths of technology and instrumental rationality. The critique of this hegemonic modernism casts a wide net, branching out from the narrowly defined modernism of literature and art into architecture, urban planning, philosophy, economy, sociology, and social engineering. It traces the same utopian fallacies in functionalism, neopositivism, and behaviorism; in LeCorbusier and the Bauhaus; in abstract and constructivist art as well as the monumental murals of Diego Rivera; in Sergei Tretyakov and Bertolt Brecht as well as Ezra Pound and Wyndham Lewis; and in political positions ranging from leftist Fordism to neoclassicist elitism.[9]

Whether motivated by postmodern critique or the search for alternative traditions of modernity, this attack on hegemonic modernism runs the risk of unwittingly reproducing the same epistemic totalitarianism that it seeks to displace. For one thing, it reduces the contradictory and heterogeneous aspects of twentieth-century modernisms to the claims of one dominant paradigm or, rather, the positions of a particular, canonical set of modernist intellectuals. For another, this attack collapses the discourse of modernism with the discourses of modernity, however mediated the two may be. That is, the critical fixation on hegemonic modernism to some extent undercuts the effort to open up the discussion of modernism from the traditional preoccupation with artistic and intellectual movements and to understand the latter as inseparable from the political, economic, and social processes of modernity and modernization, including the development of mass and media culture. In other words, the attack on hegemonic modernism tends to occlude the material conditions of everyday modernity which distinguish living in the twentieth century from living in the nineteenth, at least for large populations in western Europe and the United States.

If we want to make the juncture of cinema and modernity productive for the present debate, we need to grant twentieth-century modernity the same attention toward heterogeneity, nonsynchronicity, and contradiction which is currently being devoted to earlier phases of modernity—that is, in principle at least, since the attempt to reduce and control these dimensions is undeniably a salient feature of hegemonic modernism in so many areas. Still, if we seek to locate the cinema within the transformations of the life-world specific to the twentieth century, in particular the first half, we cannot conflate these transformations with, say, the tabula rasa visions imposed upon them in the name of an aesthetics and ideology of the machine. Modernist architecture and urban planning, for instance, may have had a tremendous, and perhaps detrimental, impact on people's lives, but it would be a mistake simply to equate modernist intention and actual social use.[10] Similarly, classical cinema may have been running on Fordist-Taylorist principles of industrial organization, functionally combined with neoclassicist norms of film style; but the systematic standardization of narrative form and spectatorial response cannot fully account for the *cultural* formation of cinema, for the actual theater experience and locally and historically variable dynamics of reception.[11]

Yet, conceiving of the relation between hegemonic modernism and modern life-world as an opposition may be as misleading as prematurely casting it in terms of an argument about reception, resistance, and reappropriation. We should not underrate the extent to which modernism was also a popular or, more precisely, a mass movement. Whether the promises of modernization turned out to be ideological, unfulfilled, or both, there were enough people who stood to gain from the universal implementation of at least formally guaranteed political rights; from a system of mass production that was coupled with mass consumption (that is, widespread affordability of consumer goods); from a general improvement of living conditions enabled by actual advances in science and technology; and from the erosion of long-standing social, sexual, and cultural hierarchies. To be sure, these promises have become staples of Western capitalist mythology and have in many ways contributed to maintaining relations of subordination in the West and in other parts of the world. But if we want to understand what was radically new and different in twentieth-century modernity, we also need to reconstruct the liberatory appeal of the "modern" for a mass public—a public that was itself both product and casualty of the modernization process.

From this perspective, the cinema was not just one among a number of perceptual technologies, nor even the culmination of a particular logic of the gaze; it was above all (at least until the rise of television) the single most expansive discursive horizon in which the effects of modernity were reflected, rejected or denied, transmuted or negotiated. It was both part and prominent symptom of the crisis as which modernity was perceived, and at the same time it evolved into a social discourse in which a wide variety of groups sought to come to terms with the traumatic impact of modernization. This reflexive dimension of cinema, its dimension of *publicness*, was recognized by intellectuals early on, whether they celebrated the cinema's emancipatory potential or, in alliance with the forces of censorship and reform, sought to contain and control it, adapting the cinema to the standards of high culture and the restoration of the bourgeois public sphere.[12]

In the following, I will elaborate on the juncture of cinema and modernity through the writings of Siegfried Kracauer and, by way of comparison, Walter Benjamin, both of whom were approximately the same age as the emerging cinema and acutely aware of the key role the new medium was playing in the struggle over the meanings of modernity. Both were writing in the Germany of the Weimar Republic, which itself has become a topos of classical modernity in—and as—crisis, as a period that rehearsed the contradictions of modernization in belated and accelerated form.[13] Kracauer and Benjamin were friends and read and reviewed each other's writings; if their correspondence is relatively slim, it is because they saw each other and talked frequently, especially during their common exile in Paris and, later, in Marseille.[14] Neither of them held an academic position: Kracauer wrote for and (from 1924 on) was an editor of the *Frankfurter Zeitung*, a liberal daily that Ernst Bloch once referred to as the "*Ur*-paper of solidity" (*Urblatt der Gediegenheit*);[15] Benjamin worked on a freelance basis for various literary journals and radio stations.

My discussion will focus on Kracauer, whose major writings on cinema, mass culture, and everyday life (hundreds of articles and reviews dating from the interwar period) are less widely known than Benjamin's few canonized texts relating to the topic. If the latter are treated in a more critical tone, this has less to do with the texts themselves than with their reception, in particular the way Benjamin's historico-philosophical construction of Baudelaire's Paris is used to elide the specifically twentieth-century dimensions of both cinema and modernity. Obviously, one cannot simply align Benjamin with a nineteenth-century genealogy of modernity and Kracauer, by contrast, with one predicated on the twentieth. Benjamin explicitly derived his construction from an analysis of the crisis of the present (and his Artwork Essay as a telescope connecting the two sites),[16] and Kracauer, conversely, also turned to the nineteenth century, notably with his "social biography" of Jacques Offenbach, in which he analyzed the genre of the operetta as a prototype of the institution of cinema.[17] Nonetheless, the bulk of Kracauer's Weimar writing is engaged with twentieth-century modernity and thus, on a rather basic level, offers a wealth of observations and reflections on cinema and mass culture that we do not find in Benjamin.[18] On the basis of his persistent reflexive-empirical engagement with contemporary reality, Kracauer represents an early attempt to conceptualize different types of modernity or competing modernities. I will try to delineate these competing modernities in Kracauer's work, referring to them in terms of his own "thought-images" of, respectively, America, Paris, and the Alps.

DISCOVERING "AMERIKA"

America will disappear only when it completely discovers itself.
KRACAUER, "Der Künstler in dieser Zeit" (1925)

In both retrospective and contemporary accounts of Weimar culture, the cinema's status as a privileged figure of modern life is often associated with the discourse of Americanism, the invocation of "Amerika" as metaphor and model of a disenchanted modernity. This term encompassed everything from Fordist-Taylorist principles of production—mechanization, standardization, rationalization, efficiency, the assembly line—and attendant standards of mass consumption; through new forms of social organization, freedom from tradition, social mobility, mass democracy, and a "new matriarchy"; to the cultural symbols of the new era—skyscrapers, jazz ("*Negermusik*"), boxing, revues, radio, and cinema. Whatever its particular articulation (not to mention its actual relation to the United States), the discourse of Americanism became a catalyst for the debate on modernity and modernization, polarized into cultural conservative battle cries or jeremiads on the one hand and euphoric hymns to technological progress or resigned acceptance on the other. Among the latter, the political fault lines ran between those who found in the Fordist gospel a solution to the ills of capitalism and a harmonious path to democracy (the contemporary concept of "white socialism") and those who believed that modern technology, and technologically based modes of production and consumption, furnished the conditions, but only the conditions, for a truly proletarian revolution ("left Fordism").[19]

In the first years of the republic, the association of cinema and Americanism was by no means established, at least not until the implementation of the Dawes Plan in 1924 and the attendant large-scale campaign of industrial rationalization according to Ford and Taylor. Around the same time, and for related reasons, Hollywood consolidated its hegemony on the German market. In a report for the *Frankfurter Zeitung* on a conference of the Deutsche Werkbund in July 1924, Kracauer presents this gathering of designers, industrialists, educators, and politicians as a site of missed connections. The conference was devoted to two main topics, "the fact of Americanism, which seems to advance like a natural force" and the "artistic significance of the fiction film."[20] Before going into details, Kracauer observes a major failure to connect in the speakers' basic approach to Americanism: They went all out to explore its "total spiritual disposition" but, true to the Werkbund's professed status as an "apolitical organization," they left the "economic and political preconditions upon which rationalization . . . is based substantially untouched." While the proponents and critics of rationalization seemed to articulate their positions with great conviction and ostensible clarity, the second topic remained shrouded in confusion. "Curiously, perhaps due to deep-seated prejudices, the problem of film was dealt with in a much more biased and impressionistic way than the fact of mechanization, even though both phenomena, Americanism and film composition, after all belong to the same sphere of surface life."

In an often-quoted passage of his semiautobiographical novel *Ginster,* Kracauer has the protagonist and his friend Otto debate questions of scientific methodology. While Otto proposes a method that emphasizes "secondary matters" (*Nebensachen*) and "hidden paths" (*Schleichwege*) so as to arrive at "scientifically cogent hypotheses," Ginster does not believe that the point is even to reconstruct an "original reality": "According to his theory, Columbus had to land in India; he discovered America. . . . A hypothesis is valid only under the condition that it misses its intended goal, so as to reach another, unknown goal."[21] The choice of example is no coincidence. The episode illustrates not only Kracauer's own approach to "reality"[22] but also his peculiar engagement with "Amerika," with capitalist-industrial, mass-mediated modernity.

Kracauer's writings prior to the mid-1920s by and large participate in the period's culturally pessimistic discourse on modernity.[23] Within a predominantly philosophical and theological framework, modernity appears as the endpoint of a historical process of disintegration, an evacuation of meaning from life, a dissociation of truth and existence which has thrown the atomized individual into what Georg Lukács has termed a state of "transcendental homelessness." Drawing on contemporary sociology, in particular on Simmel, Scheler, and Weber, Kracauer sees this process as linked to the unfolding of a progressively instrumentalized *ratio,* of abstract, formal reason detached from human contingency, which incarnates itself in capitalist economy and the corresponding ideal of "a thoroughly rationalized civilized society" (*Gesellschaft* as opposed to *Gemeinschaft*).[24]

It is significant that Kracauer elaborates his early metaphysics of modernity in a treatise on the detective novel, a genre of popular fiction which thrived on serial production and which in Germany occupied a lower rank on the ladder of cultural values than in England or France.[25] Kracauer reads this genre not from the outside, as a sociological symptom, but as an allegory of contemporary life. "Just as the detective reveals the secret buried between people, the detective novel discloses, in the aesthetic medium, the secret of the de-realized society and its substanceless marionettes." It thus transforms, by virtue of its construction, "incomprehensible life" into a "counter-image" of reality (116–117), a "distorting mirror" in which the world can begin to read its own features. When, around 1924, Kracauer begins to develop a theoretical interest in film, it is motivated in similar terms. Because of its formal capacities of displacement and estrangement, he argues, film is singularly suited to capture a "disintegrating world without substance"; it therefore fulfills a cognitive, diagnostic function vis-à-vis modern life more truthfully than most works of high art.[26] Kracauer's turn to the "surface," to a topography of the ephemeral, culturally despised products of the period, is thus already programmed into his early metaphysics of modernity, the eschatologically tinged project of registering the historical process in all its negativity.[27]

For Kracauer, following his teacher Simmel, the fascination with the surface phenomena of modern life was simultaneously a rejection of the discipline of philosophy, in particular the tradition of German idealist philosophy. Theoretical thinking schooled in that tradition, Kracauer felt, was increasingly incapable of grasping a changed and changing reality, a "reality filled with corporeal things and people."[28] Accordingly, Kracauer's despair over the direction of the historical process turns into a despair over the lack of a heuristic discourse, over the fact that "the objectively-curious [das Objektiv-Neugierige] lacks a countenance."[29] Like many of his generation, Kracauer sought such a heuristic discourse in the writings of Marx and contemporary Marxist theory, which he began to read, intensely if idiosyncratically, around 1925. But if his own writings began to take a materialist turn during those years, it was also because actual developments in the discourse of modernization were demanding a different approach.

With the introduction of Fordist-Taylorist principles of production in both industry and the service sector and the accompanying spread of cultural forms of mass consumption, the very categories developed to comprehend the logics of modernity—"rationalization," "demythologization," "alienation," "reification"—gained a new dimension; the ratio assumed a more concrete, and more complex and contradictory, face. To be sure, there had been experiments in and debates on rationalization before the advent of Americanism, in fact before World War I. And while there was a distinct push for Fordist-Taylorist methods in the mid-twenties, they were not implemented everywhere and at the same pace.[30] Yet even if thorough rationalization remained largely an aspiration and the discourse on its effects often lapsed into myth, it nonetheless assumed a powerful reality—in urban planning and architecture, in social engineering, in new cultural practices of living and leisure—which Kracauer perceived as insufficiently grasped by prevailing accounts of modernity.

It was not that the critique of Western rationality ignored capitalist modes of production and exchange. For Kracauer, however, this critique itself remained marooned in the abstractions of transcendental philosophy because it posited the *ratio* as a transhistorical, ontological category of which the current phase of capitalism was just a particular, inevitable and unalterable incarnation. He extended this reproach even to Lukács, whose *History and Class Consciousness* (1923) had persuasively fused Weber's theory of rationalization with Marx's theory of commodity fetishism and thus provided a major impulse for Critical Theory.[31] Kracauer not only rejected Lukács's notion of the proletariat as both object and subject of a Hegelian dialectics of history; he also balked at the conception of reality as a totality that the theoretical intellect presumed to know from a position outside or above. For Kracauer, the recognition of the historical process required the construction of categories from within the material; bringing Marx up to date demanded a "dissociation [*Dissoziierung*] of Marxism in the direction of the realities."[32]

Kracauer's own dissociation into the realities of modern life can be seen, at the most obvious level, in his choice of topics and areas. Beginning around 1925, his articles increasingly revolve around sites and symptoms of change: quotidian objects (the typewriter, inkwells, umbrellas, pianellas); spaces (metropolitan streets, squares and architecture, arcades, bars, department stores, train stations, subways, homeless shelters, unemployment offices); and the media (photography, illustrated magazines, film); rituals and institutions of an expanding leisure culture (tourism, dance, sports, cinema, circus, variety shows, amusement parks). As remarkable as the range of topics is the change of tone and differentiation of stance in Kracauer's writing. Although the critique of the capitalist grounding of modernization continues—and becomes fiercer by the end of the decade—the metaphysically based pessimistic and normative attitude recedes in favor of an "uncertain, hesitant affirmation of the civilizing process." Such a stance, Kracauer concludes in his essay "Travel and Dance,"

> is more real than a radical cult of progress, be it of rational origin or unflinchingly aimed at the Utopian, but also more real than the condemnations of those who romantically flee from the situation assigned to them. It [this stance] defers promises without refraining from statements; it looks at the phenomena that have emancipated themselves from their foundation not just categorically as disfigurements and distorted reflection, but grants them their own, after all positive possibilities.[33]

What particular possibilities did Kracauer perceive in the cultural manifestations of Americanism? What in this particular regime of modernization was specifically new and potentially liberatory? While Kracauer still occasionally deplores the "machinelike" quality of modern existence, he begins to be fascinated by new entertainment forms that turn the "fusion of people and things" into a creative principle. He first observes this principle at work in the live musical revues that were sweeping across German vaudeville stages: "The living approximates the mechanical, and the mechanical behaves like the living."[34] With an enthusiasm that sounds unusually close to the discourse of "white socialism," Kracauer reports on the Frankfurt performance of the Tiller Girls (actually a British troupe) whose tour inaugurated the "American age" in Germany:

> What they accomplish is an unprecedented labor of precision, a delightful Taylorism of the arms and legs, mechanized charm. They shake the tambourine, they drill to the rhythms of jazz, they come on as the boys in blue: all at once, pure duodeci-unity [*Zwölfeinigkeit*]. Technology whose grace is seductive, grace that is genderless because it rests on joy of precision. A representation of American virtues, a flirt by the stopwatch.[35]

Kracauer's pleasure in precision does not rest on an aesthetics of technology but on the social and sexual configurations this aesthetics may yield. In the planned economy of the revue, the payoff of standardization is a sensual manifestation of collective behavior, a vision—or mirage—of equality, cooperation, and solidarity. It is also a vision of gender mobility (girls dressed up as sailors), if precariously close to a retreat from sexuality. Still, Kracauer conveys a glimpse of a different organization of social and gender relations—different at least from the patriarchal order of the Wilhelmine family and the standards of sexual difference which clashed with both the reality of working women and Kracauer's own gay sensibility.[36]

The Taylorist aesthetics of the revue also suggests a different conception of the body. Writing about two "excentric dancers" (*Exzentriktänzer*) performing live in the Ufa Theater, Kracauer asserts that the precision and grace of these gentlemen's act "transform the body-machine into an atmospheric instrument." They defy physical laws of gravity and statics, not by assimilating technology to the phantasma of a complete, masculine body (the armored body of the soldier/hero), but by playing with the fragmentation and dissolution of that body: "When, for instance, they throw one leg around in a wide arc . . . it is really no longer attached to the body, but the body, light as a feather, has become an appendix to the floating leg."[37] While resonating with a desire to overcome the limitations of the "natural" body, this image is a playful variant of Kracauer's peculiar masochistic imagination, which (especially in his novels but also in his essays) again and again stages the violation of physical and mental boundaries by extraneous objects and sensations. The jumbling of the hierarchy of center and periphery in the dancer's body, as well as its prosthetic expansion, undermines both bourgeois notions of an "integrated personality" and the proliferating attempts (in sports, in "body culture") to reground "the spirit" in an organic, natural unity.[38]

Since the Fordist-Taylorist regime does not stop with the human body but takes on the realm of nature in its entirety, some of Kracauer's most interesting comments on rationalization can be found in his writings on the circus. While the circus is an Enlightenment invention and belongs to a manufactural mode of production, he notes the pervasiveness of rationalization even in an institution that was rapidly being pushed aside—and subsumed—by deterritorialized forms of media culture such as the cinema.[39] One of his articles on the Zirkus Hagenbeck, published a year before his famous essay "The Mass Ornament," reads like a sketch for that essay. Kracauer introduces the appearance of the giant menagerie in Frankfurt as an "International of animals," describing the animals as involuntary delegates from globally extended regions. They are united under the spell of Americanism:

> The fauna moves rhythmically and forms geometrical patterns. There is nothing left of dullness [*Dumpfheit*]. As unorganic matter snaps into crystals, mathematics seizes the limbs of living nature and sounds control the drives. The animal world, too, has fallen for jazz. Under the pressure of Hackanson Petoletti's thighs a thoroughbred stallion dances the Valencia and excels in syncopes, even though he's from Hanover. Every animal participates in the creation of the empire of figures according to its talents. Pious Brahmin zebus, Tibetan black bears [*Kragenbären*] and massifs of elephants: they all arrange themselves according to thoughts they did not think themselves. . . . The thickest hide is penetrated by the thinnest idea; the power of the spirit proves itself miraculously. At times it seems not only to subdue nature from behind, as it were, but to emanate from nature itself. The sea lions juggle as if animated by reason. With their pointed snouts they throw into the air and catch whatever their mentor, Captain von Vorstel, throws them: torches, balls, top hats. In-between they eat fish to strengthen their neck muscles—downright reasonable.[40]

The regime of heteronomous reason rehearsed on the backs of the animals would be merely pathetic if it weren't for the clowns whose anarchic pranks debunk the imperialist claims of rationalization: "They too want to be elastic and linelike, but it doesn't work, the elephants are more adroit, one has too many inner resistances, some goblin crosses out the elaborate calculation."[41] While their antics have a long tradition, the clowns assume an acute alterity in relation to the ongoing process of modernization; they inhabit the intermediary realm of *improvisation* and *chance* which, for Kracauer, is the redeeming supplement of that process—which has come into existence only with the loss of "foundations" or a stable order.[42]

The institution in which the clowns could engage rationalization, as it were, on its own turf was, of course, the cinema. Here the clowns had succeeded in founding their own genre, slapstick comedy, in a medium that assured them an audience way beyond local and live performances. In numerous reviews, Kracauer early on endorsed slapstick comedy (*Groteske*) as

a cultural form in which Americanism supplied a popular and public antidote to its own system. Like no other genre, slapstick comedy brought into
play the imbrication of the mechanical and the living, subverting the economically imposed regime in well-improvised orgies of destruction, confusion, and parody. "One has to hand this to the Americans: with slapstick
films they have created a form that offers a counterweight to their reality.
If in that reality they subject the world to an often unbearable discipline,
the film in turn dismantles this self-imposed order quite forcefully."[43]

Obviously, Kracauer was only one among a great number of European
avant-garde artists and intellectuals (such as the Surrealists) who celebrated
slapstick film, and their numbers grew with the particular inflection of
that genre by Charlie Chaplin.[44] Benjamin too ascribed to slapstick comedy an acute political significance, which complemented his often dutiful
and at best sporadic endorsements of Soviet film. In his defense of *Battleship Potemkin*, for instance, he puts American slapstick film on a par with
the Russian revolutionary film because it relentlessly pursues one particular "tendency": "Its polemics [*Spitze*] is directed against technology. This
kind of film is indeed comic, but the laughter it provokes hovers over an
abyss of horror."[45] When Benjamin later resumes the topic in conjunction
with his Artwork Essay, he discusses slapstick comedy's engagement with
technology in terms of the concepts of "shock" and "innervation." In this
context, Chaplin emerges as an exemplary figure, because he pioneers a
filmic analysis of assembly-line technology, a "gestic" rendering of perceptual discontinuity: "He chops up the expressive movement of the human
body into a sequence of minute innervations," a procedure that "imposes
the law of filmic images onto the law of human motorics." By practicing
such systematic self-fragmentation, "he interprets himself allegorically."[46]

Kracauer's Chaplin is neither as baroque nor as avant-garde as Benjamin's. Where the latter emphasizes allegorical mortification and "self-
alienation," Kracauer locates the appeal of the Chaplin figure in an already missing "self": "The human being that Chaplin embodies or, rather,
lets go of, is a *hole.* . . . He has no will; in the place of the drive toward self-
preservation or the hunger for power there is nothing inside him but a
void which is as blank as the snow fields of Alaska."[47] Whether from lack of
identity or inability to distinguish between self and multiplied self-images
(as Kracauer observes with reference to the hall-of-mirror scene from *Circus*), Chaplin instantiates a "schizophrenic" vision in which the habitual relations among people and things are shattered and different configurations appear possible; like a flash of lightning, Chaplin's laughter "welds
together madness and happiness."[48] The absent center of Chaplin's persona allows for a reconstruction of humanity under alienated conditions
("from this hole the purely human radiates discontinuously. . . . It is always discontinuous, fragmentary, interspersed into the organism"). A

key aspect of this humanity is a form of mimetic behavior which disarms the aggressor, whether person or object, by way of imitation and adaptation and which assures the temporary victory of the weak, marginalized, and disadvantaged, of David over Goliath.[49]

For Kracauer, Chaplin is not just a diasporic figure but "the pariah of the fairy tale," a genre that makes happy endings imaginable and at the same time puts them under erasure. The vagabond again and again learns "that the fairy tale does not last, that the world is the world, and that home [*die Heimat*] is not home."[50] If Chaplin is a messianic figure for Kracauer (as Inka Mülder rightly argues), it is important to bear in mind that he represents at once the appeal of a utopian humanity and its impossibility, the realization that the world "could be different and still continues to exist."[51] Chaplin exemplifies this humanity under erasure, both in his films and by the undeniable scope of his worldwide and ostensibly class-transcendent popularity. While Kracauer is skeptical as to the ideological function of reports of how, for instance, the film *City Lights* managed both to move prisoners in a New York penitentiary to laughter and George Bernard Shaw to tears, he nonetheless tackles the slippery question of Chaplin's "power" to reach human beings across class, nations, and generations[52]—the possibility, ultimately, of a universal language of mimetic behavior which would make mass culture an imaginative and reflexive horizon for people trying to live a life in the war zones of modernization.

Compared to Benjamin, Kracauer's interest in Chaplin and slapstick comedy—as in cinema in general—was less focused on the question of technology, nor did he conceive of technology as a productive force in the Marxian sense, let alone as a framing apparatus. He was concerned with mechanization as a socioeconomic regime and cultural discourse that, more systematically than any previous form of modernization, addressed itself to the *masses,* constituted a specifically modern form of collective. The mechanical mediation may place mass culture in the realm of "the inauthentic" (*das Uneigentliche*), but, since the road to "the authentic" was blocked anyway, Kracauer increasingly asserted the reality and legitimacy of "*Ersatz*"; the very distinction becomes irrelevant in view of the perspective, however compromised, that the mass media might be the only horizon in which an actual democratization of culture was taking place. This perspective also defines the parameters of critique: not only is the critic himself, in tendency, always a member of the consuming mass, but the media also offer the conditions for critical self-reflexion on a mass basis.

CONFIGURATIONS OF THE "MASS"

The *locus classicus* of Kracauer's analysis of Fordist mass culture is his 1927 essay, "The Mass Ornament." Here the Tiller Girls have evolved into a historico-philosophical allegory that, as is often pointed out, anticipates key arguments of Horkheimer and Adorno's *Dialectic of Enlightenment* (1947). As a figure of capitalist rationalization, Kracauer argues, the mass ornament is as profoundly ambiguous as the historical process that brought it forth—a process of demythologization or disenchantment that emancipates humanity from the forces of nature but, by perpetuating socioeconomic relations "that do not include the human being," reproduces the natural and reverts into myth; rationality itself has become the dominant myth of modern society. Unlike his fellow Critical Theorists, however, Kracauer does not locate the problem in the concept of Enlightenment as such (which for him at any rate is associated less with German idealism than with French empiricism and the utopian reason—and happiness—of fairy tales). Rather, he argues that the permeation of nature by reason has actually not advanced far enough: The problem with capitalism is not that "it rationalizes too much," but that it rationalizes "*too little*." Just as he forgoes investing in the alterity of autonomous art as the last refuge of a socially negated individuality, Kracauer rejects any attempt to resurrect precapitalist forms of community as a way out: "The process leads right through the middle of the mass ornament, not back from it."[53]

The comparison with *Dialectic of Enlightenment* at once obscures and reveals an important distinction. For the essay on the mass ornament does not just present a critique of instrumental reason and corresponding views of history as technologically driven progress; nor does it place faith in the critical self-reflexion of the bourgeois male intellect.[54] The underlying—and, in my reading, crucial—concern of the essay is the *mass* in "mass ornament." In Kracauer's rhetorical design, the Tiller Girls clearly stand for a larger social and political configuration. This configuration not only includes the abstract patterns of moving bodies in musical revues and sports displays arranged by the invisible hand of Taylorist rationality ("the legs of the Tiller Girls correspond to the hands in the factory"); it also includes the *spectating* mass "which relates to [the ornament] aesthetically and which represents nobody"—nobody, I would add, other than itself. While the mass ornament itself remains "mute," without consciousness of itself, it acquires meaning under the "gaze" of the masses, "who have adopted it spontaneously." Against the "despisers among the educated" (likely the majority of the readers of the *Frankfurter Zeitung*, where the essay was published), Kracauer maintains that the audience's "*aesthetic* pleasure in the ornamental mass movements is *legitimate*"; it is superior to the former's anachronistic investment in high-cultural values because at least it acknowledges "the facts" of contemporary reality. Even though the force of the *ratio* that mobilizes the mass is still "too weak to find [in it] the human beings and make its figures transparent to cognition," there is no question for Kracauer that the subject of such critical self-encounter has to be, can only be the masses themselves.[55]

Already in his 1926 essay on the Berlin picture palaces, "Cult of

Distraction," Kracauer's argument revolves around the possibility that in these metropolitan temples of distraction something like a self-articulation of the masses might be taking place—the possibility, as he puts it elsewhere, of a "self-representation of the masses subject to the process of mechanization."[56] Bracketing both cultural disdain and a critique of ideology, he observes that in Berlin, as opposed to his native Frankfurt and other provincial cities, "the more people perceive themselves as a mass, the sooner the masses will also develop creative powers in the spiritual domain which are worth financing." As a result, the so-called educated classes are losing their provincial elite status and cultural monopoly. "This gives rise to the *homogeneous cosmopolitan audience* [das *homogene Weltstadt-Publikum*] in which everyone is of *one* mind, from the bank director to the sales clerk, from the diva to the stenographer.[57] That they are "of *one* mind" (*eines Sinnes*) means no more and no less than that they have the same taste for sensual attractions or, rather, distractions. They congregate in the medium of distraction or diversion (*Zerstreuung*) which, in the radical twist that Kracauer gives the originally cultural-conservative concept, combines the mirage of social homogeneity with an aesthetics that is profoundly decentering and dis-unifying, at least as long as it does not succumb entirely to gentrification. In "the discontinuous sequence of splendid sense impressions" (which likely refers to an already elevated version of the "variety format"),[58] the audience encounters "its own reality," that is, a social process marked by an increased heterogeneity and instability. Here Kracauer locates the political significance of distraction: "The fact that these shows convey in a precise and undisguised manner to thousands of eyes and ears the *disorder* of society—this is precisely what would enable them to evoke and keep awake that tension which must precede the inevitable change [*Umschlag*]."[59]

It should be noted that Kracauer does not assume an analogical relation between the industrial standardization of cultural commodities and the behavior and identity of the mass audience that consumes them (an assumption derived from Lukács's theory of reification, which would become axiomatic for Adorno's critique of the culture industry and, with different valorization, for Benjamin's theses on art and industrial reproduction). For one thing, Kracauer (like Benjamin) did not object to serial production, standardization, and commodification as such, as can be seen in his many reviews of popular fiction, especially detective and adventure novels, as well as in his repeated, if sometimes grudging, statements of admiration for Hollywood over Ufa products.[60] For another, Kracauer would not have presumed that people who see the same thing necessarily think the same way; and if they did pattern their behavior and appearance on the figures and fables of the screen, the problem was the escapist ideology of German film production and the gentrification of exhibition. In other words, Kracauer's critique was aimed less against the lure of cinematic identification in general than against the cultural and political practices responsible for the unrealistic tendency of such identification, the growing denial of the discrepancies of the social process.[61]

The cinema is a signature of modernity for Kracauer not simply because it attracts and represents the masses, but because it constitutes the most advanced cultural institution in which the masses, as a relatively heterogeneous, undefined, and unknown form of collectivity, can represent themselves as a *public*. As Heide Schlüpmann argues in an important essay, Kracauer sketches a theory of a specifically modern public sphere which resists thinking of the masses and the idea of the public as an opposition (as Habermas still does in his 1962 study *The Structural Transformation of the Public Sphere*). Kracauer "neither asserts the idea of the public against its [actual or putative] disintegration and decline," Schlüpmann points out, "nor does he resort to a concept of an oppositional public sphere" (à la Negt and Kluge). Rather, Kracauer sees in the cinema a blueprint of an *alternative* public that "can realize itself only through the destruction of the dominant public sphere," that is, bourgeois institutions of high art, education, and culture that have lost all touch with reality.[62] Understandably, this construction has made Kracauer vulnerable to the charge that he naively tries to resurrect the liberal public sphere, once again bracketing capitalist interest and ideology.[63] To be sure, he adheres to political principles of general access, equality, justice, and, perhaps more so than his more orthodox Marxist friends, the right to and necessity of self-determination, that is, democratic forms of living and interaction. Yet Kracauer is materialist enough to know that these principles do not miraculously emerge from the rational discourse of communicatively competent, inner-directed subjects, let alone from efforts to restore the authority of a literary public sphere. Rather, cognition has to be grounded in the very sphere of experience in which historical change is most palpable and most destructive—in a sensual, perceptual, aesthetic discourse that allows for "the self-representation of the masses subject to the process of mechanization."

Such phrases were not uncommon among radical Weimar intellectuals; their critical usefulness ultimately depends upon the underlying concept of the subject in question. The modern mass, as a social formation which, to whatever effect, cut across boundaries of class and status, had entered public awareness in Germany only after World War I. If the revolution of 1919 had briefly mobilized the image of a powerful, active mass, the following years saw the creation of a mass primarily through the stigma of misery, culminating in 1923 with the great inflation that extended the experience of destitution and loss far beyond the industrial working class. During the short-lived phase of economic recovery, the masses began to appear less as a suffering and more as a consuming mass—the mass came into visibility as a social formation in collective acts of consumption. And since consumer goods that might have helped improve living conditions (for instance, refrigerators) were still a lot less affordable than in the United States,[64] the main objects of consumption were the fantasy productions and environments of the new leisure culture. In them, Kracauer discerned the contours of an emerging mass subject, a mass that, for better or for worse, was productive in its very need and acts of consumption.

Kracauer's concept of the mass or masses develops from one indebted to the typological constructions of contemporary social theory to a more empirical, sociologically and politically determined approach, although the former remains present in the latter as a regulative idea. This idea begins to take shape in Kracauer's cautious revaluation of elitist-pessimistic assessments of the mass from LeBon through Spengler, Klages, and Freud. Seemingly rehearsing the standard oppositions, he sets off the mass from the organic community of the people or folk (*Volk*); from the higher, "fateful" unity of the nation; and, for that matter, from socialist or communist notions of the collective. While the ideal-type of the community is composed of unique, tradition- and inner-directed individuals ("individuals who *believe* themselves to be inwardly shaped"), the mass is an amorphous body of anonymous, fragmented particles that assume meaning only in other-directed contexts, whether mechanized process of labor or the abstract compositions of the mass ornament.[65] The liberatory aspect of the mass ornament rests for Kracauer precisely in this transformation of subjectivity—in the erosion of bourgeois notions of personality which posit "nature and 'spirit' as harmoniously integrated," in the human figure's "*exodus* from sumptuous organic splendor and individual shape into anonymity."[66] The mass ornament's critique of an outdated concept of personality (including Kracauer's own early efforts to rescue it) turns the Medusan sight of the anonymous metropolitan mass into an image of liberating alienation and open-ended possibility and at times even into a vision of diasporic solidarity—that is, he sees possibilities for living where others see only leveling and decline.[67] For Kracauer, the democratization of social, economic, and political life, the possibility of the masses' self-organization, is inseparably linked to the surrender of the self-identical masculine subject and the emergence of a decentered, dis-armor-ed and disarming, subjectivity that he found exemplified in Chaplin.

This vision, however, as Kracauer knows, has more to do with the happy endings of fairy tales than with the actual social and political developments. His more empirically oriented approach to mass society focused on a group that at once personified the structural transformation of subjectivity and engaged in a massive effort of denial—the mushrooming class of white-collar workers or employees to whom he devoted a groundbreaking series of articles, *Die Angestellten* (1929).[68] Although by the end of the twenties white-collar workers still made up only one-fifth of the workforce, Kracauer considered them, more than any other group, the subject of modernization and modern mass culture. Not only did their numbers increase fivefold (to 3.5 million, of which 1.2 million were women) over a period during which the number of blue-collar workers barely doubled, but their particular class profile was also deeply bound up with the impact, actual or perceived, of the rationalization push between 1925 and 1928. The mechanization, fragmentation, and hierarchization of the labor process and the threatening effects of dequalification, disposability, and unemployment made the working and living conditions of white-collar workers effectively proletarian. Yet, fancying themselves a "new middle class," they tended to deny any commonality with the working class and instead to recycle the remnants of bourgeois culture. Unlike the industrial proletariat, they were "spiritually homeless," seeking escape from their actual situation in the metropolitan "barracks of pleasure" (entertainment malls like the Haus Vaterland, picture palaces, etc.)—the very cult of distraction to which Kracauer, three years earlier, had still imputed a radical political potential. With the impact of the international economic crisis, the employees' evasion of consciousness, as Kracauer was one of the first to warn, made them vulnerable to national socialist messages; it was these "stand-up collar proletarians" who were soon to cast a decisive vote for Hitler.[69]

The different conception of the mass is one of the most obvious distinctions between Kracauer's understanding of cinema and modernity and that of Benjamin. Like Kracauer, Benjamin sees the phenomenon of the mass manifest itself primarily in acts of consumption and reception, mediated by the fetish of the commodity (which Benjamin substantially defines from the perspective of reception rather than, as Marx did, from production and circulation). But where Kracauer's analysis focuses on the present, Benjamin projects the problematics of mass culture, art, and technology back into the nineteenth century. In this genealogy, he traces the emergence of the metropolitan masses in the writings of Baudelaire as well as Hugo, Poe, and others. Like Marx, Benjamin contrasts the urban masses depicted by the literati with the "iron mass of the proletariat": "What is at issue is not a particular class, nor any collective however structured. At issue is nothing but the amorphous crowd of passersby, the street public."[70] The ingenuity of Benjamin's reading is that he traces the presence of this urban crowd in Baudelaire's poetry as a "hidden figure," the "moving veil" through which the poems stage moments of "shock," as opposed to the literal depictions one finds in the writer's lesser contemporaries. As in Baudelaire, Benjamin sees the epochal turn toward the masses encoded in the architecture, fashions, events, and institutions of high-capitalist culture; he does not describe or analyze the masses but traces their profound impact on just about every area of cultural practice.

As is often pointed out, Benjamin's vast project of "a material philosophy of history of the nineteenth century,"[71] his never completed work on
the Paris Arcades or *Passagen-Werk,* was methodologically inseparable from
his concern with the "current crisis," that is, the rise of fascism, the complicity of liberal capitalism, and the congealing of a socialist alternative
in Stalinism. For Benjamin, it was this crisis that brought the "fate" of art
in the nineteenth century into the "now of recognition," made it recognizable as it was "never before and never will be again."[72] Within this
historico-philosophical construction, the masses appear in a number of key
theoretical tropes. One has to do with the linkage of novelty and repetition which fascinated Benjamin in the dynamics of capitalist commodity
production, in particular the phenomenon of fashion. Here, the masses
enter as the social corollary of mass production, and Benjamin draws a
direct line from the figure of the prostitute as human "mass article" to
the later revues with their exhibition of strictly uniformed "girls" (English
in the original).[73] What fascinates him in mass production, however, is a
particular dialectic of *temporality,* the return of the "always-again-the-same"
in the shocklike acceleration of the new, with which capitalism has created a highly ambivalent, explosive conjuncture of modernity and prehistory (mythical "Golden Age"/"Time of Hell").[74] Within that logic, the
cinema would seem to be an answer to the historical imagination of Blan-
qui or Nietzsche rather than to the emergence of the masses as an economic, social, and cultural subject: "The doctrine of eternal recurrence as
a dream of the immense inventions still to come in the field of reproduction technology."[75]

The mass is also figured in Benjamin's notion of the "dreaming collective" and the related image of capitalism as a "dreamsleep" that "came
over Europe and with it a reactivation of mythic powers."[76] The enormous creativity of industrialization and commodity production in the nineteenth century had generated a matrix of collectivity in the phantasmagoria of consumption. That collectivity (which, in the Arcades Project,
clearly cuts across class boundaries), however, remains "unconscious." The
masses who flock to the world fairs and other mass spectacles consist of
isolated, anonymous individuals whose "self-alienation" is only enhanced
by the "distractions" that "raise them to the level of the commodity."[77] While
Benjamin's notions of dreaming and the unconscious were indebted to
the Surrealists, his insistence on the moment of "waking up," on breaking the cycle of "aestheticization and anaestheticization" (in Susan Buck-
Morss's terms), aligns him with Kracauer's efforts toward the masses' coming to (self-)consciousness, literally, coming to their senses.[78] They had,
however, somewhat different concepts of political change: If Benjamin fused
messianic theology and Marxism into the desperate hope for a proletarian
revolution, Kracauer kept his eschatalogical yearnings mostly separate from

the critical project of getting the masses to realize themselves as a democratic public.[79] But they agreed upon what would happen if the masses *didn't* wake up, if they were to continue in their illusory dream state. As the Nazis' mass-mediated spectacles of rallies and parades brought home with terrifying urgency, fascism offered the masses an "imaginary solution" (*Scheinlösung*) to real problems and contradictions that could end only in total oppression and mass annihilation. Echoing Kracauer's argument about the remythicization of the mass ornament, Benjamin, in the epilogue to his Artwork Essay (1935–1936), elaborates on the fascist strategy of giving the masses an aesthetic "*expression,*" a mirrorlike representation, as opposed to giving them their right, that is, acknowledging their claim to changed relations of property.[80]

The third, and in my view most problematic, troping of the mass in Benjamin's writings is in the notion of a "collective innervation" of technology and the role of film in this context. The problem is not with the concept of innervation as such, the technological interpenetration of "body and image space" which Benjamin thought through more radically than any of his contemporaries (with the exception, perhaps, of Ernst Jünger);[81] rather, it is the attempt to hitch the proletariat to the cart of this process and make the cinema a rehearsal ground for polytechnical education. Like Kracauer, Benjamin is indebted to Béla Balázs's observation of a *structural* affinity between masses and cinema which is grounded in the medium's perceptual, phenomenological specificity—the insight that film, in Kracauer's words, "by breaking down the distance of the spectator which had hitherto been maintained in all the arts, is an artistic medium turned toward the masses."[82] Unlike Kracauer, Benjamin also takes over Balázs's rather more tentative assertion that, with film, capitalist society has generated a means of production which promotes that society's own abolition, and that therefore the masses addressed by the cinema converge with the revolutionary proletariat—a notion that Kracauer repeatedly criticized as both dogmatic and romantic. More systematically than Balázs, Benjamin establishes the revolutionary potential of film from an argument about the fate of art in the age of industrial-technological re/production (which does not need to be elaborated here).[83] Suffice it to say that Benjamin's concept of the masses, at least in the Artwork Essay, derives primarily from the structural qualities of technical re/production—sameness, repeatability, closeness, "shock" (vs. uniqueness, distance, "aura"), the analogy of assembly line and cinematic reception—rather than the social, psychosexual, and cultural profile of the moviegoing public.

Benjamin's concept of the masses as the subject of cinema passes over the actual and unprecedented mixture of classes—and genders and generations—which had been observed in cinema audiences early on (notably by sociologist Emilie Altenloh in her 1914 dissertation); it also ignores,

and no doubt implicitly opposes, the often condemnatory, culturally conservative attitude toward the cinema on the part of the traditional working-
class organizations, including the Communist party (although there were,
no doubt, important efforts to create a workers' cinema from the mid-
1920s on).[84] While in the nineteenth-century masses, as refracted through
the dreamworld of commodities, Benjamin can still recognize the contours of a different collective, in his assessment of the twentieth-century
masses, empirical and utopian intentions seem to fall apart. In the few
places where he actually *describes* a contemporary mass formation (as in
One-Way Street, 1928), he lapses into a pessimistic discourse that emphasizes the instinctual, animal-like yet blindly self-destructive behavior of "the
mass."[85] In a long note to the second version of the Artwork Essay, Benjamin resumes this discourse with explicit reference to LeBon and mass
psychology, as he contrasts the "compact mass" of the petit bourgeoisie,
defined by "panic-prone" behavior such as militarism, antisemitism, and
blind striving for survival, with the "proletarian mass." The latter, in fact,
Benjamin argues, ceases to be a mass in the LeBonian sense in the measure that it is infused with class-consciousness and solidarity. Ultimately,
the proletariat "works toward a society in which both the objective and the
subjective conditions for the formation of masses no longer exist."[86]

For Benjamin, the masses that structurally correspond to the cinema
coincide not with the actual working class (whether blue-collar or white-
collar) but with the proletariat as a category of Marxist philosophy, a category of negation directed against existing conditions in their totality. Hence
the "conspiracy of film technique with the milieu," which he discusses in
his defense of *Battleship Potemkin,* comes to signal the passing of the bourgeois order: "The proletariat is the hero of those spaces to whose adventures the bourgeois in the movie theater gives himself over with throbbing
heart, because he must relish the 'beautiful' even and especially where it
speaks to him of the annihilation of his own class."[87] Whether rejected in
LeBonian terms or embraced as the self-sublating empirical prototype of
the proletariat, the masses are attributed a degree of homogeneity that
not only misses their complex reality but also ultimately leaves the intellectual in a position outside, at best surrendering himself to their existence as powerful, though still unconscious, Other. Where Kracauer self-
consciously "constructs" the reality of the white-collar workers through
theorizing observation—quotations, conversations on location, his own situation as an employee[88]—Benjamin's image of the masses, whether projected backward into the nineteenth century or forward into the not-yet of
the proletarian revolution, ultimately remains a philosophical, if not aesthetic, abstraction.

One could argue that Kracauer's analysis of mass culture as white-collar
or employee culture is just as one-sided as Benjamin's linkage of film and

proletariat. After all, he himself stresses the specificity of Berlin's leisure culture as *Angestelltenkultur,* "that is, a culture which is produced by employees for employees and which is considered a culture by the majority of employees."[89] Yet, to say that this particular focus eclipses the rest of society, in particular the working class, would be as misleading as to conceive of mass culture and employee culture as an opposition.[90] Rather, Kracauer's analysis recognizes a key element by which the culture of the employees, in their self-image as new middle class, was becoming hegemonic—in its fantasies of class-transcendence, its fixation on visuality, and its construction of a social, national, and specifically modern imaginary. Responding to similar historical developments as Lacan's lecture on the mirror phase,[91] Kracauer locates the power of this imaginary in processes of identification and fantasy unmoored from class and economic interest, in the proliferation of "role-playing" as a model of social behavior.[92] The cinema offers a major rehearsal ground for new forms of social identity because of its mechanisms of perceptual identification in which the boundaries between self and heteronomous images are weakened (or, rather, recognized to be porous in the first place) and which permit the viewer to let himself or herself "be polymorphously projected."[93] While in the mid-twenties this psycho-perceptual mobility still beckons the writer with pleasures of self-abandonment, emptiness, and loss, by the end of the decade it makes him view the cinema as a transcript of contemporary mythology: "The idiotic and unreal film fantasies are the *day dreams of society* in which the true reality comes to the fore and its otherwise repressed wishes take shape."[94]

The psychoanalytic concept of repression—which Benjamin and Kracauer agreed was needed to complement Marxist concepts of ideology and the notion of "false consciousness"[95]—cuts both ways. The film fantasies not only reveal society's repressed wishes; they also participate in the repression of those aspects of reality which would disturb the delusion of imaginary plenitude and mobility: "The flight of the images is the flight from revolution and from death."[96] With the intensification of the economic and social crisis, Kracauer increasingly stresses the compensatory economy between the everyday drudgery of business and the business of entertainment: "The exact counterblow to the office machine is the colorful wide world. Not the world as it is but as it appears in the popular hits. A world from which a vacuum cleaner has removed down to the tiniest corner the dust of the everyday. The geography of the homeless shelters is born from the popular hit."[97]

The image of the vacuum cleaner is no coincidence. Kracauer remained skeptical throughout of attempts to ground visions of social change in the model of technology, in particular the functionalist school of modern architecture (LeCorbusier, Mies van der Rohe, Gropius and the Bauhaus). The "culture of glass" that Benjamin so desperately welcomed as the death-blow to bourgeois culture (and attendant concepts of "interiority," "trace," "experience," "aura") leaves Kracauer, an architect by training, filled with "scurrilous grief" (*skurrile Trauer*)—grief over the historical-political impasse that prevents the construction of apartments predicated on human needs.[98] And he responds to the functionalist crusade against the ornament (notably Adolf Loos) by showing how the repressed ornamental returns in the very aesthetics of technology which ordains the mass spectacles of chorus lines, sports events, and party rallies. In his analysis of Haus Vaterland, finally, he indicts the architectural style of *Neue Sachlichkeit*, which he finds there in exaggerated form, for its secret complicity with the business of distraction: "Like the rejection of old age, it too originates in the horror of the confrontation with death."[99] The reflection on death which functionalism evades and which Kracauer insists upon as a public responsibility is not simply an existential *memento mori*, however, but is aimed at German society's refusal to confront the experience of mass death bound up with the lost war.[100]

COMPETING MODERNITIES, HISTORICAL OPTIONS

I have so far emphasized that strand of Kracauer's reflections on cinema and mass modernity which shows his "uncertain, hesitant affirmation of the civilizing process"—his attempt to trace as yet undefined autonomous developments, however compromised; his willingness to grant them "their own, after all positive possibilities." But he was at no point ever uncritical of capitalist-industrial modernization, much as he immersed himself in the attendant new visual culture and with it the chance and challenge of an expanded horizon of experience. Especially toward the end of the decade, under the impact of the international economic crisis and the sharp rise in unemployment, the surrealist streak in Kracauer's writings on mass culture and modern living recedes in favor of an increasingly severe critique of ideology. If he had earlier shared the playful relief from burdens of tradition and hierarchy, he now stresses the inadequacy and posthumous quality of Americanist entertainment forms, specifically chorus lines and jazz.[101] In this closing section, I will return to the darker side of Kracauer's assessment of Fordist-Taylorist modernity—not to end with it as somehow more "true" or more realistic but to situate it in relation to both historically available and politically impending alternatives.

Kracauer's critique of modernization was primarily directed against the imperialism with which technological rationality seized all domains of experience and reduced them to coordinates of space and time, to "a depraved omnipresence in all dimensions that are calculable."[102] In particular, he assailed the destruction of memory advanced, in different ways, by architecture, urban planning, magazines, and photography. This critique oscillates between his earlier, culturally pessimistic stance on modernity and a recognition of the ways in which technological rationality itself was used to naturalize the contradictions of modernity, to turn it into a new mythical eternity.

The site and symbol of presentness, contemporaneity, or simultaneity (*Gleichzeitigkeit*) is the city of Berlin, the "frontier" of America in Europe.[103] "Berlin is the place where one quickly forgets; indeed, it appears as if this city has a magical means of wiping out all memories. It is the present and puts its ambition into being absolutely present. . . . Elsewhere, too, the appearance of squares, company names, and stores change; but only in Berlin these transformations tear the past so radically from memory."[104] This tendency is particularly relentless on the city's major boulevard, the Kurfürstendamm, which Kracauer dubs a "street without memory." Its facades, from which "the ornaments have been knocked off," "now stand without a foothold in time and are a symbol of the ahistorical change which takes place behind them."[105] The spatial correlate of the congealing of time and memory into a seemingly timeless present is the imperialist gesture with which newsreels, illustrated magazines, and tourism pretend to bring the whole world into the consumer's reach. The more distances are shrunk into exotic commodities, the more their proliferation occludes the view onto the "exotics" of what is close by, "normal existence in its imperceptible terribleness"; the daily life of Berlin's millions remains "terra incognita."[106]

Like Benjamin, Kracauer found a counter-image to contemporary Berlin in the city of Paris. There, the "web"—"maze," "mesentry"—of streets allows him to be a real flâneur, to indulge in a veritable "street high" (*Straßenrausch*).[107] There, the crowds are constantly in motion, circulating, bustling, unstable, unpredictable, an "improvised mosaic" that never congeals into "readable patterns." The impression of flux and liquidity in Kracauer's writings on Paris is enhanced, again and again, by textual superimpositions of ocean imagery and evocations of the maritime tradition and milieu. The Paris masses display a process of mixing which does not suppress gradations and heterogeneity; they are themselves so colorful that, as Kracauer somewhat naively asserts, even people of African descent can be at home—and be themselves—without being "jazzified" or otherwise exoticized.[108] There, too, the effects of Americanization seem powerless, or appear transfigured, as in the case of the luminous advertising (*Lichtreklame*) that projects undecipherable hieroglyphs onto the Paris sky: "It darts beyond the economy, and what was intended as advertising turns into an illumination. This is what happens when the merchants meddle with lighting effects."[109]

Paris, for Kracauer, is also the city of Surrealism and the site of a film production that stages the jinxed relations between people and things in different ways from films responding to the regime of the stopwatch. In the films of René Clair and Jacques Feyder (especially the latter's *Thérèse Raquin*), Kracauer praised a physiognomic capacity that endows inanimate objects—buildings, streets, furniture—with memory and speech, an argument that links Balázs's film aesthetics with Benjamin's notion of an "optical unconscious."[110] It is this quality, by the way, which Kracauer also extols in the best Soviet films (as in his remarkable review of Vertov's *Man with a Movie Camera*) and which he links to the Surrealist objective to "render strange what is close to us and strip the existing of its familiar mask."[111] In their dreamlike, physiognomic quality such films rehearse what Benjamin called the interpenetration of "body and image space" and what Kracauer discerned as the cinema's chance of staging shocklike, physiologically experienced encounters with mortality and contingency. Yet he also increasingly took contemporary French films to task (in particular those of Clair) for their lapses into sentimentality and artsiness, as well as for their romantic opposition to mechanization.[112]

As much as it offered the German writer asylum from the reign of simultaneity, speed, and dehumanization, Paris was not the alternative to Berlin or, for that matter, "America"; nor did Kracauer, as did Benjamin, attempt a linkage between the nineteenth-century invention of modern life and the crisis of contemporary mass modernity. Just as "Berlin" is already present in the topography of Paris, in the constellation of faubourgs and center which Kracauer traces in his "Analysis of a City Map," so does Berlin represent the inescapable horizon within which the contradictions of modernity demand to be engaged. France was, after all, "Europe's oasis" as far as the spread of rationalization and mass consumption were concerned, and Clair's "embarrassing" spoof on the assembly line (in *A nous la liberté*) was only further proof of the French inability to understand "how deeply the mechanized process of labor reaches into our daily life."[113] In his first longer essay on the French capital, "Paris Observations" (1927), Kracauer thematizes the perspective "from Berlin," sketching the perceptions of the persona of one who has lost confidence in the virtues of bourgeois life and who "even questions the sublimity of property," who "has lived through the revolution [of 1919] as a democrat or its enemy," and whose "every third word is America." While he does not exactly identify with this persona, by the end of the essay he clearly rejects the possibility that French culture and civility could become a model for contemporary Germany. "The German cannot move into the well-warmed apartment as which France appears to him today; but perhaps one day, France will be as homeless [*obdachlos*] as Germany."[114] The price of Paris life and liveliness is the desolation and despair of the provinces and the banlieux, which Kracauer describes in his unusually grim piece, "The Town of Malakoff": contemplating Malakoff's melancholy quarters, he finds, by contrast, even in the barbaric melange of German industrial working-class towns, signs of hope, protest, and a will toward change.[115] When, finally, Kracauer returns from another trip to Paris in 1931, he is animated by a political discussion on the train, and as the train enters Berlin's Bahnhof Zoo, the nightly city appears to him "more threatening and torn, more powerful, more reserved and more promising than ever before."[116] In its side-by-side of "harshness, openness . . . and glamour," Berlin is not only the frontier of modernity but also "the center of struggles in which the human future is at stake."[117]

Paradoxically, the more relentlessly Kracauer criticizes the products of mass-mediated modernity, the less he subscribes to his earlier utopian thought that, some day, "America will disappear."[118] In fact, the more German film production cluttered the cinemas with costume dramas and operettas reviving nationalist and military myths, and the more the industry adjusted to and promoted the political drift to the right, the more it became evident that "America" *must* not disappear, however mediocre, superficial, and inadequate its current mass-cultural output.[119] The constellation that is vital to Kracauer's understanding of cinema and modernity is therefore not that between Paris and Berlin, but that between a modernity that can reflect upon, revise, and regroup itself, albeit at the expense of (a certain kind of) memory, and a modernity that parlays technological synchronicity into the timelessness of a new megamyth: monumental nature, the heroic body, the re-armored mass ornament—in short, the Nazi modernism exemplified by Leni Riefenstahl.

This constellation is illustrated in the juxtaposition of two vignettes that again project the problems and possibilities of mass-mediated modernity onto an earlier institution of leisure culture, the Berlin Luna park. In an article published on Bastille Day, 1928, Kracauer describes a roller coaster whose facade shows a painted skyline of Manhattan: "The workers, the small people, the employees who spend the week being oppressed by the city, now triumph by air over a super-Berlinian New York." Once they've reached the top, however, the facade gives way to a bare "skeleton":

> So this is New York—a painted surface and behind it nothingness? The small couples are enchanted and disenchanted at the same time. Not that they would dismiss the grandiose city painting as simply humbug; but they see through the illusion and their triumph over the facades no longer means that much to them. They linger at the place where things show their double face, holding the shrunken skyscrapers in their open hand; they have been liberated from a world whose splendor they nevertheless know.[120]

Even in the shrieks of the riders as they plunge into the abyss, Kracauer perceives not only fear but also ecstasy, the bliss of "traversing a New York whose existence is suspended, which has ceased to be a threat." As I have argued elsewhere, this image evokes a vision of modernity whose spell as progress is broken, whose disintegrating elements become available in a form of collective reception that leaves space for both self-abandonment and critical reflexion.[121]

Two years later, in a May 1930 article entitled "Organized Happiness," Kracauer reports on the reopening of the same amusement park after major reconstruction. Now the attractions have been rationalized, and "an invisible organization sees to it that the amusements push themselves onto the masses in prescribed sequence"[122]—a model for Disney World. Contrasting the behavior of these administered masses with the unregulated whirl of people at the Paris *foires*, Kracauer makes the familiar reference to the regime of the assembly line. As in the Sarrasani Circus, which he had criticized in similar terms a few months earlier, this regime does not leave "the slightest gap"; there is no more space for improvisation and reflexion.[123] When he arrives at the newly refurbished roller coaster, the scene has changed accordingly. Most of the cars are driven by young girls, "poor young things who are straight out of the many films in which salesgirls end up as millionaire wives." They relish the "illusion" of power and control, and their screams are no longer that liberatory. "[Life] is worth living if one plunges into the depth only to dash upward again as a couple [*zu zweit*]." The seriality of the girl cult is no longer linked to visions of gender mobility and equality, but to the reproduction of private dreams of heterosexual coupledom and the restoration of patriarchal power in fantasies of upward mobility. Nor is this critique of the girl cult available, let alone articulated, in the same sphere or medium as the phenomenon itself (as in Hollywood's own deconstruction of the girl cult which Kracauer had celebrated in Iribe and Urson's film *Chicago*);[124] rather, it speaks the language of a critique of ideology in which the male intellectual remains outside and above the public of mass consumption.

The hallmark of stabilized entertainment, however, is that the symbol of the illusion has been replaced. Instead of the Manhattan skyline, the facade is now painted with an "alpine landscape whose peaks defy any depression [*Baisse*]." All over the amusement park, in fact, in the design above a boxing ring and that surrounding a roulette table, Kracauer notes the popularity of "alpine panoramas"—"striking sign of the upper regions which one rarely reaches from the social lowlands." The image of the Alps not only naturalizes and mythifies economic and social inequity; it also asserts a different, or rather identical, timeless Nature, a place beyond history, politics, crisis, and contradiction. Against the metaphoric, mass-mediated "urban nature" (*Stadtnatur*), with "its jungle streets, factory massifs and labyrinths of roofs," the alpine panoramas, like the contemporary mountain films, offer this presumably authentic, unmediated nature as a solution to modernity's discontents.[125] The recourse to antimodern symbols does not make this alternative any less modern: As Kracauer increasingly observes—and objects to—the return in German revues and films of the Alps, the Rhine, Old Vienna, and Prussia, of lieutenants, fraternities, and royalty, he recognizes them as a specific version of technological modernity, an attempt to nationalize and domesticate whatever liberatory, egalitarian effects this modernity might have had.[126]

In his earlier discovery of "America," Kracauer had hoped for a German version of mass-mediated modernity that would be capable of enduring the tensions between a capitalist-industrial economy in permanent crisis and the principles and practices of a democratic society. Crucial to this modernity would have been the ability of cinema and mass culture to function as an intersubjective horizon in which a wide variety of groups—a heterogeneous mass public—could negotiate and reflect upon the contradictions they were experiencing, and in which they could confront the violence of difference and mortality rather than repress or aestheticize it. Whatever stirrings of such a modernity the Weimar Republic saw, it did not find a more long-term German, let alone European, form; Berlin never became the capital of the twentieth century. Instead, "Berlin" split into irreconcilable halves: an internationalist (American, Jewish, diasporic, politically radical) modernism and a Germanic one that assimilated the most advanced technology to the reinvention of tradition, authority, community, nature, and race. When the Nazis perfected this form of modernism into the millennial modernity of total domination and mass annihilation, "America" had to become real, for better or for worse, for Kracauer and others to survive.

NOTES

The work on this essay has been generously supported by the Alexander von Humboldt Foundation. For inspiration, criticism, and support I wish to thank Bill Brown, Ed Dimendberg, Tom Gunning, Andreas Huyssen, Gertrud Koch, Helmut Lethen, Tom Levin, Alf Lüdtke, Klaus Michael, Jonathan Rosenbaum, Heide Schlüpmann, Karsten Witte, Theresa Wobbe and, especially, Michael Geyer.

1. The phrase was addressed to Félix Mesguich, the Lumières' cameraman, and is reported in his memoirs, *Tours de manivelle* (Paris: Editions Grasset, 1933); it has been cited apocryphally ever since, notably by Godard in *Le Mépris*. See Georges Sadoul, *Lumière et Méliès*, ed. B. Eisenschitz (Paris: Editions Pierre Lherminier, 1985).

2. See, for instance, Noël Burch, "Porter, or Ambivalence," *Screen* 19, no. 4 (winter 1978/79): 91–105, and other essays in part collected in *Life to Those Shadows*, ed. and trans. Ben Brewster (Berkeley, Los Angeles, London: University of California Press, 1990); Tom Gunning, "The Cinema of Attraction[s]," *Wide Angle* 8, nos. 3–4 (1983): 4–15; Charles Musser, *The Emergence of Cinema: The American Screen to 1907* (New York: Scribners, 1990); David Bordwell, Janet Staiger, Kristin Thompson, *The Classical Hollywood Cinema: Film Style and Mode of Production to 1960*

(New York: Columbia University Press, 1985), part 3; as well as Thomas Elsaesser, ed. (with Adam Barker), *Early Cinema: Space, Frame, Narrative* (London: BFI, 1990). Also see Miriam Hansen, *Babel and Babylon: Spectatorship in American Silent Film* (Cambridge: Harvard University Press, 1991), chapters 1–3.

3. Tom Gunning, "Tracing the Individual Body: Photography, Detectives, and Early Cinema," in this volume. Also see Jonathan Crary, *Techniques of the Observer: On Vision and Modernity in the Nineteenth Century* (Cambridge: MIT Press, 1990).

4. Anne Friedberg, *Window Shopping: Cinema and the Postmodern* (Berkeley, Los Angeles, London: University of California Press, 1993); also see Stephen Kern, *The Culture of Time and Space* (Cambridge: Harvard University Press, 1983); and David Harvey, "Time-Space Compression and the Rise of Modernism as a Cultural Force," in Harvey, *The Condition of Postmodernity* (Oxford, Cambridge, Mass.: Blackwell, 1989).

5. Susan Buck-Morss, "Aesthetics and Anaesthetics: Walter Benjamin's Artwork Essay Reconsidered," *October* 62 (Fall 1992): 3–41. Also see Vanessa R. Schwartz, "Cinematic Spectatorship before the Apparatus: The Public Taste for Reality in *Fin-de-Siècle* Paris," in the present volume.

6. If we take modernism, in the widest sense, to refer to the articulated intellectual, artistic, political responses to modernity and to processes of modernization, then the distinction between the terms can only be a sliding one: Baudelaire, for example, did not simply record the phenomena he perceived as saliently new and different in "modern" life but also wrote them into significance—and, as a new type of literary intellectual, was also part of them. Nonetheless, it seems important not to collapse the two terms if we wish to maintain the heuristic claim that modernity comprises the material conditions of living (regardless of what intellectuals thought about them) as well as the general social horizon of experience, that is, the organization of public life as the matrix in which a wide variety of constituencies related to these living conditions and to each other and did or did not have access to representation and power. The literature on modernity and modernism is too vast to list here; Harvey, op. cit., chapter 2, offers an original, if often unreliable, summary. Another place to start is Benjamin H. D. Buchloh et al., eds., *Modernism and Modernity: The Vancouver Conference Papers* (Halifax: Nova Scotia College of Art and Design, 1981), as well as Andreas Huyssen, *After the Great Divide: Modernism, Mass Culture, Postmodernism* (Bloomington: Indiana University Press, 1986).

7. Marshall Berman, *All That Is Solid Melts into Air: The Experience of Modernity* (1982; reprint, Harmondsworth: Penguin, 1988), pp. 36, 171. For another attempt to retrieve an alternative, preclassical modernism (in *fin-de-siècle* Orientalism, hedonism, androgyny, and decorative design), see Peter Wollen, "Out of the Past: Fashion/Orientalism/The Body," in Wollen, *Raiding the Icebox: Reflections on Twentieth-Century Culture* (Bloomington: Indiana University Press, 1993).

8. Fredric Jameson, *Postmodernism, or, The Cultural Logic of Capitalism* (Durham: Duke University Press, 1991).

9. See, for instance, Berman's attack on the modernism of the "highway," Berman, op. cit., pp. 164ff.; Harvey, op. cit., part I; Peter Wollen, "Modern Times: Cinema/Americanism/The Robot," in *Raiding the Icebox*; also see Miriam Hansen,

Ezra Pounds frühe Poetik und Kulturkritik zwischen Aufklärung und Avantgarde (Stuttgart: Metzler, 1979), part I.

10. See, for instance, recent studies devoted to urban housing estates built in Weimar Germany and their reception, that is, actual living practices developed by their largely working-class inhabitants: Adelheid von Saldern, "Neues Wohnen, Wohnverhältnisse und Wohnverhalten in Großwohnanlagen der 20er Jahre," in *Massenwohnung und Eigenheim: Wohnungsbau und Wohnen in der Großstadt seit dem Ersten Weltkrieg*, ed. Axel Schildt and Arnold Sywottek (Frankfurt, New York: Campus, 1988), pp. 201–221; idem, "The Workers' Movement and Cultural Patterns on Urban Housing Estates and in Rural Settlements in Germany and Austria During the 1920s," *Social History* 15, no. 3 (1990): 333–354.

11. On classical cinema and Fordist-Taylorist modes of production, see Janet Staiger, part II of Bordwell, Staiger, Thompson, op. cit. On cultural formations of reception, see Hansen, *Babel and Babylon*, pp. 87–98; also chapters 3, 11, 12.

12. These attempts were particularly strong in the German case; see Anton Kaes, "Literary Intellectuals and the Cinema: Charting a Controversy," *New German Critique* 40 (winter 1987): 7–33; Heinz-B. Heller, *Literarische Intelligenz und Film* (Tübingen: Niemeyer, 1985).

13. Detlev J. K. Peukert, *Die Weimarer Republik* (Frankfurt: Suhrkamp, 1987), pp. 11–12.

14. The letters collected in Walter Benjamin, *Briefe an Siegfried Kracauer* (Marbach: Deutsches Literatur-Archiv, 1987), suggest a generous, mutually respecting relationship; the difficulties of that relationship rather emerge from their correspondence with other friends, in particular Theodor W. Adorno, Leo Löwenthal, and Gershom Scholem. For some of these personal-intellectual constellations, see Martin Jay, *Permanent Exiles: Essays on the Intellectual Migration from Germany to America* (New York: Columbia University Press, 1985); see also Klaus Michael, "Vor dem Café: Walter Benjamin und Siegfried Kracauer in Marseille," in *"Aber ein Sturm weht vom Paradise her"*: *Texte zu Walter Benjamin*, ed. Michael Opitz and Erdmut Wizisla (Leipzig: Reclam, 1992), pp. 203–221.

15. On Kracauer's position in the *Frankfurter Zeitung*, see Thomas Y. Levin, foreword to Kracauer, *The Mass Ornament*, ed. and trans. Thomas Y. Levin (Cambridge: Harvard University Press, 1994), and Andreas Volk, "Siegfried Kracauer in der 'Frankfurter Zeitung': Ein Forschungsbericht," *Soziographie* 4 (Schweizer Gesellschaft für Soziologie, 1991): 43–69. On the political fate of the paper, see Wolfgang Schivelbusch, *Intellektuellendämmerung: Zur Lage der Frankfurter Intelligenz in den zwanziger Jahren* (Frankfurt: Suhrkamp, 1985), pp. 55–76; and Uwe Pralle, "Eine Titanic bürgerlichen Geistes: Ansichten der 'Frankfurter Zeitung,'" *Frankfurter Rundschau*, 20 January 1990. On the conception of the *Feuilleton* as a critical, "enlightening" address to the Weimar public, see Almut Todorow, "'Wollten die Eintagsfliegen in den Rang höherer Insekten aufsteigen?' Die Feuilletonkonzeption der *Frankfurter Zeitung* während der Weimarer Republik im redaktionellen Selbstverständnis," *Deutsche Vierteljahresschrift* 62, no. 4 (1988): 697–740.

16. See Benjamin to Werner Kraft, 28 October 1935, Benjamin, *Gesammelte Schriften* (hereafter cited as *GS*), vol. 5, ed. Rolf Tiedemann (Frankfurt: Suhrkamp, 1983), p. 1,151. The entire passage is quoted in translation in Gertrud Koch,

"Cosmos in Film: On the Concept of Space in Walter Benjamin's 'Work of Art' Essay," trans. Nancy Wenne, *Qui Parle* 5, no. 2 (1992): 62.

17. Siegfried Kracauer, *Jacques Offenbach und das Paris seiner Zeit* (1937), in English as *Offenbach and the Paris of His Time*, trans. Gwenda David and Eric Mosbacher (London: Constable, 1937).

18. Kracauer himself noted this disjunction of cognitive interests and urged Benjamin, in a review of the latter's *Origin of German Tragic Drama* and *Einbahnstraße*, to apply the "Baroque book's method of dissociating immediately experienced unities" to an analysis of contemporary reality ("Zu den Schriften Walter Benjamins," *Frankfurter Zeitung* [hereafter cited as *FZ*], 15 July 1928, rpt. in Kracauer, *Schriften* 5, ed. Inka Mülder-Bach [Frankfurt: Suhrkamp, 1990], part 2: 119–124; previously published in Kracauer's own collection of his Weimar essays, *Das Ornament der Masse* [Frankfurt: Suhrkamp, 1963], hereafter cited as *OdM. Mass Ornament*. Volume 5 of Kracauer's *Schriften* was published in three parts, hereafter referred to as 5.1, 5.2, 5.3).

19. For a sample of Weimar texts on Americanism, see Anton Kaes, ed., *Weimar Republik: Manifeste und Dokumente zur deutschen Literatur, 1918–1933* (Stuttgart: Metzler, 1983), pp. 265–286; and Kaes, Martin Jay and Edward Dimendberg, eds., *The Weimar Sourcebook* (Berkeley, Los Angeles, London: University of California Press, 1994), chapter 15. For a survey see Frank Trommler, "The Rise and Fall of Americanism in Germany," in *America and the Germans: An Assessment of a Three-Hundred-Year History*, ed. Trommler and Joseph McVeigh (Philadelphia: University of Pennsylvania Press, 1985), 2:332–342. See also Helmut Lethen, *Neue Sachlichkeit, 1924–1932: Studien zur Literatur des 'Weißen Sozialismus'* (Stuttgart: Metzler, 1970); Erhard Schütz, *Romane der Weimarer Republik* (Munich: Fink, 1986), p. 7off.; Peukert, op. cit., pp. 178–190. On the juncture of cinema and Americanism, see Thomas J. Saunders, *Hollywood in Berlin: American Cinema and Weimar Germany* (Berkeley, Los Angeles, London: University of California Press, 1994). On "left Fordism," see Wollen, "Modern Times." My theoretical approach to Americanism is indebted to Victoria de Grazia, in particular "Americanism for Export," *Wedge* 7–8 (winter–spring 1985): 74–81.

20. Kr. [Kracauer], "Die Tagung des Deutschen Werkbunds," *FZ*, 29 July 1924. Translations, unless otherwise noted, are mine.

21. [Kracauer], *Ginster: Von ihm selbst geschrieben* (1928), in *Schriften* 7, ed. Karsten Witte (Frankfurt: Suhrkamp, 1973), p. 34.

22. Kracauer's concept of "reality" is often characterized with reference to two programmatic statements from his article series on white-collar workers, *Die Angestellten* (1929): "Only from its extremes can reality be opened up," and "A hundred reports from a factory do not add up to the reality of this factory, but will always remain that—a hundred views of a factory. Reality is a construction," *Schriften* 1 (Frankfurt: Suhrkamp, 1978), pp. 207, 216. On Kracauer's "realism," see Heide Schlüpmann, "Phenomenology of Film: On Siegfried Kracauer's Writings of the 1920s," *New German Critique* 40 (winter 1987): 97–114; idem, "The Subject of Survival: On Kracauer's *Theory of Film*," *New German Critique* 54 (fall 1991): 111–126; and M. Hansen, "'With Skin and Hair': Kracauer's Theory of Film, Marseille 1940," *Critical Inquiry* 19 (spring 1993): 437–469.

23. On this phase of Kracauer's writing, see Inka Mülder's pioneering study, *Siegfried Kracauer—Grenzgänger zwischen Theorie und Literatur: Seine frühen Schriften 1913–1933* (Stuttgart: Metzler, 1985), part I; Michael Schröter, "Weltzerfall und Rekonstruktion: Zur Physiognomik Siegfried Kracauers," *Text + Kritik* 68 (1980): 18–40; see also David Frisby, *Fragments of Modernity: Theories of Modernity in the Work of Simmel, Kracauer, and Benjamin* (Cambridge: MIT Press, 1986), chapter 3.

24. Kracauer, *Der Detektiv-Roman*, in *Schriften* 1, p. 105. The phrase "transcendental homelessness" comes from Georg Lukács's *Theory of the Novel* (1920), which Kracauer reviewed twice; see the longer version, "Georg von Lukács' Romantheorie," *Neue Blätter für Kunst und Literatur* 4, no. 1 (1921/22), rpt. in *Schriften* 5.1: 117–123. The opposition of "*Gemeinschaft*" and "*Gesellschaft*," notably coined by Ferdinand Tönnies in 1886 (corresponding to oppositions of "culture" vs. "civilization" and "unity" vs. "distraction" [*Zerstreuung*]), was still highly popular after World War One and part of the anti-Americanist repertoire. See also Kracauer's epistemological inquiry, *Soziologie als Wissenschaft* (1922), rpt. in *Schriften* I, and his important programmatic essay, "Die Wartenden," *FZ*, 12 March 1922, rpt. in *Schriften* 5.1: 160–170 (also in *OdM*).

25. This treatise was written between 1922 and 1925 but not published until 1971, in vol. 1 of Kracauer, *Schriften*. An excerpt was published under the title "Die Hotelhalle" (The Hotel Lobby) in *OdM*, pp. 157–170. For a summary, see David Frisby, "Zwischen den Sphären: Siegfried Kracauer und der Detektivroman," in *Siegfried Kracauer: Neue Interpretationen*, ed. Michael Kessler and Th. Y. Levin (Tübingen: Stauffenburg Verlag, 1990), pp. 39–58.

26. See Miriam Hansen, "Decentric Perspectives: Kracauer's Early Writings on Film and Mass Culture," *New German Critique* 54 (fall 1991): 47–76. The relevant texts are, among others, Kracauer's reviews of *Die Straße* (Karl Grune, 1923), *FZ*, 3 and 4 February 1924, and his discussion of that film in another programmatic essay, "Der Künstler in dieser Zeit," *Der Morgen* 1, no. 1 (April 1925), rpt. in *Schriften* 5.1: 300–308.

27. Hansen, "Decentric Perspectives," p. 51ff. For a different reading of Kracauer's turn to the "surface," see Inka Mülder-Bach, "Der Umschlag der Negativität: Zur Verschränkung von Phänomenologie, Geschichtsphilosophie und Filmästhetik in Siegfried Kracauers Metaphorik der 'Oberfläche,'" *Deutsche Vierteljahresschrift* 61, no. 2 (1987): 359–373.

28. Kracauer, "Die Wartenden," p. 169. The rejection of philosophy, which marks Benjamin's development as well, was pervasive among German intellectuals during the postwar years; see, for instance, Margarete Susman, "Exodus aus der Philosophie," *FZ*, 17 June 1921. On Kracauer's antiphilosophical turn, see Eckhardt Köhn, *Straßenrausch: Flanerie und kleine Form: Versuch zur Literaturgeschichte des Flaneurs bis 1933* (Berlin: Arsenal, 1989), pp. 225–230.

29. Kracauer, "Künstler in dieser Zeit," p. 304.

30. See Alf Lüdtke, *Eigen-Sinn: Fabrikalltag, Arbeitererfahrung und Politik vom Kaiserreich bis in den Faschismus* (Hamburg: Ergebnisse-Verlag, 1993), pp. 244–254.

31. Martin Jay, *The Dialectical Imagination: A History of the Frankfurt School and the Institute of Social Research, 1923–1950* (Boston, Toronto: Little, Brown & Co., 1973); Eugene Lunn, *Marxism and Modernism: An Historical Study of Lukács, Brecht,*

Benjamin and Adorno (Berkeley, Los Angeles, London: University of California Press, 1982), pp. 188f., 198f.; Rolf Wiggershaus, *Die Frankfurter Schule: Geschichte, Theoretische Entwicklung, Politische Bedeutung* (Munich: Hanser, 1986), pp. 95–97; Frisby, *Fragments*, p. 123f. On Kracauer's radicalization of Simmel and the antiidealist pathos of *Lebensphilosophie*, see Rolf Wiggershaus, "Ein abgrundtiefer Realist: Siegfried Kracauer, die Aktualisierung des Marxismus und das Institut für Sozialforschung," in Kessler and Levin, op. cit., pp. 284–295.

32. Kracauer to Ernst Bloch, 27 May 1926, in Bloch, *Briefe, 1903–1975,* ed. Karola Bloch et al. (Frankfurt: Suhrkamp, 1985), I:273.

33. Kracauer, "Die Reise und der Tanz," *FZ,* 15 March 1925, rpt. in *Schriften* 5.1: 295 (also in *OdM*).

34. Rac [Kracauer], "Schumann-Theater," *FZ Stadt-Blatt,* 4 March 1925.

35. Raca [Kracauer], "Die Revue im Schumann-Theater," *FZ Stadt-Blatt,* 19 May 1925. This review notes approvingly the American influence on German variety stages and by contrast excoriates the retrograde style of the Germanic numbers. Kracauer elaborates on the bad alliance of revue genre and patriotism, militarism, maternal femininity, high culture (the *Tannhäuser* overture with lighting effects), and Viennese *Gemüt* in "Die Revuen," *FZ,* 11 December 1925, rpt. in *Schriften* 5.1: 338–342; here the Tiller Girls too fall prey to Kracauer's scathing critique (p. 340). After the 1929 crash, Kracauer emphasizes the anachronistic and "spook-like" character of American-style revues, a "simile become flesh" of an illusory economic prosperity ("Girls und Krise," *FZ,* 26 May 1931, rpt. in *Schriften* 5.2: 320–322; "Girls and Crisis," trans. Courtney Federle, *Qui parle* 5, no. 2 [spring–summer 1992]: 51–52).

36. On Kracauer's gender politics, see Heide Schlüpmann, "Die nebensächliche Frau: Geschlechterdifferenz in Siegfried Kracauers Essayistik der zwanziger Jahre," *Feministische Studien* 11, no. 1 (May 1993): 38–47. For Kracauer's gay inclinations, see his two semi-autobiographical novels, *Ginster* and, especially, *Georg* (completed in exile, 1933–1934, first published 1973 in *Schriften,* vol. 7), and his correspondence with Leo Löwenthal 1923 and 1924, in Kracauer's papers, Deutsches Literatur-Archiv, Marbach a.N. On the Tiller Girls in the context of Weimar androgyny and sexual politics, see Maud Lavin, *Cut with a Kitchen Knife: The Weimar Photomontages of Hannah Höch* (New Haven, London: Yale University Press, 1993); Kirsten Beuth, "Die wilde Zeit der schönen Beine: Die inszenierte Frau als Körper-Masse," and other essays in *Die Neue Frau: Herausforderung für die Bildmedien der Zwanziger Jahre,* ed. Katharina Sykora et al. (Marburg: Jonas Verlag, 1993). Helmut Lethen stresses the antipatriarchal implications of Americanism in his excellent study of modernist "codes of conduct," *Verhaltenslehren der Kälte: Lebensversuche zwischen den Kriegen* (Frankfurt: Suhrkamp, 1994); see, for instance, his discussion of Carl Schmitt's rejection of Americanism as "the worst form of cannibalizing the father [*Vaterfraß*]" (p. 233).

37. Raca [Kracauer], "Exzentriktänzer in den Ufa-Lichtspielen," *FZ,* 16 October 1928. On the protofascist imagination of the male body as armor, see Klaus Theweleit's by now classic study, *Male Fantasies* (orig. pub. 1977, 1978), trans. Stephen Conway (Minneapolis: University of Minnesota Press, 1987, 1989); see also Hal Foster, "Armor Fou," *October* 56 (spring 1991): 64–97.

38. For Kracauer's polemics against "body culture," see, for example, "Sie sporten," *FZ*, 13 January 1927, rpt. in *Schriften* 5.2: 14–18; also his second review of *Wege zu Kraft und Schönheit* (revised version, 1926), *FZ*, 5 August 1926, rpt. in Karsten Witte, ed., *Schriften* 2 (Frankfurt: Suhrkamp, 1984), pp. 389–399; and "Das Ornament der Masse," *FZ*, 9 and 10 June 1927, rpt. in *Schriften* 5.2: 57–67 (see also *OdM*). For examples of an alternative (though always, for Kracauer, problematic) physicality, see "Langeweile," *FZ*, 16 November 1924, rpt. in *Schriften* 5.1: 278–281 (also in *OdM*); "Der verbotene Blick," *FZ*, 9 April 1925, rpt. in *Schriften* 5.1: 296–300; "Die Eisenbahn," *FZ*, 30 March 1930, rpt. in *Schriften* 5.2: 175–179; "Abschied von der Lindenpassage," *FZ*, 21 December 1930, rpt. in *Schriften* 5.2: 260–265 (also *OdM*); "Heißer Abend," *FZ*, 15 June 1932, rpt. in *Schriften* 5.3: 82–83.

39. Kracauer reflects on the relationship between circus and cinema in his numerous reviews on circus films; see, for instance, his enthusiastic review of Max Reichmann's film *Die Manege* (1927): "Ein Zirkusfilm," *FZ*, 18 January 1928, rpt. in *Schriften* 2: 405–407.

40. Raca [Kracauer], "Zirkus Hagenbeck," *FZ*, 19 June 1926. In contrast, see his prerationalization circus essay, "Im Zirkus," *FZ Stadt-Blatt*, 8 June 1923.

41. "Zirkus Hagenbeck"; for Kracauer's identification with the clowns, see also his follow-up article, "Geh'n wir mal zu Hagenbeck," *FZ Stadt-Blatt*, 20 June 1926; and "Akrobat—schöön," *FZ*, 25 October 1932, rpt. in *Schriften* 5.3: 127–131.

42. On the significance of improvisation and chance in Kracauer see Hansen, "Decentric Perspectives," p. 70, and "With Skin and Hair," pp. 45off., 467.

43. Raca [Kracauer], "Artistisches und Amerikanisches," *FZ*, 29 January 1926. On the centrality of the slapstick genre in Kracauer's drafts and outlines, from 1940 toward his later *Theory of Film* (1960), see Hansen, "With Skin and Hair," pp. 46of., 467.

44. See, for instance, texts collected in Wilfried Wiegand, ed., *Über Chaplin* (Zürich: Diogenes, 1978); Klaus Kreimeier, ed., *Zeitgenosse Chaplin* (Berlin: Oberbaumverlag, 1978). See also Sabine Hake, "Chaplin Reception in Weimar Germany," *New German Critique* 51 (1990): 87–111; Saunders, *Hollywood in Berlin*, chapter 6, "Comic Redemption: The Slapstick Synthesis."

45. Benjamin, "Erwiderung an Oscar A. H. Schmitz," *Literarische Welt*, 11 March 1927, rpt. in *GS*, vol. 2, ed. Rolf Tiedemann and H. Schweppenhäuser (Frankfurt: Suhrkamp, 1977), p. 753. In his *Moscow Diary* he deplores the (self-)restricted range of Soviet film culture which has no room for (imported) slapstick comedy, "since it is based on uninhibited play with technology. Everything technical, however, is sacred here; nothing is taken more seriously than technology" (Benjamin, *Moscow Diary*, ed. Gary Smith, trans. Richard Sieburth [Cambridge: Harvard University Press, 1986], p. 55, transl. modified. See also Benjamin, "Zur Lage der russischen Filmkunst" [1927], *GS*, vol. 2, pp. 747–751).

46. Benjamin, draft notes relating to the Artwork Essay, *GS*, vol. 1, ed. R. Tiedemann and H. Schweppenhäuser (Frankfurt: Suhrkamp, 1974), pp. 1,040, 1,047. See also the draft notes to the Kafka essay, in which Benjamin considers Chaplin and Kafka in terms of the concept of "self-alienation" and the historical boundary marked by the demise of silent film (*GS*, vol. 2, pp. 1,256ff.).

47. Raca [Kracauer], "Chaplin" (on *The Gold Rush*), *FZ*, 6 November 1926, rpt.

in Kracauer, *Kino*, ed. Karsten Witte (Frankfurt: Suhrkamp, 1974), p. 165f.; this collection contains a number of Kracauer's extensive writings on Chaplin. On Kracauer's Chaplin criticism, see Witte, "Nachwort," in *Kino*, pp. 268–274; Mülder, *Kracauer*, pp. 99–100.

48. Kracauer, "Chaplin: Zu seinem Film 'Zirkus,'" *FZ*, 15 February 1928, *Kino*, pp. 167–170; "Chaplin," p. 66; "Chaplins Triumph," *Neue Rundschau* 42, no. 1 (April 1931); rpt. in *Kino*, p. 179.

49. The David-versus-Goliath theme is first singled out in Kracauer's review of *The Pilgrim*, "Chaplin als Prediger," *FZ*, 23 December 1929, rpt. in *Kino*, pp. 170–173. It will become a recurrent motif in Kracauer's later work, in particular *Theory of Film*, where it is linked to cinematic techniques such as the close-up and the capacity of film to give representation to "the small world of things" as opposed to the grand schemes of narrative and history.

50. "Chaplin's Triumph," p. 179. On Chaplin as a diasporic, Jewish figure, see also Hannah Arendt, *The Jew as Pariah: Jewish Identity and Politics in the Modern Age*, ed. Ron H. Feldman (New York: Grove Press, 1978), pp. 79–81.

51. Mülder, *Kracauer*, p. 100; Kracauer, "Chaplin [*Circus*]," p. 169.

52. Kracauer, "Chaplin's Triumph"; also see Kracauer, "Lichter der Großstadt: Zur deutschen Uraufführung des Chaplinfilms," *FZ*, 28 March 1928, rpt. in *Kino*, pp. 173–176.

53. Kracauer, "Ornament," pp. 62, 67.

54. Peter Wollen, for instance, argues that Kracauer's "utopian dream was of a Fordist rationality that would not be dehumanizing," but he goes on to fault Kracauer for ignoring that "the problem is that of reintegrating reason not only with truth, but with the body" (*Raiding the Icebox*, p. 56). For a different view, see Heide Schlüpmann, "The Return of the Repressed: Reflections on a Philosophy of Film History from a Feminist Perspective," *Film History* 6, no. 1 (spring 1994): 80–93; idem, "Die nebensächliche Frau," p. 46; and Hansen, "With Skin and Hair," pp. 458f., 464; see also note 38, above.

55. "Ornament," in *Schriften* 5.2, pp. 59–67; Kracauer takes up the gap between mass ornament (as object of surveillance and organization) and mass democracy (as the condition of social and economic justice) in his essay on unemployment agencies, "Über Arbeitsnachweise: Konstruktion eines Raumes," *FZ*, 17 June 1930, rpt. in *Schriften* 5.2: 190–191.

56. S. Kracauer, "Berliner Nebeneinander: Kara-Iki—Scala-Ball im Savoy—Menschen im Hotel," *FZ*, 17 February 1933.

57. Kracauer, "Kult der Zerstreuung: Über die Berliner Lichtspielhäuser," *FZ*, 4 March 1926; "Cult of Distraction," trans. Thomas Y. Levin, *New German Critique* 40 (winter 1987): 92f.

58. The term "variety format" was coined by Brooks McNamara, "The Scenography of Popular Entertainment," *The Drama Review* 18, no. 1 (March 1974): 16–24; see also Gunning, "Cinema of Attractions." Kracauer consistently defends the practice of mixed programming (live performances, shorts and features) just as he sees in live music an invaluable source of improvisation and unpredictability; see, for example, "Ufa-Beiprogramm," *FZ*, 11 March 1928; "Ein Monstretonfilm," *FZ*, 19 October 1929. In a wonderful passage on moviegoing from his novel *Georg*,

Kracauer unfolds the anecdote of the piano player who cannot see the screen and thus creates an amazing, epiphantic relation between image and music (pp. 428–429).

59. "Cult," pp. 94–95; translation modified.

60. See, for instance, Kracauer's obituary written for Edgar Wallace, *FZ*, 13 February 1932; "'Berlin-Alexanderplatz' als Film" (comparison with Sternberg, *An American Tragedy*), *FZ*, 13 October 1931, rpt. in *Schriften* 2, p. 510; "Der heutige Film und sein Publikum," *FZ*, 30 November and 1 December 1928, rpt. as "Film 1928" in *OdM*, pp. 295–310. For a similar stance, see Benjamin, "This Space for Rent," *One-Way Street* (1928), selections of which appear in *Reflections*, trans. Edmund Jephcott, ed. Peter Demetz (New York, London: Harcourt Brace Jovanovich, 1979), pp. 85–86.

61. Anon. series of eight articles, *FZ*, 11–19 March 1927, rpt. as "Die kleinen Ladenmädchen gehen ins Kino," in *OdM*, pp. 279–294; "Film 1928"; "Not und Zerstreuung: Zur Ufa-Produktion 1931/32," *FZ*, 15 July 1931; "Gepflegte Zerstreuung: Eine grundsätzliche Erwägung," *FZ*, 3 August 1931, rpt. in *Schriften* 2, pp. 500–503.

62. Heide Schlüpmann, "Der Gang ins Kino—ein Ausgang aus selbstverschuldeter Unmündigkeit: Zum Begriff des Publikums in Kracauers Essayistik der Zwanziger Jahre," in Kessler and Levin, *Siegfried Kracauer*, p. 276.

63. See, for instance, Lethen, *Neue Sachlichkeit*, pp. 102–104; Lethen has since revised his assessment of Kracauer; see his illuminating essay, "Sichtbarkeit: Kracauers Liebeslehre," in Kessler and Levin, op. cit., pp. 195–228. A more recent version of this charge can be found in Schütz, op. cit., pp. 32–33.

64. Peukert, op. cit., pp. 175ff.

65. "Ornament," in *Schriften* 5.2: 58f. (emphasis added). I am deliberately using the terminology of post–World War II American mass sociology, notably David Riesman, *The Lonely Crowd* (1950; reprint, New Haven and London: Yale University Press, 1961). Riesman describes the emergence of a new, "other-directed" character type with recourse to the "radar" metaphor for which he credits the Marxist economic historian Karl August Wittfogel, a collaborator of the Frankfurt (later New York–based) Institute for Social Research. On this connection, see Lethen, "Radar-Typ," in *Verhaltenslehren der Kälte*, pp. 235–243.

66. "Ornament," section 5.

67. See, for instance, "Abschied von der Lindenpassage," *FZ*, 21 December 1930, rpt. in *Schriften* 5.2: 260–265; (also in *OdM*); "Berg- und Talbahn," *FZ*, 14 July 1928, rpt. in *Schriften* 5.2: 117–119, trans. Thomas Y. Levin, "*Roller Coaster*," *Qui Parle* 5, no. 2 (1992): 58–60; "Proletarische Schnellbahn," *FZ*, 24 April 1930, rpt. in *Schriften* 5.2: 179–180; "Berliner Nebeneinander."

68. Published as a book in 1930, subtitled *Aus dem neuesten Deutschland* (From the Most Recent Germany), now in *Schriften* 1, ed. Karsten Witte (Frankfurt: Suhrkamp, 1971). For a more detailed account see Frisby, *Fragments*, pp. 158–172; and Benjamin's remarkable reviews, "Ein Außenseiter macht sich bemerkbar," *Die Gesellschaft* 7 (1930) I: 473–477, and "S. Kracauer, Die Angestellten" *Die Literarische Welt* 6, no. 20 (16 June 1930): 5, rpt. in *GS*, vol. 3, pp. 219–228. In addition to this study, Kracauer wrote a number of reviews and articles focusing on female

employees, e.g., "Mädchen im Beruf," *Der Querschnitt* 12, no. 4 (April 1932), *Schriften* 5.3: 60–65.

69. The term "Stehkragen-Proletarier" is used in the German translation of Kracauer's retrospective "psychological history of German film," *From Caligari to Hitler, Schriften* 2: 199; the American version (Princeton, N.J.: Princeton University Press, 1947) simply uses "white-collar workers" (p. 189). In his 1936 exposé, "Mass and Propaganda," a proposal for a "study on fascist propaganda" solicited by Adorno for the Institute for Social Research in New York, Kracauer actually differentiates among *three* groups within the "new masses" who, each in their way, responded to fascist ideology: the proletariat, the proletarianized middle class, and the unemployed. See issue no. 47 of *Marbacher Magazin* (1988), devoted to Kracauer, edited by Ingrid Belke and Irina Renz, esp. pp. 85–90.

70. Benjamin, "On Some Motifs in Baudelaire" (1939/40), GS I.2: 618, 619; *Illuminations,* trans. Harry Zohn, ed. Hannah Arendt (New York: Schocken, 1969), pp. 165, 166, translation modified.

71. Rolf Tiedemann, editor's introduction to Benjamin, *Passagen-Werk* (hereafter cited as *PW*), *GS,* vol. 5, p. 11. Also see Susan Buck-Morss's excellent study, *Dialectics of Seeing: Walter Benjamin and the Arcades Project* (Cambridge: MIT Press, 1989).

72. Benjamin to Gretel Karplus [Adorno], 9 October 1935, *GS,* vol. 5, p. 1,148; partly translated in Buck-Morss, *Dialectics,* p. 392. See also his letters to Horkheimer, 16 October 1935, and to Werner Kraft, 28 October 1935, *GS,* vol. 5, pp. 1,149, 1,151.

73. Benjamin, *PW, GS,* vol. 5, pp. 417, 427; similar (though without revue "girls") in "Zentralpark," *GS,* vol. 1, p. 668; "Central Park," trans. Lloyd Spencer and Mark Harrington, *New German Critique* 34 (winter 1985): 40. Also see Buck-Morss, *Dialectics,* p. 190ff. In his notes on the Artwork Essay, Benjamin extends the analogy to the sphere of reproduction: "The mass reproduction of artworks is not only related to the mass production of industrial goods but also to the mass reproduction of human attitudes and activities" (*GS,* vol. 1, p. 1,042).

74. On the dialectics of capitalist temporality in the *Passagen-Werk,* see Buck-Morss, *Dialectics,* part 2, especially pp. 96–109.

75. Benjamin, "Zentralpark," p. 680; "Central Park," p. 48 (transl. modified).

76. Benjamin, *PW, GS,* vol. 5, p. 494; also see Buck-Morss, *Dialectics,* chapter 8.

77. Benjamin, "Paris—the Capital of the Nineteenth Century" (1935 exposé), in *GS,* vol. 5, p. 50; in *Charles Baudelaire: A Lyric Poet in the Era of High Capitalism,* trans. Harry Zohn and Quintin Hoare (London: Verso, 1983), p. 165.

78. Buck-Morss, "Aesthetics and Anaesthetics" (see note 5, above).

79. See Schlüpmann, "Gang ins Kino," p. 275.

80. Benjamin, "The Work of Art in the Age of Mechanical Reproduction," *Illuminations,* p. 242; see also Kracauer, "Masse und Propaganda."

81. The term "innervation" appears in Benjamin's essay on surrealism, "Surrealism: The Last Snapshot of the European Intelligentsia" (orig. pub. 1929), in *Reflections,* p. 192; *PW, GS,* vol. 5, p. 777; the first version of the Artwork Essay, in *GS,* vol. 1, p. 445; the second version, *GS,* vol. 2, p. 360, 4; "Über einige Motive bei Baudelaire," *GS,* vol. 1, p. 630 ("On Some Motifs in Baudelaire," p. 175, translated as "nervous impulses"). Also see Buck-Morss, *Dialectics,* p. 117; Hansen, "Of Mice

and Ducks: Benjamin and Adorno on Disney," *South Atlantic Quarterly* 92, no. 1 (winter 1993): 38, n. 24; and Koch, "Cosmos."

82. Kracauer, review of Balázs, *Der Geist des Films*, "Ein neues Filmbuch," *FZ*, 2 November 1930; also see Kracauer's review of *Der sichtbare Mensch*, *FZ*, 10 July 1927. On Balázs's (unacknowledged) significance for Benjamin, see Gertrud Koch, "Béla Balázs: The Physiognomy of Things," *New German Critique* 40 (winter 1987): 167–177.

83. Buck-Morss, "Aesthetics and Anaesthetics"; Hansen, "Benjamin, Cinema and Experience: 'The Blue Flower in the Land of Technology,'" *New German Critique* 40 (winter 1987): 179–224; Hansen, "Of Mice and Ducks."

84. Emilie Altenloh, *Zur Soziologie des Kino: Die Kino-Unternehmung und die sozialen Schichten ihrer Besucher* (University of Heidelberg; Leipzig: Spamersche Buchdruckerei, 1914). On the proletarian film, see Bruce Murray, *Film and the German Left in the Weimar Republic* (Austin: University of Texas Press, 1992); see also Adelheid von Saldern, "Massenfreizeitkultur im Visier: Ein Beitrag zu den Deutungs- und Einwirkungsversuchen während der Weimarer Republik," *Archiv für Sozialgeschichte* 33 (1993): 21–58.

85. *Einbahnstraße, GS*, vol. 4, pp. 95–96; *Reflections*, p. 71.

86. Benjamin, "Das Kunstwerk im Zeitalter seiner technischen Reproduzierbarkeit" (second version), *GS*, vol. 7, pp. 370f.

87. Benjamin, "Erwiderung an Oscar A. H. Schmitz," *GS*, vol. 2, p. 753. Related to this surrender is Benjamin's plea, in a note on "the political significance of film" in the *Passagen-Werk*, for a "dialectical" acceptance—and transcendence of "Kitsch" in art that wants to reach "the mass"; *PW, GS*, vol. 5, pp. 499–500.

88. Kracauer's position in the *Frankfurter Zeitung* was, with the exception perhaps of a few years between 1924 and 1929, almost always precarious; yet, barred from an academic career for a variety of reasons (among them his speech impediment), he preferred being a dependent editor of a paper with a wide circulation, ranging from white-collar workers to the educated bourgeoisie, to the greater freedom he might have enjoyed at a paper like the *Weltbühne* (which repeatedly offered him an affiliation)—which, however, reached a more limited readership of mostly like-minded artists and literary intellectuals. On Kracauer's employee status, see his own account in *Georg*; and Hans G. Helms, "Der wunderliche Kracauer," *Neues Forum* 18 (June/July 1971): 28. Also see note 15, above.

89. *Die Angestellten*, p. 215. Kracauer elaborates on this culture in the chapter "Asyl für Obdachlose" (Shelter for the Homeless), which tropes on Lukacs's phrase of "transcendental homelessness." For excerpts of this chapter in translation, see Kaes, Jay, and Dimendberg, eds., *Weimar Republic Sourcebook*, pp. 189–191.

90. For the latter kind of argument, see Henri Band, "Massenkultur versus Angestelltenkultur: Siegfried Kracauers Auseinandersetzung mit Phänomenen der modernen Kultur in der Weimarer Republik," in *Zwischen Angstmetapher und Terminus: Theorien der Massenkultur seit Nietzsche*, ed. Norbert Krenzlin (Berlin: Akademie Verlag, 1992), pp. 73–101.

91. Lacan first presented his lecture at a meeting of the International Psychoanalytic Association at Marienbad in 1936; during the conference, he traveled to the Berlin Olympics to watch the fascist imaginary in action. See Buck-Morss, "Aesthetics," p. 37; David Macey, *Lacan in Contexts* (London, Verso, 1988), p. 214.

On parallels between Kracauer and Lacan, cf. Thomas Elsaesser, "Cinema—The Irresponsible Signifier or, 'The Gamble with History,'" *New German Critique* 40 (winter 1987): 65–89.

92. Kracauer, "Die kleinen Ladenmädchen," p. 280; on "role-playing" and the emergence of a managerial caste, see Kracauer's remarkable essay on the actor, "Über den Schauspieler," *Die Neue Rundschau* 41, no. 9 (1930): 429–431, rpt. in *Schriften* 5.2: 231–234.

93. Kracauer, "Langeweile" (Boredom), *FZ*, 16 November 1924, rpt. in *Schriften* 5.1: 279; also *OdM* 322.

94. Kracauer, "Die kleinen Ladenmädchen," p. 280.

95. Benjamin, "Ein Außenseiter," p. 223.

96. Kracauer, *Die Angestellten*, p. 289; see also p. 248. For his indictment of the current film production as "Fluchtversuche" or attempts to escape, see, for instance, "Film 1928."

97. Kracauer, *Die Angestellten*, p. 287.

98. See especially Benjamin's programmatic 1933 essay, "Erfahrung und Armut," in *GS*, vol. 2, pp. 213–219; Kr [Kracauer], "Das neue Bauen: Zur Stuttgarter Werkbundausstellung: 'Die Wohnung,'" *FZ*, 31 July 1927, rpt. in *Schriften* 5.2: 68–74.

99. Kracauer, *Die Angestellten*, pp. 286–287. Kracauer elaborates on the relation(s) between photography and death in "Die Photographie," *FZ*, 28 October 1927, rpt. in *Schriften* 5.2: 83–98, trans. Thomas Y. Levin, *Critical Inquiry* 19 (spring 1993): 421–436.

100. Michael Geyer, "The Stigma of Violence in Twentieth-Century Germany: A History of Man-Made Mass Death," unpublished ms; see also Hansen, "With Skin and Hair," pp. 465f., 468f.

101. See, for instance, Kracauer, "Girls and Crisis," and "Renovierter Jazz," *FZ*, 25 October 1931, rpt. in *Schriften* 5.2: 390–392.

102. "Reise und Tanz," p. 293.

103. On Kracauer's city images, see Inka Mülder-Bach, "'Mancherlei Fremde': Paris, Berlin und die Extraterritorialität Siegfried Kracauers," *Juni: Magazin für Kultur und Politik* 3, no. 1 (1989): 61–72; Köhn, *Straßenrausch* (see note 28, above), pp. 225–248; David Frisby, "Deciphering the Hieroglyphics of Weimar Berlin: Siegfried Kracauer," in *Berlin: Culture and Metropolis*, ed. Charles W. Haxthausen and Heidrun Suhr (Minneapolis: University of Minnesota Press, 1991), pp. 152–165; Anthony Vidler, "Agorophobia: Spatial Estrangement in Simmel and Kracauer," *New German Critique* 54 (fall 1991): 31–45. On Kracauer in the tradition of Weimar *flânerie*, see Karl Prümm, "Die Stadt der Reporter und Kinogänger bei Roth, Brentano und Kracauer," in *Die Unwirklichkeit der Städte: Großstadtdarstellungen zwischen Moderne und Postmoderne*, ed. Klaus R. Scherpe (Reinbek: Rowohlt, 1988), pp. 80–105; and Anke Gleber, "Criticism or Consumption of Images? Franz Hessel and the Flâneur in Weimar Culture," trans. Bill Rollins, *Journal of Communication Inquiry* 13, no. 1 (winter 1989): 80–93.

104. "Die Wiederholung: Auf der Durchreise in München," *FZ*, 29 May 1932, rpt. in *Schriften* 5.3: 71–72.

105. Kracauer, "Straße ohne Erinnerung," *FZ*, 16 December 1932, rpt. in *Schriften* 5.3: 173.

106. *Die Angestellten*, p. 298. The figure of the inversion of distance and close-ness, exotic and familiar, is pervasive in Kracauer's essays and reviews; see, for instance, "Exotische Filme," *FZ*, 28 May 1929; "Die Filmprüfstelle gegen einen Russenfilm," *FZ*, 23 July 1930, last section ("Menschen im Busch") rpt. in *Schriften*, vol. 2, pp. 438–439; "Die Filmwochenschau," *Die Neue Rundschau* 42, no. 2 (1931): 573–575, rpt. in *Kino*, pp. 11–14; "Reisen, nüchtern," *FZ*, 10 July 1932, rpt. in *Schriften* 5.3: 87–90.

107. The term "Straßenrausch" appears in Kracauer's uncanny essay, "Erinnerung an eine Pariser Straße," *FZ*, 9 November 1930, rpt. in *Schriften* 5.2: 243–248; for a description of a Berlin "street intoxication," see *Georg*, p. 487. His other major articles on Paris are "Analyse eines Stadtplans: Faubourgs und Zentrum," *FZ* (ca. 1926), rpt. in *Schriften* 5.1: 401–403; "Lichtreklame," *FZ*, 15 January 1927, rpt. in *Schriften* 5.2: 19–21; "Pariser Beobachtungen," *FZ*, 13 February 1927, rpt. in *Schriften* 5.2: 25–36; "Das Straßenvolk in Paris," *FZ*, 12 April 1927, rpt. in *Schriften* 5.2: 39–43; "Negerball in Paris," *FZ*, 2 November 1928, rpt. in *Schriften* 5.2: 127–129; "Die Berührung," *FZ*, 18 November 1928, rpt. in *Schriften* 5.2: 129–136; "Ein paar Tage Paris," *FZ*, 5 April 1931, rpt. in *Schriften* 5.2: 296–301. A number of these articles were collected by Kracauer himself in the collection *Straßen in Berlin und anderswo* (Frankfurt: Suhrkamp, 1964). Kracauer's "social biography" of Jacques Offenbach (see above, note 17), written after his occasional sojourns in Paris had turned into the hardships of exile, also belongs to this context. On Kracauer's Paris, see Mülder-Bach, "Mancherlei Fremde"; and Remo Bodei, "L'expérience et les formes: Le Paris de Walter Benjamin et de Siegfried Kracauer," tr. J. Liechtenstein in *Walter Benjamin et Paris*, ed. Heinz Wismann (Paris: Editions du CERF, 1986), pp. 33–47.

108. Kracauer, "Negerball in Paris," pp. 128f.

109. Kracauer, "Lichtreklame," p. 19.

110. Raca, "Thérèse Raquin," *FZ*, 29 March 1928, rpt. in *Kino*, pp. 136–138; "Neue Tonfilme: Einige grundsätzliche Bemerkungen" (on Clair's *Sous les toits de Paris*), *FZ*, 16 August 1930, rpt. in *Kino*, pp. 125–128 ("half-ironic expeditions through the peculiar inbetween-world [*Zwischenwelt*] in which things and people irritate, touch and caress each other" [p. 127]); "Wiedersehen mit alten Filmen: VI. Jean Vigo," *Basler National-Zeitung*, 1 February 1940, rpt. in *Kino*, pp. 120–124. On Benjamin's trope of an "optical unconscious," see Hansen, "Benjamin, Cinema and Experience," pp. 207ff., "Of Mice and Ducks," pp. 30f., 42f.; Koch, "Béla Balázs," pp. 172f.; and "Cosmos in Film," pp. 70f.

111. Kracauer refers to Vertov as a "surrealist artist who registers the colloquy that the died-away, disintegrated life holds with the wakeful things," stressing the film's affinity with states of dreaming and dying as opposed to the usually emphasized themes of technology and collectivity ("Mann mit dem Kinoapparat," *FZ*, 19 May 1929, rpt. in *Kino*, pp. 88–92). The quotation is from a fairly negative review of Clair's *Quatorze Juillet*, "Idyll, Volkserhebung und Charakter," *FZ*, 24 January 1933, partially rpt. in *Kino*, pp. 132–135; Kracauer's understanding of Surrealism is indebted to Benjamin's 1929 essay, to which he occasionally alludes.

112. Kr[Kracauer], "Neue Filme," on Clair's *Le million, FZ*, 18 May 1931, rpt. in *Kino*, pp. 128–130; "Rationalisierung [on Clair's *A nous la liberté*] und Unterwelt," *FZ*, 27 January 1932, rpt. in *Kino*, pp. 130–132.

113. "Rationalisierung," p. 131. On the historical context of France's resistance to "mechanization," see Richard F. Kuisel, *Seducing the French: The Dilemma of Americanization* (Berkeley, Los Angeles, London: University of California Press, 1993).

114. Kracauer, "Pariser Beobachtungen," pp. 25, 35.

115. Kracauer, "La Ville de Malakoff," *FZ*, 30 January 1927, rpt. in *Schriften* 5.2: 22–24.

116. Kracauer, "Ein paar Tage Paris," p. 301. For a similar turn, see "Die Wiederholung" (The Repetition), a companion piece to "Erinnerung an eine Pariser Straße" which contrasts Berlin's presentist modernity with Munich's dreamlike evocation of the past and culminates in a veritable flight or escape back to Berlin.

117. Kracauer, "Berliner Landschaft," *FZ*, 8 November 1931, rpt. in *Schriften* 5.2: 401; also see "Unfertig in Berlin," *FZ*, 13 September 1931, rpt. in *Schriften* 5.2: 375.

118. Kracauer, "Der Künstler in dieser Zeit," *Der Morgen* 1, no. 1 (April 1925), rpt. in *Schriften* 5.1: 300–308. Ernst Bloch resumes this formulation in "Die Angst des Ingenieurs" (1929), *Gesamtausgabe* (Frankfurt: Suhrkamp, 1977), 9:352.

119. See, for instance, "Film 1928," pp. 296, 309f.

120. Kracauer, "Berg- und Talbahn," pp. 117–118, "Roller Coaster," p. 59.

121. Hansen, "Decentric Perspectives," pp. 75–76.

122. Kracauer, "Organisiertes Glück," *FZ*, 8 May 1930.

123. Raca [Kracauer], "Zirkus Sarrasani," *FZ*, 13 November 1929. This piece relates to his earlier articles on the circus, e.g., "Zirkus Hagenbeck" (see above), in a similar way as "Organized Happiness" does to "Roller Coaster." The analogy between circus aesthetics and Fordist-Taylorist methods of production is made more explicitly and single-mindedly than in the earlier article; the symptom of the slippage between playful parody and dead-serious thoroughness is "the elimination [*Ausfall*] of the clowns": "There is no time for the clowns, we have to rationalize too much. Improvisation will soon no longer be granted any place."

124. Raca [Kracauer], "Girldämmerung," *FZ*, 22 June 1928. Much as it betrays the writer's own ambivalence toward (New) women, this review once more demonstrates Kracauer's interest in Fordist mass culture's potential for critical self-reflexion, which was not limited to the genre of comedy but, as in this case, could also occur in social drama. The review concludes with the sentence, "American miracles happen in Hollywood."

125. Kracauer, "Worte von der Straße," *FZ*, July 1930, rpt. in *Schriften* 5.2: 201. On the mountain film, see Eric Rentschler, "Mountains and Modernity: Relocating the *Bergfilm*," *New German Critique* 51 (fall 1990): 137–161; for Kracauer's polemic against the mountain film genre, see *From Caligari to Hitler*, chapters 9 and 21, and, by contrast, his early, rather enthusiastic review of Arnold Fanck's film *Der Berg des Schicksals*, "Berge, Wolken, Menschen," *FZ Stadt-Blatt*, 9 April 1925. For an attempt to rescue the Alps from the discourse of reactionary *kitsch*, see Ernst Bloch, "Alpen ohne Photographie" (1930), *Gesamtausgabe*, vol. 9, pp. 488–498.

126. For an instance of such domestication in the genre of the musical, see Karsten Witte, "Visual Pleasure Inhibited: Aspects of the German Revue Film," trans. J. D. Steakley and Gabriele Hoover, *New German Critique* 24–25 (fall/winter 1981/82): 238–263.

CONTRIBUTORS

Richard Abel teaches cinema studies and cultural studies in the English department at Drake University. His books include *French Cinema: The First Wave, 1915–1929* (1984) and *When the Ciné Goes to Town* (1994).

Leo Charney is visiting assistant professor of film studies at the University of Iowa. He is completing a manuscript titled "Drift: Empty Moments in Modernity and Cinema."

Margaret Cohen is associate professor of comparative literature at New York University. Her publications include *Profane Illumination: Walter Benjamin and the Surrealist Revolution* (1993) and *Spectacles of Realism* (1995), of which she is a co-editor. She is completing a study titled "Why Was There No French Women's Realism?"

Jonathan Crary, a founding editor of Zone Books, is associate professor of art history at Columbia University. Author of *Techniques of the Observer*, he is currently completing a book on the problem of attention in the late nineteenth century.

Tom Gunning teaches film history in the department of radio, TV and film at Northwestern University. He is the author of *D. W. Griffith and the Origins of American Narrative Film* (1991) and numerous articles on early cinema. He is currently working on a book about early cinema and modernity.

Miriam Bratu Hansen is Andrew W. Mellon Professor in the Humanities and director of the film studies center at the University of Chicago. Her most recent book is *Babel and Babylon: Spectatorship in American Silent Film*

(1991, 1994). She has also published on German cinema and film theory and is working on a study on the Frankfurt School's debates on film and mass culture.

Alexandra Keller is a doctoral candidate at New York University in cinema studies. She is writing a dissertation on postmodernism, genre, and the post-Reagan Western.

Jeannene Przyblyski is completing her Ph.D. in art history at the University of California, Berkeley. She has published on "Courbet, The Commune, and the Meaning of Still Life in 1871." She is currently at work on a book-length study of photography and the Paris Commune.

Erika D. Rappaport is assistant professor of history at Florida International University. She is currently completing a study of gender, shopping, and department stores in Edwardian London.

Mark B. Sandberg is assistant professor of scandinavian studies and film studies at University of California, Berkeley. He is currently working on a book about visual culture in turn-of-the-century Scandinavia.

Vanessa R. Schwartz is assistant professor of history at the American University in Washington D.C. She is completing a book on popular realism in mass culture in *fin-de-siècle* Paris.

Ben Singer is assistant professor of film studies at Smith College. He is completing a study of sensational melodrama and the social profile of American cinema in the teens.

Marcus Verhagen has a Ph.D. in art history from University of California, Berkeley. He has taught at University of California, Berkeley, and Mills College and is currently preparing a book on modernism, mass culture, and the comic arts.

INDEX

Designer: UC Press Staff
Compositor: Prestige Typography
Text: 10/12 Baskerville
Display: Baskerville